GREEN-LITE

Green-lite

Complexity in Fifty Years of Canadian Environmental Policy, Governance, and Democracy

G. BRUCE DOERN, GRAEME AULD,
AND CHRISTOPHER STONEY

Carleton Library Series 234

McGill-Queen's University Press
Montreal & Kingston • London • Chicago

ISBN 978-0-7735-4581-6 (cloth)
ISBN 978-0-7735-4582-3 (paper)
ISBN 978-0-7735-9748-8 (ePDF)
ISBN 978-0-7735-9749-5 (ePUB)

Legal deposit fourth quarter 2015
Bibliothèque nationale du Québec

Printed in Canada on acid-free paper that is 100% ancient forest free
(100% post-consumer recycled), processed chlorine free

McGill-Queen's University Press acknowledges the support of the Canada
Council for the Arts for our publishing program. We also acknowledge the
financial support of the Government of Canada through the Canada Book
Fund for our publishing activities.

Library and Archives Canada Cataloguing in Publication

Doern, G. Bruce, 1942–, author
    Green-lite: complexity in fifty years of Canadian environmental policy,
governance, and democracy / G. Bruce Doern, Graeme Auld, and
Christopher Stoney.

(Carleton library series; 234)
Includes bibliographical references and index.
Issued in print and electronic formats.
ISBN 978-0-7735-4581-6 (bound). – ISBN 978-0-7735-4582-3 (paperback). –
ISBN 978-0-7735-9748-8 (ePDF). – ISBN 978-0-7735-9749-5 (ePUB)

1. Environmental policy – Canada – History – 20th century.
2. Environmental policy – Canada – History – 21st century. I. Auld,
Graeme, author II. Stoney, Christopher, author III. Title. IV. Series:
Carleton library series; 234

GE190.C3D64 2015   363.700971   C2015-904276-3
                                              C2015-904277-1

This book was typeset by Interscript in 10.5/13 Sabon.

Contents

Charts and Tables

CHARTS

TABLES

Abbreviations

AAFC	Agriculture and Agri-food Canada
ADM	assistant deputy minister
AECL	Atomic Energy of Canada Ltd
AES	Environmental Protection Service
AIT	Agreement on Internal Trade
ANAC	Aboriginal and Northern Affairs Canada
AQA	Air Quality Agreement (Canada-US)
ASC	Aquaculture Stewardship Council
BCF	Building Canada Fund
BQ	Bloc Québécois
CBD	Convention on Biological Diversity
CCCI	Cities and Climate Change Initiative
CCPA	Canadian Chemical Producers Association
CCS	carbon capture and storage
CDRM	Cabinet Directive on Regulatory Management
CDSR	Cabinet Directive on Streamlining Regulation
CEAA	Canadian Environmental Assessment Agency
CEAC	Canadian Environmental Advisory Council
CEC	Commission on Environmental Cooperation (NAFTA)
CEPA	Canadian Environmental Protection Act
CESD	commissioner of the environment and sustainable development
CETA	Canada-EU Trade Agreement
CFI	Canada Foundation for Innovation
CFIA	Canadian Food Inspection Agency
CFIB	Canadian Federation for Independent Business

CIAC	Chemical Industry Association of Canada
CIHR	Canadian Institutes of Health Research
CIPO	Canadian Intellectual Property Office
CIWP	Canada Infrastructure Works Program
CMHC	Canada Mortgage and Housing Corporation
CNSC	Canadian Nuclear Safety Commission
CORE	Commission on Resources and Environment (British Columbia)
CSA	Canadian Standards Association
CSIF	Canada Strategic Infrastructure Fund
CTF	Canadian Taxpayers Federation
CUFTA	Canada–US Free Trade Agreement
CWS	Canada Wildlife Service
EACSR	External Advisory Committee on Smart Regulation
EAP	Economic Action Plan
EARP	Environmental Assessment Review Process
EC	Environment Canada
ECE	Economic Commission of Europe
EMR	Energy, Mines and Resources
ENGOS	environmental non-governmental organizations
EPA	Environmental Protection Agency (US)
ERCB	Energy Resources Conservation Board (of Alberta)
ETC	Environmental Technologies Canada
FCM	Federation of Canadian Municipalities
FDA	Food and Drug Administration (US)
FEARO	Federal Environmental Assessment Review Office
FSC	Forest Stewardship Council
FTE	full-time equivalent
GAA	Global Aquaculture Alliance
GATT	General Agreement on Tariffs and Trade
GDP	gross domestic product
GHG	greenhouse gases
GIF	Green Infrastructure Fund
GM food	genetically modified food
GMI	Global Mining Initiative
GST	Goods and Services Tax
GTF	Gas Tax Fund
HRSDC	Human Resources and Skills Development Canada
ICME	International Council of Metals and the Environment

ICMM	International Council on Mining and Metals
ICSP	Integrated Community Sustainability Plans
IEA	International Energy Agency
IFOAM	International Federation of Organic Agriculture Movements
IIED	International Institute for Environment and Development
IISD	International Institute for Sustainable Development
IJC	International Joint Commission
INFC	Infrastructure Canada
IP	intellectual property
IPCC	Intergovernmental Panel on Climate Change
IWC	International Whaling Commission
JCPC	Judicial Committee of the Privy Council
KOA	Knowledge Outreach and Awareness (Programs)
LOS	legitimate objectives (in trade agreements)
MAC	Mining Association of Canada
MMSD	Mining, Minerals, and Sustainable Development
MOU	memorandum of understanding
MSC	Marine Stewardship Council
NAFTA	North American Free Trade Agreement
NEB	National Energy Board
NEP	National Energy Program (1980–84)
NGO	non-governmental organization
NIMBY	not in my back yard
NPM	New Public Management
NRC	National Research Council Canada
NRCan	Natural Resources Canada
NRTEE	National Roundtable on Environment and Economy
NSB	New Substances Branch
NWRC	National Wildlife Research Centre
OAG	Office of the Auditor General
OECD	Organization for Economic Cooperation and Development
PBO	parliamentary budget officer
PCO	Privy Council Office
PMO	Prime Minister's Office
R&D	research and development
RAN	Rainforest Action Network
RIAS	Regulatory Impact Assessment System

RRD	responsible resource development
RSA	related science activities
S&T	science and technology
SD	sustainable development
SFI	Sustainable Forestry Initiative
SFT	Speech from the Throne
SMES	small and medium-sized enterprises
SR&ED	Scientific Research and Experimental Development Tax Credit
SSHRC	Social Sciences and Humanities Research Council
SUD-Net	Sustainable Urban Development Network
TBS	Treasury Board Secretariat
TBT	technical barriers to trade
TRM	technology road map
UNEP	United Nations Environment Program
UNFCCC	United Nations Framework Convention on Climate Change
UN–HABITAT	United Nations Human Settlements Programme
WCR	world class regulator
WHO	World Health Organization
WIPO	World Intellectual Property Organization
WMI	Whitehorse Mining Initiative
WTO	World Trade Organization
WTO-TRIPS	World Trade Organization Trade-Related Intellectual Property System
WWF	World Wildlife Fund (or World Wide Fund for Nature outside North America)

Preface

This book is the product of the authors' individual and collaborative work on environmental policy in Canada and internationally over the last four decades. During this extensive period of reading, discussion, and interviews, we owe numerous debts of thanks, gratitude, and learning to many individuals and to many agencies and institutions involved directly and indirectly with the story of Canadian environmental policy, governance, and democracy.

We are also grateful to many environmental academics and practitioners from across Canada and internationally. We have drawn on their scholarly research, which we cite and debate throughout the book. In particular, we would like to thank co-authors from previous works whose research and ideas have informed this book. Jeff Kinder, Monica Gattinger, Tom Conway, Robert Hilton, and Tamara Krawchenko deserve special recognition and thanks for their contributions.

We also thank the two McGill-Queen's University Press–chosen peer reviewers for their extremely valuable comments and recommendations on an earlier version of the manuscript. They have without a doubt helped make it a better final analytical product.

A continuing intellectual and personal set of thanks are owed to colleagues and staff at our home academic institutions, the School of Public Policy and Administration at Carleton University, and the Politics Department, University of Exeter, in the United Kingdom.

G. Bruce Doern, Graeme Auld, and Christopher Stoney
January 2015

GREEN-LITE

Introduction and Analytical Framework

This book provides an in-depth historical examination of Canadian environmental policy, governance, and democracy over the past five decades, covering the Harper, Chrétien-Martin, Mulroney, and Trudeau prime ministerial eras. Trudeau's initial era is recognized as the beginning of the age of federal attempts to intervene and manage environmental issues and concerns on a national scale. More recently, as Canada becomes what the Harper government calls an energy "superpower," questions arise concerning the near-term future and longer-term issues regarding Canada's environmental choices, challenges, and consequences.

Within a comparative and international context, we examine how environmental policy, governance, and democracy have emerged through increasing numbers of environmental regimes (six are identified and examined in this book). The concept of regimes is now used often in political, policy, and governance scholarship and is applied mainly to highlight more complex meso-level institutional realms, including: types of democracy; political executive structures; international relations; regulatory domains; budgetary systems; or more particular cross-governmental policy areas such as risk, safety, and science and technology (May 2007; Harris and Milkis 1989).

Increasingly complex, the six environmental regimes involve diverse policy ideas and content, spatial, and scalar realms of public and private power, complex governance processes and structures, and contending and overlapping forms of democracy in an Internet age. We examine how and why Canadian environmental policy has changed, for the better or for worse in terms of key policy and governance patterns, and what changing normative and contested assessments have come to mean. Our own assessment of Canadian federal environmental policies and influence is captured by the term *green-lite*. The term reflects the sub-optimal nature of federal stewardship from an environmental perspective and the tendency for other levels of government and the private and not-for-profit sectors to assume greater responsibility for environmental policy in the absence of strong and sustained federal leadership, but for other reasons as well. It is also in part a reflection of the gap between federal environmental discourse and rhetoric on the environment and the influence and impact of federal policies.

Green-lite is mainly for academics and students interested in the development and evolution of Canadian environmental policy, governance, and democracy in the age of environmentalism from 1960 to the present. However, we have kept in mind governmental and business readers who regularly follow environmental issues, and citizens and interest-group participants who benefit from environmental policy progress and who are harmed by policy failure at the global, national, provincial, and local levels.

The book is the first to provide an integrated, historical, and conceptual examination of Canadian environmental policy and governance over many decades and the underlying complexity of the challenges and choices. Complexity is a basic characteristic of the environmental policy story over the entire period examined; it has not emerged only recently. Now in its sixth decade, the story of environmental policy in Canada is intricate and varied and is without doubt a story that needs a strong federal focus and extended multi-level and multi-scalar governance focus. We therefore include considerable and necessary provincial and city-local government coverage throughout; at the same time, space limitations preclude a full comparative examination of all Canadian cities, provinces, and territories. Provincial policies are, however, a significant analytical and empirical feature throughout the book. They appear in our discussion of the prime ministerial Liberal and Conservative agendas, environmental assessment policy in the analysis of Environment Canada, the analysis of the evolution of the Energy-Environment and Natural Resources–Environment regimes, and the final regime chapters dealing with cities and urban sustainability, infrastructure, and NGOs (non-governmental organizations), markets, and businesses. Overall, multi-level and multi-scalar environmentalism and governance, and hence key provincial features, are also examined.

ANALYTICAL FRAMEWORK

Our overall contribution centres on the development and use of a three-part analytical framework consisting of (1) green-lite as an initial heuristic for exploring and understanding the complexity of Canada's environmental policy and governance patterns over a fifty-year period; (2) environmental regimes defined as broad integrated systems of environmental ideas, organizations, interests, policies, and policy instruments; and (3) three key elements of the regimes that help elucidate the nature of policy, governance, and democratic change and inertia within and across the six environmental regimes we examine. Before turning to the framework and an explication of our green-lite concept, we offer three critical definitions.

We define *environmental policy* as statements, laws, rules, and programs intended to reduce and prevent pollution and related adverse impacts on nature and natural capital. Such policy encompasses a widening set of environmental content, normative concerns, and values. Environmental policy is made by multiple levels of government, by private corporations and business interest groups, and by environmental non-governmental organizations (ENGOs). Environmental policy can be direct as defined above, or it can consist of de facto hyphenated policies that emerge from other policy fields and policy-makers, such as those on energy, natural resources, trade, transportation, innovation, fisheries and oceans, food and agriculture, cities, communities, and infrastructure.

Environmental governance is a subset of the broader concept of overall governance that emerged in the literature on politics, policy, and public administration over the past thirty years (Aucoin 1997, 2008; Rhodes 1997). In one sense, governance can be expressed simply as an effort to recognize more explicitly that governing involves more than government, more than the state, and more than public policy pronounced and implemented by the state and its bureaucracies. It also implies the state playing a role characterized at times more by steering than rowing and by more explicit efforts to improve service delivery, but in addition it still implies the continued need for a strong state and state-led capacities (Bell and Hindmoor 2009).

Environmental democracy is defined broadly to include all the main values, criteria, and arenas of democratic participation and engagement in existence in the Canadian political system. These include: elected, representative, Cabinet-parliamentary democracy;

federalist democracy; interest group pluralist democracy; civil society democracy; and direct democracy, including burgeoning Internet-based social media networks (Gidengil and Bastedo 2014; Pal 2013; Bickerton and Gagnon 2009; Williams 2009; Rainie and Wellman 2012).

Chart 0.1 previews the analytical journey, beginning with the contextual background as shown and then moving to the analytical framework devised to assess the six environmental regimes.

Green-lite

Green-lite is a heuristic concept. It is centred on aspects of complexity that facilitate an examination of Canada's environmental policy and governance patterns. We stress from the outset that environmental policy encompasses far more than a simple linear expression of objectives followed by implementation consequences and impacts. It involves at a minimum the five policy and governance patterns previewed below.

Green-lite is the overall basis through which, in the wake of our full empirical analysis, we argue that Canada's performance has been relatively modest and sometimes lagging. The book thus investigates the transformations and inertia that have occurred in Canadian environmental policy, democracy, and governance. We explore the extent to which current concerns raised about environmental retreat and inadequacy, or the redirection of the federal government's role on the environment, represent a shift to green-lite features or whether environmental policy has always been more variegated and understated.

Table 0.1 provides preview illustrations of the five main green-lite types of complexity regarding environmental policy and governance patterns.

It must be stressed that green-lite as a heuristic concept does not imply there has been no green or environmental policy progress. Environmental progress has occurred in Canada. The establishment of Environment Canada and the environmental assessment processes were both important developments, to name just two. However, green-lite elucidates that progress remains a struggle due to complexities of several basic kinds. We make these clear in the book by documenting the fluctuating fortunes of environmental issues on the Canadian political agenda over time (see chapter 2)

Chart 0.1: Analyzing Canadian environmental policy, governance, and democracy

CONTEXT	ANALYTICAL FRAMEWORK	SIX ENVIRONMENTAL REGIMES
Conceptual foundations (chapter 1) • Environmental ideas • Political economy of environmental policy • Environmental democracy and governance in a networked Internet world *Canada's environmental policy and democracy in Liberal and Conservative prime ministerial eras (chapter 2)* *International environmental policy: Canada-US relations and global agreements and agendas (chapter 3)*	*Green-lite as an analytical heuristic concept re: five policy and governance patterns in environmental policy complexity* • Ends-means calculus and conflict • Complex boundary realities and therefore hyphenated environmentalism • Diverse and conflicting temporal realities • Diverse nature of, and triggering points for, environmental agendas • Complex multi-scalar and spatial governance and democracy coordination and conflict dynamics *Environmental regimes* • As complex realms of mainly hyphenated environmental policy ideas, institutions, processes, interests, and policy instruments • As vertical and horizontal in direction and scope within government • As diverse scalar and spatial realms *Regime elements* • Environmental ideas, discourse, and agendas • Environmental power structures, democracy, and governance • Science, evidence, knowledge, and precaution	Change and inertia across 40 to 50 years in the: • Environment Canada–Centred Regime (chapter 4) • Energy-Environment regime (chapter 5) • Natural Resources–Environment Regime (chapter 6) • Federal–Cities Urban Sustainability Regime (chapter 7) • Federal–Municipal Infrastructure Sustainability Regime (chapter 8) • NGO, Market, and Business– Environment Regime (chapter 9)

Table o.1: Preview of types and illustrations of green-lite as heuristic concept regarding environmental policy and governance patterns

---

Complex policy "ends-means" calculus and conflict

• The frequent reality that key players see the policy *means* (instruments, approaches, and compliance provisions) as *ends* in themselves, and thus there is often no simple separation of broad, stated ends/purposes from highly valued, preferred means

• The creation of multiple ends/goals and discourse in statute development and law and in delegated law (regulation) when environmental policy must be interpreted and administered by more than one department or agency

• The increasing resort to using guidelines as soft co-regulation and co-governance approaches, especially with firms and industry associations but also with environmental organizations

Complex boundary realities: Hyphenated environmentalism

• The notion of complex boundaries in even defining what the environment is – in short, in determining or securing agreement about what is inside or outside the field as an overall policy field

• The reality that environmental policy is virtually always a hyphenated policy field, which means that most expressions of such policy involve the values of multiple agency mandates as expressed in statutes, policies, rules, and changing discourse

• The notion that core environment departments such as Environment Canada are fundamentally horizontal and cross-governmental in policy aspirational terms but must deal with numerous departments in a complex Cabinet that are more vertical and sectoral and that, at best, see only environmental matters as a smaller component in their mandates

Diverse and conflicting temporal realities

• The diverse temporal features of environmental policy where time can imply centuries and epochs, or intergenerational notions; or time expressed in terms of shorter-term electoral cycles, budgetary cycles, policy evaluation periods, and day-to-day statements of politically expressed progress, defensiveness, and failure

• The notion that environmental policy goals and ideas can focus on cleanup and remediation or prevention, and sometimes both

• The vast temporal scope, and legitimacy, of claims of safety regarding the long-term storage of nuclear and uranium wastes or carbon capture and storage

Diverse nature of, and triggering points for, environmental agendas in the context of wider policy and political-economic agenda processes

• Environmental policy can be triggered at any given time by both broad-scale environment-economy concerns and by harms and risks specific to an industrial sector or environmental issue, ranging from lead in gasoline, to the effects of biofuels for deforestation, and asbestos and human health

- The practical realities of how environmental public opinion, media coverage, and environmental agendas relate to political party agendas, to government agendas across minority or majority government cycles, and to specific major agenda-setting occasions such as the Speech from the Throne and annual Budget Speeches, federal-provincial first minister summits, and G-8 and G-20 global summits
- The short tenure in office of environmental ministers (eighteen months on average) as a separate feature of agenda-setting dynamics in the government and within Environment Canada

Complex multi-scalar and spatial environmental governance and democracy coordination and conflict dynamics

- Multilateral and bilateral federalist and local forms of governance and democracy regarding numerous simple versus more complex pollutants
- Cross-border (international and intra-national) scalar and spatial scope and manageability of water, land, air, and related realms of natural environmental capital
- Planetary scale and scope of global eco-politics and possible solutions regarding issues such as climate change, biodiversity, and species at risk

and in international environmental dynamics and agreements (see chapter 3). The larger part of the empirical evidence emerges in the analysis of the six environmental regimes. Our conclusions then draw out the empirical confirmations of the value of the green-lite concept examined in relation to the five policy and governance patterns and the resulting complexity.

Environmental Regimes

Environmental regimes are complex realms of mainly hyphenated environmental policy ideas, institutions, processes, interests, and policy instruments. The six regimes mapped and examined empirically are the:

- Environment Canada–Centred Regime (chapter 4)
- Energy-Environment Regime (chapter 5)
- Natural Resources–Environment Regime (chapter 6)
- Federal–Cities Urban Sustainability Regime (chapter 7)
- Federal–Municipal Infrastructure Sustainability Regime (chapter 8)
- NGO, Market, and Business–Environment Regime (chapter 9)

The first three regimes have the longest histories, reaching back forty to fifty years. The last three, although they have a longer lineage than one might initially think, tend to have consolidated in the past twenty to thirty years, and they each involve lessened federal control, though not a lack of federal involvement. Moreover, the three newer regimes required space and opportunities to gain traction and perhaps even consolidate; historically, however, we see that they often simply lay beside, underneath, or on top of the earlier regimes. We also look at the content and evolution of each regime and the overlaps and interactions among them. Environmental policy has been a hyphenated world descriptively, empirically, and politically from day one. These overlapping regimes compel us to look across multiple forms of delegated governance and democracy. These range from federal departments in the context of Cabinet parliamentary government to arm's-length agencies and public-private co-governance arrangements and networks; they also include provinces and cities and complex spatial, scalar, and regional decision-making arenas.

Environmental regimes, therefore, involve diverse environmental content and decision-making that is much larger and more complex than a single federal "environment" department or agency, and it is beyond the scope of one book to address them all in detail. For example, we do not examine other hyphenated environmental regimes through chapters centred on transportation, or trade, or food, or fisheries and oceans, though aspects of these emerge as illustrative examples. We examine the six defined environmental regimes as noted above because we consider them to be the most relevant and influential. However, because of political-economic debate, academic theory and discourse, and institutional politics, there are bound to be both agreements and disagreements about the precise boundaries and importance of such regimes.

Indeed, as indicated, boundary issues and overlaps are also often a key feature in the analyses of green-lite analytical complexity and empirical challenges. Some regimes such as infrastructure-related regimes have a longer lineage (such as in the history of oil and gas pipelines); these are now, however, a growing focus and/or are contending for analytical and practical recognition in academic environmental analysis. The same applies to regimes centred on cities and communities and on NGO, market, and business-driven certification systems.

Regime Elements

Environmental regime *elements* are basic important features that help understand some of the trajectories of environmental policy change and inertia, and they also provide related insights into the green-lite concept discussed above. The three main elements examined are:

- Environmental and related policy ideas, discourse, and agendas
- Environmental power structures, democracy, and governance
- Science, evidence, knowledge, and precaution

Each of the three elements is needed to provide a thorough account, but each poses different challenges regarding qualitative and quantitative evidence and the time periods being covered. As mentioned earlier, there are some overlaps among these elements. For example, ideas such as "natural capital" and "biodiversity" are relevant to both the ideas element and the science and evidence element.

The mixes of dominant and contending *environmental and related ideas, discourses, and agendas* are found in historical and still relevant contests among ideas such as "polluter pays" and sustainable development and green plans. These and other varied discourses and ideas also show up in the changing content of ministerial speeches such as those on "ethical oil" or "responsible resource development." Ideas about environmental policy and regulation appear in Speeches from the Throne; in interest-group, think-tank, and academic papers; and in the diverse kinds of sound-bite discourse developed by the media, Internet bloggers, social media networks, and political parties in partisan discourse and more recently in unremitting attack politics and continuous campaigning. Ideas that emerge briefly or continuously in central policy and budgetary agendas are also important, as are periods when environmental ideas, hyphenated or not, are not mentioned.

Environmental regimes also contain both entrenched and shifting systems of *environmental power structures, democracy, and governance*. Within the state, public power can involve the impacts of minority versus majority governments; it also encompasses the extended power of prime ministers over the Cabinet, compared to earlier periods or as exercised with greater focus in some regimes rather than others. The changing power relations faced by Environment Canada in relation to other economic and resource departments and agencies is a key part of the federal environmental story and is mirrored as well at the provincial, city, and international levels.

Private power focuses typically on the power of business, Canadian and global, including its preferred ministers and departments for focused policy lobbying such as Finance, Industry Canada, and natural resource ministries. However, understanding business power requires considering tensions among big business and small and medium-sized firms and Canadian versus foreign firms, including state-owned foreign firms. Green industry sectors and markets are also a part of the changing business power domain. Environmental NGOs and related consumer and medical-health interests are an additional source of power and influence, albeit usually not on as sustained or well-funded a basis as business. Governance as a concept in environmental policy regimes is increasingly and quintessentially about the interactions of public and private power and diverse kinds and norms of democracy; therefore, it involves complex co-governance arrangements and agreements with market stakeholders and social interests and networks.

Varied and changing kinds of *science, evidence, knowledge, and precaution* also underpin the structure of different environmental regimes. They are essential in assessing proposals for new environmental policies and regulations and in assessing new specific products, projects, and processes. But there are also conflicts among these terms. We assess these conflicts when considering questions such as the loss of evidence, or indeed the claimed death of evidence on environmental matters.

On science-based governance in different environmental regimes there must be analytical respect for the diverse meanings inherent in science-based government, including notions of research and development (R&D), related science activities (RSA), innovation policies, public goods, and linear and non-linear conceptions of science and technology pursued variously by front-line regulatory assessors, government labs, firms, universities, and foundations (Doern and Kinder 2007). Science-based governance also interacts with intellectual property "invention-centred" analysis and decisions regarding the correct delineation of private property and public good realms for knowledge regarding the environmental commons.

The role of science versus other forms of evidence and knowledge is an intricate feature of environmental regime development and inertia. *Ex-ante* regulatory assessment involves forms of benefit-cost analysis by economists and related required forms of regulatory impact analysis (RIAS) (Radaelli 2009; Mihlar 1999). The science and arts of *ex-post* regulatory program evaluation and even more difficult life-cycle analysis also loom large.

Aspects of transformational technologies are embedded in our conceptions of science-based and evidence-based environmental governance. They help define what new technologies (such as fracking or carbon capture and storage) consist of and also some of their characteristics as shape-shifting new "sectors" or horizontal transformational parts of all sectors, such as information technologies and environmental reporting (Phillips 2007).

The pairing of science-based and evidence-based governance with precautionary governance is necessary in several analytical senses. The precautionary principle, as indicated above, emerged as an explicit governance norm in environmental policy, national and international, partly to counter trade-related notions of sound science. As a governing norm and procedure, the precautionary principle stresses the need to respect the realities of scientific uncertainty and the need to not proceed with some projects, products, or processes when there is a risk of harm, even though scientific certainty about the risk is lacking.

MAIN QUESTIONS AND ARGUMENTS

Three principal questions are addressed in this book: (1) How, why, and to what extent has Canadian environmental policy, discourse, governance, and democracy changed in the last fifty years? (2) How does the multi-scalar nature and complex interaction of environmental regimes influence our ability to assess environmental policy? (3) Is environmental science and evidence declining as a factor and determinant in the conduct of environmental policy and in the development of environmental agendas?

We advance six related arguments. The first argument centres on our main green-lite discussion of policy complexity outlined above and its overall view of Canadian environmental policy and governance patterns across the fifty-year period.

Second, we contend that Canadian federal environmental policy was once nominally centred on Environment Canada; however, power and policy have increasingly been ceded to the prime minister and other central agencies in both the Chrétien-Martin and Harper eras and to other ministers and departments functioning in other environment-related regimes (as outlined below).

Third, we argue that Canadian environmental democracy – defined as criteria and venues of participation and consultation with groups,

interests, and citizens – has become increasingly fragmented and
diffuse. This may seem contradictory when seen against the above
argument about strong prime ministerial executive dominance. But
in other ways it is not. A primary driver of this change is the greater
importance of networked and Internet relations and a proliferation
of ways of understanding democratic practice in Canada, which
includes the growing presence and contending legitimacy of five criteria and venues of Canadian democracy: Cabinet-parliamentary
representative democracy; federalist democracy; interest-group pluralist democracy; civil-society democracy; and direct democracy,
including Internet-centred social media and networks. It also involves
conflicts and cooperation among such criteria and venues.

Fourth, we show that the importance and power of Canada's natural resources and the staples theory that underpins them continues
to significantly influence, drive, and often weaken overall environmental policy, particularly regarding the needed steps to develop
green industries and alternative green energy sources.

Fifth, we argue overall that Canada's environmental policy cannot
be understood without examining an ongoing rescaling of environmental governance, democracy, politics, and policy. Decisions have
been downscaled to the provincial and municipal level with implications for what priorities are set, how decisions are made, and what
outcomes ensue. Decisions have also been up-scaled to the supra-
national level, to intergovernmental and non-governmental processes and actors. On the latter, for instance, Canada's position in
the global economy as a major exporter of staple resources, such as
fish, food, oil, minerals, and forest products, exposes Canada to new
and old forms of international pressures. Most importantly, decisions being made through international supply chains by individual
companies, collections of companies, and multi-stakeholder private
regulatory initiatives are becoming critical venues shaping and sometimes surpassing the importance of Canada's public policy processes
at both the federal and provincial levels.

To understand the multiple and complex trajectories of environmental policy in Canada, we argue that a careful understanding of
this rescaling must be juxtaposed to the ongoing transformation of
Canada's federal environmental regimes (Auld 2014). This rescaling
is also prominent in the areas of green energy policies at the provincial level, regarding natural resources in particular (Hessing,
Howlett, and Summerville 2005), and in key urban sectors such as

construction, waste and infrastructure, and public transit (Steinberg 2013; Gladstone, Kennedy, and Abele 2013).

Sixth, environmental science has always had to compete for access and attention with other forms of evidence, knowledge, and practice, within Canada and internationally. However, we argue that there has been a significant change in the role of science and evidence in environmental policy and agendas in the current Harper era. In part this change involves the use of related knowledge regarding economics and cost-benefit analysis but also risk-benefit concepts and advocacy. It is, however, even more the product of communications strategies and related central control and the presence of permanent campaigning and attack politics and the explicit muzzling of federal scientists in the environmental field in particular.

THE EMPIRICAL ANALYSIS OF TWENTY-FIVE POLICY GOVERNANCE HISTORIES

We clearly build on other important related published sources (academic, think tank, governmental, and interest group, and non-governmental organization) that have examined more particular features of Canada's environmental policy, governance, and democracy, in addition to crucial studies of international developments. Canada is certainly examined in an international environmental context, but we do not conduct a full head-to-head comparison with other countries throughout the book. By integrating our areas of expertise and academic perspectives, we also build on, but considerably extend, our past work on environmental policy.

At its core we examine empirically twenty-five policy/governance histories traced over the relevant periods of coverage in the six environment-regime chapters (see table 0.2). These provide both scope and depth in the overall forty- to fifty-year empirical analysis of environmental policy and governance. In addition, environmental agendas are examined in chapter 2 on prime ministerial eras, and six other international policy and governance histories are examined contextually in chapter 3. These include: Canada-US environmental policy relations; the Great Lakes; biodiversity; international conventions and protocol-setting processes and agendas; environmental-trade agreements; climate change and the Kyoto Protocol and post-Kyoto eras, and the high Arctic.

Table 0.2: The six environmental regimes and illustrative policy/governance histories

Environmental regimes	Illustrative policy/governance histories
Environment Canada–Centred Regime (chapter 4)	• Early Environment Canada units: staying and leaving (1971 to late 1980s) • Department as networked; environment-economy institution (1990 to 2002) • Environment Canada and diverse prime ministerial and central policy controls and influences (2002 to 2013) • Environment Canada as a changing science- and evidence-based department • Environmental assessment of projects
Energy-Environment Regime (chapter 5)	• Nuclear energy (1950s to present) • The National Energy Board (1959 to present) • Federal energy departments as lead players (1966 to present) • The Harper era (2006 to present)
Natural Resources–Environment Regime (chapter 6)	• Resource promoter (and regulator?) (1867 to 1970s) • Changing terms of the relationship (1980s) • International sustainable development agenda (1992 to 2006) • From sustainable development to responsible resource development (2006 to 2013)
Federal–Cities Urban Sustainability Regime (chapter 7)	• A pre-sustainable development era (late 1960s and 1970s) • Early sustainable development and environmental concerns (1979 to 1993) • Cities and communities New Deal era (1993 to 2006) • Demise of explicit cities focus in recession and open federalism era (2006–2013)
Federal–Municipal Infrastructure Sustainability Regime (chapter 8)	• Infrastructure as nation building (post–First World War to 1960s) • Unsustainable urban growth: federal government as municipal banker (1960s to 1970s) • Early sustainable development and environmental concerns (1979 to 1993) • Green infrastructure and the New Deal (1993 to 2006) • Changing agendas, but "green" infrastructure dollars still flow (2006 to 2013)
NGO, Market, and Business–Environment Regime (chapter 9)	• Roots of discontent (1960s to 1970s) • Trying to gain influence (1960s to 1980s) • Rise of private governance and co-governance (1990 to 2013)

Our twenty-five policy and governance case histories draw empirically on numerous reports and studies of Canadian and international environmental policies and issues by academic, think tank, and governmental entities, complemented by our own research, including a large number of interviews with environmental regime officials and players across the six regimes.

The historical content of the empirical chapters broadly covers a fifty-year period, mainly chronologically but often and necessarily by moving back and forth between earlier periods to more recent developments in the Harper and also Chrétien-Martin prime ministerial eras. We sometimes reference even earlier historical events, given their foundational influence on Canada's current environmental policies. The regime chapters also include key features of the Canadian constitution and federal-provincial law and rule-making powers and conflicts and, as previewed above, provincial developments as well as cities and local government in a multi-scalar context. Although we cannot analyze all provincial or individual city initiatives here in a full comparative way, we believe our framework and conclusions will encourage others to do so, thereby adding to this fifty-year study and coverage of Canadian environmental policy, governance, and democracy.

The book thus empirically investigates the transformations and forms of change and inertia that have occurred in Canadian environmental policy, governance, and democracy. Guided by our green-lite concept, we examine questions about the federal government's environmental role. Is its role in retreat? Is it being redirected? Or has the situation always been more variegated and understated? Such questions can be further extended to assess and understand emerging and evolving concepts of environmental rights, sustainability, consumption, nature, and naturalness (Walker 2012; Wiles 2007). In discussing such questions and issues, we inevitably shed some light on means as well as ends, particularly in the context of policy implementation and evaluation.

The book is organized into two parts. Part One consisting of chapters 1, 2, and 3 examines key contextual aspects of the analysis, including the book's conceptual foundations; it also covers the prime ministerial eras of environmental policy, Canada-US relations, and international environmental negotiations and agreements. Part Two provides in chapters 4 to 9 the empirical analysis of six key changing environmental regimes and our twenty-five policy histories. Conclusions are offered in chapter 10.

PART ONE

Conceptual Foundations and Historical Context

1

Conceptual Foundations

INTRODUCTION

This chapter lays out the conceptual foundations that inform our study of environmental policy, democracy, and governance in Canada. We examine the foundational literature with three purposes in mind: to provide context for the book's readers, to pave the way for aspects of our regime analysis and analytical framework, and to provide initial examples of our green-lite concept.

The foundational literature, combined with our empirical research, led to the development of the book's three-part analytical framework presented in the book's introduction: green-lite as a heuristic analytical map for complex environmental policy and governance patterns, environmental regimes, and regime elements. This conceptual review draws on academic, governmental, and other studies that are historical, contemporary, Canadian, and comparative. The literature emerges from diverse social science disciplines and fields, including political science, economics, law, sociology, public policy, science and technology policy, governance, and public administration. The environmental regime analysis in Part Two of the book draws on other, more particular, policy-relevant literature as well.

Three conceptual literature streams provide a crucial theoretical and applied environmental policy, governance, and democracy foundation. These streams are: environmental ideas; the political economy of environmental policy; and environmental democracy and governance in a complex, networked Internet world. We explore each briefly to detail its links and overlaps and show how they are foundational for our analysis overall. Table 1.1 previews the content to be discussed.

Table 1.1: Conceptual foundations in brief

Environmental ideas
- Conservation ethics
- End-of-pipe cleanup and related remediation
- "Polluter-pay" principle
- Limits to growth
- Sustainable development (SD)
- Science-based decision-making
- Precautionary principle
- Low-carbon economy
- Natural capital and the environmental commons
- Green industries

The political economy of environmental policy
- Capitalism and business power: interest groups and corporations
- Prime ministerial, Cabinet, and executive power at the federal and provincial level
- Aboriginal peoples
- Environmental federalism
- Cities and communities
- Global eco-politics, rescaling, and the changing logic of collective action
- Consumer power and green consumption
- Environmental NGOs and think tanks
- Scientists as a power and influence base

Environmental governance and democracy in a complex, networked, Internet world
- Contending democratic criteria and arenas
- Environmental agenda-setting
- Networks, the Internet, and theories of complexity
- Policy, governance, and time: life-cycle approaches
- Environmental science–based governance as applied to policies, projects, product, and process assessments and approvals
- Environmental governance and varied policy instrument dynamics
- Changing types of environmental regulation

ENVIRONMENTAL IDEAS

Environmental ideas are reflected in formal policy statements; in theoretical concepts, some of which become formal scientific or policy paradigms; in changing departmental names and mandates; in emerging environmental discourses defined as a "shared way of looking at the world" (Dryzek 2013, 5) or as ways of reframing policy to gain greater consensus or to reinforce differences (Fischer 2003); and in media and partisan sound-bites and political communication strategies. Few, if any, of these ever leave the field of discourse and advocacy within environmental policy in Canada and internationally; in total, they reflect green-lite features of environmental policy. While ideas that emerge from the environmental sphere are central, others also matter. In Part Two, we necessarily discuss ideas regarding energy, resource, and northern development, and key ideas about competitiveness, innovation, and economic development. These ideas include liberalized energy markets, energy security, regional fairness and burden sharing, and, recently, discourse characterizing Canada as an "energy superpower" and as a supporter and source of "ethical oil."

Conservation ethics were an early normative foundation that predates the formation of core departments such as Environment Canada; they have had a presence throughout Canada's history. Indeed, conservationists came to Environment Canada in 1971 when staff and mandates were transferred from the Department of Energy, Mines and Resources (Doern and Conway 1994). As an idea, conservation ethics were also pre-eminent in Canada's early national and provincial parks, and they are apparent in forms of citizen science provided by bird and wildlife watchers and in many Aboriginal hunting and fishing practices (Kinder 2010; Henderson 2013).

End-of-pipe cleanup and related remediation ideas have been central from the outset of the environmental age. They focus on the cleanup of pollution emissions and effluents that have already occurred and done harm, as well as any remediation necessary to remove contamination from soil, surface water, or groundwater sediment. In addition, they have links to the *polluter-pay principle* and Pigou and other economists' concepts regarding externalities, in this case negative externalities. The policy instruments associated with these ideas are end-of-pipe control measures achieved through requirements for "best practicable technology" regarding new industrial plants but not old existing industrial plants (Doern and Conway 1994). In short, cleanup and "polluter-pay" ideas are linked to further practical questions, such as how fast cleanup occurs, whether payment is by the polluter alone, or indeed whether it occurs at all (Helm 2003).

The limits to growth paradigm featured prominently in environmental debates in the 1960s and 1970s, as articulated by international entities such as the Club of Rome (Meadows et al. 1972). It argued that ever-growing economies and industrial production were ultimately incompatible with a clean environment, as was unlimited and inadequately regulated energy use. This idea lost favour in later decades, but concerns about how much growth is tolerable and sensible for the planet and for specified ecosystems are perennial in environmental-economy debates and advocacy and resistance strategies. It undergirds, for instance, projects such as the Global Footprint Network, which annually calculates the resource-use footprint of human society (see www.footprintnetwork.org).

Using different discourse and involving a more explicit and even deeper discussion of the limits and dangers of trying to use technologies to solve climate change, debate has emerged about the "anthropocene" gap (Galaz 2014). The anthropocene gap refers to the geological limits of the earth's current ecosystem, subject increasingly to human-made challenges and harms when, as Hayden (2014) argues, even green growth is not enough. In related ways, official studies by global bodies such as the World Bank (2012; Revkin 2014) are also expanding the basis and scope of these issues.

Sustainable development (SD) refers to policies anchored in preventive and intergenerational ideas about environmental harms and benefits. As articulated especially by the Brundtland Commission (1987) in the late 1980s, SD is an idea and paradigm that aims to ensure, across governance areas, that the environment and its ecosystems are left in at least as good a state for the next generation as they were for the current generation (Boutros et al. 2010; Lafferty and Meadowcroft 2000). Cast somewhat more loosely, such policies are often seen by governments as those that balance the economic, social, and environmental effects of policies – the "triple bottom line" (Toner 2000). In the process of practising SD approaches, environmental harms such as endangered species have been identified, and policy solutions have been extended to explicit international and national policies about preserving biodiversity, albeit with results that are very mixed or often difficult to discern (Stoett 2012).

In more specific energy policy terms, sustainable development is tested initially against the basic concept of whether Canada has made progress in even reducing energy use on a per capita basis over the past forty years, or as evidenced by other measures of energy efficiency. Since such per capita usage has actually increased marginally or has produced only sluggish gains in some sectors but not others, there is clearly much more to do (International Energy Agency 2004; Doern 2005). When the Kyoto Protocol and its requirements for reductions in greenhouse gas emissions are added as a core test of sustainable development, then the Canadian record is bad in basic emission terms, because Canadian emissions increased by over 24 per cent in the period from 2002 to 2010, and indeed the Harper government formally announced Canada's withdrawal from the Kyoto Protocol obligations in 2011 (see chapter 2 and 3).

In addition, sustainable development criteria have been implanted in federal policy and decision processes, in some statutory mandates, and in some reporting activities by departments (Commissioner of the Environment and Sustainable Development 2012; Toner and Meadowcroft 2009; VanNijnatten 2002). Sustainability values are also often expressed in terms of environmental rights and justice per se (Boyd 2012; Walker 2012), rights and concepts of justice that apply to pollution cleanup and prevention and that are intergenerational and applying therefore to present and future populations. In some related policy fields (e.g., biotechnology), sustainable development ideas have also been expressed under concepts such as stewardship and respect for life (Doern and Prince 2012). Thus some changed policy processes are in place but certainly not major changes in policy outcomes; this pattern of halted transition, we suggest, reflects the green-lite reality at play in Canada today (Bregha 2011; 2006; Boutras et al. 2010).

Science-based decision-making is a pervasive idea in that much of environmental policy is underpinned by a belief in the need for independent science and technology knowledge as practised by scientists and technical experts, both to identify harms, risks, and pollutants and to develop ways of eliminating or minimizing adverse effects and also preventing pollution from occurring in the first place. Such decision-making also is rooted in an idea in international and internal trade policy, where it was intended to ensure that environmental and health protections were based only on science and were not an avenue for new forms of anti–free trade protectionism (Trebilcock 2011; Braithwaite and Drahos 2000). Science-based decision-making was a key part of early environmental assessments of projects and also of policy-making, but these assessment tasks were also featured by broader evidence-based decision-making, including risk-benefit analysis (Howlett 2011; Hood, Rothstein, and Baldwin 2001). The nature of the science also became much more complex and inter-disciplinary, as environmental policy and regulation was applied to ever more complex pollutants and hazards, many of which were interacting (Kinder 2010). Thus differences and uncertainty emerged as governments moved from dealing with relatively simple harms, such as lead or mercury, to later ones, such as greenhouse gases and biodiversity, species at risk, and related complex habitats and ecosystems.

The precautionary principle is an environmental decision-making idea that allows policy-makers, regulators, and scientists to take provisional risk-management measures when an assessment points to the likelihood of harmful environmental and health effects and there is a lack of scientific certainty (Vogel 2012; Saner 2002. The European Union has been particularly strong in formally and infor-mally endorsing this idea in EU law in areas such as food policy, in part in response to direct pressure and actions by the European Parliament. The principle has also been adopted in Canadian federal laws and policies, but Canada has been much more cautious, in part because of the stronger forces and pressures that support the above-mentioned idea of science-based decision-making. Nonetheless, pre-caution is always embedded in the underlying policy discourse in the environmental realm, as new products and production processes emerge (Doern and Prince 2012). Indeed, Stirling (2013, 2) argues, "Precaution reminds us that innovation is not a forced one-track race to the future. Instead, like biological evolution, technical prog-ress entails constantly branching paths ... the notion of exclusively science-based decisions under uncertainty is an oxymoron."

Low-carbon economy goals and related energy ideas comingle in the environmental domain because of the underlying reality that energy policy as a whole refers to policies aimed at influencing and shaping the supply of energy sources and fuels, the demand for them by energy-users, and, ever more importantly, the environmental impacts of energy use (Helm 2012; Bridge and Le Billon 2013). The low-carbon economy refers to efforts to reduce the use the energy sources with the worst greenhouse gas emissions (such as coal and fossil fuels) so as to reduce the threats of climate change and also generate a newer, more renewable energy mix to anchor the economy and generate innovation and prosperity (Hayden 2014; Giddens 2011; National Roundtable on the Environment and the Economy 2011b). The climate-change literature examines diverse and complex combined kinds of economic and social issues, including distributional aspects, biodiversity, shale gas and fracking technology, and adaptation related to floods and risk-management in extreme events (Dryzek, Norgaard, and Scholsberg 2013; Brooks 2013; Cohen and Fullerton 2013; Maes et al. 2013; and Keskitalo and Carina 2013).

As we detail in chapter 5, the Energy-Environment Regime covers energy-resource domains, sources and fuels such as oil and natural gas, coal, hydroelectricity, nuclear energy, and a host of alternative or renewable sources such as biofuels, fuel cells, solar energy, wind power, and biomass, and also energy-efficiency and conservation measures and activities (Clark 2013). Energy policy also involves global, national, and regional politics, where past and current conflicts over prices and energy security influence views of what future environmental-energy policy should and should not be (Eberlein and Doern 2009; Doern and Gattinger 2003).

Natural capital and the environmental commons are closely linked ideas. Natural capital is defined by one environmental agency as "the land, air, water, living organisms of the earth's biosphere that provide us with ecosystem goods and services, imperative for survival and well-being" (International Institute for Sustainable Development 2013, 1). Such capital is normally not accounted for in conventional economics and measures of national and global wealth. The environmental commons is cast in ways similar to those of public goods, where private property concepts, laws, and rules are unworkable and harmful (Brousseau et al. 2012). The environmental commons and the avoidance of the tragedy of the commons has found frequent expression by advocates and scholars, most notably the work of Elinor Ostrom (1990, 2012), which has examined numerous situations where common resources are managed in the absence of control via public authority or private property rights. Studies of water, oceans, fisheries, and air have borne out these challenges of management in diverse international spaces and over long periods of time (Castree 2014; Clancy 2011, 2014). Recently, the Global Ocean

Commission (2014), an expert and politically high- profile body whose membership includes former Canadian prime minister Paul Martin, published a major report on the deteriorating state of the world's oceans and fisheries and how to rescue this crucial and complex part of the environmental commons.

The climate change debate and negotiations and the advocacy of sustainable development as a policy paradigm are quintessentially about such kinds of natural capital and the environmental commons, and so are various overall concepts of resource stewardship. Federal environmental advisory bodies such as the National Roundtable on the Environment and the Economy (NRTEE 2003) have tied concepts of natural capital to earlier notions of nature conservation. NRTEE identified many continuing barriers to the adoption of a natural capital concept, including a failure to integrate the true costs and benefits of nature in federal decision-making. Among its recommendations was the need for spatial concepts such as "conservation planning for whole landscapes" (NRTEE 2003, 43).

Green industries as an explicit idea and goal emerged in two senses. First, there was an environmental sector emerging, in part because tougher environmental regulations were creating a market for firms to solve environmental problems and generate new, greener production processes. Second, even firms or sectors with bad pollution records could become greener industries gradually. Later, studies and NGO pressures were also extending the notion of the non-renewable sector to a more explicit reference to "green industries" as such and to discourse that spoke of "the green race" globally, and to "climate prosperity," and of how Canada "needs to be ready" (NRTEE 2011b). This links to explicit arguments that Canada not bind its energy and climate-change policies in lockstep with the United States, which is the Harper government's preferred approach (NRTEE 2011b; MacDonald 2011). Meanwhile, Canadian initiatives on green industries were mainly provincial and, in comparison with those of other countries such as Germany and Sweden, were weak and scarcely noticeable (Rivers and Jaccard 2009; Lipp 2007).

THE POLITICAL ECONOMY
OF ENVIRONMENTAL POLICY

The political economy of environmental policy literature refers to broad interpretations of stages in environmental development where the focus is on the macro- and also meso-level relations of power between the state and capitalism and between the state and society federally and provincially (Winfield 2012; Coleman and Skogstad 1990). It also relates to so-called meta power paradigms defined as "power over power, transformative and structuring power" (Burns and Hall 2012), including as it relates to sustainability (Burns 2012). The presentation is broadly chronological, but it must be stressed that most of the issues and arguments are still in play as interests that are themselves institutions in the governance structure debate and characterize the ideas and power structures involved. Environmental policy entered a core structure of political-economic power in Canada and globally and sought to change and reshape it and was in turn itself reshaped across the forty to fifty years being examined.

Capitalism and Business Power: Interest Groups and Corporations as Institutions

Capitalism is clearly at the centre of the environmental policy story, as it is in other policy fields. As an organizational system centred on markets, profits, property rights, and corporations as limited liability institutions, capitalism defines and creates opposition to and support for environmental policy. The analysis of globalization and national environmental policy intervention is also highly relevant here, both in general and in particular sub-realms of environmental policy and their particular structures of global political power (Wijen et al. 2013). A recent and hotly debated book that frontally relates capitalism with climate change is Naomi Klein's *This Changes Everything* (Klein 2014). She makes the case that capitalism is the institutional driver of climate change, the dominant threat to the survival of the planet, arguing that market-based approaches and carbon trading will not be the saviours of the planet. She argues that the changes to our relationship with nature and one another that are required to respond to the climate crisis humanely should be catalysts for broader human and democratic change, including pulling back strongly from capitalism in its modern neo-liberal form. Others engaged in similar previous analyses may see Klein's future as one possibility but not a predetermined one, given the contradictions inherent in capitalism (Newell and Paterson 2010).

The business corporation as an institution in particular has both direct and indirect political power and social power (Wilks 2013). It wields power via its capacity to invest and disinvest, via business ethics, and via its strategic plans and its relations with shareholders and investors. Understanding environmental political economy through the concept of varieties of capitalism is also highly relevant (Hall and Soskice 2001). Within Canada, particular provinces have historically exhibited different kinds of capitalism, ranging from more state-centred varieties in Quebec and Saskatchewan to market-oriented varieties in Alberta and Ontario. Canada, being subject to the power of American businesses and earlier British capital overall, and in particular industries, has been a central theme (Clarkson 2009). The study of Canadian natural resource industries under Innis's staples theory and under more recent theories of national resource-based, centre-periphery relations easily resonates in the environmental policy mosaic in general, including policies in the north and high Arctic (Hessing, Howlett, and Summerville 2005; Byers 2009; Abele 2011; "The Melting North" 2012).

The notion of *regulatory capitalism* has also emerged conceptually and empirically (Braithwaite 2005, 2008; Levi-Faur 2005) and is highly relevant to understanding environmental policy and governance and its green-lite features. It seeks to differentiate regulatory capitalism from the neo-liberal capitalism era of the 1970s and 1980s. It seeks to capture the fact that regulation, including environmental regulation, is growing markedly but is less a feature of state rule and enforcement alone and much more a system of co-regulation between the state and business interests and firms as partner institutions but also other non-state interests and networks (Doern, Prince, and Schultz 2014; Grabosky 2012).

Business power in the environmental domain involves a changing array of corporations and business interests. The configuration of business interests includes interest groups, sectors, and firms that have been long-term traditional polluters in sectors such as oil and gas and minerals. These sectors' core instincts have been to lobby against robust environmental policy and regulation. But the nature of business power in environmental matters has become more complex because, in part at least, business interests are more divided and differentiated (Faulkner 2008; Doern 2005). At present, they include: growing industries such as the telecom and IT sector that see themselves as clean; pressure and requirements from financial, insurance, and securities industries that firms make known their environmental liabilities; the sustainable development strategies of some leading innovative firms and the growth of environmental industries, in short, firms that profit from tough new regulations and the development of new technologies that address environmental problems.

While energy business interests certainly contain firms that are polluters and greenhouse gas emitters, they also include key firms known to be environmentally progressive and that see economic opportunity in new green environmental technologies as alternatives to the carbon economy (Macdonald 2011). Globally, huge firms such as British Petroleum (BP) symbolically changed their logo to mean "beyond petroleum," with the hope to pursue strategies quite different from those of, say, Exxon. Nonetheless, BP was the undoubted corporate villain in the huge oil spill in the Gulf of Mexico in the southern United States in 2010. But some subtlety and nuance is needed in looking at global firms. BP was an innovator on one front. It was a big proponent of market-based solutions to environmental problems, such as climate change. It was a leader on this file and helped promote it in Europe, as it saw this initiative aligning with its business strength. BP did not, on the other hand, have strength on the technical side of the oil business, as the 2010 disaster showed, something where Exxon is seen as a stronger player. In Canada, companies such as TransAlta have developed strategies for profiting from emission reductions and alternative technologies, and there are other examples along these lines as well.

Energy industry associations further illustrate the complexity and diversity of contemporary interests lobbying in the environmental policy field overall. Key national lobbies such as the Canadian Electricity Association, which used to consist of a handful of big, mainly provincially owned utilities, now also consist of many dozens of smaller firms that are entering the restructured and liberalized electricity markets (Dewees 2009). They have diverse views about the energy-environment trade-offs and linkages and how to profit from them. In a different way, core energy lobbies such as the Canadian Association of Petroleum Producers (CAPP) lobby in ways that recognize their diverse mix of small and large energy players, some of which see themselves as being in the environmental industries sector. CAPP has crafted and lobbied for its own approaches to more incentive-based environmental policy and regulation, which recently includes carbon sequestration.

The Canadian environment-energy business lobby is also characterized by some divisions between powerful multinational oil companies (the majority US foreign owned) and the more numerous, smaller oil and gas companies that tend to operate at the exploration phase of oil and gas development. Core links to the US energy industry lobby are, as a result, built into Canada's environmental politics, all the more so as the US government and American multinational oil firms have their eye firmly on Alberta's oil sands as a vital part of current and future strategic energy supply for the United States. The ever-growing level of Canadian natural gas exports to the United States also ensures a central US market and lobbying presence in Canada's internal environment-energy industry politics. In recent years, China and its state and private firms have become additional players in energy and resource markets, as it seeks to meet insatiable, fast-growing demands for energy and resources to meet its booming economies.

While the above discussion gives us a core sampling of concepts and institutions regarding business power and capitalism, it will be necessarily augmented in later chapters, including the account in chapter 6 of natural resource institutions, and in chapter 9 of combined business and environmental institutions functioning in the NGO, Market, and Business–Environment Regime, often through negotiated certification systems.

Prime Ministerial, Cabinet, and Executive Power at the Federal and Provincial Level

This domain of overall political executive power has been central to understanding environmental policy and its inevitable hyphenated nature. We see this in more detail in chapter 2 on federal prime ministerial eras. Federally, the themes here are quite diverse. With hindsight, the Mulroney Conservative era has been seen – even by environmental groups – as Canada's most progressive green era. The current Harper era is seen thus far as a period of environmental policy retrenchment. Analyses of executive power on environmental matters have stressed from the outset that Environment Canada, within the Cabinet and its committees, has been surrounded by a sea of critics and interests working through other departments, including Natural Resources Canada and Industry Canada (Doern and Phidd 1983). Indeed, when the Cabinet had an "environment committee," it was composed mainly of this broader array of ministers. This, among other reasons, is why we need to look at the six regimes examined in Part Two of the book regarding our conceptions of green-lite complexity. Most of them flow out of changes in executive power and structure and related new understandings of expanding but also hyphenated environmental policy.

In the Harper era, with the Conservatives' anti-Kyoto stance and Canada as an energy superpower discourse, the Cabinet or its committees has had exceedingly little say. Energy-environmental policy has been under the direct personal control of the prime minister to a considerable extent, as have other key decisions. Earlier eras, to be sure, also exhibited this centralized power to some extent. The period from 1980 to 1984, following the oil crisis of 1979–1980, was characterized by massive federal intervention by means of the Trudeau Liberals' National Energy Policy (NEP), a policy strongly opposed by energy interests in Alberta and Western Canada overall (Doern and Toner 1985). Then, in 1985, Mulroney-led federal energy policy was decidedly pro-market but augmented by the discourse, if the not the actions, of sustainable development, including the quite highly praised Mulroney Conservatives' 1990 Green Plan (Toner 2000; Doern and Conway 1994).

Aboriginal Peoples

The structure of interests concerning Aboriginal peoples has also changed in the environment-energy context. Treaties, land claims, and related self-governance aspirations in Canada's regions has conferred on Aboriginal peoples mixes of direct sovereign powers along with territorial governance, shared authorities, and delegated responsibilities (Abele and Prince 2006). These provisions have been accompanied by a quite different set of views about energy and resource development, compared to the debate in the Berger Commission era of the 1970s (see details in chapter 5). Aboriginal peoples increasingly tend to favour development, provided there is local control over employment, benefits, and investment (Coates et al. 2008). Indeed, more recently, Henderson (2013) has made the case that locally based clean-energy approaches are becoming, and could increasingly become, a defining feature of Aboriginal life. On other aspects of energy policy such as climate change, there are major concerns, because Aboriginal peoples in the north are already experiencing adverse climate change effects yet see little action from the federal government, whose focus since 2006, paradoxically, has

been on the economic opportunities and sovereignty issues in opening up the Northwest Passage to shipping and commerce because of
the melting of the ice due to climate change (English 2013; Abele
2011; Byers 2009).

Environmental Federalism

Environmental policy, governance, and democracy in Canada is
environmental federalism on a de facto basis. The Canadian constitution of 1867 emerged before governments knew about environmental matters or tried to deal with them. So both levels of
government have been involved since the 1970s, initially creating
environment departments and then gradually establishing federal
and provincial environmental assessment regimes for projects and
regulations and control practices for particular local, regional, and
national pollutants (Harrison 1996). As environmental matters
increased and became more complex, mechanisms for federal and
provincial environmental ministers to meet, discuss, and coordinate
policies emerged.

Canada's environmental policy and basic politics are influenced
profoundly by conflicts between major energy *producer* regions / provinces (and related energy business interests whose centre of power
has been in the oil and gas sector and now, in particular, the oil sands
sector) and other more populous *consumer regions,* provinces,
and interests, especially Ontario and Quebec. These clashes have
been especially important when energy prices have risen suddenly
and sharply, as they did in 1973 and 1979, and again in recent
years. Such conflicts surface in a central way over Canada's climate change policies and the issue of burden-sharing among provinces and their main industries (MacDonald 2011; Canada West
Foundation 2010). Inter-regional pressures also have arisen over
nuclear energy. Canada's CANDU reactor was developed through
federal support for R&D. Although actual reactor sales and use have
been confined mostly to Ontario, Canada's main nuclear province
(Bratt 2012; Doern, Dorman, and Morrison 2001). And Canada's
vast and diverse forest endowments are spread across Canada's
provinces (Luckert, Haley, and Hoberg 2012).

The inherent multi-level governance attributes of the federation
extend outwards to Canada's adherence to trade agreements and
a growing number of environmental agreements that deal with

particular pollutants and ecosystems (see chapter 3). These attributes further extend downwards to major cities and local governments. They also extend to spatial spheres and areas defined by particular air, water, and land and production-plant realities. But in *federal-provincial* jurisdictional terms, energy and natural resource jurisdiction resides overwhelmingly at the provincial level regarding energy and resource laws, and primary tax jurisdiction as well. When Canadian energy and resource federalism is compared to that of other federations, Canada tends to come in at the highly decentralized end of the comparative jurisdictional and related political power equation (Eberlein and Doern 2009). Moreover, since provincial resource and energy endowments are vastly different, it also means that any resulting or possible federal-provincial arrangements or agreements (spending or regulatory) are bound to be variously bilateral, partially multilateral, or wholly multilateral, depending on key spatial realities such as dealing with offshore petroleum development, and fisheries and oceans and fresh water (Clancy 2011, 2014; McGrane 2013). The federal government, for its part, has more limited jurisdiction, but constitutionally, it does have some entry points for laws, spending, and rule-making in constitutional fields such as the conditional spending power; the trade and commerce power; the generalized peace, order, and good government provision; and via some aspects of foreign and international policy, including trade and security, and varied treaty areas.

On the environment side, this extended multi-level governance system is shaped by the fact that multilateral environmental agreements are each different, because they deal with different specific pollutants/emissions or environmental practices. This means that Canada confronts a diversity of soft and hard law rules as part of its international obligations. Such agreements range from the Great Lakes, to acid rain, and the ozone layer, and extend to the most complex of them all, the UN Framework Convention on Climate Change and its associated instruments, such as the Kyoto Protocol (Harrabin 2012).

Cities and Communities

Cities and communities are a part of the power and governance structure within provinces and nationally. The core literature is relevant here, both in this primary constitutional sense and in

environmental terms and concerns about local pollution and congestion, and urban renewal and other expressed green-related issues
(Graham and Andrew 2014; Stoney and Graham 2009; Tindal and
Tindal 2004; Wolfe 2003; Axworthy 1971). A more particular impetus came from the processes and report of the Brundtland Commission (1987) and from its later urban- and community-focused
Agenda 21 processes, studies, and proposals (United Nations 1992),
including concepts such as human settlements. In later phases, literature on cities and communities that focused on urban spaces and
also regional-city clusters in innovation-environment literature are
also relevant for our analysis (Wolfe 2009; Bradford 2004a). The
analysis in chapter 7 of the Federal–Cities Urban Sustainability
Regime and in chapter 8 of the Federal–Municipal Infrastructure
Sustainability Regime draw on this core literature but also on other
relevant analytical material on cities and communities.

Global Eco-Politics, Rescaling, and the Changing Logic of Collective Action

Global eco-politics is a conception of global environmental and governance challenges first developed by Pirages (1978) and recently
expanded and examined more fully by Peter Stoett (2012). In Stoett's
view, global eco-politics "conveys the inherent complexity of the
task: the centrality of collective action problems, the wide range of
actors, the technical and scientific challenges and opportunities, and
the need for both leadership and widespread legitimacy" (8).

"Rescaling" refers to a body of literature that argues that globalization is causing a rescaling of such collective action problems that
they are no longer very well matched to the scale of the nation state.
As Cerny (1995) explains, "The more that the scale of goods and
assets produced, exchanged, and/or used in a particular economic
sector or activity diverges from the structural scale of the national
state – both from above (the global scale) and from below (the local
scale) – and the more that those divergences feed back into each
other in complex ways, then the more that the authority, legitimacy,
policy making capacity, and policy implementation effectiveness of
states will be challenged from both without and within" (597). Not
surprisingly, this kind of political economy theory has usefully
found its way into diverse policy fields, including environmental
policy, climate change, and urban and local government (Brenner

2009; Andonova and Mitchell 2010; Okereke and Bulkely 2009; Bulkely 2010).

The extended discussion in this book of green-lite features takes us into these global eco-politics and rescaling realities and also ambiguities. It extensively explores these features in the discussion of environmental federalism and cities and communities as human settlement areas in key regime chapters 6, 7, 8, and 9. Before this, though, these features are apparent in chapter 3 regarding the Arctic north and the complex structure of particular pollution- and hazard-centred protocols and also features of trade agreements and their treatment of environmental matters.

Consumer Power and Green Consumption

Consumer interests and citizen-consumers are also germane to the basic political economy of environmental policy. A key point to note is that there are more arenas for the expression of consumer interests, precisely because markets have gained a greater hold in the national and global economy. Consumer-citizens mount continuous challenges, increasingly via social media, regarding the quality of consumption, in short, not just what products are made but how they are made in environmental or related quality of production terms (Webb 2004; Princen, Maniates, and Comca 2002). This can extend to whether investors, small and big, will invest in firms with bad or dubious environmental records. Some of these developments and dynamics are also a linked to the story of how environmental voluntary codes and eventual private governance-certification developments occurred in the forestry sector but also earlier in the chemical industry. But in these regimes, environmental NGOs were the bigger force for change and not consumer interests per se. These are a key part of chapters 6 and 9 but also emerge in our discussion of international environmental policy in chapter 3.

Environmental Non-Governmental Organizations and Think Tanks

On the core environmental NGO side of the equation of private-public interest-oriented power and influence are even more numerous and varied organizations and associations, increasingly with complex networks and alliances with US and international environmental

NGOS (Paehlke 2010; Pralle 2003; VanNijnatten and Boardman 2002). NGOS still seek to mobilize national and global pressure and public opinion to ensure that Canada's environmental policy on energy and other policy fields is progressive. However, the strategies of groups such as Greenpeace, Energy Probe, Pollution Probe, the Sierra Club, the Pembina Institute, the Canadian Arctic Resources Committee, and the David Suzuki Foundation can differ enormously. Environmental advocates also function in and through advisory bodies such as the federal government's National Roundtable on the Environment and the Economy, in numerous local and provincial-regional settings, and in business and industry co-governance settings and arrangements (Auld and Cashore 2013). Compared to even a decade ago, such interests, while still maintaining overall pressure, are much more literate about, experienced with, and prepared to consider varied ways of dealing with energy-environmental problems, from direct regulation to incentives and tradable permit systems. Canada's Green Party is also a presence and in the 2011 federal general election saw their Leader, Elizabeth May, elected to Parliament.

Cross-border Canada-US environmental-energy lobbying on pipelines has reached complex levels of intensity. The proposed Keystone XL oil pipeline to bring Alberta oil sands petroleum south to Texas encountered strong environmental opposition in Nebraska regarding its planned route in that state. This quickly became a partisan and pre-election issue in the United States in the run-up to the November 2012 elections, resulting in a decision by the Obama administration to reject the proposal, at least regarding that part of the pipeline route. Somewhat in response to this decision, the Harper government began to speak more frequently about exporting Canada's oil to China. The Harper government also took a hard political line regarding the Northern Gateway pipeline proposal hearings by the National Energy Board. The pipeline to the BC coast would allow expanded Canadian gas exports to Chinese and Pacific Rim markets. The Harper government launched a strong criticism that labelled some Canadian environmental groups as unpatriotic, regarding their opposition and their alleged links to funding and support by US environmental groups (Toner and McKee 2014). The complex structure and formation of such NGOS using international market pressure and alliances with groups in the United States and numerous countries is mapped in more detail in chapter 9 and is simultaneously a feature of rescaling and thus green-lite complexity.

Scientists as a Power and Influence Base

Perhaps the hardest interest to pin down in the political economy of environmental policy is that of scientists inside and outside of government, and internationally. Individual scientist advocates such as David Suzuki and those who may be members of environmental roundtables and panels, or who have strong university-based reputations, exert considerable advocacy influence, and certainly media coverage in the identification of environmental risks and sustainable development needs. Moreover, federal scientists in both Natural Resources Canada (NRCan) and Environment Canada, as well as in global bodies, which form around particular environmental agreements such as climate change, exert influence (Kinder 2010; Doern and Kinder 2007; Doern and Reed 2000).

However, as discussed later, there is considerable evidence in recent years that federal scientists are being muzzled and controlled by federal communications policies and personnel centred in the Prime Minister's Office and in relevant science-based departments (O'Hara and Dufour 2014). These practices are also tied to the much-greater presence and practice of "continuous attack politics" (Toner and McKee 2014). There have also been major cuts to government science, with a report by the Professional Institute of the Public Service of Canada (2014) characterizing them as the "disappearance of Canadian public interest science" in the Harper era. Major cuts had also occurred under the Liberals' mid-1990s program review, which had also hit Environment Canada in a major way (Enros 2013; Swimmer 1996).

ENVIRONMENTAL POLICY, DEMOCRACY, AND GOVERNANCE IN A COMPLEX NETWORKED INTERNET WORLD

The third foundational stream of literature is reviewed and mapped to convey key aspects of how environmental policy, democracy, and governance function in an increasingly complex and dynamically networked Internet world (Aucoin, Jarvis, and Turnbull 2011). The potential for green-lite complexity is high.

Conceptual literature on environmental democracy and governance in a networked, Internet world is inevitably interwoven with broad and specific features of democracy and governance and network formation. This is especially the case with the notion of modern networked governance, when it is contrasted more generally with hierarchies and markets as fundamental ways of organizing societies and economies. Complexity analysis also depends upon the exact design of environmental programs and the complementary use of other policy instrument mixes, all aligned so that desired impacts (such as pollution reductions, sustainable development, or positive environmental-health effects) are achieved in ways that link with basic incentives for efficiency, innovation, and economic growth, for political legitimacy and public support (Coglianese 2010; Conference Board of Canada 2010a; Jaccard 2006).

Contending Democratic Criteria and Arenas

Claims about democratic governance in any policy field, including environmental policy, have to confront at least five criteria and arenas of democracy with various notions of democratic deficits and imperfections (Gidengil and Bastedo 2014; Pal 2013; Lenard and Simeon 2012; Doern and Prince 2012; Dryzek and Dunleavy 2009). The five criteria and arenas of democracy are as follows. First, *representative democracy*, which in the Canadian case is Cabinet-parliamentary democracy, where the public interest is claimed to reside in elections and majoritarian decision-making. Second, *federalized democracy*, where politics and policy divide constitutionally between national and provincial governments, yielding both conflictual and cooperative joint action and various kinds of bilateral and multilateral federalist bargains and diverse views of democratic action. Third, *interest group pluralism*, where democracy emerges through the continuous interplay of interest group institutions and players of numerous kinds involved in lobbying, engagement, and consultation with government and with each other. The focus here tends to be on business groups but also consumer interests and the determination at any time of what constitutes the public interest. Fourth, *civil society democracy*, where democracy is said to arise if broader social NGOs of numerous kinds are involved, including environmental, human rights, indigenous, and women's groups, principally those representing the weak and marginalized in society, many of which take up the language of equality-seekers and rights-holders in general and also under the Charter of Rights and Freedoms. Fifth, and finally, *direct democracy*, where democracy occurs, where individual citizens, voters and non-voters, express their views and have influence through their own individual actions, and through polling, focus groups, social on-line networks, and as citizens and as consumers functioning in the marketplace as environmentally and health-conscious consumers. They also include individual scientists involved as critics and even as whistle-blowers within government and private firms.

These diverse, partly overlapping, and often conflicting criteria and arenas are certainly a part of our analysis of the twenty-five policy histories and across the six regimes examined in Part Two of the book.

Environmental Agenda-Setting

Environmental agenda-setting needs to be seen in the context of broader conceptual theories of agenda-setting. Overall, the broader theories of agenda-setting are anchored in complex interactions between politicians and policy-makers, the media, and the public. More specifically it is seen in relation to the issue attention cycles and spans of different players, including voters and citizens, and to framing and reframing processes, and also to the role of the mass media interacting with the communication strategies of governments (Eisler, Russell, and Jones 2014; Wolfe, Jones, and Baumgartner 2013; Howlett 1998; Kingdon 1995). For example, its dynamics have been cast as "punctuated equilibrium" agendas where policy stays stable for long periods while, in a punctuated fashion, some policies change quickly and dramatically (Baumgartner and Jones 1993; Jones and Baumgartner 2005, 2012). Agenda-setting is also being examined in relation to the growing role of Internet-centred social media in Canada and globally (Chu and Fletcher 2014).

When environmental issues are examined in such conceptual contexts, certain characteristics emerge. Soroka (2002) shows the increased salience of environmental issues in Canada in the late 1980s due to the impact of national and international environmental events but also shows how it has lower salience in most periods, including the 1970s. He compares it with inflation as an issue, suggesting that the environment should be more open to media influence to periodically set the agenda or force governments to pay attention. He notes that "most individuals will not experience environmental problems every day" (268). Other comparative literature seeks to differentiate in environmental news media the difference between metacycles and issue cycles (Djerf-Pierre 2013). Metacycles "refer to the major fluctuations in attention to the entire domain of environmental issues over time, while issue cycles refer to the oscillation in attention pertaining to single issues" (495).

Such a single issue, albeit a big one, is climate change. Harrison and Sundstrom (2010), and contributing authors to their volume, look at its comparative politics. Climate change has seen increased salience in public opinion terms in Canada, but the fate of national policies, in Canada and elsewhere, is also a product of a struggle between ideas and self-interest and also different notions of time regarding predicted impacts versus costs (Harrison 2010).

Another single, agenda-setting issue that has been examined is Canadian water exports (Bakenova 2004). In this case, water exports as an issue had a relatively low position on the overall national and environmental agenda in the forty years between 1960 and 2002. But it frequently became a policy problem, due to international and federal-provincial events and pressures, and thus had a "persistent pattern of presence" (5). There were frequent pressures to make this a quintessential environmental issue that would result in the banning of water exports (to the United States, especially). But governments "never fully precluded the possibility of water export" (5), even though there was environmental opposition and international arguments about water security for some countries, or regions within countries, and even thought the economic feasibility of water exports from Canada was ambiguous.

On basic environmental opinion polling in Canada, the Canadian Opinion Research Archive (2013) is of interest regarding polling by Environics from 1985 to 2009. When asked, "In your opinion, what is the most important problem facing Canadians today?," only 2 to 4 per cent of Canadians responded "environment/pollution" for most of this period. The main exception was in 1989 and 1990, the years of the Mulroney green plan gestation and announcement. The figure identified crept up to 7 to 8 per cent for the Harper years covered. Not surprisingly, throughout this period, Canadians responded at near the high 40 per cent range for those issues identified as the economy and unemployment. In several years, health care was identified as the most important problem. Environmental issues were never that important for citizens, with the exception of the green plan years. The environmental questions defined the environment as "environment/pollution," with later mentions of "climate change," but only for a few survey periods and with climate change registering at about 2 per cent when listed on its own. We return to such agenda-setting dynamics in our discussion in chapter 2 on the environmental priorities of the four prime ministerial eras, as revealed by Speeches from the Throne and Budget Speeches. They are also germane in other regime chapters as green-lite complexity features.

Networks, the Internet, and Theories of Complexity

Networks, including environmental networks, have received increasing analytical attention in the study of economic and social institutions and thus are important for understanding contemporary debates on environmental policy content, consequences, and governance (Henman 2011; Svantesson 2011). They are increasingly bound up in the economic and social transformative influence of the Internet and linked to theories of complexity (Coleman and Blumler 2009).

In political and policy analysis, some authors initially cast networks as a particular inner feature of broader arrays of so-called policy communities (Coleman and Skogstad 1990). Policy communities were developed as an analytical category that went beyond traditional interest or lobby groups to embrace broader environmental and other NGOs. Later analyses have broadened networks to some extent to encompass scientific expertise and the roles of universities (Howlett and Ramesh 2003; Montpetit 2009).

Meanwhile, in economic and related fields, networks are being analyzed in a much broader context, contrasted with markets and hierarchies as basic modes of social and economic organization (Agranoff 2007; Benkler 2006; Thompson et al. 1991). *Hierarchies* are associated with bureaucracy, especially traditional Weberian state bureaucracy – hence, with systems of top-down superior-subordinate political and administrative relations accompanied by formal rules, with related forms of civil service bureaucracies essential to representative Cabinet-parliamentary and other systems of democratic government (Aucoin 1997). *Markets* are organized on the basis of "voluntary" means of exchange tied to money, commerce, and the making of profits, but with key rules and protections for property rights and transactions provided by the state. *Networks* are contrasted with both of the above, in that they are forms of organization characterized by non-hierarchical and voluntary relations based on trust, and commonality of shared interests and values where profit is not a defining characteristic (Agranoff 2007; Thompson et al. 1991). Hierarchies, markets, and networks are being increasingly combined in very complex ways.

Some attributes of networks as an institutional mode are expressed in terms of constructing *partnerships,* including environmental partnerships. Such partnerships can be truly voluntary, but more often they take on the form of policy-induced or required contractual or quasi-contractual partnerships between/among public and private sector entities and interest groups. In this context, they acquire some of the characteristics inherent in markets or hierarchies as well (Kinder 2010), and they are also a key part of the previously mentioned theories of regulatory capitalism where co-regulation is the norm.

The Internet as a defining and increasingly dominant and enabling technology and infrastructure has become a crucial engine of and site for social and economic network formation, for designed systems of e-commerce and e-governance, and for fast-forming kinds of social media such as Google, Facebook, and Twitter. It is the heartland of "big data," with such data accumulating at unbelievable rates, such that up to 90 per cent of the world's data and information have emerged in the last five years (Haldane 2013; Etzioni 2012). The Internet and its presence is transformational in the most profound ways. It is both an infrastructure and the home base of new theories and practices, positive and negative, regarding information and modern science (Naughton 2012; Floridi 2014; Coleman and Blumler 2009).

For many public and private interests, including environmental lobbies, the Internet has greatly reduced the costs of communication and joint action. It has also fostered new avenues for direct democracy by individual citizens, including via social networks (Rainie and Wellman 2012; Borins and Brown 2008). But this also means that critics of environmentalists, environmental NGOs, and environmental advocacy are also mobilized and enabled in new ways. Analyses of networks in public policy and in the conduct of science and research bring out the tendency for networks to be increasingly complex, embedded with transaction costs and related layers of bureaucracy. This is bureaucracy not necessarily of the hierarchical kind but rather of a more horizontal, transactional, and vertical kind (Flinders 2008; Doern and Kinder 2007).

Theories of complexity per se have been developed and debated within the natural and engineering sciences and their subdisciplines and also enter considerations about society and social innovation. They also are a part of public policy theory in the twenty-first century. Authors such as Geyer and Rihani (2010) and Morcol (2012) advocate complexity theory based on their view that too many policy-makers and policy scholars treat policy and governance systems as being orderly, predictable, and controllable. But complexity notions have also been needed, as Pal (2013) argues, in matters of policy and decision-making where the need is to model chaos in the face of accidents, floods, terrorism, crises, and epidemics in environmental, public health, and infrastructure protection. Norberg and Cumming (2012) also use the idea of complexity to analyze sustainable development in diverse policy fields; Walby (2007) uses it to examine the nature of what she refers to in social policy terms as "multiple intersecting social inequalities."

Indeed, concepts of complexity are a part of the literature on public policy and governance, without complexity theory being centrally or overtly used. Naughton (2012), in his analysis of the Internet, refers to complexity as the "new reality" but also argues that it is not easy to unpack complexity and hence it is hard to understand or predict (162–3). He also points out that Nobel economist Herbert Simon (1962) had much earlier written about the challenging "architecture" of complexity, well before the onset of the Internet. Last but not least, it is useful to note the basic conceptual fact that innovation policy (economic and social) and related features of network-based clusters have been defined from the outset as being non-linear. They are thus complex, whether one has a theory of complexity or not.

Policy, Governance, and Time: Life-Cycle Approaches

Concepts of time in public policy-making and governance capture temporal periods that include: immediate short-term crises (real and manufactured); diverse temporal notions of what "capital" means, regarding investment in physical infrastructure, human and natural/

environmental capital in different intergenerational periods, and even epochs; decision cycles related to business cycles, political-electoral cycles; and fiscal budgets that are annual and cyclical or structural.

Doern, Maslove, and Prince (2013) have utilized notions of temporal budgeting in the Canadian fiscal and budgeting system, including how aspects of structural innovation policy often was downplayed and papered over because of these dynamics. But the literature on policy, governance, and time has early roots in policy and social analysis. Edelman's work (1977, 1988) deals with both crises and the political use symbolic politics and discourse to advance and skew issues and policy critics. Auld (1985) was one of the first academics in Canada to advance the need for improvement-investment funds rather than annual spending and real capital budgets to pay for different kinds of capital that had long life cycles and replacement dynamics. Work by Gaudreault and Lemire (2003) show continuing problems with tracking and investing in physical capital in Canada, federally and provincially. And, under recent infrastructure-centred deficit- and recession-era "stimulus" programs, there have been limited but also controversial claims that such funding is helping community, environmental, and social innovation (Bennett 2012).

Life-cycle approaches are also a part of the temporal dimension of environmental and environmental health policy, with built-in complexities of the green-lite kind. They have emerged more specifically in related environment, health, and food realms of rulemaking and compliance linked to notions of innovation (Health Canada 2006, 2007a; NRTEE 2011a). The life-cycle concept means moving away from a single "point in time" pre-market assessment system for products and processes to one that also followed products and processes in post-market phases, including their ultimate environmental final-use phases. For example, the federal blueprint for renewal in health and drug regulation advocated moving to a product life-cycle approach, regulatory interventions *proportional* to risk (a process that would require revamping the product categorization system), in concert with a proactive and enabling regulatory system, so as to not only keep pace but to be ahead of the trend, where possible, partly through greater regulatory foresight programs and activities regarding new and changing technologies (Health Canada 2006, 7–24). Another version of life-cycle analysis by Ireland, Milligan, Webb, and Xie (2012) also calls for an ongoing analysis and appreciation of how any regulatory agency faces different and changing challenges, depending on whether it is in its infancy, high-growth, mature, or declining stage.

Environmental Science-Based Governance as Applied to Assessing Policies, Projects, Infrastructure, Product, and Process Assessments and Approvals

The nature of environmental science-based governance has revealed the necessarily different decision-making rhythms and cycles in assessing diverse objects of assessment. These include the assessment of Cabinet-approved *policies* (statutory and non-statutory) where sustainable development reviews are in place. They relate to physical *projects and infrastructure* that are subject to federal and provincial environmental-assessment law and processes (Doern 2007a). They also relate to large numbers of product and process assessments, mainly at the premarket stage, but increasingly at the more elongated post-market stages as well. Environmental harms and benefits can be central to these assessment processes, or they can simply be one feature of them. This can also be the case with patent and related intellectual-property system assessments of what constitutes public property–centred inventions, as opposed to products and processes that are seen by others as public goods and common property resources. In all of these spheres of central or partial environmental content, there are also vast differences in the volume of decisions being made annually or over any longer period.

The nature of the science and technology being brought to bear is also a part of this governance aspect. In some contexts and phases it is research and development (R&D) activity per se that is involved, as conducted by both regulatory departments and agencies and by private corporations and university researchers. In other areas it is far more likely to be related science activities (RSA), where the science and knowledge are lodged more in the brains of front-line environmental and other scientists and their networked relations with fellow RSA practitioners across the government and in other countries and international agencies. Indeed, Environment Canada has been characterized as being mainly a performer of RSA (Kinder 2010; Doern and Kinder 2007). In still other contexts, such as regarding environmental industries and innovation clusters, the norms and expertise relate as well to concepts of innovation and smart regulation at both the product and process level.

Environmental Governance and Varied Policy Instrument Dynamics

By definition, environmental governance involves the deployment and use of all of the main policy instruments: regulation, taxation, spending, and persuasion/information. There is a complex literature on such instrument choices and mixes and the often difficult "means-ends" debates they raise (Doern, Prince, and Schultz 2014). Regulation is the most frequently deployed instrument in environmental policy and is discussed in more detail in the next section. But environmental taxation has been a feature, particularly in the debates about green taxation, as a way to put a cost on various environmental emissions and also with regard to how the tax system (deductions and tax expenditures), as designed or through tax-system inertia, affects businesses in different industrial sectors, including tax preferences that favour carbon emitters. As we shall see further in chapter 2's discussion of prime ministerial eras, the issue and, to date, the political illegitimacy of environmental taxes has been a major feature of environmental governance in the Harper era.

Public spending is also an environmental governance issue, not only in the sense of the public spending needed to underpin regulation, but also the spending devoted to environmental research and technology development, such as carbon sequestration and more recently fracking, but also to support energy conservation.

Regarding taxation, of course there have been tax measures (rates, deductions, tax credits) that have built up gradually and produced, later summarized in a rather oblique way under data and debates about *tax expenditures* (Lester 2014; Finance Canada 2010). In our review of Budget Speeches in chapter 2, we shall see any number of specific measures, such as accelerated capital expenditure write-offs or cancelled ones that could be pro- or anti-environmental in intent and impacts. A more recent stimulus-like tax initiative was the 2009 Home Renovation Tax Credit that provided environment/conservation measures for individuals but was temporary. A longer-standing tax measure that can help in some energy-environment/green industries is the two-decade-old Scientific Research and Experimental Development (SR&ED) Tax Credit. And there are any number of deductions and rate incentives for energy and resource companies that are the foundation for how they make investments and calculate profits in Canada and in comparison with other countries.

The idea of environmental taxes and tax shift is now a fairly old one but in Canada not a politically successful one. Canadian economists such as Ross McKitrick have argued for what he labelled "double dividend" environmental taxation (McKitrick 1997, 2011). The double dividend arises by putting a tax on pollution emissions (the environmental dividend), and the resulting tax revenues are used to finance tax reductions in other taxes elsewhere in the economy (producing a second efficiency and allocative dividend). Even so, such appealing ideas almost always get translated into arguments about "tax grabs" and tax-burden sharing. This happened in the 2008 run-up to the federal election, where Liberal leader Stéphane Dion advocated an environmental tax and designated it as a source of expenditure revenue federally for new social spending. The Harper Conservatives easily linked such environmental tax ideas to its political base in Alberta, where earlier 1980 federal Liberal NEP energy-related tax measures were cast as an unfair and offensive intervention into provincial energy matters.

Nonetheless, the underlying issue of where federal environmental tax and related support measures go, or tend to cluster, has long been a focus of criticism. A report by the commissioner of the environment and sustainable development (2000) examined what it called government support for "energy investments." On both the tax and spending sides, it concluded, "With a few exceptions, federal government support today for energy investments, including support through the tax system, does not particularly favour the non-renewable sector over the renewable sector" (3). But the "few exceptions," in effect some of the tax underbelly referred to above, were not discussed in much detail or weighed in the overall scheme of things.

Environmental policy instruments related to the use of persuasion, exhortation, and information provision are also a part of the foundational literature on environmental governance. For example, the original environmental assessment policies of the Government of Canada were expressed initially as guidelines; however, these were then forced into a statutory form after environmentalists took the issue to the Supreme Court of Canada, which decided that these guidelines were indeed laws (Docrn and Conway 1994). But guidance-like instruments are still very much a part of environmental governance in Canada and internationally regarding particular harms and hazards, depending on their stage of progress or inertia on the environmental agenda and on their inherent complexity.

Changing Types of Environmental Regulation

As noted above, regulation is often the most discussed and debated aspect and instrument of environmental governance, and therefore its many phases of development and particular types are a key underpinning to our discussion in the empirical chapters in Part Two of the book. Early initial environmental regulation in the 1960s and 1970s was a part of *public interest regulation,* which refers to the era beginning in the 1960s when the birth of the progressive regulatory state emerged (Eisner 1993; Harris and Milkis 1989; Stanbury 1980). The larger public interest, as opposed to private business interests, was given political expression in regulations dealing with consumer safety and product safety, nuclear safety, and the environmental assessment of projects and of environmental health and safety.

Regulatory capture theory emerged in the 1950s as a theory that critiqued public utility regulation by focusing on the underlying dynamics of power between and among regulated businesses, regulatory bodies, and consumers. Capture theory initially centred on a theory by Bernstein (1955) that regulators *gradually tended to be captured* by the industries they were regulating. It was gradual in that the regulator went through a kind of life cycle, beginning with public interest vigour, then gradually working out a comfortable modus vivendi with the industry, and eventually morphing into a regulator captured by industry interests and enjoying the quiet life, with significant career interchange between the regulator and the industry. Notions of capture have continued to be a part of regulatory analysis, and even of everyday non-theoretical discourse about the presumed habits of regulators, even though the complexity of regulatory systems arguably makes capture much harder to describe and prove empirically (Etzioni 2012; Hancher and Moran 1989; Doern et al. 1999). This is an issue to which we return in some of our environmental regime chapters.

However, environmental governance has also been influenced by a succession of views and advocacy regarding the strengths and weaknesses of particular kinds and modes of regulation, such as those noted further below. For example, *command and control regulation* involves a normative approach or claim of the existence of too many and too detailed input or process-oriented kinds of rules, a kind of detailed "one size fits all" approach, even though the industries, firms, communities, and individuals being regulated faced numerous diverse situations and contexts. The charge that regulation was too command-and-control oriented was often made regarding early environmental regulations (Stanbury 1980). There were many reasons for the subsequent effort to change the approach to regulation – business pressures and budget cutbacks – but underpinning it there was also a sense that reform had to follow the simple, everyday logic of practical situations (Braithwaite and Drahos 2000).

This critique and lobbying led to the advocacy and practice of various types of so-called *incentive-based regulation*. They recognized explicitly the complex cost and production situations facing firms, industries, and consumers. The growing presence and importance of international trade rules has resulted in rule-making premised on regulating outputs and *performance* rather than on prescriptive, detailed command-and-control rules (Sparrow 2008; Doern and Johnson 2006). *Cap-and-trade* systems, as defined earlier in the chapter, is a particular form of incentive-based economic regulation of growing but also controversial importance in the environmental and related energy fields, including climate change policy (Murray, Newell, and Pizer 2008). In effect, the "cap" component is a form of "command," in that it sets some agreed or defined limit on emissions. The "trade" component allows firms with good environmental records to sell pollution rights or permits on the market to firms whose environmental records are less well developed. This reduces the overall costs of compliance and takes into account the different economic situations of different companies. Cap-and-trade is nonetheless a controversial concept, in part because of issues regarding exactly how stringent the cap is, and the scope and coverage of industries (nationally, internationally, and regionally), and also because, in partisan political battles, it is often and usually quite incorrectly labelled rhetorically as a tax, and in particular a tax on corporations. In addition, views depend on whether permits are given out for free or are auctioned.

Management-based regulation even more explicitly recognizes that regulation is increasingly process oriented and is a matter of de facto co-governance with private firms and related interests and organizations (Coglianese 2008; Bennear 2007). Its underlying concept is "to deploy regulatory authority in a way that leverages the private sector's knowledge about its particular circumstances and engages with firms in developing their own internal procedures and monitoring practices that respond to risks" (Coglianese 2010, 160). Examples of this approach occur in several regulatory realms, including environmental-food regulation, where it has arisen in part because of the growing complexity of food production and supply chains nationally and internationally.

Regulatory cooperation and harmonization has itself been an increasing part of regulatory ideas, advocacy, and strategies in the environmental governance realm. In principle and practice, it relates to both international linkages and coordination, and also within Canada, among the provinces and territories, including key aspects of reducing interprovincial barriers by opening up Canada's internal trade (Doern 2005). Regulatory cooperation refers to a wide range of institutional and procedural frameworks to build more integrated systems for rule-making and implementation. Several federal departments and agencies, including Environment Canada, Agriculture, and Agri-Food Canada, have developed such cooperative arrangements.

Regulatory harmonization refers to processes leading to a country agreeing through negotiation to adopt common laws and rules with other countries. Such regulatory harmonization is especially present in and encouraged by various trade laws, agreements, and organizations (e.g., WTO, the Uruguay Round Agreement, the General Agreement on Trade in Services, and NAFTA), but it is also present in other policy fields. Regulatory cooperation can also occur if countries and sub-national jurisdictions engage in mutual recognition agreements where each party agrees to recognize the regulations of the other party, even though they are not identical or fully harmonized.

The greater use of voluntary codes and private standards and certification systems constitutes a further approach centred on promoting the greater use of such codes and related private standards as a complementary instrument of environmental, consumer, and marketplace reform in the context of multi-level global governance (Marx et al. 2012; Tollefson, Gale, and Haley 2008; Webb 2004). Voluntary codes are non-legislatively required commitments, including certification processes and reporting, as well as "naming and shaming" tactics developed by non-state and state actors. Such codes have been developed in many areas, including those environment-related ones developed for the chemical industry, forests, and fisheries.

In some cases, firms, industry associations, and/or NGOs devise their own codes of behaviour standards on products and production processes and then ensure their public monitoring. In other cases, government agencies are involved in both the drafting and monitoring. The need for codes and standards as a preferred or complementary tool of rule-making was also becoming more evident under the impetus of e-commerce and the general development of the Internet, and also in the context of the above-mentioned development of complex food-supply chains. This was because codes often were a faster way to respond to marketplace change that involved global, cross-national commerce (Büthe 2011). Normal international law-making and regulation simply took too long, and hence some progress could be made through codes and related approaches.

The federal government also had to respond to, take part in, or monitor other initiatives emerging from other stakeholders, including combined environmental and consumer NGOs. These groups were increasingly launching their own standard-setting, certification, and code development in competition with official state-sponsored processes and then using market forces to generate support for their preferred code or market outcome. This occurred in an area such as forest management, where sustainable practices were central (Luckert, Haley, and Hoberg 2012). Chapter 9 provides an extended necessary discussion of these certification dynamics in the NGO, Market, and Business–Environment Regime.

CONCLUSIONS

In this chapter we have set out the conceptual foundations that underpin the analysis of Canadian environmental policy, governance, and democracy set in an international and comparative context. Three broad streams of literature have been briefly surveyed: environmental ideas; the political economy of environmental policy; and environmental democracy and governance in a complex, networked Internet world. We reviewed the foundation literature to provide a background for the reader, to underpin our regime analysis and analytical framework, and to offer initial examples of our green-lite concept.

Our aim is to extend these foundational concepts through our own analytical framework that has to maintain considerable breadth and historical perspective, but also has to be constrained and sharpened into a manageable and persuasive analysis. As set out in the book's introduction, our analytical framework involves in particular: the concept of *green-lite* seen in relation to complexity and the nature of changing and growing environmental challenges; the identification and analysis of six key environmental *regimes;* and also, within each regime, the three *elements* that help us understand key contributing drivers of regime change and inertia.

2

Canadian Environmental Policy
and Agendas in Liberal and Conservative
Prime Ministerial Eras

INTRODUCTION

To provide an initial historical context, we take a basic look at Canadian environmental policy and agendas in Liberal and Conservative prime ministerial eras covering the last four to five decades. Canadian environmental democracy and governance are also a part of this history, as are national, federal-provincial, and international policies and institutions, each influencing the timing and content of the others. The more detailed Canada-US relations and international context is presented in chapter 3, and we return to many of these and other policy agenda issues in more detail in the environmental regime chapters in Part Two of the book.

This chapter surveys the major federal environmental policy laws, statements, plans, strategies, and changes in the last three decades of the twentieth century and the first decade-and-a-half of the twenty-first century. This historical analysis reveals both continuities and key differences across Liberal and Conservative governments and prime ministerial eras, as environmental policies emerged and expanded in scope, but also as environmental issues retreated from political and policy agendas or shifted or were reframed into new kinds of political and policy discourse. It is replete with green-lite features, as environmental agendas are forged by a complex interaction among governments, the media, and public opinion.

Important aspects of multi-level governance also appear in this historical narrative as national, international, provincial, urban and local, and newer regional/spatial levels emerged. With them, new forms of multi-scalar coordination and conflict materialized as environmental policy became more complex, embracing both direct environmental policies and also hyphenated and indirect ones in particular related policy fields.

The chapter proceeds first in terms of the time periods of the main federal prime ministerial and governing political party eras: the Trudeau Liberals from 1968 to 1983, the Mulroney Conservatives in the 1984 to 1992 period, the Chrétien and later Martin Liberals from 1993 to 2005, and finally the Harper Conservatives from 2006 to the present. The prime ministerial eras reveal aspects of, and evidence regarding, environmental policy; however, such policies can be understood fully only by further locating them within and across broader fiscal, economic, and social agendas present in each era. The economic and social agendas, and environmental issues within them, can also be revealed in policy- and reform-agenda strategies related to taxation, regulation, and public spending. These too are a necessary part of our historical account of each prime ministerial era.

We also present an empirical analysis of environmental policy and agendas via a close look at the environmental content and discourse of thirty-one Speeches from the Throne (SFTS) from 1968 to 2013, and also forty-eight Budget Speeches from 1970 to 2014. SFTS are the broadest, quintessential, agenda-setting expression of priorities and values by the federal government to Parliament and to the Canadian people. They do not occur annually but rather at approximately eighteen-month intervals as new sessions of Parliament begin. SFTS tend to be thematic narratives centred on new or changed laws and ways of expressing agendas and priorities.

Budget Speeches, by contrast, are atypically in February or March of each year. They are thematic as well, but also more economy-focused, and contain numerous specific tax and expenditure measures – new, altered, or cancelled (Doern 2009). These can be large, medium, or small, not to mention gesture-like and applicable for diverse time periods (e.g., small amounts for a couple of years; very big amounts but for time commitments of seven to ten years and thus likely well beyond the current government's tenure in office). Some can be tracked easily but many also disappear into the fiscal mists.

Thus, among our findings regarding a review of all thirty-one SFTS is the general strong proclivity of all prime ministers to stress economic and fiscal priorities well ahead of environmental ones. Environmental sections or mentions in SFTS tend to come in the last third of SFTS, the one exception being the 1989 Mulroney SFT, where it is prominently listed as the second item very early on. Regarding Budget Speeches, which are usually much longer and more detailed, the chapter shows the relatively greater number of environmental and related measures in budgets on both the tax and spending sides of the fiscal equation. But these are typically also listed as a lower priority, given the larger macro-economic growth or recession posture that dominates the budget or indeed several budgets across the four prime ministerial eras.

The analysis of SFTs and Budget Speeches is underpinned by the discussion in chapter 1 regarding the theory and dynamics of agenda-setting and its interaction with media and public opinion and further shows some of the green-lite complexity of the book's overall analysis (Jones and Baumgartner 2012; Harrison 2010; Soroka 2002; Bakenova 2004). Chapter 1's agenda literature also showed that when Canadians are polled about what they regard as the most important national issues, environmental issues were not generally ranked highly, except in the late 1980s (Canadian Public Opinion Research Archive 2013).

PRIME MINISTERIAL AND POLITICAL PARTY ERAS: ENVIRONMENTAL POLICIES, IDEAS, AGENDAS, AND REFORMS

The Trudeau Liberals

The Trudeau Liberals launched Canada's formal environmental policy age with the establishment of Environment Canada in 1970–71 but through their majority governments of 1968–72, 1974–79, and 1980–84 and a minority government interregnum of 1972–74 they did not systematically attend to environmental policy and governance (Doern and Conway 1994; Boardman 1992; Paehlke and Torgerson 1990). Under its initial "Just Society" and rational decision-making ethos, Trudeau focused on distancing his government from the seemingly chaotic decision-making of the previous Pearson Liberal minority government and also pushed reforms for greater public participation. Some of these changes were also built on earlier 1960s developments that were partly environmental and also partly on a growing sense among Canadians that they were in a new prosperous age and could afford to deal with new problems and challenges (Whittington 1980).

However, in the early and mid-1970s the Trudeau Liberals were forced into a policy agenda centred on wage and price controls as Canada (and the global economy) faced hyper-inflation that was not amenable to normal central bank monetary policy or to fiscal policy. And from 1980 to 1983 the Trudeau government aggressively launched initiatives that ranged from constitutional repatriation and the Canadian Charter of Rights and Freedoms to the National Energy Program as a partial response to a global energy crisis in the wake of tripling oil prices, and an industrial strategy centred on resource mega projects (Doern and Toner 1985).

The Trudeau environmental record and agenda had some strengths. Trudeau himself had good initial environmental instincts and interests, some arising from his own life as an active and adventurist nature enthusiast and outdoorsman. He also met early on with members of the Club of Rome and had considerable sympathy with its "limits to growth" arguments and advocacy of a needed new environmental age.

He took a personal interest in and strongly supported the establishment of the Department of the Environment in 1970–71 (now referred to as Environment Canada). Trudeau was actively involved in the early internal mandate debate about the department and seemed initially to favour those advocating a resource-conservation ethic, which included making the national Parks Service a part of the department, much to the chagrin of senior parks officials. Quickly, however, the more imperative core mandate became the need for pollution cleanup and related remediation.

Nonetheless, in its first five years, the Trudeau government could genuinely take credit for beginning Canada's environmental policy era. It also established in 1972 the Canadian Environmental Advisory Council (CEAC) as a direct advisor to the minister but also one that would provide a more careful and constrained point of access for the growing number of environmental NGOs but without the latter having direct representation (Doern and Conway 1994, 106).

Another key environmental policy centred on the environmental assessment and review of new projects involving federal law and/or funding. Here the Trudeau era story was one of support but of a much more cautious nature, particularly as the Canadian economy weakened in the later 1970s. The Environmental Assessment Review Process (EARP) had begun but was weak structurally and was not backed by statutory powers (Schrecker 1984, 1991; Couch 1988).

Moreover, several provinces were starting their own processes and hence there were federal concerns about duplication of processes for the same project. There was also Cabinet concern that the federal process not be as radical and aggressive as those approaches already adopted in the United States by the Environmental Protection Agency (EPA). Trudeau and his central agencies, the PCO and PMO, were also developing horizontal regulatory policies and required that Environment Canada's EARP system also implement the government's policies aimed at reducing the regulatory burden on the private sector. It was, in short, to avoid red tape and delay (Doern and Conway 1994, 201–2).

While Canada-US initiatives on Great Lakes pollution cleanup began in the Trudeau era, as did some action on regulating toxic substances and some early recognition of the pollution caused by acid rain, the Trudeau era also saw the Parks Service taken away from Environment Canada and the enactment of the Fisheries Act, from which came many of its regulatory powers regarding water that were given to a new Department of Fisheries (now Fisheries and Oceans Canada).

In its last years, from 1980 to 1984, the Trudeau Liberals' major decisions on the Charter of Rights and Freedoms, the National Energy Program, and the above-mentioned mega-project industrial strategy meant that they had virtually no directly expressed environmental content. The Charter was a major and historic achievement and facilitated a "rights oriented" political discourse and also court cases but few on environmental rights, nor were such rights central to the Charter itself. The NEP had a massive energy policy focus on federal intervention, including in the northern Canada Lands but with nary a word mentioned about the environment. Similarly, the 1983 federal budget's mega-project strategy, which sought to drive an economic recovery by supporting large resources-led developments queuing-up for approval, also scarcely mentioned environmental issues (Doern 1983).

The Trudeau era thus had promising environmental beginnings, but then a long decline in effective policy and regulation symbolized a green-lite approach, whereby each initiative had to struggle for traction and support against other economic and resource ministers and their departments and business interests. It had some support from environmental groups, but such support was often skeptical about the department as "their" nominal home base inside the government (see chapter 4).

The Mulroney Conservatives

The two Mulroney Conservative majority governments from 1984 to 1988 and 1988 to 1993 fostered an environmental agenda that largely lay dormant in their first term in office but then peaked in the 1988–93 period with the 1990 Green Plan, by far the most ambitious federal environmental initiative (Gollner and Salee 1989; Conway 1992; Macdonald 1991). The realities of other policy and fiscal challenges in the Mulroney era left some room for environmental matters but only episodically. First, for their entire period in office, the Mulroney Conservatives had to deal with large fiscal deficits, the largest in Canadian history (Doern, Maslove, and Prince 2013). This meant that funds for new initiatives, environmental or otherwise, were scarce, except for the $3 billion 1990 Green Plan and an increase in the budget for the Department of Forestry (see chapter 6).

Its other signature policy battle in its first term was over free trade, including the Canada-US Free Trade Agreement and the 1988 election, which was a virtual referendum on free trade (Doern and Tomlin 1991). Later it negotiated the North American Free Trade Agreement (NAFTA) (Trebilcock, 2011). Free trade had environmental policy and political links, first, because the environmental lobby joined and often led the opposition to free trade, and second, during the policy clashes about environment and trade, they advocated the need for environmental protections. Only the insistence of the newly elected US president Bill Clinton secured the environmental side deal in the 1993 NAFTA package that was opposed by the Mulroney government and was only reluctantly agreed to when the new Chrétien Liberals came to power in 1993.

The second Mulroney term agenda centred on a major restructuring of the Canadian economy, initially through tax reform and the introduction of the Goods and Services Tax (GST) and key deregulatory moves in fields such as telecommunications, airlines, and railways. But the Mulroney agenda also was caught up in attempted constitutional reforms that led to stark failure with both the Meech Lake and Charlottetown accords and to an eventual crushing election defeat in 1993. Given these big agenda preoccupations, it is remarkable that environmental matters even came into the attention span of the government.

However, in 1988, Brian Mulroney as prime minister took a considerable personal interest in the environmental policy domain.

Following the 1988 election he made the minister of the environment a member for the first time of the Cabinet's Priorities and Planning Committee. He appointed Lucien Bouchard as the minister of environment, a Quebec MP who was arguably the most dynamic environment minister in Canadian history. He immediately began work on what became the $3 billion 1990 Green Plan. The impetus for the Green Plan was helped considerably by a series of environmental crises and accidents internationally, including the Bhopal chemical disaster in India, and the Chernobyl nuclear reactor meltdown in the Soviet Union.

The environment featured in the 1989 Mulroney Speech from the Throne, but the Green Plan was not announced until late in 1990, separate from both Budget Speeches and Speeches from the Throne (Doern and Conway 1994). In 1988, however, the Conservative government established the National Round Table on Environment and the Economy, with its legislative mandate put in place five years later by the Chrétien Liberals. NRTEE replaced the above-mentioned Canadian Environmental Advisory Council, established in 1972, to give environment and economy issues a better linked-policy focus.

The $3 billion 1990 Green Plan stressed the new global realities of environmental problems and also rode the highest public opinion polling of environmental issues by Canadians, both before and after its announcement. The Green Plan advocated the concept of sustainable development and contained a comprehensive series of goals and more than 100 specific initiatives (Canada 1990; Hoberg and Harrison 1994). The projects included the regulation of up to forty-four priority toxic substances in five years, and plans to reduce the generation of waste in Canada by 50 per cent by the year 2000. The Green Plan also helped give Canada a lead role in the 1992 Rio Earth Summit (see chapter 3).

In addition to the Green Plan pinnacle, the Mulroney era included the establishment of three new national parks, Bruce Peninsula, Grasslands, and South Moresby (May 1990; Doern and Conway 1994). The Green Plan committed the Mulroney government to even more national parks. The Conservatives also secured in 1989 a long-sought acid rain agreement with the United States, largely and ultimately through Mulroney's close personal relationship with US president Ronald Reagan.

In addition, the Green Plan led to the development of environmental assessment processes on all federal *policies,* not just projects.

The Conservatives also crucially had secured, following court cases launched by environmental groups, the eventual passage of the Canadian Environmental Assessment Act. Focused on projects, it gave a statutory base to the former non-statutory EARP system mentioned above, but in a way that increased ministerial discretion, alleviating concerns arising from the court challenges (see chapter 4). The Canadian Environmental Protection Act had already also been passed in 1987, which provided a stronger lever to deal with the toxic substances agenda.

While the Mulroney environmental agenda had its own slow gestation, it did result in an environmental record that resulted in Mulroney being named in 2006 the greenest prime minister in Canadian history, by a panel of environmental experts organized by the publication *Corporate Knights* ("Brian Mulroney" 2006; Heaps 2006). Elizabeth May, the MP and Green Party leader agrees with this view and attributes it partly to Mulroney's willingness to listen and consult (De Sousa 2011). May had been an advisor to an early Mulroney-era environment minister, Tom MacMillan.

The Chrétien and Martin Liberals

The three Liberal majority governments of Jean Chrétien (with Paul Martin as minister of finance) and the Paul Martin minority government from 2003 to 2005 witnessed initial high environmental aspirations in its 1993 election campaign Red Book agenda centred on support for the idea of sustainable development (Liberal Party of Canada 1993). The Liberals established in 1995 the commissioner of the environment and sustainable development, whose office was within the Office of the Auditor General and hence a new parliamentary watchdog agency (see chapter 4). However, good environmental intentions succumbed to the immediate first-term de facto agenda, when the government focused on dealing with the huge, now fifteen-year-old federal fiscal deficit and also accumulating debt via major expenditure cuts under program review (Swimmer 1996).

From 2000 to 2003, the Liberal agenda was also focused on finding ways to foster economic growth in the new innovation economy. Indeed, this was the central theme of its first post-election Speech from the Throne in 2000 and later of its policies and reforms to the federal regulatory system – reforms cast as *smart regulation,* including the need to foster environmental industries. Sustainable development featured in its second and third Red Book election campaign agendas, and also appeared in the reform mandate of reorganized departments such as Natural Resources Canada (NRCan) and a new Fisheries and Oceans Canada (Doern 1993a; Doern and Gattinger 2001; Clancy 2011).

When the brief Martin minority government period began after a bitter leadership battle between Martin and Chrétien, its early agenda focused on democratic reform, the knowledge economy, Aboriginal affairs (a policy file chaired by Martin), and with general expressions of support for a more integrated approach to social, economic, and environmental policy (in short, sustainable development cast as the "triple bottom line" referred to in chapter 1). The first Martin Speech from the Throne did contain, under the heading of building a twenty-first-century economy, further support for sustainable development, including commitments to the Kyoto Protocol and a ten-year $3.5 billion program to clean up contaminated sites (Doern 2004a). This agenda was quickly overwhelmed by the Chrétien-era sponsorship scandal and the public inquiry into it that Martin had ordered. The latter issue more than any other led to the defeat of the Martin Liberals and the election early in 2006 of the Harper Conservatives.

During the full Chrétien-Martin era from 1993 to 2005, environmental policy was sheltered under a combined sustainable development and innovation economy/smart regulation mix of ideas and discourse. However, independent analyses of the environmental record have pronounced it as being more akin to "saving face" (Stefanick and Wells 1998); or simply weak and spotty at best (Gallon 1996). Moreover, the Liberal's mid-1990s Program Review process to cut spending included severe cuts to government science including cuts of about 30 per cent to Environment Canada's science and research (Swimmer 1996; Kinder 2010).

Some new environmental initiatives were realized including the establishment of two new national parks. In the Martin agenda, his personal focus on cities was seen as having some new spatial and related environmental positives and raised the prospects for potentially promising though somewhat vague future impacts (see chapter 7) including the links of the cities agenda to public infrastructure (Bradford 2004a).

However, the Chrétien-Martin era of environmental policy was increasingly and ultimately being tested against the issue of climate change and the promised reduction of greenhouse gas (GHG) emissions. On this central issue, the Liberals revealed a difficult and often duplicitous agenda (see chapters 3 and 4). On the one hand, Chrétien in particular lent rhetorical support to the global climate-change agenda, and the need to reduce GHG emissions and to achieve the commitments of the Kyoto Protocol, which for Canada were to reduce emissions by 6 per cent from 1990 levels by the 2008–12 period. On the other hand, however, Canada ratified the protocol only in 2002 as Chrétien was leaving office, and the 6 per cent reduction commitment was seemingly crafted not by careful thought and analysis but rather by a desire to look morally superior to the United States. Moreover, Canada's GHG emissions actually *increased* massively during the Liberal era by over 24 per cent, placing it among the worst performers among OECD countries (Jaccard 2014; Macdonald, VanNijnatten, and Byorn 2004; Rivers and Jaccard 2009).

The Harper Conservatives

The Harper minority governments from 2006 to 2011, and its majority government since May 2011, developed their version of environmental policy. The Conservatives' approach to environmental policy developed amidst overall political and economic challenges and its own agenda that increasingly centred on the promotion of oil sands energy and natural resources development, effectively burying environment under the rubric of responsible resource development (RRD) (Toner and McKee 2014). Canada, in the Harper government's view, sought to be an "energy superpower" and a provider of "ethical oil." In the process, Harper became Canada's first "bitumen" prime minister.

The Conservatives' initial agenda, however, was anchored on a five-point program of accountability, following Harper's defeat of the Martin Liberals in 2006 over the sponsorship scandal but also on promised reductions of the Goods and Services Tax (GST), a promise easily available from the large budgetary surplus inherited from the Liberals. The Harper government showed some initial policy interest regarding a "made in Canada" national water strategy in its 2006 electoral platform, but the water-management agenda quickly dissipated (Cargnello et al. 2014). In its 2008 SFT, Harper promised to ban all bulk water exports (Forest 2010), an issue that had been on the agenda at a persistent but low level for decades (Bakenova 2004). However, such a ban has not happened and, more-over, the Harper government revealed no central environmental plans during its first two years. There were some specific initiatives (see Budget Speeches analysis below), and there was certainly sharp partisan duelling in the House of Commons when Stéphane Dion, first as environment minister and later as Liberal leader, made environmental issues, including the need for green taxes, a key area of Liberal criticism of the Harper Conservatives.

In many ways, Harper as prime minister was becoming de facto his own environment minister (Calamai 2007; Brownsey 2007). Environmental public opinion was at a higher level of saliency than normal because of climate change issues, but it did not last for long, as the international banking and global economic crash of 2008 came to dominate federal and global politics and agendas (Harrison 2010).

However, there were two lower-profile environment-related policies revealed through early changes in Harper's overall regulatory policy. In 2007, the Harper government announced its Cabinet Directive on Streamlining Regulation (CDSR) (Canada 2007). It stressed that the government's first two commitments to Canadians in the CDSR are that, when regulating, the federal government will (1) protect and advance the public interest in health, safety, and security, the quality of the environment, and social and economic well-being of Canadians, as expressed by Parliament in legislation; and (2) promote a fair and competitive market economy that encourages entrepreneurship, investment, and innovation.

The statement implied both a rank ordering of these ideas and goals but also a sense of balance needed between them in an enabling knowledge-based innovation economy. These two values remained central when the Conservatives introduced a replacement Cabinet Directive on Regulatory Management (CDRM) in 2012. But they were made more complex and diffuse by the addition of several other stated goals and values related to its regulatory red-tape reduction agenda (Doern, Prince, and Schultz 2014, chapter 4).

A second change in the CDRM and elsewhere, compared to earlier federal regulatory policy, is that regulatory policy and governance is to be governed by a broader "life cycle" notion of regulation. Under this concept the historic pre-market emphasis in health- and environment-related policy and regulation was now to be complemented by much-needed post-market monitoring through the full cycle of production and use, including the ultimate later closure of plants and mining facilities (Health Canada 2006; NRTEE 2011a). Analysis by NRTEE (2011a) suggested that such policies were certainly desirable and needed but also largely aspirational to date.

A further early Harper era initiative was the passage by Parliament in 2008 of the Federal Sustainable Development Act. Its basic principle in section 4 stated, "The Government of Canada accepts the principle that sustainable development is based on ecologically efficient use of natural, social and economic resources and acknowledges the need to integrate environmental, economic and social factors in the making of all decisions of the government." Among its provisions was the establishment of a Sustainable Development Office in Environment Canada to report on progress on the implementation of the Federal Sustainable Development Strategy.

When the global banking and economic crisis began in 2008, the Harper agenda shifted in a minority government context, to issues such as the fast-growing fiscal deficit, the development of the economic stimulus and related infrastructure program, and the Conservatives' Economic Action Plan (Curry and McKenna 2014). This agenda shift sought to maintain economic growth, deal with the recession, and tackle specific issues such as the auto industry bailout and more regulatory streamlining via red-tape reduction. The agenda was noticeably devoid of environmental goals, and indeed most accounts of the 2008–11 period found the Conservatives and Harper himself keeping issues such as climate change and the Kyoto Protocol to a minimalist level (Jaccard 2014; Craik, Studer, and VanNijnatten 2013). This included a low profile at the 2009 Copenhagen climate change summit and Canada's eventual decision in 2012 to withdraw from the Kyoto Protocol.

Harper's climate change policy was increasingly tied to a kind of "made in the USA" approach, in that Canada's revised strategy for GHG emissions mirrored the US commitment to reductions of 17 per cent below 2005 emissions by 2020. The intent was to stay in sync with US inactions, given the trade dependence of the Canadian economy on the US market and US competition (Macdonald 2011). Electorally, Harper suffered not a bit for this minimalist view, given that he won his majority in the 2011 election, and given that climate change and environmental issues were scarcely an issue in that election campaign. Green-lite agenda realities are thus revealed in Harper's climate-change minimalism, as it was in the Chrétien-Martin era's climate-policy duplicity, exacerbated by both government's delays in even starting policy implementation, with the result that announced plans were literally impossible to complete and more expensive. As Jaccard (2014) has convincingly argued. "We knew that the Liberal government of Jean Chrétien should have implemented effective policies right after signing Kyoto in 1997. It takes at least a decade to significantly reduce emissions via energy efficiency, switching to renewables, and perhaps capturing carbon dioxide from coal plants and oil sands. Each year of delay jacks up costs ... Just like Mr Chrétien, however, Mr Harper failed to immediately implement the necessary policies ... instead of honestly admitting that it won't achieve its 2020 target, the Harper government still pretends that it will" (Jaccard 2014, 1–2).

By 2011 and into the Conservative majority government era, the Harper positioning on the environment was a mixture of hyphenated environmental gestures that included an announced new national park (this time an existing part provincial and part municipal park near Toronto) and a northern and Arctic strategy, including the prime minister's annual late summer visits to the north, always with expressed combined economic-environmental concerns and always linked to the issues of Aboriginal peoples (see chapter 3).

The Conservatives had earlier introduced streamlined approval of major resource infrastructure projects, an initiative run out of Natural Resources Canada through its Major Projects Management Office. It focused on creating a single window for approvals. When the federal economic stimulus program was underway in the 2009–11 period, steps were taken to waive environmental assessment requirements for projects, again so as to speed their journey into a quick shovel-ready state of implementation (Pal 2011b). On the other hand, some local-level assessments of stimulus program projects indicated modest environmental benefits did occur, as defined in varied community terms (Bennett 2012).

After securing a majority government in the 2011 election, the Conservatives developed a more explicit policy of responsible resource development (RDD) that supported resource exports and was coupled with policies creating one environmental or regulatory assessment and not two or more at federal and provincial levels. This notion of one-step efficiency and more streamlining explicitly raised the issue of how fast is fast enough for such assessments to be both environmentally effective and economically efficient (Clarke et al. 2013). This full package was part of the Conservatives' huge omnibus budget bills, which were rammed through Parliament in 2012 and included changes that weakened environmental provisions in the Fisheries Act at the bidding of energy business interests (Toner and McKee 2014) and diminished environmental regulation in other key ways as well. Budget cuts to Environment Canada and other resource departments have also been underway as part of the Harper austerity program. Cuts included the abolition of the National Round Table on Environment and the Economy.

The Harper government also launched a highly aggressive agenda against environmental regulatory processes and environmental groups (Toner and McKee 2014; Goar 2013). These strategies and changes also extended to threats under Canada's charity tax laws in which some environmental groups had their charity status challenged by the government as the result of purported political activities to which the funds were being directed. These attacks also sought to label these groups as radicals and thus delegitimize their voices in key regulatory processes – such as the NEB's review hearings for the proposed Northern Gateway pipeline – because the groups had funding relations with US foundations.

However, following the re-election of US president Barack Obama in 2012, there was expressed second-term interest by Obama in making progress on climate change and environmental policy. This was slow to emerge, but in 2014 Obama announced planned measures that he could implement by presidential executive powers ("Climate Change" 2014; Baker and Davenport 2014). The Harper agenda is now having to confront both potential higher US climate and emission-reduction standards and the reality of environmental opposition in the US to the planned Keystone XL pipeline that will ship oil sands to the southern United States (De Souza 2013). Moreover, in Canada in 2013 there were also major political protests (see chapter 5) from Canada's Aboriginal peoples centred on both treaty rights and environmental concerns and also regarding the Northern Gateway pipeline being planned for the West Coast shipment of oil and gas to the booming Chinese and Asian markets (Canada West Foundation 2013b).

Last but not least, there was growing provincial and private-sector pressure that Canada needed some kind of new national energy and resource strategy that would have to be informed by both sustainable development and cap-and-trade emission-reduction policies and practices and concerns about water use and fracking (Brownsey 2013). The final report of the outgoing commissioner of the environment and sustainable development (2012) concluded that the government had weakened the environmental processes a step too far, and a new rebalancing was needed to meet global competition in energy and natural resources from countries with better sustainable development regimes (chapter 1).

By late 2014, Nanos Research public opinion polling was also showing that large percentages of Canadians saw the need for more balanced federal leadership regarding both energy and environmental policy and for an end to polarized arguments between energy companies and environmentalists (Galloway 2014). A national dialogue was needed. Even conservative news media such as the *National Post* were drawing attention to the growing criticism within Conservative Party circles led by former Reform Party leader Preston Manning in his capacity as the head of the Manning Centre for Building Democracy (Hopper 2015). He was advocating "pricing pollution" policies as a way to increase Conservative party support on environmental matters.

The Harper government also had to increasingly face the new reality of plummeting international oil prices, with forty-dollar oil foreseen as a likely key feature for several years ahead, given the combined effects of the US shale gas supply revolution and the strategy of Saudi Arabia as the de facto head of the OPEC cartel opting to keep world prices low to drive out high-cost countries and producers ("Sheiks v Shale" 2014). In this context Harper asserted in the House of Commons that "under the current circumstances of the oil and gas sector, it would be crazy economic policy to do unilateral penalties on that sector" (quoted in Whittington 2014, 1). Harper was reminded that he used the "crazy" label when asked about stronger emission control rules several years earlier when prices were at $100 per barrel and hence posed the obvious retort about when crazy ends and better policy begins.

Harper era climate change–related GHG emission reduction actions were and are weak. Environment Canada's 2013 emission trends report (Environment Canada 2013b) tried to make a good story out of a bad record. It reiterated the government's Copenhagen Accord commitment to reduce its GHG emissions to 17 per cent below 2005 levels by 2020. But the report stresses early on that the "government's approach is to encourage strong economic growth and job creation while achieving our environmental objectives" (1). It stresses that Canadian GHG emissions decreased by 4.8 per cent between 2005 and 2011 but only later in the report was it noted that these reductions were achieved mainly by provincial actions, particularly in Ontario. The report notes that Canada "will continue to make progress ... in implementing its sector by sector approach to regulate emissions" (2). But the fast-growing GHG emissions of the oil industry was not one of those sectors, as the Alberta-centred oil sands industry strongly and successfully lobbied Ottawa not to implement such emission reductions in 2012 and 2013 (Jaccard 2014; McCarthy 2013c; Simpson 2013a, 2013b).

SPEECHES FROM THE THRONE, BUDGET SPEECHES, AND NATIONAL ENVIRONMENTAL AGENDAS

Our second way of tracking and assessing federal environmental agendas through the four main prime ministerial eras is through a more detailed look at Speeches from the Throne and Budget Speeches. We look at statements from each agenda occasion and then comment on them further in relation to agenda-setting dynamics, discourse, reframing, and issue management, as underpinned by chapter 1's discussion of agenda setting.

Speeches from the Throne

Regarding the place or mention of an environmental agenda in the history of Speeches from the Throne (SFTs), one can see its periodic and changing presence in the thirty-one SFTs since Trudeau came to power in 1968 and extending to the 2013 Harper Throne Speech (see table 2.1).

It must be stressed that our reading of all the thirty-one SFTs confirms the general proclivity of all prime ministers to stress economic and fiscal priorities ahead of environmental ones and indeed of most other policy fields. Environmental sections or mentions in SFTs tend to come in the last third of SFTs, the one exception being the 1989 Mulroney SFT, where it is prominently listed as the second item very early on. This is of significance, because an SFT is written and crafted by political leaders who seek to convey the policy and thematic essence of their plans and priorities as a new session of Parliament begins and of how they wish to express it.

These agenda strategies also centre on their sense of media coverage and what issues are pressing for attention by the media but also by opposition parties. The need to differentiate the government's position and to communicate it to voters in a sea of critics means that careful attention is paid to issue framing and issue management, sometimes for the longer term, but often just to chart a way through short-term political winds and storms. SFTs do not tell us anything about whether newly expressed mentions and policies are implemented, although of course many items are implemented in some fashion.

Table 2.1 conveys in a different way the basic story of the four prime ministerial eras. The Trudeau era SFT story shows an initial environmental presence in its first five SFTs, including the establishment of the Department of the Environment, and then no mentions at all in its next seven SFTs. The Mulroney era shows a slow start in its first term but then the burst of 1989–90 in the Green Plan era.

Environmental priorities are mentioned in seven of the eight Chrétien-Martin SFTs, so they are more consistently present during the 1994 to 2005 period. Discourse is centred on the balanced economic and environmental goals of a sustainable development kind, but also environmental security and the Kyoto Protocol.

The Harper era's six SFTs since 2006 show environmental content in four of the six priority occasions. A shift in discourse and policy is evident in the reference to adopting more "responsible" approaches to both environmental regulation and climate change. The mention of a National Conservation Plan in the 2011 SFT suggests a possible new direction or emphasis. But in the 2013 SFT, all environmental matters were expressed as sub-features of the Harper government's responsible resource-development initiatives and discourse.

One of the more consistent features of SFTs in all prime ministerial eras is expressed interest by all of them in new national parks as part of their own political legacy. In earlier political eras it was often said that a prime minister's core political patronage views were best captured in the expression "If it moves, pension it; if it doesn't, then pave it." "Park it" may now be added to form a trilogy. This would be a tad unfair, because there is ample evidence that national parks are indeed environmentally valuable and supported by political

Table 2.1: Environment as expressed priority in Speeches from the Throne in Trudeau, Mulroney, Chrétien-Martin, and Harper eras

---

Trudeau SFTs (12) 1968–83

• Some mention in first five SFTs (1968–73) and none in last seven SFTs (1974–83)

• Reference variously to national parks, the problem of pollution, the rehabilitation of water resources, bills on pollution in oceans and the atmosphere, new Department of Environment, three new national parks (and seven since 1968), environmental impact, Environmental Contaminants Act and Canada Wildlife Act, and protection of natural environment

Mulroney SFTs (5) 1984–93

• No mention in first and third SFTs (1984, 1988)

• Limited reference in 1986 SFT to reform of National Parks Act

• Major priority (ranked second) in 1989 SFT and most extensive in any SFT in 1968–2013; referred to environmental imperative; establishment of NRTEE; toxic chemical regulation under Canadian Environmental Protection Act; new water legislation; acid rain deal with the United States; and Montreal ozone layer protocol

• Final SFT in 1991 referred to Green Plan of 1990, asserted that environment and economic prosperity are "fully compatible" goals and central to our decision-making

Chrétien-Martin era SFTs (8) 1994–2005

• No mention in 1997 SFT

• Considerable mention in the other seven SFTs

• Initial reference in 1994 SFT to "integrated approach to economic, social, environmental, and foreign policy"

• Major section in 1996 SFT titled "environmental security" and also referred to environmental technologies, Law of the Sea Convention, new national parks, and international environmental leadership

• 1999 SFT referred to Kyoto commitment to reduce GHG emissions, species at risk and natural habitat, government operational goal of being a "model of environmental excellence," and cleanup of federal contaminated sites

• Final three SFTs (2001, 2002, and 2004) refer variously to improved research on ground water; challenge of climate change; ten new national parks; streamlined Canadian Environmental Assessment Act; clean water and air; and the One Ton Challenge program for emissions at individual level

Harper SFTs (6) 2006 to present

• No mention in two of five SFTs (2006 and 2009)

• Section in 2007 SFT on Improving the Environment and Health of Canadians and included commitment to reduce GHG emissions by 60 to 70 per cent by 2050; promise of support for biofuels; tougher enforcement needed because this is main reason why past environmental laws have not worked

- 2008 SFT advocates a "responsible approach" to climate change; greater use of technology so that 90 per cent of electricity in Canada is produced from "non-emitting sources"
- 2011 SFT (after majority government victory) refers to how natural environment shapes Canada's national identity; seeks public engagement to create National Conservation Plan; advocates new clean energy projects and Rouge Valley national park to be established in Toronto area
- 2013 SFT, no environmental section but in its major "resource development" promises, it asserts that such development must "respect the environment"; measures included that will enshrine the "polluter-pay" system into law; set higher safety standards for companies operating offshore; and reintroduce the Safeguarding Canada's Seas and Skies Act to protect our oceans and coasts

leaders and Canadians as a whole. In short, they are not superficial and do not conform to green-lite criteria, though Canada continues to struggle to protect areas representing the diversity of ecotypes across the country. And if one measures parks as an instrument to help conserve and protect threatened species and habitats, then the assessment of parks becomes more complicated.

Budget Speeches

Table 2.2 shows environmental priorities and agendas as reflected in forty-seven Budget Speeches across the four prime ministerial eras from 1970 to 2014. As is the case with SFTs, environmental themes and initiatives are rarely shown as highly ranked items in most Budget Speeches most of the time. Rather they tend to be expressed later in the speeches, at times with their own heading, but often just quickly mentioned and listed as measures on the tax and spending side.

Specific tax measures often take the form of accelerated capital cost allowances, some of which are intended to support oil and gas and natural resource industries, and hence may not be environmentally beneficial, but others that are more targeted measures on quite specific "environmental" or "clean" or "renewable" fuel use such as solar power, ethanol, and methanol but also for individuals purchasing monthly transit fares rather than using cars. Accelerated capital cost allowances are also often eliminated, perhaps included in budgets to ensure level playing fields for different competing fuel sources.

Table 2.2: Environment as expressed priority in 48 Budget Speeches in Trudeau, Mulroney, Chrétien-Martin, and Harper eras

Trudeau Budget Speeches (16) 1970–84

- No direct "environmental" mentions in thirteen of sixteen Budget Speeches
- Periodic reference to "pollution reduction" and "natural resources measures"; oil and gas pricing and conservation; "energy self-reliance" and "energy self-sufficiency" by 1990
- Budgetary measures typically smallish and often centred on accelerated capital allowance measures or tax write-offs (e.g., use of industrial wastes as fuel sources; tax breaks for use of solar-powered water heaters)
- 1975 Budget had expenditure cuts to all departments, including Environment Canada
- Tax breaks and tax increases in different years for mining and oil and gas industries
- 1980 Budget included $4 billion Western Canada Fund, with projects for energy and resource development and some pollution-reduction initiatives in the west; renewable energy technology incentives; establishment of Enertech Canada
- Two Budget Speeches in both 1974 and 1978, mainly because budgetary and inflation and energy price shocks were making it impossible to plan spending and tax measures for longer than six months

Mulroney Budget Speeches (9) (1985–93)

- No direct "environmental" mentions in eight of nine Budget Speeches
- $3 billion Green Plan announced late in 1990 but not in a budget
- Relatively minor reference to Green Plan in later budgets, including 1992 Budget under measures for a "healthier environment," and in 1991 when notice given that Green Plan spending would be spread over six years rather than five
- Other selective tax and spending measures (amidst continuous high deficits) regarding Western and Atlantic Energy Accords (post-NEP); cancellation of federal home insulation program because of adverse health effects in insulation material being used; Environment Canada program to eliminate lead emissions in gasoline by 1992; some funds for global warming and water quality research, and for sustainable forests; incentives for ethanol and methanol as an "environmental benefit"

Chrétien-Martin era Budget Speeches (9) 1994–2005

- No direct environmental mentions in five of nine Budget Speeches
- Spending cuts announced in 1995 Budget for departments, including 30 per cent for Environment Canada; later shown in 1996 Budget Speech as a 38 per cent cut
- Parks Canada Agency established; accelerated cost allowance tax rules for mines and oil sands; tax changes to ensure level playing field for renewable energy and conservation

- Sustainable development highlighted in 1997 Budget related to energy efficiency, including $425 million Canada Infrastructure Works Program; tax deductions in environmental trusts; establishment of Canada Foundation for Innovation, with some later SD and environmental infrastructure research at universities
- 1998 Budget reference to Aboriginal peoples, addressing their "environmental challenges"; some funding for climate change research and emission trading systems
- 2000 Budget "initiatives to develop new environmental technologies and improve environmental protection," including $700 million over three years for projects and for Climate Change Action Fund, Sustainable Development Technology Fund, and Foundation for Climate and Atmospheric Science
- 2001 Budget initiatives on Strategic Infrastructure and the Environment, including doubling of funding to Green Municipal Energy Fund, Green Municipal Investment Fund
- 2003 Budget announced $3 billion to "promote SD and a healthy environment," including $16 million for Northern Science; $2 billion for Climate Change Action Fund for Canada; support for alternative fuels, including ethanol, but also "reducing resource sector corporate tax to 21 per cent"
- 2004 Budget included new post-SARS Canadian Public Health Agency for public health emergencies; a communities initiative; $4 billion over ten years to clean up contaminated sites
- 2005 Budget highlights "environmental sustainable development" as key to "better health," and develop a "green economy and sustainable communities" with $5 billion committed, including $1 billion Clean Fund for GHG reduction; $200 million over five years for wind power; $920 million over fifteen years for biomass energy
- Cities and communities initiatives funded by share of gas tax revenues

Harper Budget Speeches (9) 2006–14

- No direct "environmental" mentions in four of nine Budget Speeches
- 2006 Budget gave accelerated capital cost allowance for forestry bioenergy; $400 million over five years to combat pine beetle infestation and to strengthen competitiveness of forest sector; $5.5 billion over four years for Infrastructure; donations of ecologically sensitive land made under the Ecogift program exempted from capital gains tax
- 2007 Budget committed to "investing in Canadians, preserving and protecting our environment," including $1.5 billion Canada Eco Trust for Clean Air and Climate Change projects with the provinces and territories; $2 billion over seven years for production of renewable fuels; hiring of fifty more environmental enforcement officers; $10 million to create and expand protected areas in NWT (boreal forest and habitat for caribou herds); new National Water Strategy and $400 million funding; Infrastructure Advantage program

Table 2.2: Environment as expressed priority in 48 Budget Speeches in Trudeau, Mulroney, Chrétien-Martin, and Harper eras (*continued*)

- 2008 Budget contained measures for Canadian sovereignty in the Arctic and for "ensuring a cleaner healthier environment"; supporting communities in "traditional industries" so that forestry sector can be "model of environmental innovation and sustainability"; $250 million for carbon capture and storage initiatives with provinces; $330 million for Aboriginal communities safe drinking water; $21 million for more effective environmental enforcement

- 2009 Budget referred to initiatives on "a more sustainable environment" new Clean Energy Fund; focus on Canada Action Plan stimulus and infrastructure mandate (some with environmental content/potential)

- 2010 Budget gave some attention to Green Jobs and Growth package, including clean energy; environmental protection in the North and in the Great Lakes; $100 million for Next Generation Renewable Power Initiatives

- 2011 Budget (one pre- and one post-election majority government) referred to further investments in a "cleaner energy economy" and to "protecting Canada's natural environment," with over $1 billion committed, including $27 million for Environment Canada weather services

- 2012 Budget focused on "responsible resource development" but "while safeguarding the environment" and ensuring the "safety and security of Canadians as energy resources are developed

- 2013 Budget focus again on "responsible resource development" but also "protecting Canada's natural environment and wildlife," including new Rouge Valley Park in Toronto area

- 2014 Budget section on "responsible resource development," including mention of "conserving Canada's natural heritage," and also particular items such as building more snowmobile trails, and resurfacing the Trans-Canada Highway through a national park

Each of the four prime ministerial eras contains both tax and spending initiatives in budget speeches and plans. But in eras of deficits and spending restraint (as in most of the Trudeau and Mulroney eras), tax measures were the preferred instrument, to some extent. But other than the $3 billion Mulroney-era 1990 Green Plan (which, as mentioned, was not announced in a budget speech), the Trudeau and Mulroney eras had only limited new or newish environmental spending plans on offer. Larger environmental spending initiatives increasingly expressed in terms of sustainable development began to appear in Chrétien-Martin-era budgets, especially after the federal deficit ends and fiscal surpluses became the norm from 1998 to 2006.

Table 2.2 draws initial attention to specific "environmental" mentions in Budget Speeches and shows no direct mentions in thirty of forty-seven budgets. Interestingly, the Harper era has more explicit environmental mentions in more budgets than the three previous prime ministerial eras. These were more to set out specific initiatives but may also have emerged to overcome criticism of the government's weak climate change record. More recent Harper budgets also, as we have seen, used the policy discourse of clean energy and responsible resource development as a signature policy discourse.

Finally, it is important to note the gradual presence in Budget Speeches and plans of *infrastructure* programs (starting in 1997) but continued in both the Chrétien-Martin and in the Harper eras, with considerable attention given to them as new departures. Various *cities and communities* agendas were also linked to infrastructure measures or to other more specific programs. *Aboriginal peoples* and related environmental issues also received greater attention, as did Arctic sovereignty and northern development. Natural resources and conservation issues and discourse were also present. We leave to later chapters the more detailed discussion of these features and program structures for environmental policy and how to characterize and assess them.

CONCLUSIONS

The chapter has examined federal environmental policy and agendas in the main federal prime ministerial and governing political party and partisan eras, the Trudeau Liberals from 1968 to 1983, the Mulroney Conservatives in the 1984 to 1993 period, the Chrétien and then Martin Liberals in the 1993 to 2005 period, and finally the Harper Conservatives from 2006 to the present. The prime ministerial eras reveal environmental policy, but such policies can be fully understood only by locating them within and across broader economic and social agendas present in each era, which typically have garnered a much higher priority overall across all four prime ministerial eras.

The analysis of SFTs and Budget Speeches is underpinned by the discussion in chapter 1 regarding the theory and dynamics of agenda-setting and its interaction with media and public opinion and further shows some of the green-lite complexity features of the book's overall analysis.

Thus, our analysis of the environmental content of Speeches from the Throne from 1968 to 2013 shows one major "up" and a lot of downs and/or stasis on environmental matters, both across and within prime ministerial periods. It has also shown that in almost all of its modest periods of salience, SFTs tend to show environmental priorities only in the latter third of such speeches. However, the prime ministerial eras including the SFTs also convey the gradual mention and advocacy of early conservation and pollution cleanup ideas, and then the greater, usually concurrent reference to notions of sustainable development and integrated economic and environmental approaches and also clean energy and responsible resource development.

The analysis of Budget Speeches reveals somewhat greater environmental direct mentions, but again more in later parts of otherwise economically and fiscally focused priority- and agenda-setting occasions for annually detailing political and policy narratives. Quite specific tax and spending initiatives do emerge in most budgets, depending on how much room for manoeuvre there is on each side of the fiscal equation in any given year and over longer periods where the macro economy exhibited more dominant battles and challenges over deficits and recessions but also hyper-inflation and even over surpluses.

The chapter has shown some of the international influences in national environmental agendas, including the Kyoto Protocol and acid rain, but we need now to proceed to a more detailed understanding of these global and regional features (especially vis-à-vis the United States), a task to which chapter 3 is devoted.

3

International Environmental Policy: Canada-US Relations and Global Agreements

INTRODUCTION

An account of the changing nature of international environmental policy, and Canada's role in shaping it and responding to it, is crucial for understanding our analyses of the six environmental regimes in later chapters. Some of these international dimensions have been apparent in chapters 1 and 2; however, we need a clearer sense of the basic contours of how international environmental policy has evolved over the past five decades. While our focus is on the policy story, we also refer to the nature of international relations and power and to the governance structures that changed it and were produced by it.

Indeed, many conceptual and theoretical perspectives have been developed to assess international environmental policy (Dryzek 2013; Wijen et al. 2013; Volger 2013; Elliott 2004; Held et al. 1999). Strands of international relations (IR) theory offers a focus on power and *real politique* concerns of states, both in general and in environmental matters. Theories of *globalization* show how domestic policy choices are influenced by strong and complex international forces, including economic liberalism, but also global public-interest civil-society forces, and also transformative technologies such as the Internet and biotechnology. Global international environmental policy has also been analyzed, as previewed in chapter 1, by concepts of *eco-politics* cast literally and necessarily as planetary-level concerns for the earth as an ecosystem and for its survival in the face of massive common resource challenges, and the earth as the supplier of crucial forms of ecological goods and capital. Each strand takes

interest in the fast-changing types and forms of multilevel governance and multi-scalar challenges at play, as nation-states negotiate,
compete, and cooperate as unitary states, federalized states such
as Canada, and complex multi-state political entities such as the
European Union.

When speaking about the politics of the earth, Dryzek (2013), in
his advocacy of a "discourse approach," begins by arguing that
"environmental issues do not present themselves in well-defined
boxes labelled radiation, national parks, climate change, biodiversity, rainforest, heavy metal pollution and the like ... environmental
problems tend to be interconnected and multi-dimensional" (9).
Complexity is Dryzek's analytical watchword, arguing globally that
"the more complex the situation, the larger the number of plausible
perspectives upon it – because the harder it is to prove any one of
them wrong" (9).

Complexity in these diverse views of international reality and also
this chapter overall further underpins the green-lite approach developed for this book and its Canadian regime analysis. This chapter
elucidates this complexity in the six international environmental
policy and governance histories explored, such as the mix in the
energy system of a large technical system (Hughes 1987) with high
potential for politicization, a large part of which is genuinely related
to the environment and ecosystem (Eberlein and Doern 2009).

Understanding Canada's international environmental policy story
requires tracing its evolution in relation to both multilateral and
Canada-US relations (Boardman 2002). The latter includes the
changing role of the United States as a neighbour and as the global
superpower in the early decades being covered. But under globalization and related forces, the United States now functions under a
multi-polar global power structure that increasingly is shaped by
China, India, Brazil, and East Asian countries and economies, as well
as by the European Union. In international governance terms, these
latter changes are symbolized by the decline of the G-8 and the rise
to prominence of the G-20 bloc of wealthy economies.

The analysis proceeds in six sections that capture the evolution of
an increasingly complex international environmental policy system.
First, we examine some core features of Canada-US environmental
policy relations. Second, we trace the basic complex trajectories and
features of multilateral environmental negotiations and agreements.
Third, the policy and governance history of biodiversity is studied

globally and in relation to Canada's efforts as a signatory to the UN Convention on Biological Diversity. Next we explore the core characteristics and developments in international trade and environment processes and agreements. The fifth section considers climate change, the Kyoto Protocol, and the post-Kyoto world. The sixth section scrutinizes recent interest in the Arctic North and the global and regional dynamics it fosters about de facto climate adjustment, environmental control, economic development, and impacts on northern indigenous peoples in the eight countries (including Canada) that border the Arctic. Conclusions then follow.

CHANGING CANADA-US ENVIRONMENT POLICY RELATIONS

It is axiomatic that Canada's international environmental policy, governance, and politics is greatly shaped by relations with the United States (Hoberg 2002a; Bernstein and Cashore 2002; Doern and Conway 1994). The United States is Canada's most important trading market partner, and the countries are linked through shared terrestrial, aquatic, and marine ecosystems. Such linkages have implications for a host of policy domains. In electricity, for instance, there are more Canada-US north-south grids and safety systems than there are east-west ones within Canada (Dewees 2005). No major oil and gas pipeline in Canada has been developed, built, and even environmentally regulated without de facto joint American and Canadian decisions having to be made at both the national and provincial and state levels or without American and Canadian corporate investment. Increasingly, Canada-US agriculture and food supply chains extend deeply into the other's borders from the proverbial farm gate to plate. American-led technologies such as the Internet have changed communications and campaigning tactics, globally, cross-border, and nationally, about environmental and all policy issues, and especially via the increasingly pervasive role of social media.

The cross-border lobbying also involves complexities for Canada. There is rarely one-stop shopping for any lobby in any democratic political system, but this is particularly true in the United States. First, US federalism means several states from Maine to Michigan to Washington are at the front lines of sharing the 4,800-kilometre common political border, and many more states are at the front lines of sharing environmental borders and ecosystems. Second, the nature of its political system, particularly the separation of powers (e.g., the independent power of Congress and the role of the courts) and the realities of very short and always looming electoral cycles, creates many points of access and veto points that Canadian interests must attend to when interacting with the United States.

Hoberg's (2002a) suggested strategic framework for understanding Canadian-American environmental relations is useful for this chapter and those on specific regimes to follow. He outlines six mechanisms of US influence that can occur and have done so, singly or in combination: physical environmental; policies and actions through emulation (elite driven or activist driven); diplomacy; trade agreements; economic integration and harmonization pressures; and cross-border lobbying (170–3).

For Canadian environmental interests, the United States has, at different times, been an environmental hero and villain, both in political rhetoric and environmental policy practice (Hale 2010; Clarkson 2009; Doern and Gattinger 2003). The 1962 publication of Rachel Carson's seminal book *Silent Spring* brought the issues of pesticide use and the chemical industry to the fore in Canada; in many ways, it marked the birth of the modern environmental age. This was due to the compelling evidence and argument anchored in Carson's science but also because of the exposure it received by American mass media, especially television. Such coverage was watched by Canadians as much as Canadian media; indeed, some of Canada's main environmental NGOs emerged initially in the 1960s and 1970s as creations of parent US environmental NGOs (Paehlke 2010) (see chapter 9).

Previous chapters highlighted these other American environmental impacts. These include, for instance, the emergence of Canada's nuclear industry in the post-war era and the impact of nuclear reactor safety concerns following the Three Mile Island partial nuclear meltdown in Pennsylvania in 1979 (Doern and Morrison 1980). American influence of a different kind also occurred, as shown in chapter 2, through the desire in the early Trudeau era that early environmental assessment *not* be as radical as the progressive law-based role of the US Environmental Protection Agency (EPA), compared to Canada's guideline approach to environmental assessment. And of course we have provided an initial sense of the current Harper-era bitumen-centred multiple pipeline strategy with fast-changing US energy changes and market dynamics linked to fracking and rapidly increasing US oil and gas supplies.

In this section, we look illustratively at three earlier diverse Canada-US environmental policy examples that still resonate today: the Migratory Birds Convention and related wildlife issues; Great Lakes water quality; and acid rain. Key aspects of these core relations are apparent in later policy histories detailed in the chapter, including Canada-US relations in biodiversity, trade, and environment; climate change; and the melting Arctic.

Early US influence on environmental policy, well before the environmental age, can been seen in the 1916 Migratory Birds Convention, which was negotiated by the United Kingdom and the United States for the protection of migratory birds in North America. It was amended in 1995 by a Canada-US protocol that encompassed provisions for Aboriginal and treaty rights for Aboriginals in Canada and the United States (Burnett 2011; Doern and Kinder 2007; Dagg 1974). The impetus for the convention in the United States (and Canada) came from front-line activists concerned about the hunting of migratory birds and the need to preserve them. Indeed, at that time, when the Dominion Wildlife Service of 1947 was created (in 1950 changed to the Canada Wildlife Service) and up to the present, migratory and resident birds have been viewed as crucial components of Canadian ecosystems, because the status of their populations can indicate overall environmental health (Burnett 2011; Doern and Kinder 2007; Canadian Wildlife Service 2000).

The US-Canada trajectory continues with a long-term history of cross-border partnerships and research and monitoring cooperation now extended to related forms of conservation and watershed protection by the CWS and also in concert with Parks Canada and Fisheries and Oceans Canada and their separate and joint planning strategies (Bickis 2008). The North American Waterfowl Management Plan and the North American Bird Conservation Initiative have also fostered interactions between North American agencies and NGOs.

While such cross-border grassroots political pressure and involvement has always been a feature of the migratory bird story, there were weaknesses when cross-border groups sought to use NAFTA side-agreement processes that allowed citizens (NGOs, individuals) to file submissions alleging that one or more of the three NAFTA counties was failing to effectively enforce its environmental law (see further discussion later in this chapter). The Commission for Environmental Cooperation (CEC) dealt with these. In the cases that Wilson (2003) analyzes, two submissions alleging failure were submitted, one against the United States and one against Canada. While noting that groups viewed the CEC process as rather weak, Wilson does add that "these cases indicate nonetheless that the procedure still has some limited usefulness as a way of highlighting implementation failures" and closes by recommending that "NGOs that do choose to invest in pursuing a citizen submission would be advised to combine these efforts with other approaches to mobilizing public pressure (1).

The Great Lakes were another focal area for US-Canada cooperation. Early formal cooperation began with the 1909 Boundary Waters Treaty, administered by one of the longest-serving environmental bodies, the International Joint Commission (IJC) (Clamen 2013). Under its governing treaty, the IJC was concerned mainly with water quantity (i.e., water levels), but it has since addressed water quality related to pollution protection and restoration. The massive St Lawrence Seaway project also flowed from this bilateral cooperation. The project has been associated with major adverse environmental effects due to flooding and water diversions (Macfarlane 2014; Alexander 2009).

In terms of institutional legitimacy, the IJC earned considerable support, because it was a truly bilateral entity with both the giant, more populous United States agreeing that it and the smaller Canada would each appoint three members to the commission. Early on, and in the decades since, water quantity and levels were vital as major economic and population growth (especially in the United States) in cities and elsewhere threatened the viability of such water resources. Thus a fairly principled view emerged that neither country should takes actions unilaterally that might have adverse impacts on the other. As a result the IJC functioned for the most part as a consensus-oriented and expert body. It also evolved to develop complex relations with numerous state and provincial governments and with environmental NGOs. It would also arbitrate between the two countries when asked. However, the IJC was subject to criticism about the quality of some of its decisions on certain sensitive and often large-scale projects (Botts and Muldoon 2005).

The 1972 Great Lakes Water Agreement between Canada and the United States was signed just as Environment Canada was being created (Sproule-Jones 2003; Doern and Conway 1994). It had been preceded by joint scientific research on water quality by the two countries and also by considerable cooperation by Canadian and US environmental NGOs as they lobbied for an agreement, especially those in the Great Lakes bordering US states and Canadian provinces. Given the more than forty joint water boundary areas, and changing pollution threats and water-level concerns at play with the Great Lakes, not all challenges were solved or even addressed. Great Lakes issues saw improvement in water quality, but then also new pollution threats with the lakes as both an economic and social resource, including its importance to tourism and to ecological biodiversity. These ongoing challenges are apparent in the toxic algae bloom that spread in parts of Lake Erie in August 2014, which threatened wildlife and drinking water for communities such as Toledo, Ohio.

The third example of Canada-US environmental policy and eco-politics centred on acid rain, the popular name for a complicated environmental hazard involving emissions of sulphur dioxide (SO_2) and nitrogen oxides (NO_2). After fifteen years of political and scientific debate between the two countries, a Canada-US Air Quality Agreement (AQA) was signed in 1991, including an Acid Rain Annex. A 2012 Progress Report on the agreement concludes, as had earlier reports, that since 1991, "there have been large reductions in SO_2 and NO_x emissions on both sides of the border with subsequent reductions in ecosystem acidification and improvements in air quality" (Air Quality Committee 2012, 1).

Acid rain in Canada in particular, unlike some other pollutants, "was quintessentially middle class because its most visible presence was in central Canada's middle income cottage country. The image of dying lakes was one to which many Canadians could relate directly whether as cottage owners or as visitors to the summer home of a friend or relative" (Doern and Conway, 1994, 148). This was largely true in the United States as well; however, the core eco-politics in the two countries was different and more divisive on acid rain, compared to water levels in the Great Lakes. For Canada, the main US source of SO_2 was coal-fired plants in the Midwestern states such as Ohio and West Virginia. They were also the pollution source for Americans harmed by acid rain in the New England states (Regens and Rycroft 1988). Within Canada, the primary source of acid rain was smelter owners such as INCO, Ontario Hydro,

Falconbridge, and Algoma. Emissions from some of these sources also affected the United States. These differences in turn influenced the nature of pollution-control approaches being advocated and/or rejected.

Overall, the politics in both countries was complicated, multi-levelled, and multi-scaled. This was despite early science documenting the adverse impacts of acid rain, science that was often cooperative and joint between the two countries' scientists and also internationally (Alm 2000; Glode and Glode 1993; OECD 1977; Science Council of Canada 1977). Getting acid rain onto the agenda and having it stay there for long enough in both countries was difficult, given different agenda-setting occasions and opportunities (Gibson 1990; Park 1989; Doern 1993a). Acid rain was also initially a part of the 1979 Convention on Long-Range Transboundary Air Pollution (LRTAP), which was more exhortative than regulatory.

Canada pressed for joint action with both the Carter and Reagan administrations. In 1980 a Coalition on Acid Rain was formed in Canada to give extra impetus to the issue both vis-à-vis the United States and also within Canada. In the last months of the Carter administration, Canada secured a memorandum of intent committing the two countries to cooperative steps to combat acid rain and that included provisions for notification and joint research.

The Reagan era brought considerable stalemate politics, partly because of Reagan's deregulatory and pro-market ideology and agenda, but in this initial 1980 to 1984 period, there was no clear sailing on the Canadian side of the border, given that this was, as chapter 2 has shown, a period when the Trudeau Liberals were not giving environmental issues much attention. There were also problems at the Ontario provincial level, given that the Canadian sources of acid rain were located in Ontario. When the Mulroney Conservatives took office, at the Reagan-Mulroney Shamrock Summit early in 1985, the two leaders agreed on the commonality of the acid rain problem and appointed special acid rain envoys.

There was some research-funding progress in the aftermath of this summitry; however, it was not until the George Bush Administration that the Canada–United States Air Quality Agreement was signed in 1991. Bush had presented himself as an environmental president, and the ultimate agreement on the acid rain issue came from his successful leadership, along with Congressional support, that brought into being the new US Clean Air Act with its more concerted control measures.

Migratory birds, the Great Lakes, and acid rain as examples of Canada-US environmental policy relations, and the additional examples that arise in the policy and governance histories in the rest of this chapter, show the vital importance of joint action by the United States and Canada. They also illustrate the complex and different ecosystem realities that had to be addressed in the context of shifting, larger, cross-border, and global agendas.

GLOBAL ENVIRONMENTAL SUMMITRY, AGENDA SETTING, AND NEGOTIATIONS

International environmental policy has many bases. It emerges from environmental summits and agenda-setting processes led by state-to-state forms of international relations and globalization pressures and dynamics (Wijen et al. 2013). It involves cooperative and conflictual non-state interactions among environmental NGOs and business interests. It involves accounts of the emergence of an age of ecology and of the relations between nature and power in global and local historical settings (Radkau 2008, 2014). And it takes shape and form via environmental treaties, including multilateral conventions and associated protocols and regional and bilateral agreements (Sands and Peel 2012; DeSombre 2011; Nagtzaam 2009; Elliott 2004; Young 2001). Table 3.1 shows at a glance a historical trajectory of key summits, agendas, agreements, and protocols. Of course we cannot discuss all of them in this chapter or in the book as a whole, but the range and order of these events, processes, and policies is important. Nor can we discuss all the various international organizations involved.

While important and illustrative, the table 3.1 list by no means reveals all the international environmental agreements around the world, globally, regionally, and multilateral or bilateral. Stoctt (2012) assembles a "rudimentary chronology" that is four pages long, begins in 1815 with a legal framework regarding navigation of the Rhine River, and ends in 2013 with the International Year of Water Cooperation (32–6). Another current database indicates that there are at present over 1,100 multilateral, 1,500 bilateral, and 250 "other" environmental agreements (Mitchell 2013).

Our list begins with international processes related to parks and protected areas, a phenomenon introduced in the analysis of Canadian prime ministerial eras in chapter 2. The Stockholm

Table 3.1: Selected list of international environmental policy summits, conventions, protocols, and agenda-setting events

- World Conferences on National Parks, starting with 1962 World Parks Congress
- 1972 Great Lakes Water Quality Agreement
- 1972 Stockholm UN Conference on Human Environment
- 1972 United Nations Environmental Programme
- 1972 World Heritage Convention
- 1979 Convention on Long-Range Trans-Boundary Pollution
- 1982 UN Convention on the Law of the Sea
- 1985 Vienna Convention for the Protection of the Ozone Layer
- 1987 Brundtland Commission report and consultations
- 1987 Montreal Protocol on Substances That Deplete the Ozone Layer
- 1990 World Meteorological Convention and Intergovernmental Panel on Climate Change
- 1991 Global Environmental Facility
- 1992 United Nations Conference on Environment and Development Rio Earth Summit
  - Agenda 21
  - Convention on Biological Diversity
  - Convention to Combat Desertification
  - Declaration of Forest Principles
  - Framework Convention on Climate Change
  - Rio Declaration
- 1995 NAFTA side agreement on the environment and formation of Commission on Environmental Cooperation
- 1996 Ottawa Declaration and formation of the Arctic Council
- 1997 Kyoto Protocol, under the UN Framework Convention on Climate Change
- 2000 Biosafety Protocol (under the Convention on Biodiversity)
- 2000 Natura 2000 established as ecological network of special protected areas in the European Union
- 2002 World Summit on Sustainable Development
- 2005 International Marine Protected Areas Congress
- 2009 Copenhagen Climate Change Process and Agreements
- 2011 Durban Climate Change Process and Agreements
- 2012 Doha Climate Change Process and Agreements
- 2012 Rio+20 Earth Summit
- 2013 Warsaw Climate Change Process and Agreements
- 2014 Lima Climate Change Process and Agreements
- 2014 United States–China Climate Accord

Conference in 1972 was pivotal in getting the environment on the global agenda, had major Canadian involvement and advocacy, and was headed by Canada's Maurice Strong. It established the agenda-setting model for later summits in that they each involved thousands of state delegates and NGO and business participants accompanied by massive media coverage. The Stockholm Conference was followed by a series of summit-like processes that took place in 1987, 1992, 2002, and 2012 (Birnie, Boyle, and Redgwell 2009; Wapner 2003).

The sample of conventions and protocols in table 3.1 shows the emergence of needed responses to hazards and "tragedies of the commons" (Ostrom 1990, 2012) and pollutants in the domains of air, water/marine, and land or terrestrial (Auld, Kurzydlo, and Steiner 2013). Also glimpsed is a sense of the increasing complexity of the pollutants and hazards, including biodiversity and climate change, but with none of the other earlier conventions dealing with hazards or harms being simple or easy to solve by cleanup and remediation or prevention. Not included in such illustrative lists are the environmental disasters emanating from wars and armed conflict or from nuclear accidents and environmental-health crises such as mad cow disease and other pandemics (Dryzek 2013; Stoett 2012; Doern and Reed 2000).

The only international environmental agency mentioned above is the United Nations Environmental Programme (UNEP). However, the regime chapters later in this book bring out the roles and influence of other agencies and international organizations in forestry, urban sustainability, and business and NGO certification measures centred on international market pressure and leverage. Formed in 1972, UNEP describes its role as providing "leadership to encourage partnership in caring for the environment by inspiring, informing and enabling nations and peoples to improve their quality of life without compromising that of future generations" (UNEP 2013, 1). While certainly a significant player in key environmental conventions and protocols, there has always been tension between this kind of historic facilitative and often soft law role and whether it or some replacement agency needs to evolve into a "World Environmental Organization" (WEO) with a more comprehensive regulatory role analogous to what the World Trade Organization (WTO) is for global trade. A WEO has been both advocated and opposed by environmental scholars (Biermann and Bauer 2005). We return to this issue in the section below on trade and environment policy, but first we need a final further contextual sense of patterns of international environmental decision-making for international conventions and protocol setting.

Table 3.2 provides a sense of the stylized or potential agenda and decision stages involved, stretching over many years or decades, that begin with early awareness of an environmental hazard or harm, usually as identified by scientists but also by other front-line observers and chroniclers. The extended stages are mixtures of agenda-setting and then sequences of negotiations, the order of which will depend on whether protocols are needed or judged to be viable within the broader or parent convention.

But the nature of negotiations and steps is also a function of a still more nuanced set of dynamics (Young 1999, 2001). DeSombre (2011) suggests that these dynamics include the interests of actors, power of actors, number of actors, issue structure, problem characteristics, issue linkage, and environmental aid and economic sanctions (14–24). Also important are the crafting, use, and abuse of diverse forms of environmental discourse (Dryzek 2013).

A key reality in all of this is also the fact that the signatories to environmental agreements involve different sets of countries, depending on their interest in a given pollutant, either as a source of the pollution, as a country adversely affected by it, or their moral and practical sense of being able to engage in negotiations at a given time. There is rarely an overall parent or supra environmental agreement composed of all counties because of the nature of both the hazard and its particular political economy configuration, and the system of eco-politics involved. Some come close, as we see first with the Convention on Biodiversity; others have smaller numbers of signatories, as we see in the other policy and governance histories that follow in this chapter and in later regime chapters.

BIODIVERSITY AS A GLOBAL AND CANADIAN ECO-POLITICS AND GOVERNANCE CHALLENGE

The Convention on Biological Diversity (CBD) was adopted in Nairobi, Kenya, in May 1992, opened for signature at the UNEP Rio Earth Summit in June 1992, and entered into force on 29 December 1993 (CBD 1992; Stoett 2012; Boyd 2011; Dale and Hill 2011). Canada was an active advocate of the CBD and Prime Minister Brian

Table 3.2: Stages in international environmental convention and protocol setting

1. Early awareness and scientific identification of hazard

2. Global recognition of problem

3. Convening of meetings to develop a convention

4. Development of major ministerial statements of concern

5. Development of convention: actual negotiating sessions; between-negotiations study and lobbying, and later adoption and ratification

6. Development of strategy for regulation and control

7. Development of protocols if needed or viable; actual negotiating sessions; between-negotiations study and lobbying and later adoption and ratification

8. Development of control measures

9. Development of funding mechanism

10. Enforcement

11. Built-in review, feedback, and discovery of links to related or new hazards and pollutants

12. Renegotiation of treaty

Adapted from Doern 1993b, 30.

Mulroney was the first leader to ratify the convention. Unusually among many environmental agreements, the early initiative for identifying and pushing for the CBD came from developing countries, in large part because biodiversity tends to be richest near to the equator. As Stoett's examination of the CBD as a system of eco-politics points out, these equatorial regions "collectively hold roughly four-fifths of the world's biodiversity" and thus "held uncharacteristically efficacious bargaining power" (Stoett 2012, 50).

The Rio Earth Summit was well named, and biodiversity captured a central place in its aspirations for the planet. Biodiversity is the shorthand term for biological diversity, which is "the variety of species and ecosystems on Earth and the ecological processes of which they are a part" (Canada 1995a, 5). The three components of biodiversity are ecosystem, species, and genetic diversity. Ecosystems in turn "perform functions that are essential to human existence such as oxygen and soil production and water purification" (Canada 1995b, 5). We focus here on the CBD overall and Canada's efforts to implement both the spirit and the complexity of its features and challenges. In addition, however, the CBD led to other negotiated protocols, such as that on biosafety relating to biotechnology and in particular to the trans-boundary movement of any living organism (Doern 2000a).

Under the CBD, signatory countries had to submit a biodiversity strategy and then regularly report on it to UNEP and also internally within Canada. We look at a sample of these briefly, beginning with Canada's initial strategy submitted in 1995 under the Chrétien Liberals. The early parts of the strategy discuss the vital importance but also the complex nature of the task, and the strategy ends with Canada's vision and guiding principles for its biodiversity strategy.

Canada's response began with the establishment of a Federal-Provincial-Territorial Biodiversity Working Group "with a mandate from parks, environment, wildlife and forestry ministers" (Canada 1995b, 5). There was also a Biodiversity Advisory Group composed of key stakeholders and ten expert focus groups to provide advice on specific CBD articles (5). The conclusions from this process were that "federal, provincial and territorial governments, in cooperation with members of the public and stakeholders, will pursue the strategic directions set out in the Strategy according to policies, plans, priorities and fiscal capacities" (6). The first part of this statement is positive and aspirational. The second half is highly conditional, given that it centres critically on multi-level governance, including cities and communities. The strategy's reference to the overall reach of biodiversity encompassed diverse "employment goals and human needs and desires" (including eco-tourism and outdoor recreation), but also key notions of spiritual importance and national identity. Effective biodiversity strategies were presented as a form of "insurance for the future" (9).

Like many strategies and policies, but understandable, given the "wicked problems" of biodiversity and eco-politics (Stoett 2012, chap. 3), even the aspiration levels are complex. Thus the 1995 Canadian strategy speaks of a vision, eleven guiding principles, and twelve strategic directions. The *vision* is for Canada to be a "society that lives and develops as a part of nature, values the diversity of life, takes no more than can be replenished and leaves to future generations a nurturing and dynamic world, rich in its biodiversity" (Canada 1995b, 13). Among the eleven *guiding principles* are that "biodiversity has ecological, economic, social, cultural and intrinsic values" and that "development decisions must reflect" such values (14). They also include the principle that the "knowledge, innovations and practices of indigenous and local communities should be respected, and their use and maintenance carried out with the support and involvement of these communities" (14). Among the twelve *strategic directions* are the "use of ecological planning and management approaches on landscape/waterscape-level planning," and "through research, increase our understanding of the status, genetic diversity, and ecological relationships of species and populations to improve ecological planning and management" (18).

Given these honestly important but complex, aspirational, and multi-level governance implications, it is not surprising to see mixed results, as Canada has later reported on its challenges to the CBD Secretariat in Montreal and other audiences. For example, Canada's fourth report to UNEP in 2009 contained a chapter that focused on the "mainstreaming of biodiversity in Canada," a term used to reflect "examples of the growing number of players addressing biodiversity on a diversity of fronts" (Environment Canada 2009, ii and chap. 3). It reported that "scientists have identified over 70,000 species occurring in Canada's diverse ecosystem and as many more remain to be identified" (1), but also stressed that "much of the Canadian economy is built on natural resources" and that Canada, like other countries, was fostering the emerging "bio-based economy including genomics, biotechnology and pharmaceutical industries" (1).

An Environment Canada report (2012b) provides an audit and evaluation of biodiversity policy and priorities for the department. It first concluded that at the federal, provincial, and territorial (F/P/T/) level there had been a "recent trend towards reduced levels of ... senior management engagement on biodiversity (Environment Canada 2012a, 3). The same was true in the department where a lack of clear direction was reported. The study noted that mainstreaming had occurred to a degree at the federal, provincial, and territorial levels of government, and even more extensively at the local level, where Environment Canada wields only limited direct influence (3). Evidence, it observes, suggests that Environment Canada has made progress in achieving immediate and intermediate outcomes, which provides optimism that final outcomes on biodiversity conservation in Canada and globally can be achieved. Still, the report recognized that threats "continue and long term work is needed" (3–4). The report's only recommendation was that there was a need to establish "a mechanism or forum for horizontal discussion and coordination of biodiversity issues within the department" (4).

The commissioner of the environment and sustainable development (CESD) published a comprehensive report (2013a) that is much more damning and unambiguous about the federal government's performance. Regarding the linked biodiversity, species at risk, and also protected areas, the commissioner concludes, "We've looked at these topics in a number of audits since 1998. Our findings have been consistent: despite significant efforts over the years and progress in some areas, there is still much to be done to meet key legislative responsibilities, deadlines and commitments. This report finds many of the same issues, and I see a wide gap between the government's commitments and the results achieved" (3), much of the shortfall found in Environment Canada's own data. The CESD argues overall that "ground-breaking approaches are needed" and that "without concerted and committed efforts, more key species and critical spaces will be lost" (5).

At the international level, assessments of the CBD have also pointed to serious gaps and indeed to compelling problems of even doing basic things both at the CBD level globally and in large groupings of countries such as the European Union. For example in 2002, signatory countries meeting in Johannesburg agreed to "achieve by 2010 a significant reduction of the current rate of biodiversity loss at the global, regional and national level" (Santamaria and Mendez 2012, 209). These authors also show that "funding limitations and knowledge gaps forced biodiversity conservation to focus at the operational level, on the static definition of species still predominant in the biological sciences – considered to be the most prominent and readily recognizable form of biodiversity" (208). By 2010, the reduced goal had itself not been realized. Santamaria and Mendez argue that the "intensity and speed of human alterations to the planet's ecosystems are yielding the static ahistorical view of biodiversity obsolete. Human reactions frequently trigger fast evolutionary responses, drastically affect extant genetic variation (most often depleting it), and result in the ongoing establishment of new communities and co-evolutionary networks for which we lack past analogues" (216).

Stoett's analysis of the CBD draws attention to several features of its structure and progress, which include the work of 173 countries that have submitted the required reports on national plans and outcomes; the CBD Secretariat based in Montreal "is recognized as the flagship institution in the global quest for the protection of biodiversity" (Stoett 2012, 54); the "democratic legitimacy of the convention has improved with the remarkable increase in participation of indigenous and nongovernmental groups" (55); and the Global Environmental Facility (GEF) has been a key funding source for CBD activities. However, Stoett also concludes, "The complexity of the underlying problem and the secretariat's limited formal autonomy should impose realistic expectations on any evaluation of its impact as a knowledge broker and even more as a capacity builder" (55). Overall, Stoett argues, "The continued decline of diversity is frightening, shameful ... It is not a pretty picture but that should not resign us to the impoverishment of the earth's remarkable biodiversity" (59–60).

Thus, overall, at both the global level and with regard to Canada's involvement in the CBD, the picture is quite similar for both aspirational values and implementation challenges. The convention is quintessentially global and indeed planetary in its eco-politics imperatives. Some progress is being made, but complexity and difficulty are massive and subject to simple or rational cause-and-effect performance logics. Canada's early commitment was strong, but its performance has been weak, difficult to assess, and temporally complex.

INTERNATIONAL TRADE AND ENVIRONMENT: SEPARATE AND LINKED WORLDS

For the purposes of this chapter, we need to appreciate some of the separate and linked characteristics of the trade-environmental realm of international policy and governance, with trade also serving here as a useful surrogate for other kinds of international economic policy.

First, the *core focus* of the trade realm is that it seeks through state action to control and restrain *governmental* behaviour. An initial early focus of the General Agreement on Tariffs and Trade was on tariffs (essentially a border tax) and their gradual reduction through several rounds of GATT negotiations (Trebilcock 2011). A later focus was on subsidies, which countries had used in the name of industrial policy, defence policy, and regional policy, and which of course had numerous good and adverse impacts, intended and unintended, on international trade (and on pollution).

The core focus of environmental policy, by contrast, is to solve or manage environmental harms through state action, to control and restrain the *behaviour of markets,* meaning both firms/producers and consumers. The state can also be a producer and consumer, and so controlling the behaviour of governments in this further sense is also a part of environmental policy. But mainly it is the state that is regulating and/or seeking to induce and persuade firms and consumers to pollute less and to produce and consume in a more environmentally sustainable way.

Second, *time of origin* is also a relevant characteristic, in that the international trade policy system started under GATT in the post–Second World War era. In contrast, the main cluster of international environmental policies and institutions started mainly in the 1970s and hence had to play "catch-up" as environmental interests and advocates sought to find their own international space and scale, depending on the nature of hazards being addressed.

Third, the *degree of institutionalization* of the two international policy systems is quite different. Trade policy is much more institutionalized in the World Trade Organization (WTO), with 159 countries as signatories to the agreement forged in the Uruguay Round, and bound in particular by its dispute-settlement processes. The dispute-settlement system anchors the greater extent of institutionalization, in that it is much more rules-based and has dispute panels and time limits than it was initially. International environmental policy has no equivalent to the WTO. The UNEP plays a facilitative, coordination role alongside a host of other specialized UN organizations and agencies, such as the Food and Agricultural Organization, UN-Water, the International Maritime Organization, and many others. Chapters to follow detail the work of other international organizations in the forest and mining sectors, as well as private and co-governance initiatives led by NGOs and business.

Fourth, the *conception of borders* is different, though each is becoming more complex. International trade policy has evolved from trade "at the border" (tariffs, quantity protection) to trade "over the border" via national treatment and other provisions and hence into virtually all heretofore or previously domestic policy fields. Environmental "borders" rarely coincide with national or sub-national political borders. Instead they relate, as chapter 1 has shown, to ecological borders and flows and hence to different realities of space and scale.

Fifth, the issue of *handling "legitimate objectives" (LOs) regarding health, safety, and environment* is increasingly germane in trade agreements. In the international trade realm, such LOs are considered policy rights that sovereign states can legitimately pursue in the public interest. Of course, this is precisely how environmentalists believe such policies should be carried out. The qualifier in trade agreements is that when LOs are pursued, they must be carried out in the least trade-distorting manner possible, by adhering to rules and processes regarding *technical barriers to trade* (TBT). These processes in turn centre on differences of view on the role of science, evidence, and knowledge in decision-making, as well as concepts such as the precautionary principle (Trebilcock 2011; Trebilcock, House, and Eliason 2013).

The political power logic for TBT chapters was underpinned by the expectation that if nations could no longer use *tariffs* as key vehicles of protection, or *subsidies* either, two of the past favoured protectionist devices in the policy tool kit, they would look into the now diminished tool kit for others. These "others" such as health and safety and environmental provisions could serve as the weapon of choice, deployed either directly or indirectly. In short, nations and key interests within them would always have some reasons to protect rather than to liberalize trade, and indeed such technical barriers were being deployed. LOs were policy rights but also had to be regulated somehow within trade agreements (Heydon 2012). The WTO agreement also includes LO provisions regarding sanitary and phytosanitary measures (SPS Agreement). These are measures for food safety and animal and plant health measures, as defined in their own separate agreement. However, these kinds of measures are very TBT-like (Epps 2008).

In the Canadian case, it is also worth noting that LO provisions are contained within the Agreement on Internal Trade (AIT) negotiated between the federal government and the provinces (Doern and MacDonald 1999). LO provisions go to the heart of overlaps and conflicts between free trade federalism, environmental policy in a federation, and federalist democracy, including provisions for dispute settlement (Doern 2007a, 2013).

Meanwhile more and more countries were also signing other regional or bilateral trade agreements, each of which required WTO approval, but each of which could be somewhat different, as long they were liberalizing trade overall. This has certainly included Canada, where bilateral trade agreements were concluded with Chile, Colombia, and Peru. But much more crucially, the Harper government is currently negotiating major agreements such as the Canada-EU Trade Agreement (CETA) and the Trans-Pacific Partnership Free Trade Agreement (TPP). Foreign investment protection agreements have also been a part of this agenda and have been heavily implicated in concerns over the role of Canadian mining companies operating in Latin American and African countries (Gordon and Webber 2007). We return to this in chapter 6.

It must be stressed at this point that trade agreements as a real and perceived business and corporate agenda received an enhanced focus when the WTO was formed and became a rhetorical and political focus for anti-globalization and also pro-environment critics. The Seattle protests in 1999 and then a series of high-profile protests at other G7 Summit meetings in 2000, 2001, and 2002 meant trade regime defenders were put on the defensive, largely on the grounds that the WTO (and other institutions of global governance) were cast as undemocratic in the sense that NGOs and civil society were said to be largely shut out of its decision-making. In contrast, others argued that "ecological modernization" was occurring in the global economy, with some environmental benefits therefore tied in and feasible under globalization (Hajer 1995; Mol 2001).

The larger "trade and" agenda was also a key feature of the expanding trade regime culture and agenda. This referred again to the broadening content of agreements that increasingly included "trade and" services, "trade and" investment, intellectual property, etc., and that anticipated still further extensions into realms such as competition policy. These issues in the overall GATT Uruguay Round agreement resulted in separate related agreements on these subjects and in part to WTO-linked institutions. Many of these changes increasingly were seen by some critics as being the product of US power and aggressive unilateralism, in short, raw hegemonic American political and economic power especially vis-à-vis intellectual property (Sell 1998).

To complete the trade-environment section, NAFTA and the NAFTA-related provisions regarding the Commission for Environmental Cooperation (CEC) require mention. We have already seen in chapter 2 that this environmental side agreement appeared largely at the insistence of the Clinton administration. Among the CEC provisions are processes whereby citizens of any of the three NAFTA countries can request reviews by the commission where they believe that one or more countries are not implementing their own environmental policies and rules. While not strong, these provisions have been used, they have led to the publication of reports and studies, and they have contributed to a naming and shaming process to shine a light on non-compliance or to enhance effective environmental protection (Kirton and MacLaren 2002; Levasseur 2002). For instance, a Canadian group, West Coast Environmental Law group, recently argued that the weakening of federal environmental laws and enforcement by the Harper government means that Canada is not adhering to its NAFTA obligations regarding the maintenance of high environmental standards (Hume 2013). The CEC also reports more generally on a wide range of environmental and sustainable development issues involving one or more of the three member countries. It, along with other national and international environmental entities, has to navigate through intricate and complicated processes regionally and globally (Blasiger and VanDeveer 2012; Biermann and Siebenhuner 2009).

CLIMATE CHANGE POLICY, THE KYOTO PROTOCOL, AND A POST-KYOTO WORLD

Climate change policy has been central to international environmental policy over the past three decades. Moving from an early gestation stage that led to the UN Framework Convention on Climate Change (UNFCCC) to binding targets for developed countries in the Kyoto Protocol, it now defines an era that many are calling a post-Kyoto world. At the centre of this world is the changing core political-economic relations between developing and developed countries, mainly in the form of emerging large powerful countries and regions such as China, India, Brazil, and East Asia that are now fast developing and hence large producers of greenhouse gas emissions. These and other developing countries are outside the Kyoto Protocol, largely because they had successfully argued that it was wealthy Western countries that had created the problem. But in the post-Kyoto world, this no longer works as a starting point for either discussions or solutions (Dryzek, Norgaard and Schlosberg 2013; Giddens 2011; Helm 2012). We look at each of these stages with reference to global developments, and Canada's role in them told largely and necessarily in the context of Canada-US climate-change relations.

The adoption of the Framework Convention on Climate Change in 1992 and the negotiation of the Kyoto Protocol in 1997 followed years of international policy and economic analysis and decades of global scientific research to examine whether and how human emissions of greenhouse gases are causing climate change (Grubb, Vrolijk, and Brack 1999). The 1979 World Climate Conference created the World Climate Research Programme to help stimulate research. Then, in 1988 the Intergovernmental Panel on Climate Change (IPCC) was established. The IPCC's successive reports provided the scientific underpinning, first, for the UNFCCC, and second, for the Kyoto Protocol and other outcomes and agreements of the UNFCCC's annual Conference of the Parties (COPs) and various ad hoc working groups and subsidiary bodies. The IPCC's first assessment report was published in 1990, the second in 1996, and the third in July 2001; others have followed since.

Assessments made by the IPCC, composed of several hundred scientists from around the globe, produced a strong scientific consensus that more and more governments were beginning to accept, though not yet act upon with firm commitments. In short, even though the Kyoto Protocol had been adopted in 1997 with targets for reductions of greenhouse gas emissions for a group of developed countries, the protocol was slow to begin. But all parties knew that, at its core, the Kyoto Protocol was mainly regulatory and rule-based, in that targets for reductions were required. Accordingly, some countries, institutions, and interests were already beginning to change their behaviour in anticipation of eventual commitments. But policy solutions as a whole and the character of the policy mix, including its specific regulatory provisions, would emerge in more detail only after prolonged and protracted negotiations among initially 178 countries (now almost 200) and with enormous pressure coming from national and international environmental NGOs and scientists. As we have seen in our discussion of agenda setting, countries in the Kyoto Protocol processes faced intricate issues of national interest, and regional interests within countries, as well as issues of timing on economic and fiscal policy. This was and is certainly true for Canada (Harrison 2010).

The Kyoto processes were also anchored in the IPCC's science-based work. This combined and linked work identified all the other possible actions that countries and stakeholders could take, some combination of which would be needed to deal with the problem and, equally important, would be needed to forge a consensus on which a negotiated and enforceable global agreement could emerge among the parties. This was because the final complex package had to meet not only the core test of reducing greenhouse emissions but also of doing it in a way that was economically efficient (hence the need for flexible, incentive-based regulation and other technological measures) and equitable, especially between developing and developed countries, but also *within* countries. But agreement within countries varied enormously and hence was also part of the overall complex calculus and dynamics.

An IPCC policy-makers working group had early identified the portfolio of actions available. Many of these action were significant and difficult, but others were frequently labelled as "no regrets" actions, since they would be beneficial and relatively costless, no matter what future negotiations might hold. These included phasing out distorting policies, such as some subsidies and regulations, non-internalizing of environmental costs, and distortions in transport pricing, cost-effective fuel-switching measures, such as renewables, and enhancing forest sinks or reservoirs and related forest management and land use practices (Grubb, Vrolijk, and Brack 1999).

Canada's strategies were proceeding in tandem through newly created domestic institutional processes. Many research- and technology-oriented activities began in the early 1990s. But after the 1997 Kyoto Protocol was negotiated, Prime Minister Chrétien and the premiers and other first ministers directed the federal, provincial, and territorial ministers of energy and environment "to examine the impacts, costs and benefits of implementing the Kyoto Protocol, as well as the options for addressing climate change" (National Climate Change Process 2000, 2). They were to do so under "a guiding principle that no region should bear an unreasonable burden from implementing the Protocol" (2). Thus was implanted at the political level the central importance of a guideline rule on equity considerations among Canada's regions, analogous to the larger "equity" debate in the global negotiations among countries. Such a guideline rule was undoubtedly needed in an overall national unity sense, but it was especially imperative for accommodating Alberta. Alberta was already rhetorically casting Kyoto as "another National Energy Program," the strongly opposed 1980 Trudeau-era interventionist policy. And of course Alberta knew that it was the province at the heart of the carbon-producing part – albeit not the core carbon-using part – of the Canadian economy. This directive from first ministers resulted in the establishment in 1998 of the National Climate Change Process referred to above.

One further element of Canada's approach to the Kyoto Protocol negotiations and implementation, nationally and internationally, was the issue of carbon sinks. Canada sought – and at the 2001 COP in Bonn, eventually obtained – agreement for the crediting of carbon sinks for removing carbon dioxide from the environment. This was based on the fact that plants and trees "breathe in" and store CO_2 from the atmosphere, and thus forests and agricultural soils that absorb and store CO_2 are known as "carbon sinks" under the Kyoto Protocol. Canada wanted credit for enhancing sinks. Credit for carbon sinks became a key negotiating issue on several levels: moral, political, and economic. The EU and many NGOs sought to exclude them on the grounds that this was not real greenhouse-gas emission-reduction and that indeed it was based, in the view of some, on dubious or not "credible science." Canada and other countries with large forests such as Australia, Japan, and Russia supported the inclusion of carbon sinks. In the end, the Bonn 2001 agreement included them under certain conditions.

In 2002, the larger politics, symbolism, and practical realities of Kyoto commitments became more starkly revealed as the Chrétien government and the provinces faced the now more looming and immanent deadline of Canada actually signing on to specific commitments. Several past and current positions converged and collided. The first was that Canada's initial Kyoto commitments had always been based partly on a desire to simply look better than the United States and thus to convey foreign and green policy virtue to the rest of the world. When the Bush administration abandoned Kyoto in June 2001 and announced its own largely market- and incentive-based alternatives in February 2002, the Chrétien government was in a sense hoist on its own petard. Not only was the Bush administration saying that it did not really care much about how it *appeared* to the rest of the world, it meant that Canada's Kyoto position now had to be crafted in the light of the fact that its oil and gas industry (mainly Alberta's oil and gas exports) could be put at a comparative disadvantage in its main market, the United States, and that other Canadian industries centred in Ontario might face similar disadvantages if they had to pay higher environment policy–induced energy costs than their US competitors.

These issues and other dynamics, coupled with the availability and demonstration effect of the Bush administration's alternative to Kyoto, helped sow the seeds of a "made-in Canada" alternative to

Kyoto as well. The Alberta Conservative government began seeking support among the provinces and in Ottawa for a package of initiatives that would reduce and lower emissions, but that would rely more on the development of alternative technologies and would be calibrated to keep Canadian energy competitive in US markets. Such technologies included carbon capture and storage technologies (Meadowcroft and Langhelle 2011).

By the autumn of 2002, a larger business coalition, the Canadian Coalition for Responsible Environmental Solutions, had been formed. Though critical of the lack of specifics in the federal approach to Kyoto, neither it nor the Alberta alternative was any more specific. The Bush anti-Kyoto policy also prompted Canada to add a further caveat to its eventual signing on. This came in the form of a federally suggested Canadian need to get "clean energy" credits for energy that it exported to the United States, such as natural gas and hydroelectric power, which replaced dirtier US alternative sources of supply from coal- and oil-fired energy.

The Kyoto Protocol was agreed to by 178 nations in December 1997, but it did not enter into force until 2005, when Russia ratified. Canada did not ratify it until 2002, when the Chrétien Liberals undertook to reduce Canada's greenhouse gas emissions by 6 per cent below its 1990 levels, averaged over the 2008 to 2012 period. Given weak and even non-existent actions, that commitment by 2005 amounted to a needed 26 per cent reduction, since Canada's actual emissions had soared. As Daniel Schwanen emphasized, the core problem was how to achieve the reductions: "Unfortunately, the Kyoto targets were set without reference to the cost of meeting them (or of their potential benefits relative to those of following alternative scenarios of emissions reductions and time frames). Considering how far Canada is from reaching its Kyoto target, and how closely the emissions of the principal GHGs (green house gasses) resulting from human activity are linked with the growth and type of economic activity the country has typically enjoyed, a serious attempt at meeting the commitment within a given timetable would likely involve significant changes in the economy and even in Canadian lifestyles" (Schwanen 2000, 1).

The short-lived Martin Liberal government did little in the 2004 to 2006 period; and, from 2006 on, the Harper Conservatives, with their power base in Alberta, have not found it particularly difficult to give little priority to the climate change file. Following the

December 2009 Copenhagen COP, where prime minister Stephen Harper kept a low profile and assigned his environment minister, Jim Prentice, to do most of the difficult and embarrassing talking, Canada announced what its new targets on cuts to greenhouse emissions were going to be. These reductions would be 17 per cent from 2005 levels by 2020, and replaced the older Harper government targets announced in 2007 that were to reduce emissions by 20 per cent from 2006 levels (Galloway and Vanderklippe 2010).

At the 2011 Durban COP, Canada maintained its basic strategy, and only after the conference did the Harper government announce that it was pulling out of the Kyoto Protocol. It suffered little or no adverse political impacts from this decision, in the sense that it won the 2011 election and a majority government, in an election where none of the opposition parties made the environment or Kyoto an issue, in the midst of the global and Canadian fiscal and banking crisis.

The new Canadian emission-reduction targets, now outside Kyoto, are intended to follow and fit within the Obama administration's climate-change emission-reduction goals (both base year and targets) but without any guarantee that these would actually become US policy, following Congressional debate and jockeying. This Harper government position had been presented fairly consistently and hence easily attracted the label of a "made-in-the-US" climate change policy. Hence, if there was a crisis, it would be for the Canadian economy, were Canada not to harmonize its policies with those of its biggest market, the United States.

In a real sense, Harper's climate-change minimalism ran counter to expressed Canadian public opinion that supported stronger action and targets but rarely using crisis discourse in any sustained way. The Harper Conservative view is underpinned by a desire to project Canada internationally as a global energy superpower, to protect the national and regional economic engine of the Alberta oil sands, and to support its own Western Canadian political base, even though it interspersed such support with periodic gentle comments that the oil sands had to be more environmentally responsible. Moreover, the Conservatives easily found political cover (and still arguably can) by pointing out that the Chrétien and Martin Liberals' Kyoto commitments brought increased emissions, not reductions (Rivers and Jaccard 2009).

The 2010 Speech from the Throne and Budget Speech revealed the hard tactical calculus on climate change. Climate change was the final item in the 2010 SFT, and thus the Conservatives were virtually daring the Opposition parties and voters to think and vote differently from the Tories. But the SFT shifts a touch by saying that Canada aspires to be a "clean energy" superpower rather than an "energy" superpower, the language still preferred in the Budget Speech (Doern and Stoney 2010).

In 2011, as we noted earlier, the government's own National Roundtable on the Environment and Economy again argued that Canada should proceed with a "made-in-Canada" climate-change regulations approach, rather than a de facto "made-in-the-USA" policy based on broadly harmonizing eventual US regulations (NRTEE 2011b). If anything, Harper environmental policy, as it relates to energy and climate change, plays even more to an appeal to its core Alberta and Western Canadian base. This was especially the case when Harper's then newly appointed environment minister, Peter Kent, went out of his way to assert explicitly that Canada was a source of "ethical oil." In any event, as emphasized above, the Harper Conservatives won a majority government in the 2011 federal election, with climate change barely registering in either partisan dispute or voter opinion.

The overall politics of the Kyoto Protocol also centred on the fact that developing countries were not a part of the protocol, on the grounds that it was essentially the developed Western countries that had created the problem and that, moreover, developing countries would need expanded energy growth as they themselves grew and hopefully prospered economically. Increasingly, by mid-decade, and following the 2005 Gleneagles G-8 summit, the Bush administration, backed by big US energy interests, began forging an alternative and also "beyond" Kyoto small coalition around the Asia-Pacific Partnership on Clean Development and Climate. It consisted of Kyoto non-signatory countries, which crucially included China and India, the two developing but dynamic and fast-growing economies whose energy needs were insatiable but whose fast-growing GHG emissions could also negate climate change progress in other ways. Indeed, key advocates of the Kyoto Protocol saw it, even if implemented successfully, as merely the first in a series of steps that would be needed to tackle climate change in the decades beyond the protocol end date of 2012 (Grubb, Vrolijk, and Brack 1999). Current and near-term energy policies are clearly being influenced by the climate change debate, but such policies are always premised partly as well on long-term energy projections and scenarios already sketched out above. A central question in assessing these scenarios is whether countries are planning for, or moving towards, a low-carbon economy. The notion of what *low carbon* means and whether it can be achieved is, of course, itself contentious.

The term *low-carbon economy* also implies the question of how fast such a movement or progression might occur. The speed of the transition to "low(er) carbon" is driven by the power of established producer interests, and their alliances with governments, and the counter-pressure of new energy producer and manufacturing interests and environmental lobbies and their alliances with governments. The Canadian emission-reduction failure was due largely to policy and regulatory failures of actions that really began to take implementation shape only in 2002 and later. But it was also due to abject political and policy failure by the Chrétien Liberals. Canada's higher population growth and also better overall economic growth was also a factor in Canada's greenhouse gas emissions growth (Rivers and Jaccard 2009).

The international context of climate-change policy shifted and broadened further in recent years. The United Kingdom's 2007 Stern Report broadened the debate through its quite extensive, though controversial, assessment of the economics of climate change (HM Treasury 2007). The G-8 Heiligendamm (Germany) Summit also managed to ease the US administration into a broader acceptance of the science of climate change, though not of any hard regulatory approaches. The Doha COP in December 2012 produced an agreement "with a historic shift in principle but few genuine cuts in greenhouse gases" (Harrabin 2012, 1). The agreement included a provision whereby developed wealthy nations would move towards compensating poor nations for losses caused by climate change. The Kyoto Protocol is extended to 2020 but processes were also put in place for it to be replaced by 2015 by a new treaty committing both rich and poor nations to deal with climate change and greenhouse gas emission reductions. But even integrated multi-level strategies in a North American regional context are difficult and contentious (Craik, Studer, and VanNijnatten 2013).

At the 2013 COP in Warsaw, the talks were influenced by both longer-term changing coalitions among countries and by immediate events. The coalitional changes saw the continuing emergence of dozens of smaller island and coastal states already affected by climate change (Dryzek, Norgaard, and Schlosberg 2013). The giant Philippine typhoon gave increased credibility to the call for climate justice. Looking ahead to the 2015 Paris climate talks, when a replacement for the Kyoto Protocol is to be agreed on, the Warsaw agreement outlines a proposed system for pledging emission cuts and also a new mechanism to tackle the human cost of rising seas, floods, stronger storms, and other expected effects of global warming (Myers and Kulish 2013; Jolly 2013).

Broadly similar dynamics also characterized the Lima Conference of the Parties in early December 2014, but with even more pressure for an agreement that would pave the way for the definitive agreement in Paris in 2015. It had been preceded by the release of the IPCC's 2014 report, with IPCC scientists issuing their starkest warning yet, calling for fossil fuels to be phased out by 2100 (McGrath 2014). The report stressed that "continued emission of greenhouse gases will cause further warming and long-lasting changes to all components of the climate system, increasing the likelihood of severe, pervasive and irreversible impacts for people and ecosystems" (quoted in Gillis 2014b, 7). Some further unexpected momentum came from China and the United States, the world's two leading polluters, when they announced on 11 November 2014 a joint plan to reduce emissions. The plan was seen by both countries as one that would pressure all nations to make their own emission plans and reductions (Landler 2014). These developments contributed to the Lima agreement, where for the first time developing and developed nations signed up to publishing national plans for curbing carbon dioxin emissions but with environmental groups arguing that these plans were still voluntary and of course still awaited the final definitive Paris 2015 negotiations (Connor 2014).

Other published research is also important in this changing climate-change context, including the implications of limiting and keeping global warming to the 2 degrees centigrade level throughout the twenty-first century. A study by McGlade and Elkins concludes that "globally, a third of oil reserves, half of gas reserves, and 80 percent of current coal reserves should remain unused from 2010 to 2050" (McGlade and Elkins 2015, 1). And crucially for Canada, oil sands reserves form a large part of the posited "should remain unused" category. So also should oil and gas reserves in the Arctic. The study also suggests that carbon capture will not be of much use (Harrabin 2015).

In Canada, the global climate-change developments, and the related US environmental actions by President Obama discussed in chapter 2, were also putting pressure on the Harper government heading into a 2015 Canadian election to improve its dismal climate change record (see also chapter 5 on the Energy-Environment Regime).

THE ARCTIC, THE "NORTHS," AND THE "SOUTHS" IN A REGIONAL AGREEMENT

A further and more recent manifestation of international environmental policy centres on the melting Arctic Ocean as a result of climate change, and the environmental Aboriginal developmental issues and impacts involved for the eight counties that border the Arctic. And within those countries it involves each of their usually distant, less populous "norths" and their populous and politically central "souths." In Byers's (2009) definitive account, it involves the central question of "who owns the Arctic," in the sense of sovereignty, but also private property and the global commons where complex public goods have to be defended and managed. It involves rescaling in major ways, including the fact that most southerners in each of the countries have never visited their northern and high Arctic realms. It is therefore in many ways "out of sight and out of mind," except for periodic media coverage of receding ice, snow, and endangered polar bears. The most recent international regional institution established for the Arctic is the Arctic Council, whose member countries include Canada, the United States, Russia, Denmark (including Greenland and the Faroe Islands), Finland, Iceland, Norway, and Sweden (Arctic Council 2013). As John English's compelling account shows, the Arctic Council was both a Mulroney Conservative and Chrétien Liberal initiative and hence had full Canadian bipartisan international impetus (English 2013). The forerunner to the council was a 1989 meeting initiated by Finland to discuss with the eight countries cooperative measures to deal with the environment. This led to both science and research work on the environmental issues already evident and produced the Arctic

Environmental Protection Strategy. Observer countries from other parts of the world were also involved, and thus there are already broader dynamics regarding the further "internationalization" of the Arctic Council (English 2013).

It was in the Ottawa Declaration of 1996 that the Arctic Council was formerly established to provide "a means for promoting cooperation, coordination and interaction among the Arctic States, with the involvement of the Arctic Indigenous communities and other Arctic inhabitants on common Arctic issues, in particular issues of sustainable development and environmental protection in the Arctic" (Arctic Council 2013, 1).

Environmental concerns are therefore pivotal, but the notion of climate change "adjustment" as a term for the melting Arctic hardly does justice to the total task at hand and to the new worlds that other interests now see as exciting economic opportunities, including the opening of sea routes between the Atlantic and Pacific (Jones 2013). The changing Arctic agenda also involves new oil and gas exploration and supplies, and new access to minerals and other natural resources, including access to new fishing grounds and stocks. Some of the latter is Pollyannaish in the extreme, but it is already enough to raise deep concerns among environmentalists in the north and globally ("The Arctic" 2012, 2013). Concerns are also building about what Berkman (2010, 2013) refers to as the need to prevent an "Arctic Cold War." Charles Emmerson's comprehensive assessment of the Arctic and its present and future concludes that "a battleground does not mean war, but it does mean conflict and competition: political, economic, cultural and diplomatic" (Emmerson 2011, 344).

This concern about conflict arises in part because in the formation of the council the crucial concerns by some about preserving peaceful relations was deleted in the talks leading to its formation (Berkman 2013). These concerns centred on US-Russian relations and history and also their military capacities to back up sovereignty claims, but there is also NATO interest in the new sea routes and the possibility of conflict (Emmerson 2011). Indeed, the discourse used by Berkman (2010) is centred on *environmental security* and is further captured in a compelling summary view: "The Arctic Ocean is the most challenging maritime environment to govern in the world, and the challenges will only grow as the diminishing sea-ice leads to an increase in the volume, frequency and diversity of human activity in the Arctic Ocean increases the likelihood of grounding collisions, pollution, disputes, illegal trade, piracy, illegal human trafficking, and disease transmission. In the maritime arctic, current navigation regulations, enforcement capability, domain awareness and infra-structure fail to adequately prevent and respond to these rising threats" (Berkman 2009, 1).

An early 2013 set of conclusions by Arctic environment ministers regarding Arctic change and its global effects spoke of climate change and ocean acidification as well as the related need to deal with short-lived climate pollutants. It also took particular note of the need to prevent contamination in the Arctic from the long-range movement of persistent organic pollutants. Action is also needed to sustain biodiversity (Environment Canada 2013c). While economic benefits are seen by key interests regarding the melting Arctic, other studies point to huge potential economic costs. One of the latter, published in *Nature*, reports on economic costs around the world due to the release of large amounts of methane, a powerful green-house gas, from the thawing permafrost (Whiteman, Hope and Wadhams 2013; Connor 2013).

Canada has begun a two-year period as chair of the Arctic Council, but some early accounts are casting this as Canadian leadership of a "pro-development" Arctic Council (Bennett 2013). This is probably not an unfair comment, given the Harper government's own Arctic and northern strategies (Abele 2011).

The Harper era has seen the articulation, with strong prime ministerial involvement, of a northern strategy tied to a defence of Canada's Arctic sovereignty, including Harper's effort to have the North Pole, agreed as part of Canada's territorial jurisdiction. Harper's strategy for the north also includes climate change and environmental protection, including the role of a new Canadian High Arctic Research Station (Byers 2009; Coates et al. 2008). Considerable prime ministerial interest in Aboriginal issues had occurred during the brief Paul Martin Liberal-era minority govern-ment, but there was only limited follow-through in the precarious minority government politics and policy situation of the Harper era from 2006 to 2011 (Abele 2011). It remains to be seen how Harper's strategies might shift, given its larger oil and gas pipeline agenda vis-à-vis the United States and its view of environmental regula-tion being recast as responsible resource development and efficient regulation. It was therefore significant both in symbolic and political-economic terms when, in December 2013, Harper gave considerable public emphasis to his plan that Canada would claim territorial jurisdiction of the North Pole under the UN Convention of the Law of the Sea (Chase 2013a, 2013b). This occurred despite expert opinion that this claim was highly likely to be invalid (Byers 2014).

Greenpeace Canada has criticized the first draft Arctic Council treaty dealing with blowouts and oil spills, such as the kind that occurred in the 2010 Deep Water Horizon disaster in the Gulf of Mexico. Described as a treaty on the Marine Oil Pollution Preparedness and Response in the Arctic, the still vague draft, if approved, would still have to rely on individual states to set crucial drilling safety and liability limits (Koring 2013). Canada's National Energy Board launched a public review very soon after the Deep Water Horizon disaster occurred, to assess Canada's safety and environmental preparedness for offshore drilling in the Canadian Arctic. Its final reports identified both serious gaps and potential suggested solutions in the even more difficult and daunting melting ice context of the Arctic (National Energy Board 2011a, 2011b).

CONCLUSIONS

This chapter has provided an account of the changing international environmental policy and Canada's role in shaping and responding to it, not just in the last five decades of the environmental age but also in a Canada-US context stretching back to the early 1900s. The international environmental and policy context for Canada involves the continuing importance of Canada-US relations, as two neighbouring states and peoples who share intricate environmental and ecological problems and challenges. The analysis has shown again the need to trace and track both direct and indirect or hyphenated environmental policy in relation to international relations and numerous and ever-increasing numbers of international environmental agreements. From the outset, we have stressed that international environmental relations are examined through literature and scholarly approaches informed by international relations, globalization, and eco-politics theory and practice. The six fairly representative international policy histories examined in this chapter show complexity as the norm, some successes, and also failures and intense political conflict, as new hazards are discovered and remedies sought, and as agendas change or fail to gain consensus. International relations in this field always include international science and technology relations across boundaries, borders, and ecosystems.

Each of our six examined policy histories – Canada-US relations, biodiversity, global environmental summitry and conventions, trade and environment, climate change, and the Arctic – is important in its own right. It also feeds contextually into the analysis of the six environmental regimes and their green-lite features. The first of these in chapter 4 examines the Environment Canada–Centred Regime.

PART TWO

Empirical Analysis
of Six Environmental Regimes

4

The Environment Canada–Centred Regime

INTRODUCTION

The first environmental regime to be examined is the Environment Canada–Centred Regime. Canada did not have an environment department until 1971, so the core empirical story covered in this chapter deals with more than four decades of progress, delays, inertia, and cooperation and conflict in environmental policy, governance, and democracy. Chapter 3 showed that the department played a major national and international role in the 1992 UNCED Rio Summit and in the Canada-US Great Lakes environmental agreements and progress. Concurrently, it achieved only sluggish results on biodiversity policy. But we need to see the Environment Canada–Centred Regime in more detail in terms of its changing mandates and laws, as seen through four policy and governance histories.

The notion of the regime being Environment Canada–*centred* by definition means that the department was not a hermetically sealed as an entity or policy, political, governance, and democratic regime (Enros 2013; Doern and Conway 1994). The department was and is in a sense an entity within the state that aspires to be an environmental central agency at the heart of government, but with other central agencies and ministers never allowing the department to attain this central status for very long. But in another sense, the department also needed allies and others to see themselves as "environment" departments. The central agencies and power centres include, of course, at a minimum the prime minister, the Prime Minister's Office (PMO), the Privy Council Office (PCO), the Department of Finance, and the Treasury Board and its secretariat. Other Cabinet ministers and their departments and their related interest-group power structure in the Canadian economy also had diverse views about when to cooperate with and when to oppose Environment Canada in the agenda-setting, tax, expenditure, and regulatory processes of government and democracy. We have also noted in earlier chapters that environment ministers stay in post for an average of a year and a half. These short terms reflect green-lite features, since complex high turnover rates of leadership are unlikely to foster high environmental policy salience or performance. Civil servants in the department can do only so much without concerted ministerial leadership and support.

The core and linkage aspects of the regime can be seen via an initial summary look at how Environment Canada's mandate evolved and was described across the five decades. These mandates are expressed in core statutes; statutes where the department shared roles with other departments; regulations; and agreements, including funding agreements. Later, as the Internet emerged and as websites became commonplace, mandates were also expressed as visions and multi-level mission statements, based on core statutes, but often embellished in aspirational ways well beyond statutory provisions and language.

In its early years the Environment Canada mandate was centred mainly on the Department of the Environment Act, the Fisheries Act, the Canada Water Act, and the Clean Air Act. But it also described itself as an advisor on other statutes administered by other federal departments, including the Motor Vehicles Act and the Pest Control Products Act.

By the early 1990s, the department's direct legislative base had been extended to include the Canada Wildlife Act, the Canadian Environmental Protection Act, but also statutes such as the International Rivers Improvement Act, and the Migratory Birds Convention Act. Its advisory roles by then included other laws such as the Arctic Waters Pollution Prevention Act, the Canada Shipping Act, and the Transportation of Dangerous Goods Act, to name only a few. In 2002, the department had fourteen acts that were its own mandate responsibility, by then including the Canadian Environmental Assessment Act, discussed later in this chapter.

At present, the Environment Canada mandate is based on about twenty statutes, including the Species at Risk Act, the Wild Animal and Plant Protection and Regulation of International and Interprovincial Trade Act, the Federal Sustainable Development Act, and the Canada Foundation for Sustainable Development Technology Act. The current departmental website also explains that the department administers over eighty regulations and hence is "one of the Government of Canada's most active regulators" (Environment Canada 2013a). On the regulatory front, it notes the provisions of the government-wide Forward Regulatory Plans, the Cabinet Directive on Regulatory Management (formerly the Cabinet Directive on Streamlining Regulation), the Red Tape Reduction Plan, and the Canada–United States Regulatory Cooperation Council.

In what follows we detail a nuanced analysis to better understand the origins and evolution of the Environment Canada–Centred Regime as a whole, drawing attention where appropriate and relevant to green-lite features. The analysis chronologically reviews three basic periods: 1971 to the late 1980s; 1990 to 2002; and the last decade from 2003 to 2013–14. We then look at two more particular aspects in a somewhat less chronological fashion across the more than forty years of Environment Canada, namely its evolution as a science- and evidence-based department, and as a department and ministry carrying out and advocating the environmental assessment of projects. Finally, we look at overall illustrative summary evidence from the historical events as they relate to the three regime elements examined in this book. Conclusions then follow.

1971 TO THE LATE 1980S: FORGING THE EARLY ENVIRONMENT CANADA – UNITS WANTING TO STAY AND WANTING TO LEAVE

The department's early gestation and evolution from 1971 to the late 1980s involved the movement of new and old units to and from the remit of Environment Canada (Whittington 1974, 1980; Conway 1992; Doern and Conway 1994). These developments and pressures shaped the structure and mandate of Environment Canada and hence of environmental policy.

The initial constituent units within the department included:

• The *Atmospheric Environmental Service* (AES), which came from the Department of Transport as a meteorological or weather service organization, but gradually became a global research entity as climate change and other environmental hazards emerged

- The *Environmental Protection Service* (EPS), which was born in the department as its main manifestation of a regulatory department, in contrast to many of the other services below that saw themselves as resource-management and conservation-oriented services, and thus in their own way houses of preventive sustainable development (SD), even though the later official discourse and paradigm of SD did not emerge until the late 1980s
- The *Fisheries Service*
- The *Land Forest and Wildlife Service*, which reflected the fact that Environment Canada's organizational components were first assembled by order-in-council in 1970 under the Department of Fisheries and Forestry
- The *Water Management Service*, which had roots in the Department of Energy, Mines and Resources

The department, as a new, de facto, merged holding company, had to forge these services into a coherent environmental entity. However, each service struggled and competed with each other over needed spending and managerial resources and also how to define and manage the core mandate purposes regarding protection versus conservation and renewable natural resource management. These struggles were joined and refereed to some extent by central agencies of the federal government, including key officials leading these early-stage developments in the PCO, PMO, and Treasury Board Secretariat. It will also be important to refer back to these struggles in later chapters when we discuss each of the other hyphenated environmental regimes.

The Fisheries Service eventually left Environment Canada in April 1979 and is now a restructured part of the current Fisheries and Oceans Canada (Lane 2000). As a compensating swap for this loss, the department was given the Parks Service, which had been a part of the Department of Indian Affairs and Northern Development (now Aboriginal Affairs and Northern Development). But. like the Fisheries Service, the Parks Service also campaigned to get out and left Environment Canada eventually in 1993 to be a part of Heritage Canada but then found its way back as an arm's-length agency reporting to the minister of the environment. The Forestry Service also moved to Agriculture Canada (now Agriculture and Agri-food Canada) in 1984, in part because of its own campaigning, but also because the central agency players began to seek a more visible presence for the forestry sector in the Cabinet to reflect its importance to the Canadian economy.

While the temptation is strong to see these shifts as a form of bureaucratic musical chairs, each department had genuine differences in its front-line view. The Parks Service viewed itself as both a nature conservation and service-oriented agency centred in tourism and local spatial and regional development, all the more so when new national parks were increasingly created by successive governments. The Fisheries Service had developed further strong dual traditions to support and foster fisher interests, but also to protect fish as a food product, both in health and environmental terms as a renewable resource (Lane 2000; Schott 2004; Clancy 2011). The Forestry Service also saw itself in natural resource and conservation terms. As well, even though forests fell largely under provincial jurisdiction, emerging imperatives still needed greater and more visible federal attention in industry/producer issues and environmental ones.

Our brief preview above of Environment Canada's changing statutory base also reveals the gradual search for different kinds of statutory capacity. Early statutes focused on air, water, and land. But some of these early statutes, such as the Canada Water Act and the Clean Air Act, were enabling rather than containing powers of regulation. "Enabling" meant that budgets and staffing could be mobilized but only as far as central and departmental budgetary agencies would allow. It also permitted agreements to be fostered and implemented. The Fisheries Act had greater regulatory intent and potential, but other regulatory statutes such as the Environmental Contaminants Act were quite weak and ineffective until the later Canadian Environmental Protection Act was passed (Conway 1992). Environmental assessment, as we see further below, was also quite timid, since it took the form of a policy guideline for over twenty years rather than a statute.

These early in-and-out movements and genuine differences in mandate preferences and priorities certainly had green-lite complexity features, as each contending unit sought advantage in the early environment age. So also did some of the enabling statutes that had some money but not much, if any, regulatory powers.

1990 TO 2002: THE DEPARTMENT AS A NETWORKED ENVIRONMENT-ECONOMY INSTITUTION

From 1990 to approximately 2002, Environment Canada saw its national priority zenith and budgetary heyday in the $3 billion 1990 Mulroney-era Green Plan, discussed in chapter 2. We focus on key developments in this period, but occasionally we note later developments beyond it, including the nature of reporting on performance by the commissioner of the environment and sustainable development (CESD) and the National Round Table on Environment and Economy (NRTEE), both of which were established in this period.

The first point to stress about this period is that the Mulroney Green Plan provided the department with new resources (in what was otherwise an era of fiscal deficits), but it allocated even larger budgetary resources to other departments in the now-broadening Environment Canada–Centred Regime. In addition, NRTEE was established as a visible and active advocate of sustainable development and of environmental-economy linkages, networks, and consensus-based approaches (NRTEE 2013; Toner and Frey 2004). The CESD, housed in the Office of the Auditor General of Canada, was also formed in the mid-1990s.

NRTEE and the CESD were institutions initiated by Environment Canada, but their purposes were government-wide and economic and societal in scope; they were also expressions of the spirit of the late 1980s international Brundtland Commission (Boutros et al. 2010). Broadly pro-environment, each nevertheless had the proviso in general and in specific decisions that environmental ideas/values were being considered with economic and social considerations, hence the triple bottom line. In short, this could enhance the environment or water it down in the name of these conjoined values, in our terms a green-lite feature of considerable import and also difficult to assess both content and consequences overall or in particular policy- or decision-making.

The CESD's twenty-one reports since 1997 have scrutinized federal environmental and sustainable development policy (CESD 2013b). The office has also been an avenue through which petitions from individual Canadians are received, assessed, and reported on. The CESD's main reports showed some examples of progress across the government, but they often pointed out departments' sluggish efforts to present and assess their sustainable development policies and strategies. In his last report as commissioner in 2012, Scott Vaughan concluded that natural resource development and exports were proceeding at such a pace that "environmental protection is failing to keep pace with economic development" (CESD 2012, 5). In his first report as the new commissioner, Neil Maxwell, was also close to presenting a scathing criticism of Harper-era policy on biodiversity, where he saw "a wide gap between the government's commitments and the results achieved" (CESD 2013a, 2) and that several gaps were "striking" and required several "ground-making approaches" that were long overdue (2 and 3).

Overall, NRTEE for its part had more scope and freedom than the CESD, and thus its more than fifty reports were diverse and offered constructive forms of public advice on subjects such as climate, water, energy, biodiversity, governance, and the Kyoto Protocol Implementation Act (NRTEE 2013). As noted in chapter 2, NRTEE was abolished in 2012 as a part of the Harper government's budget cuts but also because, at the time, the government was not keen to receive more advice, given its weak climate-change and Kyoto-implementation policies and activities.

By this time, in addition to the environmental assessment of projects, departments were also mandated to conduct prior "strategic" or medium-term environmental assessments of all federal *policies and plans* but with only at best modest results and degrees of enthusiasm (Bregha 2006, 2011).

In the mid-1990s under the Chrétien Liberals, Environment Canada had also seen major expenditure and resource cuts, including up to 30 per cent in its science and technology budgets after the deficit reduction decisions made during the program review (Doern 2000b). But in this period, the department also had an expanded statutory and interdepartmental mandate and the need to carry out its core functions and purposes. The federal government's major 1993 restructuring review also changed the department's external mandate linkages through the creation of Natural Resources Canada as a new integrated effort to support Canada's energy, forestry, and mineral resources and industries (see chapter 6). This also ensured that NRCan had a sustainable development mandate in concert with that of Environment Canada (Doern 1993a). A newly reconstituted micro-economic department, Industry Canada, was a further product of program review and contained a sector branch on environmental industries (Doern 1996).

In 1998, Environment Canada described its mission as that of making "sustainable development a reality for Canada" and that "in order to help present and future generations of Canadians live and prosper in an environment that needs to be respected, protected, and conserved, we undertake programs to reduce risk to human health and the environment; provide weather forecasts and warnings and emergency preparedness services; and give Canadians the tools to build a greener society" (Environment Canada 1998, 7). Unlike its earlier traditional hierarchical nature, the department was now describing itself as being governed by a *matrix manage-ment* approach. Its seven headquarters organizational units and five regional operations are crosscut by three "business lines" defined as a healthy environment, safety from environmental hazards, and a green society (8).

The three program-centred units or services were the same as mentioned earlier. Science underpinned each, but with the broader research science and monitoring residing in the AES and ECS, and with EPS having a more operational function tied to direct regula-tion. But the business-lines element portended ample opportunities for both cooperation and conflict as actual decisions were made. The department was also science-based at the time because 90 per cent of its spending focused on science and technology (S&T), some 17 per cent of this directed at fostering new knowledge and technology. The department's staff of about 4,400 consisted of 70 per cent with sci-ence and technical backgrounds (Doern 2002). But, as Enros (2013) amply shows, the role of environmental science in Environment Canada was much more complex and multi-dimensional than these raw figures suggest (see more below).

2002–2014: ENVIRONMENT CANADA AND DIVERSE PRIME MINISTERIAL AND CENTRAL INFLUENCES IN THE CHRÉTIEN AND HARPER ERAS

Through two recent examples, we focus here on the last decade of Environment Canada being subject to diverse influences from the political, policy, and administrative centre. It is worth remembering that being ignored by the centre may or may not be advantageous. Regardless of what the centre does, the department must still do its job and handle an evolving mandate (Enros 2013).

For example, as discussed in chapter 2, the picture from 1971 to about 1988 was one of an initial burst of prime ministerial environmental policy interest and emphasis in the early 1970s but then its virtual demise during the larger part of the Trudeau era and for most of the first Mulroney government from 1984 to 1988. This period was also one of large federal deficits, and hence calls for more environmental spending were hard to make to unconvinced central treasuries. This had little to do with environmental policy per se: it simply reflected a firm shift to other priority concerns and imperatives. The same thing happened in the mid-1990s, and it also occurred in the 2008 financial crisis to the present recession-and-deficit-reduction period. Green-lite realities can arise and have arisen from these larger fiscal and macro-economic imperatives.

Fiscal austerity was also a key factor in the Chrétien years. As the twenty-first century dawned, a key Chrétien government priority was the innovation economy. Closely linked was the concept of *smart regulation* to support and foster such an economy through innovation-centred regulation and funding, which easily linked to the concept of sustainable development and to continuous rhetorical expression. These pressures from the centre were benignly and gently positive for Environment Canada, and its policy statements and reporting easily adopted them.

However, as seen in chapter 3's account of international environmental policy, prime ministerial and central agency interventions were often mercurial, ill-timed, and duplicitous. Thus Prime Minister Chrétien delayed and then, as he was close to leaving office, committed Canada to GHG emission reductions under the Kyoto Protocol. These were honoured in neither the Martin nor in Harper years. The severe mid-1990s Liberal program review that resulted in 30 per cent budget cuts, especially to the department's science capacity, had already undermined the commitment and ability to achieve ambitious targets.

But these are not the only instances of recent policy controls and influences from the centre. It is also important to see how Environment Canada has formally presented and defended its mandate and agenda, in part through annual budgetary plans and priorities exercises, and through ad hoc exercises at redefining or recasting its mandate under central pressure and departmental anticipation of central pressure. Consider two examples: its latest accountability report on plans and priorities, and its recent process for establishing and fostering the department as a "world-class regulator." Further examples of this kind are examined in the final historical sections on the department as a science- and evidence-based department, and regarding the environmental assessment of projects.

Turning to the plans and priorities reports, the department in the Harper era describes its mandate as that of providing a "clean, safe, and sustainable environment for Canadians. The Department works in partnership with others to fulfil its mandate through a variety of activities, including conducting research on water and air quality, monitoring Canada's natural environment, developing regulations to reduce greenhouse gas emissions, maintaining biodiversity, increasing the number of protected areas within Canada, and providing advance warning of severe weather events" (Environment Canada 2013a, 5). The department reiterates its own statutory base but again stresses that the department "is a key partner for other federal departments with secondary or shared responsibility" (6).

The plans then refer immediately to the department's five key environmental indicators "to represent at a high level, progress in delivering a clean, safe, and sustainable environment for Canadians" (Environment Canada 2013a, 7). Targets are then shown for indicators of air quality, climate change, severe weather events, biodiversity, and water quality. The department's strategic outcomes are set out and described in relation to its "program alignment architecture," the new replacement terminology for the earlier discourse of "matrix management."

Three environmental priorities are then set out for 2013–14, all of which are said to reflect the department's *stewardship mandate*," but stewardship is not defined as such. In addition, the department identifies *potential risks* that its programs may face. The first of these are risks regarding "engagement" with its domestic and international partners and stakeholders "at the same time as the department continues to meet the government's plan to return to fiscal balance" (Environment Canada 2013a, 11). A second risk to be faced is "business continuity" regarding its round-the- clock services to domestic and international partners. And finally, it drew attention to a skills risk regarding the recruitment, development, and retention of employees, especially in scientific and technical fields. The planning budget for the department showed that its budgetary expenditures for 2013–14 total $959.4 million but with planned reductions down to $846 million for 2015–16. Its FTE equivalent staff levels are 6,518 but will be reduced to 6,221 by 2015–16 (12).

It is of interest historically to note that Environment Canada had a budget of $564.3 million in 1979–80 (Whittington 1980, 102). So even taking into account inflation and a different program structure over the thirty-three years thereafter, these current budgetary amounts (and related staffing profiles) look prudent, to say the least (Enros 2013, appendix 1 and 2). More recently, an analysis of federal spending from 1996–97 (just after program review cuts) to 2010–11 showed that Environment Canada's spending had increased only from about $630 million to $795 million, compared to much higher growth rates for Natural Resources Canada (Doern, Maslove, and Prince 2013, 191).

Environment Canada, of course, is very much a regulatory department. In 2011–12 it launched a review to help meet its "objective of operating as a World Class Regulator (WCR)" (Environment Canada 2012a). It is difficult to tell whether this WCR process was occurring to help counteract growing external criticism, given that the Harper government was increasingly charged with weakening environmental protection and for muzzling its scientists (Gatehouse 2013). The muzzling referred to specific processes whereby communications and political staff told government scientists what they could say at public events, a restriction that most had not experienced before (O'Hara and Dufour 2014).

The department's WCR criteria were presented as "evidence-based decision making, effectiveness, efficiency, transparency, and adaptability" (Environment Canada 2012a, 1). A working group was charged with developing a review (ibid.). This was followed by an assessment of the report by an internationally recognized American regulatory scholar, Professor Cary Coglianese (2012a); the department then published a response to his assessment (Environment Canada 2012c).

The WCR criteria were based on a literature review and department-wide consultations with its officials. The project set out to "engage the EC community in the identification of concrete actions to: strengthen EC's regulatory processes and outcomes; institutionalize the goal of becoming a world class regulator; and improve the Department's reputation and credibility as a regulator" (Environment Canada 2012a, 8). Internal teams of regulators then conducted a self-assessment of four categories of regulatory action: "Chemicals

Management Plan Risk Management Measures; Vehicle Emissions Regulations under the Canadian Environmental Protection Act; Regulations under the Migratory Birds Convention Act; and Environmental Emergency Regulations" (9). These were each assessed against the five WCR criteria. Interestingly, policies and regulations for the mitigation of climate change were not chosen, the area most under criticism.

The report concludes first that "the analysis identified strengths in all aspects of the Department's regulatory process and confirmed EC's solid foundation and capacity to embark on our WCR journey" (Coglianese 2012a, 2). Several short-term actions were identified for improvement in data collection and information gathering; instrument selection; performance measurement; streamlining of regulatory amendments; and transparent communication of decisions (2). Within and across these actions, more specific gaps and challenges were identified. Some were focused on administrative detail but some were more substantive, such as the need to provide "further clarity regarding the scrutiny of Confidential Business Information/ Sensitive Information claims" (5). The identified need to "optimize the process for making amendments to regulations" and to "minimize regulatory costs and burden" resonated with wider recent Harper government regulatory reform directives and red-tape reduction studies (Doern, Prince, and Schultz 2014).

The Coglianese assessment of the department's report was positive overall, but it also drew attention to the need for analytical caution. He argued that "what constitutes 'world class' is both more complicated and contested ... [and that regulatory quality] is more than just a quality of the product ... but rather it is the quality of an interaction between government and society" (Coglianese 2012a, 4). He also identified criteria not selected by Environment Canada in the WCR exercise, including no explicit consideration being given to "fairness" and in particular to how it relates "to the equitable distribution of the costs and benefits of a regulation" (6). Coglianese also expressed concerns about the WCR report's definition of efficiency as "achieving the desired environmental objectives at the lowest cost possible" by arguing that "efficiency is actually what arises" when a regulatory instrument is "likely to result in benefits that outweigh costs" (7).

The department's brief response to the Coglianese assessment agreed with some of his critiques but disagreed with his view of what efficiency meant. And with regard to "distributional fairness," the department's response was that it "is an underlying principle of our constitution and is an important consideration in policy development, including Canadian federal regulatory processes. However, at present, it is a criterion that is difficult to define, measure, and operationalize" (Environment Canada 2012c, 2). This may well be true in some sense but no more so than other criteria that were selected such as "effectiveness" and "adaptability."

Controls and influences from the centre are by no means related to just policy and organization. There are also positional moves, the chief of which is the prime minister's monopoly power to change ministers. The average eighteen-month turnover of environment ministers has already been noted, and most ministers arrive in office knowing that none of their predecessor has stayed for long. A ministerial change in a summer 2013 Cabinet shuffle saw Prime Minister Harper remove Peter Kent as minister and install Leona Aglukkaq, the first Aboriginal Canadian to hold the office. This was done in part out of political calculus that she would be better positioned to persuade the United States about Canada's good intentions on the Gateway XL pipeline and also among Aboriginal peoples regarding the Northern Gateway pipeline on Canada's West Coast (McCarthy 2013b). But prime ministerial positional politics were also evident when Harper removed his newly appointed environment minister from his new economic prosperity committee of Cabinet (Wingrove 2013).

ENVIRONMENT CANADA AS A CHANGING SCIENCE-AND EVIDENCE-BASED DEPARTMENT

The three previous sections have examined the Environment Canada–Centred Regime through three selected periods in Environment Canada's departmental evolution. Here, we look across the entire forty-to-fifty-year history but with a focus on its evolution as a science- and evidence-based department. This is not a simple story, because it must deal both with what the department's science and technology roles and capacities were or needed to be as its mandate changed and grew, and also a linked understanding of how broader government-wide science-and-technology and related innovation economy policies and paradigms were reinforcing the department's tasks or often harming and distorting them. The full story also involves the need to see Environment Canada from the outset as both a science- and evidence-based entity, with the latter including social science evidence but also forms of front-line evidence from external citizen, NGO, and professional knowledge-holders (Enros 2013; Doern and Conway 1994). While it is common for authors to see evidence-based knowledge as a more recent feature, in fact it has been a part of the department's DNA from the outset.

In its early years, as we have seen, the science and evidence base of the department was centred on the mainly scientific and technical socio-economic staff who came to the department from the other government departments mentioned above. Thus, early on, Whittington observed that "although the functions of the new department officially include the carrying on of established programmes related to the 'management' of natural resources such as marketing research and assistance to the fishing and forest industries, the overall focus of the department has shifted significantly towards the protection and enhancement of the quality of the environment" (Whittington 1974, 212). The establishment of the EPS was intended to provide several points of contact between the department and the public, including an education role.

As the department acquired its other statutory mandates described earlier, such as those regarding water and wildlife, it immediately had to have diverse science and knowledge capacities to meet its regulatory and monitoring obligations. It also had to find ways to acquire and share science, analysis, and data with other departments with shared mandates on a statute-by-statute basis. An analysis of Environment Canada in 2000 also drew attention to the "stretching of green science" and to the reduction of "patient science" versus the expansion of "science on demand" (Doern 2000b). The analysis pointed to five changes in the 1990s: less money and fewer internal staff resources because of the program review cuts; the need for scientific effort to match immediate policy and events within the department and across the government (i.e., the science-on-demand dynamic); less freedom to roam regarding longer-term research based on the instincts of scientists (i.e., the patient science dynamic); the greater presence of global science, which put departmental scientists in touch daily with their counterparts in other countries; and the shift away from repeated measuring activity regarding monitoring science to the greater use of statistical sampling approaches (293–5). To these one could easily add the inherent tension between the continuing core Environment Canada mandate roles of cleanup and remediation versus preventive sustainable development of the balanced environmental, economic, and social development kind, often termed the "triple bottom line."

Environment Canada's Science Plan (Environment Canada 2007) also tells an interesting story of the way the department viewed its science strategy and its capacities in the wake of broader conceptions of what sciences and evidence were needed. In 2005 a departmental science review panel recommendation in the Martin Liberal era led to the establishment of the Science and Technology Branch and brought much of the department's science under one assistant deputy minister. The 2007 Science plan followed fairly quickly and set out "a vision for managing and conducting Environment Canada's science over the next 10 years" (Environment Canada 2007, vii). The summary mission statement for the department is "to deliver the high quality knowledge, information and data that enable the Minister, the Government, the Department, and other decision makers to enhance the *safety* of Canadians, protect the *quality of the natural environment,* and advance Canada's *long-term competitiveness*" (vii, emphasis added). The policy goals and discourse change considerably in this first Harper-era statement about environmental science. Even though the department had always had to develop and deploy evidence and knowledge, it was often described only as a science-based department (Enros 2013). However, in the above 2007 Science Plan, the mission statement does not use the word *science* except as part of its "vision" for the plan.

This is also true for the discourse used to characterize the department's three strategic directions that were identified for the department's "science." These were expressed as: (1) developing an integrated monitoring and prediction capability, including "moving to finer time and spatial scales for predictions and analysis"; (2) understanding cumulative risks, including "multiple stressors interacting over time" and the "risks to, and opportunities for, Canada's long term competitiveness resulting from a changing environment"; and (3) managing risks, optimizing opportunities, and building resilience, including "understanding the costs and benefits of the various risks" (Environment Canada 2007, viii–ix). While understandable in many ways, these strategic directions were very complex and contained green-lite features relating to both temporal and boundary realities. The report then goes on to reiterate the standard facts about the department's science being 70 per cent of the budget and two-thirds of its employees. But it also stated in somewhat more detail that two-thirds of the science was not R & D but rather covers "a variety of *non-research science activities* including weather forecasting, risk assessments, regulatory activities, data collection and environmental monitoring, emergency preparedness, and *S & T knowledge brokering*" (1, emphasis added). "Non-research" science included related science activities (RSA) in other federal S & T reports and thus included the science knowledge in the brains and experience of mainly front-line science and knowledge professionals typically interacting daily with their counterparts in other national and intergovernmental bodies but also universities, businesses, and interest groups (Kinder 2010; Doern and Kinder 2007).

The Science Plan highlighted as well that the department's science had to reflect the government's latest Federal S & T Framework and its three core principles; *alignment* to reflect and support the priorities of Canadians; *linkages* built on effective collaborative relationships; and *excellence* by producing the "highest quality, leading edge, credible and unbiased environmental science" (Environment Canada 2007, 4). The Science Plan stated then that "above all, we must demonstrate transparency and openness in how we conduct our scientific activities" (4).

Structurally, Environment Canada became in the Harper era a more complex managerial entity. It now has eight units headed by assistant deputy ministers (ADM), five of which are more policy and managerially oriented and three of which are the modern locales of its historic three initial science-focused services. The main regulatory environmental protection roles are headed by an ADM for "environmental stewardship." The ADM for Science and Technology has the main atmospheric and water realms, as well as the overall S & T policy coordination role. The third ADM heads up the Meteorological Service of Canada (Environment Canada 2013b).

But beyond these developments and aspects of the 2007 Science Plan, one needs to locate the department's science- and evidence-based features in relation to the development and evolution of particular departmental science labs and units. Although beyond the scope of this chapter, a review of some literature and studies elucidates the value of looking at these labs in greater depth. The Doern and Kinder (2007) history and assessment of federal labs and science-based agencies included four Environment Canada entities: the Environmental Technology Centre (ETC) in the field of environmental regulatory protection; the National Wildlife Research Centre (NWRC), regarding front-line sustainable development; the Water Survey of Canada (WSC); and the New Substances Branch (NSB). Regarding the histories of the ETC and NWRC over twenty years or more, the analysis details how the labs dealt with and interpreted basic and changing items in what the authors referred to as a "policy menu" (Doern and Kinder 2007). This menu included: S&T innovation/commercialization policies; sustainable development and environmental policies; parent department mandate and political-economic contexts; macro and micro budgetary management policies; and changing policy-induced linkages with universities, business, other governments, and communities. The analysis of the WSC and NSB focused on the changing nature of monitoring and the conduct of the related science activities (RSA).

The policy selecting and juggling of menus was unavoidable for middle-level science managers; it produced varied, good, bad, indifferent, or often undetectable policy outcomes. Some policy menu items were adopted as discourse but not as concerted actions. Budgetary aspects could not be ignored. Sometimes, they led to major cuts, and at other times they offered new, relatively small funding sources/programs, which labs could access only with partners. Regulatory functions, such as in the home base of the ETC, had to continue a compliance focus, whereas the dictates of flexible smart regulation were downplayed. The NWRC had a long history that predated Environment Canada, but its front-line wildlife monitoring also had to depend on front-line citizen science from bird-watchers and other knowledge holders. Then, partly in response to federal science policies urging better linkages and relocation of federal science labs closer to universities, the NWRC found itself moved to new facilities at Carleton University.

In the Harper era, the notions of science and broader kinds of evidence were given more play and focus in two ways. The first was in the senses referred to in the 2007 Environment Canada Science Plan. But it was also reflected as discussed in chapter 1 by the Conservatives' early embrace, aspirationally at least, of life-cycle approaches to all health and environmental regulation in its overall regulatory policies. These implied both pre-market and post-market science and a very extended and networked evidence-based capacity that extended well beyond the department, and other federal departments into the provincial domain, including a vast array of health professionals.

However, the second sense in which the "evidence" debate emerged centred on arguments about the "death of evidence." These included the notion that environmental policy and indeed policies of many related kinds were increasingly centred not on systematic knowledge and research but simply on opinions, on fabricated evidence of the moment. It was tied also to the greater presence of continuous attack politics and the muzzling of scientists by the communications staff at the centre of prime ministerial government and of Environment Canada (Gatehouse 2013; O'Hara and Dufour 2014; Toner and McKee 2014).

ENVIRONMENTAL ASSESSMENT OF PROJECTS: FRONT-LINE DEMOCRACY, EFFECTIVENESS, AND RESPONSIBLE RESOURCE DEVELOPMENT

We now look at environmental assessment policy, law, and regulation as a manifestation of the Environment Canada department and ministry mandate historically over forty years and as an integral feature of the Environment Canada–Centred Regime. Here, a central concern is how this area of work positioned the department to influence projects in any and every federal government department and, by extension, affect diverse sectors of the economy and diverse locations, regions, and spaces in Canadian society. As a preventive mechanism, it is, in many ways, the quintessential test for environmental policy and governance. Its history is replete with green-lite features but also some environmental progress. We trace it as a four-stage story across the four decades being covered: the early inability for twenty years to get a federal environmental assessment law passed; the era of federal and provincial environmental assessments until about 2003–4; the Chrétien-era review of environmental assessment under a smart regulation lens and discourse; and the Harper government's 2012 major revisions to the Canadian Environmental Assessment Act under strategy for responsible resource development.

The need for environmental assessment was initially given a high philosophical priority by the Trudeau Liberal government, including as a stated commitment at the 1972 Stockholm Conference. The example of US legislation was seen at first as the exemplary policy and law. But almost immediately the early dynamics and cases in the United States began to chasten the Trudeau Liberals because of possible adverse court-centred litigation effects and costs. The government pulled back immediately (Doern and Conway 1994, chap. 9). This hesitation led to the establishment of the Environmental Assessment and Review Process (FARP) based on a guideline approach and administered by the department's Federal Environmental Assessment and Review Office (FEARO). The process was centred on federal projects that either fell under federal jurisdiction or involvement in federal spending. This drove an immediate need for different kinds of scope for assessments, many that entailed minor screening and others that were comprehensive.

From the outset, however, this softer, green-lite governance-guidance regime had little legitimacy, particularly in the eyes of environmental groups, for its weak public involvement provisions and processes (Whittington 1974; Leiss 1979). The nature and efficacy of environmental participation and democracy were thus central from the outset and indeed tended to focus on environmental assessment policies and rights, but these concerns and failings have gone well beyond environmental project assessment across the four decades (Adkin 2010; Boyd 2012). The literature on the nature of environmental assessments per se had also addressed a range of democratic and policy concerns, including the role of traditional ecological knowledge regarding Aboriginal peoples (Usher 2000), the links between formal assessment and other kinds of learning via public involvement (Diduck and Mitchell 2003), and overall concerns about the inadequacy of public participation, as seen by environmental NGOs, project proponents, and governments (Stewart and Sinclair 2007).

Several environment ministers in the late 1970s and early 1980s sought to introduce a legislated approach but were resisted by the political centre, federal departments and their ministers, and related business interests. Other federal departments were not interested in or did not support these horizontal intrusions into their policy domains. But meanwhile, many provincial governments in Canada had passed their own environmental assessment laws as statutory laws, not as guidelines. By the mid- to late 1980s, the case for a federal legislative approach received publicly expressed support by the 1985 McDonald Royal Commission on the Economic Union and

Development Prospects for Canada. But the real impetus came instead from the Rafferty-Alameda and Oldman River court cases and rulings in 1989 and 1990. Environmental groups brought both cases to the courts. The essence of the court rulings was that the guidelines order, which underpinned the federal approach, was a binding legal requirement (Schrecker 1991). For the same reasons identified above about concerns over increased litigation, a renewed interest in legislation emerged in part to re-establish a more discretionary approach to environmental assessments. By 1992 the Canadian Environmental Assessment Act had been approved by Parliament. The Canadian Environmental Assessment Agency (CEAA) was established in 1994.

The overall mandate of the agency, as expressed in 2007, is to "provide Canadians with high quality environmental assessments that contribute to informed decision making in support of sustainable development" (Canadian Environmental Assessment Agency 2007, 3). Its president reports directly to the minister of the environment and functions under the Canadian Environmental Assessment Act, the Canada-Wide Accord on Environmental Harmonization and bilateral agreements with provincial governments, and international agreements, including the United Nations Economic Commission for Europe Convention on Environmental Impact Assessment in a Transboundary Context.

The principle of self-assessment is the basis of the federal environmental assessment regime. Thus federal departments and agencies conduct their own assessments in their mandate areas, drawing on their expertise in these areas. Often several departments can be involved in reviewing the same project. Assessments by departments and agencies must occur before they carry out a project; provide financial assistance to enable a project to be carried out; sell, lease, or otherwise transfer control or administration of land to enable a project to be undertaken; or issue authorizations to enable a project to go forward. The number of assessments ranges from 6,000 to 7,000 annually, and since the act came into effect in 1995, over 50,000 projects had been assessed by 2007 (Canadian Environmental Assessment Agency 2007, 9).

Environmental assessment is seen primarily as a project-planning tool to help eliminate or reduce potential harm to the environment resulting from the above-noted forms of federal involvement. Federal legislation provides for four types of environmental assessment

– screening, comprehensive study, mediation, and assessment by a review panel – with most projects only triggering a screening review. The Comprehensive Study List Regulations under the act identify those projects likely to result in significant environmental effects and thus require a comprehensive study assessment. Screenings can take several months, whereas comprehensive studies require about a year, and review panels can take over a year (External Advisory Committee on Smart Regulation 2004, 100).

The 2003 Chrétien Liberal–era amendments to the Environmental Assessment Act resulted in several changes in response to a decade or more of criticism:

- The creation of a federal environmental assessment coordinator role
- A mandate to establish a Quality Assurance Program to examine federal assessments
- The requirement to create an Internet database of all federal environmental assessments
- Mandatory follow-up programs for specified projects
- Tools to deal efficiently with projects that have inconsequential effects
- A more certain comprehensive study process
- More opportunities for public participation in the comprehensive study process supported by participant funding; and use of regional environmental studies (External Advisory Committee on Smart Regulation 2004, 101)

In 2005, a follow-up Cabinet Directive on Implementation of the Canadian Environmental Assessment Act took effect, to ensure that the administration of the act results "in a timely and predictable environmental assessment process that produces high quality environmental assessments" (Canadian Environmental Assessment Agency 2007). This directive was an interim measure until other legislative amendments to achieve consolidation took effect. Thus, though efficiency and timeliness were the overriding goals, the directive also had to specify that it did not fetter the powers, duties, functions, or discretion of federal authorities.

In the 2007 federal budget, the Harper Conservative government announced that it was creating a Major Projects Management Office to streamline the review of large natural resource projects. With an investment of $60 million over two years, "the Government seeks to cut in half the average regulatory review period from four years to about two years, without compromising our regulatory standards" (Department of Finance 2007b, 2). The CEAA's 2006–7 plans stressed that an "increase in demand for energy is likely to result in more energy-related development projects" and that "environmental assessment is a useful tool for ensuring that the Government's climate change policies are considered in project development and that projects take into consideration the potential effects of changes in climate" (Canadian Environmental Assessment Agency 2007, 12). Green-lite features were present in these combined changes in that increased speed and efficiency were being sought by both the Liberals initially and then even more so by the Harper Conservatives. but added to it was a climate-change add-on assessment of an utterly unspecified kind and complexity.

Mapping the environmental assessment system has thus far referred only to its federal government aspects. The provinces also have policies and regulations regarding environmental assessment. Assessing them is beyond the scope of this chapter, but certain key features warrant mention. First, most provinces tend to have their environmental assessments carried out by one agency rather than using the federal government's self-assessment process for its departments and agencies. Second, there are inevitable areas of split and overlapping jurisdiction. Canadian federalism's constitutional division of powers was devised well before governments even had environmental policies. The split jurisdiction nonetheless found its way into practice in areas of provincial natural resource development within provincial borders, largely because provinces owned natural resources. But even in this sphere, there are areas of federal jurisdiction for projects that cross interprovincial and international boundaries and in projects that affect fish habitat and navigable waters. This is multi-level, scalar complexity incarnate.

Coordination problems in this kind of multi-level regulation have been subject to protest for many years. One initial response to complaints about multiple assessments of the same project, serious time delays, and different assessment criteria was the establishment of the Sub-agreement on Environmental Assessment under the Canada-Wide Accord on Environmental Harmonization. The purpose of this sub-agreement is to "promote the effective application of environmental assessment when two or more governments are required by their respective laws to assess the same proposed project. It includes provisions for shared principles, common information elements, a defined series of assessment stages and a single assessment and public hearing process" (External Advisory Committee on Smart Regulation 2004, 103).

There has been some progress under these coordination mechanisms such as the joint review of some oil sands projects by the federal government and the Alberta Energy and Utilities Board; however, overall, when the Advisory Committee on Smart Regulation conducted its review of environmental assessment in 2004, it heard in no uncertain terms from industry and NGOs about serious problems with the assessment process, including timing, information requirements, and public participation (EACSR 2004, 102–4).

The smart regulation study's review stressed that "the environmental assessment process is one of the issues about which the Committee heard the most complaints and it was viewed as a key priority for regulatory reform by many industry and environmental non-governmental organizations ... It also heard scepticism over whether the recent changes to the CEAA would make the environmental process much more effective or, in some cases, even more cumbersome" (EACSR 2004, 101).

The smart regulation study concluded overall that the remaining problems warranted a new approach that moved "beyond harmonization and towards a single, nationally integrated approach encompassing federal, provincial and territorial processes" and that such an idea "was generally supported by both industry representatives and non-governmental organizations during our consultations" (EACSR 2004, 104).

If such reforms were not carried out, the committee argued that the "credibility of the assessment process will continue to erode and its effective use will be jeopardized" and that, moreover, there was a crucial need for conducting "a more holistic assessment of a project and enabling the development of expertise in this area ... and also improve the consideration of cumulative impacts of several projects on a single eco-system and ensure that the environmental assessment process adapts to new scientific advances and changing circumstances" (EACSR 2004, 104–5).

In short, "holistic" meant more complex in temporal and in eco-system terms as a green-lite reality.

Clearly such reforms would require almost unprecedented cooperation and coordination within the federal government and between and among the federal government, the provinces, and the territories. It would also require statutory change and regulatory-legal change, not to mention significant resource commitments.

Once it had a majority government, the Harper Conservatives made major changes in the Canadian Environmental Assessment Act 2012, one of dozens of legislative changes in its massive 2012 omnibus budgetary legislation, Bill C-38. The CEAA's overview leads off with the central purpose of the changes. The new law "offers an updated, modern approach that responds to Canada's current economic and environmental context. It implements several elements of the Government's plan for Responsible Resource Development to modernize the regulatory system and for natural resources to be developed in a responsible and timely way for the benefit of all Canadians" (Canadian Environmental Assessment Agency 2013, 1).

The 2012 legislation reiterates some key previous practices, including the provision that the responsible authority for an assessment rests with the Canadian Nuclear Safety Commission (for nuclear projects), and the National Energy Board (for international and interprovincial pipelines and transmission lines), or the CEAA for all other designated projects. But among the key changes are new timelines, which stipulate that the government must complete its assessment work in 365 days through the CEAA; or in 24 months through an assessment by a review panel, to which the minister of the environment may refer a designated project that "may cause significant adverse environmental effects" (CEAA 2013, 2). Public participation is adversely affected by these new timelines, but the legislation makes other changes in participation, including the provision of "a new comment period in the initial steps when the Agency is determining whether an environmental assessment is required" (2). Review panels are required to hold public hearings "during which *interested parties* can participate," but direct participation by the public is not on offer for these public hearings. This led to an August 2013 lawsuit by environmentalists in the Federal Court to strike down changed provisions in the National Energy Board Act that limit participation to affected parties but not the wider public (McCarthy 2013a).

Public participation provisions are also a feature of changes that improve cooperation and communication with Aboriginal peoples. In addition, "environmental effects" for Aboriginal peoples include effects that "cause changes to their: health and socio-economic conditions; physical and cultural heritage; current use of land and resources for traditional purposes; or structures, sites or things that are of historical, archaeological, paleontological or architectural significance" (CEAA 2013, 3).

The final and arguably most significant changes are in what the Harper government refers to as "federal-provincial integration" under which the minister of the environment, if satisfied that the substantive requirements of (the legislation) can be met by a provincial process and if that province requests it, must allow for the substitution of the federal environmental assessment process by the provincial process. The minister would make a decision about the project "using the environmental assessment report prepared by the province" (CEAA 2013, 3).

These and related approaches were aimed at supporting "the goal of one project, one review" (CEAA 2013, 7), and in this context the overall natural resource-led strategy to "balance the economic potential of the resource sector with safety and environmental protection" (7). But these changed: partly reduced and partly expanded environmental assessment tasks overall will also soon face a significant cut in the agency's spending and its human resources. In 2013–14, the agency's budget stood at $31.192 million, but with planned spending for 2015–16 shown as greatly reduced to just over $17 million. Its full-time equivalent staff will shrink from 241 at present to 160 in 2015–16 (9).

THE THREE REGIME ELEMENTS

In the context of the above historical narrative and forms of evidence, with the aid of table 4.1 we can now provide a closer summary of the three regime elements being used as a part of the book's analytical framework. We analyze and comment briefly on each in turn.

Environmental Ideas, Discourse, and Agendas

Conservation ideas emerged from the outset in the constituent units brought together from other departments. Pollution control, cleanup, and related remediation as ideas loomed larger as regulatory control statutes became more numerous. Sustainable development as an idea and discourse certainly took hold from the late 1980s on, but often with its preventive thrust softened by discourse on defining it as a

Table 4.1: The Environment Canada–Centred Regime and the three regime elements: Selected summary highlights

PERIODS EXAMINED	*The three analytical elements*		
	POLICIES, IDEAS, DISCOURSE, AND AGENDAS	POWER STRUCTURES, DEMOCRACY, AND GOVERNANCE	SCIENCE, EVIDENCE, KNOWLEDGE, AND PRECAUTION
1971 to late 1980s	• Conservation and resource management • Regulatory pollution control/remediation • Sustainable development in late 1980s after Brundtland Commission	• Units wanting to stay and leave department • Parks Canada in, out, and in "ministry" • Early Trudeau active support, but then ended • Enabling laws versus regulatory laws • Large deficits for most of the period	• Units entering were science monitoring–based • Science and evidence base for regulatory roles, and for enabling agreements and environmental public education
1990–2002	• Environmental industries • Environment-economy • Intergenerational ideas of sustainable development • Respecting, protecting, conserving to reduce risk to human health and environment	• NRTEE and CESD formed and report regularly • Program review makes 30% cuts to environmental science • NRCan formed as integrated resource department • Matrix management system practised to coordinate NRCan's business lines	• AES and ECS as monitoring science services/branches • EPS as regulatory pollution control branch • 17% of S&T for new knowledge and technology
2003–13	• Innovation economy and smart regulation as discourse • Clean, safe, and sustainable development for Canadians • Regulations to lower GHG emissions	• Chrétien late decision to ratify Kyoto but then no action to reduce GHG emissions, which increase substantially under Liberals and Harper Conservatives • Governance linked to five key environmental indicators	• Cuts to departmental budget and staff in 15% range by Harper government • WCR review emphasizes overall evidence base of department and new data capacities

	• "Stewardship" mandate • Awareness of risks and opportunities due to environmental change • Responsible resource development discourse in Harper era after majority government achieved	• "Program alignment architecture" system rather than matrix management • Harper-era budget and staff cuts but not as severe as under earlier program review • World-Class Regulator (WCR) exercise and review conducted	• Scientists muzzled under Harper communication and control approaches
Department as science and evidence–based player (1971 to present)	• Delivering high-quality knowledge, information, and data • Integrated monitoring and predictive capacity • Cumulative risks • Costs and benefits of risks • Excellence as criterion of S&T advice and performance	• Patient science versus science on demand • Greater interactions with global science • ADM for S&T • 2007 Science Plan • Departmental labs and agencies and their policy menu pressures and choices • Concerns and debates about the death of evidence	• Own core science and technology • Shared science and technology with other departments and levels of government • Closer links with universities and peer-reviewed science
Environmental assessment of projects (1971 to present)	• Environmental assessment seen as preventive approach • Democracy and participation role in the assessment process • Self-assessment cast as planning tool • Liberal-era smart regulation and need for more integrated federal-provincial processes • Conservative-era "one assessment" idea and time limits • Responsible natural resource development in Harper 2012 change to legislation	• Impacts on and pushback from several economic sectors • Early Trudeau support reduced in response to concerns about more radical US approach and litigation • EARP process and FEARO as illegitimate and failed guideline approach for first twenty years • ENGO-led court cases lead to statutory base and Canadian Environmental Assessment Agency in 1994 • Provincial laws in place early on • Harper Canadian Environmental Assessment Act 2012 passed	• Diverse core science and local project knowledge involved in over 50,000 projects since 1995 • Science and evidence feeding into four potential degrees and time scales of assessment • Recent projected cuts to CEEA budget and staff

balanced triple bottom line among environmental, economic, and social factors and considerations.

Other ideas and forms of discourse also emerged, including notions of environmental stewardship, smart regulation for a green industries and innovation economy era, and also, more recently, responsible resource development.

Environmental Power Structures, Democracy, and Governance

Power structures, democratic values, and governance challenges and changes have also emerged as causes of change and features of inertia and conflict. Prime ministerial power and interest has been both beneficial and harmful, but periods of low or non-existent interest have impacts as well, some good and some negative or undetectable. The regime has been shown in power and governance terms to have been influenced by the fiscal centre via major spending surges, as in the 1990 Green Plan, and by long-lasting deficit conditions, but also by the establishment of periodic smallish spending funds accessible only if the department partners with others.

Democratic values have been shown in the regime analysis to be central to the origins of the environmental age and therefore to the department, but also at times of a sluggish record, such as in the twenty years before Canada had a proper environmental assessment act. But democratic values have been challenged and contested in more recent periods, such as in the Chrétien and Harper eras, through assertions of prime ministerial Cabinet-parliamentary democratic primacy rather than other forms of pluralist interest group or civil society democracy.

Governance challenges and changes have also been captured in the history overall through the ways in which the environmental regime has been influenced by reorganizations and public management shifts from classic hierarchical modes of operation (but in the context of extremely high ministerial turnover, with environment ministers staying for an average of eighteen months) to internal *matrix management* systems and forms of program alignment architecture. We have also seen changes in the communications strategies of governments aligned to controlling what scientists can say, when, and to whom, but also website mandate discourse that can be shifted and broadened with vision statements more often than statutes can.

Science, Evidence, Knowledge, and Precaution

The analysis of the regime's characteristics regarding science, evidence, knowledge, and precaution is shown to be more nuanced and complex than one might first have thought. Its budgetary and staff structure easily means that it remains a science-based department. Yet early on, as its regulatory mandate and powers took hold, it was also an evidence-based department, having to possess and bring to bear technical, cost-benefit, and related social science evidence. And in areas of its mandate such as wildlife and migratory birds, it had always depended on front-line citizen science and observation. One of the more interesting features is that the chapter does not reveal much overt use of the precautionary principle as such in its website, its statutes, or most international agreements. The department is much more likely to use the discourse of sustainable development as a broad cover when complex forms of science, evidence, and scientific uncertainty are present. Since this occurs increasingly, it is perhaps accurate to say that the department has to practise precaution, even without having to recite the principle.

CONCLUSIONS

The Environment Canada–Centred Regime has been mapped in relation to the core origins and dynamics of Environment Canada as a department aspiring to be at the centre of Canadian environmental policy, but also buffeted and shaped continuously by entrenched political and economic centres of power and influence, including prime ministerial power and other core central agencies. Overall it marks out strong green-lite features arising from policy and governance patterns, particularly those dealing with complex boundary realities. The initial survey of its statutory base detailed the laws (and regulations) that define its own responsibilities, which, from the outset, forced it to interact with other federal departments and several industries, regions, and spatial domains across Canada. It has also shown the shared statutory advisory roles with other departments that had the primary role in other statutes assigned to them in fields such as transportation, fisheries and oceans, energy, and international and interprovincial trade, to name only a few.

Space limitations mean that the chapter has not examined every statute and its origins and implementation history, but we have sampled some, and the statutory mandate in total provides ample evidence why the regime is centred in Environment Canada but not confined to it. This central fact is reinforced by other environment policy regimes in the chapters to follow.

In our review of policy histories in the regime's development, the longer historical picture of its role as a science and evidence-based entity and of its environmental assessment mandate has provided an important reality. It has elucidated the ways in which mandate features, such as core policy ideas and discourses, have not so much been replaced but rather have been layered over or beside the initial ideas that shaped the department and broadened and made more complex its purposes and thus its criteria for assessment results and success.

The account of the regime's structures of power, democracy, and governance have added further to our understanding of how prime ministerial power and central agency influences have both supported and buffeted the regime. Democratic norms and criteria are diverse and can both support and conflict as they interact. These relate both to prime ministerial and Cabinet systems of representative democracy and also to pluralist and citizen-centred democracy in diverse forums for environmental policy development and project assessments. Governance ideas and changes have been revealed mainly with regard to structural reorganizations but also to systems of "matrix management" and program "alignment architecture," both as genuine concerns and as management-speak.

The underlining story of the regime suggests that Environment Canada is most accurately seen as having been both a science-based and evidence-based department from the outset, rather than as just a more recently revealed or focused on dual feature. Nonetheless, the chapter has shown the extent to which the Environment Canada–Centred Regime has had, for very good reasons, to develop and use new forms and types of data related to diverse risks, including cumulative risks and changing environmental hazards. Holistic approaches are seen as necessary but highly complex.

Green-lite complexity policy and governance patterns, particularly of the "means-ends calculus" kind, have been shown to emerge from the outset of Environment Canada's history via the early "in-and-out movements" of agencies to and from the department and genuine differences in mandate preferences and priorities. These also had green-lite features in their complex boundaries, as each contending unit sought advantage in the early environment age. So also did some of the enabling statutes that had some money but few, if any, regulatory powers. It also had evident environmental weaknesses in the nearly twenty years when Canada's environmental assessment processes had good intentions but no effective statutory basis until 1994. But even under the post-1994 statutory system, the law itself introduced considerable ministerial discretion about the types of assessments that might occur.

The idea of sustainable development is an overall positive in the regime's structure, but it is also replete with applied green-lite challenges that arise form its triple bottom-line trade-offs on environmental, economic, and social values. To these expressions of trade-offs, we have seen later ones expressed as safety, sustainability, and long-term economic competitiveness.

Quite raw green-lite realities in agenda-setting terms have also arisen from larger fiscal and macro-economic imperatives, mainly involving cuts in the department and its science capacity at least three times overall, in the Trudeau, Chrétien, and Harper eras. Last but not least, temporal green-lite features have been present in concepts of environmental assessment speed and efficiency. In the last decade, such speed and efficiency goals were sought by the Liberals initially under smart regulation rationales, and then even more so by the Harper Conservatives under the dictates of responsible resource development, but to which they added a climate-change add-on assessment criteria of an utterly unspecified kind.

5

The Energy-Environment Regime

INTRODUCTION

The Energy-Environment Regime consists of an interacting array of departments, agencies, policies, laws, and governing instruments where environmental ideas are often part of the regime structure but rarely dominant. In some ways the Energy-Environment Regime predates the Environment Canada–Centred Regime examined in chapter 4 in that, federally, issues about oil and gas pipelines and their routing and safety but also atomic or nuclear energy extend back to the 1950s and late 1960s. Coal was also a focus of national energy policy well before the Second World War (McDougall 1982). The same is true for Canada as a whole, regarding electricity production centred within provinces and under provincial jurisdiction, and encompassing major hydroelectric projects as province-building and renewable energy policies (Netherton 2007; Froschauer 1999; Armstrong and Nelles 1986). And of course energy as a natural resource is constitutionally controlled mainly by the provinces. The federal government meanwhile possesses actual and potential jurisdiction over international trade and exports and also aspects of interprovincial energy trade and environmental and safety regulation (Doern and Gattinger 2003).

Energy policy and its complex governance system seeks to influence behaviour at numerous stages of energy production and consumption, from R & D, exploration, and initial extraction, to processing, transportation, use in homes, public institutions, and commercial establishments, and the disposition, reduction, management, and remediation of wastes, effluents, and emissions (Gattinger 2012;

2013; Eberlein and Doern 2009). Such policies are aimed at influencing and shaping the supply of energy sources and fuels, demand for energy from various users, and the environmental impacts of energy use. Energy policy thus covers sources and fuels such as oil and natural gas, coal, hydroelectricity, nuclear energy, and a host of alternative or renewable sources such as hydroelectricity, biofuels, solar energy, wind power, and biomass. Technological developments related to shale gas and related hydraulic fracturing or "fracking" approaches and carbon capture and storage (ccs) are also a part of the regime story (Prud'Homme 2014). Energy policy also covers global, national, and regional politics where past and current conflicts over prices and security influence views of what future policy should and should not be (Helm 2012; Yergin 2012).

Compared to the Environment Canada–Centred Regime, the Energy-Environment Regime involves a more complex structure of energy ministries centred on a parent department, while including multiple arm's-length regulatory bodies as well. This is true federally and provincially, and in total for Canada it means an array of well over fifty energy agencies with partial environmental mandates (Doern and Gattinger 2003).

In addition, as will be evident in the analysis that follows, the commingling of energy-environment ideas, paradigms, and discourse include those such as safety, conservation, sustainable development; renewable non-fossil fuels; clean and cleaner energy; long-term storage of wastes; and different versions of energy security, and burden and benefit sharing nationally and regionally. It involves visions and realities of energy as a north-south issue within Canada and vis-à-vis exports to, and imports from, the United States. It is also an internal Canadian east-west and "coast to coast to coast" realm of development and ecological concern regarding Canada's water and oceans (Clancy 2011, 2014).

Table 5.1 lists the main federal energy policy statutes that are under the responsibility of the minister of natural resources. Some were previously in the domain of the energy department, Energy, Mines and Resources (EMR), formed in 1966 and functioning until 1992, when it was succeeded in 1993 by Natural Resources Canada (Doern 1981; Doern and Gattinger 2001).

The National Energy Board legislation and core nuclear safety laws are traceable back to the 1950s and 1960s. The core body of laws authorize and yield dozens of regulations and regulatory

Table 5.1: Main federal energy policy legislation

Arctic Waters Pollution Prevention Act

Canada Foundation for Sustainable Development Technology Act

Canada-Newfoundland Atlantic Accord Implementation Act

Canada–Nova Scotia Offshore Petroleum Resources Accord Implementation Act

Canada Oil and Gas Operations Act

Canada Petroleum Resources Act

Cooperative Energy Act

Energy Administration Act

Energy Efficiency Act

Energy Monitoring Act

Hibernia Development Project Act

National Energy Board Act

Northern Pipeline Act

Nuclear Fuel Waste Act

Nuclear Liability Act

Nuclear Safety and Control Act

Oil Substitution and Conservation Act

Source: Natural Resources Canada 2013b.

programs. Space does not allow us to examine all of these laws, but we will refer to some of them, and of course we are interested in the scope of their content as an initial defining feature of the regime.

The "environment" as a word does not appear directly in the title of any of these laws; they are all statutes focused more on industry development and governance. But environmental aspects are clearly a part of such laws and rules under evolving concepts of pollution prevention, safety, waste management, and sustainable development. This chapter presents a necessarily selective account of key developments and aspects of the Energy-Environment Regime through an examination of four policy and governance histories. It builds on other aspects already introduced in earlier chapters regarding climate change policy and the Kyoto Protocol, other international agreements, Canada-US energy relations, and Environment Canada–centred laws such as those relating to environmental assessment. The analysis is broadly chronological and draws on published histories of various kinds and time periods, depending on how such histories provide the context for any given author's particular energy field or policy case study focus. These include histories of issues such as national pipeline debates and decisions, the creation and later privatization of Petro Canada, the 1980 National Energy Policy, climate change and Kyoto, nuclear energy, and hydroelectric power, exports, and changing electricity markets, and federal-provincial energy relations. Several green-lite features are highlighted in the narrative and also in the chapter conclusions.

The chapter begins with nuclear energy and its policy and governance structure, then examines the National Energy Board and its evolution in the Energy-Environment Regime. Both developments are surveyed across a span of fifty to sixty years. The third section examines the regime through the prism of the two "energy"-policy parent departments, first EMR and then NRCan. The coverage here goes from the mid-1960s to 2005 energy-environment priorities under the Trudeau Liberals and the Mulroney Conservatives regarding EMR, and under the Chrétien and Martin Liberals on NRCan. The fourth section covers the Harper era regarding energy policy, first in the context of technology-driven energy-environment issues centred on biofuels, carbon capture and storage (CCS), and shale gas in relation to hydraulic fracturing (or "fracking") technology, and then in relation to further analysis of the Conservatives' "responsible resource development" approach. This strategy is entwined with pipeline projects, proposals, and options such as the Keystone XL Pipeline to the US Gulf Coast, the Northern Gateway pipeline regarding possible Chinese and East Asian markets from British Columbia, and a belated interest in pipelines to Eastern Canada. Environment issues in this policy agenda were often sublimated and recast as safety and clean energy issues. Pipeline construction and major hydroelectricity projects are complex infrastructure projects and thus serve also as early precursors to the even broader discussion of infrastructure in chapter 9's account of the Federal–Municipal Infrastructure Sustainability Regime.

Also woven into this most recent Harper period have been federal efforts to avoid anything that looked or sounded like federally led intervention via national energy strategies, even though there were emerging provincial- and industry-led initiatives that wanted such a national strategy (Brownsey 2013; Gattinger 2013; Mowat Centre 2013). These historical regime developments are then related to the book's three elements framework. Conclusions then follow.

1950s TO PRESENT: NUCLEAR ENERGY
AND ENVIRONMENT AS EARLY
AND CONTINUING REGIME ISSUES

Nuclear energy and environmental issues are arguably the earliest manifestation of the Energy-Environment Regime. They emerged from the Second World War in which Canada became a strategic player in the US-led war effort to develop the first atomic bomb (Bothwell 1988). The resultant post-war peaceful use of nuclear power emerged through the role of Atomic Energy of Canada Limited (AECL), a federal Crown company (Doern and Morrison 1980). The main user by far of CANDU reactors for domestic energy supply has been the Province of Ontario. Single reactors are also in operation in New Brunswick and Quebec. Canada's nuclear power industry is a mixture of its home-developed CANDU heavy water reactor, its possession of large uranium reserves and exports, and a globally important nuclear medicines component (Bratt 2012; Doern and Morrison 2009).

While Ontario domestic electricity needs were the main focus during nuclear energy's first four decades, exports were also seen as an additional opportunity and a way to ensure that CANDU would be globally competitive. Early nuclear sales to India in the 1970s were also bound up in controversy, because they occurred before India's nuclear tests had been backed by India's adherence to international nuclear proliferation treaties. In the early 1990s the domestic market dried up. But export markets opened up and became AECL's main focus (Bratt 2008; Morrison 2001). However, globally, CANDU reactors have a small market share and are competing with larger players with more dominant reactor technologies.

Significant changes to Canada's nuclear policy have occurred over the last six decades. A key factor shaping these changes has been the evolution of Canadian energy policy from an earlier era of, in effect, "fuel by fuel" policy (oil, gas, nuclear, coal, uranium, etc.) to a concern about inter-fuel substitution. Here the focus is on an integrated view of natural resources and sustainable development and full-scale or managed competition. This includes, crucially, as we see later in this chapter, the introduction of competitive electricity markets in Alberta and Ontario (Dewees 2009; Pineau 2009). It is now a critical determinant of the nuclear industry's future in Canada and elsewhere, including Canada's possible links with the US reactor business, as many reactors there undergo refurbishment and as some new reactors seem likely to be built under US energy plans. On the ever-closer links with environmental policy and sustainable development, Canada's nuclear industry faced the proverbial double-edged sword. On the one hand, it faced, as does the global nuclear industry, the historic concerns of legitimacy centred on reactor safety, the control of nuclear weapons proliferation globally, and the still unresolved and costly environmental and ethical issues of the safety and long-term storage of nuclear wastes (Durant and Johnson 2010; Stoett 2003). On the other hand, the climate change debate allows the nuclear industry to position itself more readily as a green energy source, compared to carbon-based sources such as oil and gas. This argument has also been made by climate change advocates, many of whom see nuclear power as a key part of the effort to reduce GHG emissions (International Energy Agency 2013b). This potentially broadens the underlying rationale for government support to preserve and strengthen the nuclear energy industry in Canada, and in other countries that have a nuclear power option, to include environmental factors. But in Canada, this potential has been characterized for some time as a "precarious opportunity" at best (Doern, Dorman, and Morrison 2001, chap. 1).

A recent review of the nuclear energy sector (Public Policy Forum 2014) reached quite similar conclusions, concluding that "the future of global nuclear power is uncertain" and that "the future of Canada's nuclear energy sector is unclear" (6). It offered the view that among the most serious challenges "is the need to attain and maintain the social license to build nuclear reactors" but that the sector had "few political champions" (6). This observation resonates with other views about "new energy," including old "new energy" such as nuclear power as it struggles on its way to markets in the face of limited action on climate-change GHG emission-reductions and other forms of energy inertia (Wald 2013).

Until the late 1980s there was an explicitly recognized partnership between federal nuclear policy and activity and the Ontario Government, either directly or through Ontario Hydro (Bothwell 1988; Doern and Morrison 1980). As Ontario Hydro built its first CANDU reactors, there was considerable positive collaboration, including contributions from Ontario to the R&D of AECL through joint projects and through the nuclear fuel waste R&D program. Ontario Hydro also contracted a lot of work on its CANDU stations to AECL, although it took over more of it in the late 1970s as AECL became more focused on markets outside Ontario.

The anti-nuclear attitude of the NDP provincial government from 1990 to 1995 and the concomitant changes in senior management at Ontario Hydro were also significant developments. A decision was made to shut down seven older CANDU units, in order to focus technical expertise and trained manpower on the twelve newest plants. The key in the new competitive Ontario electricity market was that CANDU reactors would have to compete with newer, mainly gas-fired sources of electricity generation, which now enter the Ontario electricity market under private ownership. AECL was affected negatively by these choices on any domestic CANDU reactor sales but also positively, because new opportunities for commercial service and refurbishment emerged as Ontario tried to get its nuclear plants into competitive shape, and to penetrate the neighbouring US market.

In each of these situations, the two key arguments made about nuclear power were increasingly made in combination: (1) nuclear provides the cheapest, *baseload* power for electric utilities, and (2) it is an energy source that is immensely positive in the climate change stakes because it does not emit significant greenhouse gases. AECL's argument is centred in the latter case on the evidence that each year a CANDU 6 reactor avoids the release of 4.8 million tons of carbon dioxide, compared to natural gas (AECL 2008).

Compared to the previous Liberal governments since 1993, and despite its minority government status from 2006 to 2011, the Harper government has in one sense quite openly supported nuclear power as a part of Canada's overall energy mix (Doern and Morrison 2009), but coupled with Harper preferences for a reduced state-led production role. In other senses, however, it has not been supportive because it has no intention of implementing any climate-change and energy-pricing policies that would help provide the appropriate conditions for nuclear to be used in sensible and relevant economic and environmental situations (Public Policy Forum 2014).

Support for nuclear has some basis in Prime Minister Stephen Harper's occasionally forceful rhetoric that Canada is an "energy super-power." In this case Canada's CANDU technology and its large uranium reserves are seen as a part of the energy mix, including significant future energy exports. But the willingness to tout nuclear power has also been manifest in more particular ways that did link it to both climate change and to technology and innovation policy. The first Harper-era minister of natural resources, Gary Lunn, strongly supported the nuclear option. Lunn argued that there were very good opportunities for nuclear in the future. And he stressed that AECL was working on a "fourth genera-tion" of nuclear reactors that would extract more energy out of nuclear fuel to minimize the storage of radioactive waste. Lunn also intimated that a nuclear reactor might be used to replace or reduce the use of natural gas for power generation and steam used to extract Alberta oil sands. Some oil sands companies tentatively suggested such a possibil-ity, though it would be many years away from fruition and it would be a highly controversial step nationally and within Alberta.

However, federal nuclear policy took on a somewhat peculiar and unusual tangent early in 2008 when the federal government fired the head of Canada's nuclear regulatory body, the Canadian Nuclear Safety Commission (CNSC). The dismissal concerned a dispute over regula-tory safety delays for one of AECL's research reactors at Chalk River, which was crucial in the production of medical isotopes. Canada sup-plied over 70 per cent of the global market for such isotopes (Calamai 2008), and a severe shortage of supply was looming. The head of the CNSC argued correctly that her mandate did not deal with the isotopes; the CNSC mandate was only about nuclear reactor safety. The govern-ment put its emphasis on the isotope problem and had new legislation passed on an emergency basis to allow the reactor to resume operations so that the isotopes could be produced and exported.

The firing controversy aired some larger underlying issues in AECL and its relationships with the regulator and the government (Calamai 2008). For the government, these relationships centred on its failure to fund AECL's investment needs for current and new reactor develop-ment, in part because the Conservative government had concerns about its managerial competence. This in turn fed into issues about whether AECL ought to be wholly or partly privatized.

However, the link to climate change policy has come from the Conservative government's view that nuclear reactors remain a key part of Ontario's overall energy policy. The federal government cannot directly dictate such a policy in Ontario, but it has taken one step within federal jurisdiction that must somehow begin to be taken, regardless of whether or not Canada has a nuclear energy future. This step is to begin to deal with long-term storage and management of nuclear wastes, its ultimate political Achilles heel in environmental terms.

In June 2007, the Harper government accepted the federal Nuclear Waste Management Organization's (NWMO) recommended approach for managing used nuclear fuel in Canada, which includes the isolation and containment of used nuclear fuel deep in the earth, with an option for temporary shallow underground storage. The NWMO is now mandated to begin planning and designing a site selection process collaboratively with Canadians, which will take years. But by 2013 not much had happened in real terms. More importantly, as Durant and Johnson have noted (2010), the overall policy and consultation processes, involving multi-scalar levels and realms, communities, and Aboriginal peoples, have failed to deal with ethical and social issues. These include in profound green-lite temporal terms involving storage of wastes over hundreds of years, where legitimacy and trust is massively difficult, if not impossible to garner.

A further potential development under the Conservative federal government has centred on efforts to partially privatize AECL, by selling its commercial reactor business to a private firm. In 2011, SNC-Lavalin CANDU Energy, an SNC-Lavalin subsidiary, agreed to buy certain assets of AECL's commercial reactor division for $15 million; the deal also required royalty payments to the federal treasury from future new-build and life-extension projects. AECL retained its past liabilities (SNC-Lavalin 2011). The deal sought to establish a strategic partnership that would be linked to the expected Ontario decisions to build new reactors as part of its overall energy strategy. Alas, these expected decisions by a deficit-fighting Liberal Ontario government are highly uncertain. Nonetheless, for SNC-Lavalin, the main attraction is the acquisition of new intellectual property linked to reactor design, waste storage, and fuel recycling, and highly qualified nuclear engineering and research personnel. Some 1,200 employees from AECL have moved to CANDU Energy. But things are never simple in the nuclear reactor field, in either the reactor sale business or elsewhere, in part because of the costs of such power and the remaining links of federal subsidized research capacity and jobs in AECL's Chalk River facilities.

Interwoven with all of these historical phases and developments are the impacts of periodic international nuclear reactor disasters/meltdowns. None has yet happened in Canada, but each of the major global ones have had impacts on Canada, including the 1979 Three Mile Island accident in the United States, the 1986 Chernobyl reactor disaster in the Ukraine, and the 2011 Japanese nuclear reactor collapse in the face of both regulatory human error and an earthquake and a tsunami. In green-lite terms, these are also temporal features centred on periodic nuclear accident-driven crises. These disasters immediately affect markets and nuclear regulatory safety approaches, including those at the Canadian Nuclear Safety Commission. They also become linked to ideas, policies, and practices regarding *nuclear safety liability*. Indeed, the most recent nuclear policy announcement by the Harper government has been to increase the liability for Canadian nuclear reactors to as much as $1 billion, compared to the current absolutely puny limit of $75 million (Galloway 2013).

1959 TO PRESENT: THE NATIONAL ENERGY BOARD AS MARKET FACILITATOR, AND SAFETY AND ENVIRONMENTAL ASSESSMENT REGULATOR

Seeing the Energy-Environment Regime story through the role, policies, and evolution of the NEB as the primary federal regulator is a necessary task in this chapter. We trace key phases of stability and change in its role when there was no federal energy minister or department as such, and when it functioned in concert with energy departments, first EMR and then NRCan. (The broader EMR and NRCan policy and governance roles are examined further in the next section of the chapter.)

Following recommendations from two royal commissions, the NEB was created in 1959 with expectations that it would develop a national energy policy (Lucas 1977, 1978). However, the only concrete component of the mandating NEB Act legislation was a comprehensive set of regulatory powers, which included licensing the construction of interprovincial and international pipelines and electric power lines; licensing the export and import of electric power, oil, and natural gas; and approving rates, tariffs, and tolls for companies it regulated. It was through the exercise of these powers that the NEB was expected to enunciate a national energy policy (except for nuclear energy).

Pipeline and international power-line licence applicants were required to convince the NEB that they were "required by the present and future public convenience and necessity" (s. 44). This role is underscored by some of the requirements the applicants were required to establish in order to obtain a licence, which included:

- the availability of oil and gas to the pipeline, or power to the international power line ... ;
- the existence of markets, actual or potential;

- the economic feasibility of the pipeline or international power line;
- ... the extent to which Canadians will have an opportunity of participating in the financing, engineering and construction of the line; and
- any public interest that in the Board's opinion may be affected by the granting or the refusing of the application. (s. 44)

While the NEB was the regulatory centrepiece, provision was made for a continuing major role for Cabinet. The exercise of all of the NEB's powers was made subject to Cabinet approval. In short, the NEB did not have final decision-making power on granting pipeline certificates, export or import licences, or the charges to be levied by regulated energy companies; those decisions had to be approved by Cabinet before taking effect. However, the Cabinet's power of approval was a "negative" power inasmuch as Cabinet could veto NEB decisions but not substitute or vary those decisions (Schultz 1977). In some respects, particularly those related to tariff or rate regulation, the NEB's original powers are the normal powers associated with the regulation of a public utility. However, in addition to the licensing criteria cited above, what made the NEB different was also the emphasis on the implied purpose of the new energy regulator, which was to plan the energy sector (NEB Act, s. 22 (1)). However, energy regulation in the 1960s was a tight closed shop network comprising the regulator and the immediately regulated. Others seldom were tempted, nor were they encouraged, to enter the NEB community in this first decade (Doern and Gattinger 2003).

Regarding its policy role, the NEB chose to concentrate on one role, that of promoting the export of natural gas and oil to the United States. As McDougall has noted, the board embraced an "export orientation" as its primary concern in this period. As he states, "The board revealed that it was more concerned with expanding the volume of export sales than with realizing the full value of those sales ... In the area of pipeline construction, the board made several decisions to approve new or expanded pipeline facilities that were explicitly justified, at least in part, with reference to the favourable impact they would have on the future marketability of Canadian oil and gas in the United States" (McDougall 1982, 99). This role did not garner much opposition because there appeared to be enough oil and gas to satisfy Canadian consumers at reasonable prices. For most of this decade as well, there was little demand, inside or outside of government, for a broader national energy policy.

Several changes emerged, however, in the 1970s in how others were viewing the NEB. First, traditional participants before the NEB began to challenge the board's "export orientation" (McDougall 1982). First, large industrial users, such as BC Hydro, and representatives from the consuming provinces expressed concern that their residents and industrial consumers would suffer from a too liberal policy of exports (ibid.). Second, the board's ability to manage the emerging conflicts was made even more complicated with the emergence of consumer and environmental groups with different ideas that challenged the promotional emphasis the board had adopted. These new interests brought new ideas and a democratic insistence that they had a right to both participate in board hearings and have their views taken into account.

The mid- and late 1970s were characterized by oil and energy turbulence globally, which resulted in first a doubling and then a tripling of world oil prices (Doern and Toner 1985). These energy price and supply shocks changed national energy policy and the NEB's role in it beyond recognition. The issues ranged from conflicts between energy-producing and energy-consuming provinces and citizens, foreign ownership of energy companies, Canadian energy self-sufficiency and the question of exports to the United States, the distribution of revenues between the federal government and energy-producing provinces as a result of the sudden and drastic rise in oil prices, the urgency of northern energy development and its impacts on Aboriginal peoples, and the appropriate mix of environmental standards. Against this period of turbulence, it was obvious that the idea of an expert-based, non-political regulatory agency such as the NEB designing a national energy plan was dead.

The Department of Energy, Mines and Resources had been established in 1966, but it too had been reluctant to be a national energy policy-maker (see more below). But the need for change was made clear in 1980 when the newly elected Trudeau Liberal government unveiled its National Energy Plan (Doern and Toner 1985). This was an economic-energy policy and regulatory regime based on a set of ideas that constituted a fundamental break with those that had been central to the previous era. The primary ideas were, first, promoting security of energy supply that went beyond sufficiency; second, Canadianizing the energy sector to reduce to 50 per cent the extent of foreign control; and finally, redistributing the benefits of the greatly increased world price in oil through revenue-sharing amongst all Canadians to meet the objective of fairness, rather than permitting all the benefits to accrue to the energy-producing companies and provinces.

The primary policies to give effect to those ideas included petroleum incentive grants to encourage Canadian corporate exploration and development, a reservation of a 25 per cent interest for the federal government in any oil or gas found in the newly designated Canada Lands in the North and the Arctic, a special place for the federal Crown corporation, Petro Canada, which had been established earlier, and finally not relying on market mechanisms to set and distribute the pricing of energy, especially oil.

A combination of existing and new institutions was used to pursue and implement the new set of policies. Among the new institutions were the Canada Oil and Gas Lands Administration, the Office of Industrial and Regional Benefits, the Petroleum Incentives Administration, the Petroleum Monitoring Agency to monitor the extent of foreign ownership, and a strengthened Northern Pipeline Agency, created in 1978 to supervise pipeline development. One key characteristic of some of these agencies was that while they played an indirect regulatory role, they were created in large part to plan development.

The NEB played no role whatsoever in formulating the NEP. It was completely shut out of policy development, and its regulatory roles were further reduced by the creation of new regulatory and energy-policy implementation institutions. Henceforth, its primary role was to be limited to the traditional regulatory role in interprovincial pipeline tolls and the prevention of market power abuse.

The Mulroney government deregulated key aspects of energy policy because of its strong opposition to the Liberal NEP (see more below), but it kept the NEB's core pipeline utility regulatory functions. Importantly it gave it strengthened environmental and safety regulation mandates. As a result, the NEB in the Mulroney era returned to a changed version of the quieter life that characterized its first decade. The NEB was also moved out of Ottawa and relocated to Calgary, where it still functions in the heart of the Canadian energy industry, and it was increasingly funded by industry fees rather than by taxpayers (Doern 1999; Doern and Gattinger 2003). It also sought to be more business-like under the growing ethos of

reinvented government and aspects of the New Public Management
with its greater customer- and client-service focus but still while
viewing energy as an essential service networked industry.

The Mulroney period also saw the development of joint federal
and provincial offshore regulators to deal with the developing offshore oil and gas industry. Thus new sectoral regulators such as the
Canada-Newfoundland Offshore Petroleum Board and the Canada–
Nova Scotia Offshore Petroleum Board were established (Clancy
2011; Sinclair 2010. But offshore energy regulation had to be quintessentially energy- and environmental-regulation virtually from the
outset, in part because of different kinds and complexities of risk,
centred on the oceans and the fisheries and hence on a different array
of global energy exploration and production companies, but also
shipping and common property resource players and communities
in Atlantic Canada. Such regulation reflects green-lite realities centred on the tragedy of the commons and complex multi-scalar coordination problems. They were certainly far from being solved in the
more pro-environmental Mulroney era, and, as we see further below,
they have been harmed further by Harper-era weakening of the
Fisheries Act in the name of responsible resource development
(Clancy 2014).

The NEB's expanded environmental regulatory role was triggered
by the passage of the federal Canadian Environmental Assessment
Act in 1995. As we have seen in chapter 4, the NEB was henceforth
a "responsible authority" under the act and thus had to coordinate
its assessments jointly with Environment Canada's Canadian
Environmental Assessment Agency. The NEB was also required to
find its own way of practising *sustainable development* (SD), a policy commitment of Natural Resources Canada, its quite new parent
department established by the Chrétien Liberal government in 1993
(Doern 1993a).

The NEB finessed this SD pressure in a green-lite "ends-means" con-
trived manner in that it was very reluctant to see its statutory mandate
contain SD obligations, but it did argue in its annual reports that it
did in fact practise it in the "triple bottom line" sense of the concept
(National Energy Board 2001, 24). In later reports in both Liberal and
Harper eras, the NEB has also argued that its goal was *sustainable
energy development*, which may or may not mean sustainable development but does harken back, especially in an Alberta historical context, to early oil and gas–conservation ideas and measures.

From 2002 to the present, the NEB's changing view of itself is captured partly in sample annual reports, as it both chronicles and responds to new pressures and market dynamics during the later Chrétien years and then during the Harper minority and majority governments. For example, the 2004 annual report states that the NEB's overall purpose is to "promote safety, environmental protection and economic efficiency in the Canadian public interest within the mandate set by Parliament in the regulation of pipelines, energy development and trade" (National Energy Board 2005, 1). This same statement also leads off the first Harper NEB annual report for 2007 (National Energy Board 2008, 1).

However, by the time of the 2011 Harper-era report, the NEB's stated purpose is reordered to "regulate pipelines, energy development and trade in the Canadian public interest" (National Energy Board 2012a, ii). The safety and environmental aspects of its mandate are mentioned in the next "goals" section. This expressed reordering may be the NEB's reading of the federal political tea leaves where, as we have already seen, the Harper era has been featured by a strong pro-energy development and resource-export ethos and set of policies cast increasingly under the discourse of Canada as an energy superpower. It was reiterated as well in a 2012 Senate report, titled *Now or Never*, argued why Canada must act urgently "to seize its place in the new energy world order" (Standing Senate Committee on Energy, the Environment and Natural Resources 2012). Such "export the raw resource" positions make no effort to discuss or support the obvious counterweight to this position, which is to devise and design policies and financing to support the upgrade of Canada's oil resources to value-added more sustainable refined products produced in Canada (Canadian Academy of Engineering 2012).

However, these are not the only ways in which successive reports capture and reflect the NEB's more recent approaches and the ways they have been expressed. On its core role, the 2004 report referred to how it both needs "to *protect* and *enable* in order to achieve outcomes that are in the public interest" (National Energy Board 2005, 1). The enabling function "implies a responsibility to *make possible*" (1–2) and hence is a somewhat gentler substitute for the NEB's developmental role for the energy industry. The report also cited the NEB's Liberal-era smart-regulation approaches that include the greater deployment of goal-oriented, performance-based regulation and service standards. However, in more particular substantive ways, the report also drew attention to key issues and engagement challenges, such as high and volatile energy prices, strained infrastructure (given new oil sands production), and Aboriginal legal rights.

Early on, the 2007 NEB annual report highlighted the board's risk-based life-cycle approach that "relates to a company's performance as well as the scope of regulatory oversight required through the life cycle of a project" (National Energy Board 2008, 1). But the board also referred to its establishment of a Land Matters Consultation Initiative, a general growing problem but one triggered by angry and aggressive landowners, in Alberta in particular, defending their property rights against energy company development encroachments. Such property rights and related land- and resource-management and boundary issues had often been important in Alberta politics. By the time of the 2011 annual report, the NEB was stressing its needed broadening approaches in public engagement (National Energy Board 2012a, 1–2). By 2011, the Land Matters initiative had resulted in the board forming a Land Matters Group, which was drafting approaches to company involvement programs.

This renewed consultation approach included pre-eminently consultations on Canadian Arctic offshore drilling. Two NEB reports late in 2011 set out the information that the board would need to assess in any future applications for Arctic offshore drilling and drew out other lessons that it and Canada needed to learn from the major 2010 US oil spill disaster in the Gulf of Mexico (National Energy Board 2011a, 2011b).

More broadly, the board also drew attention to how it has taken steps in getting companies to develop "a strong safety culture through a management systems approach" (National Energy Board 2012a, 2, 14). The dynamics of the oil sands era were also revealed through the fact that the applications to the board for approvals and licences had doubled over the previous year.

These recent NEB realities and developments also easily cross over with changes in the Alberta energy regulatory system. Indeed both the NEB and Alberta's current Energy Resources Conservation Board (ERCB) are both based in Calgary close to the heart of the oil and gas and oil sands industry. Based partly on growing criticism by environmentalists and others about its environmental capacities in the face of the Alberta energy boom, Alberta announced changes in

2013 to its energy-environment regulatory system by creating a new body, the Alberta Energy Regulator, to replace the ERCB. Despite its "Energy" title, the new board would combine the regulatory powers in one agency previously conducted by two provincial departments, Alberta Environment and also Sustainable Resource Development (Tait 2013a; Alberta Energy 2013). Interestingly, the new statute governing this changed governance structure is called the Responsible Energy Development Act. The changes can be traced back to a longer two-year regulatory enhancement project and a related consultation process. However, the actual workings of the new regulator remain a work in progress, given exactly how its additional component staff resources from the environment and natural resource ministries will fare vis-à-vis the larger staff components of the long-established and prestigious former ERCB. It also depends on which kinds of environmental, conservation, and risk-management concepts versus energy-efficiency concepts will prevail as decisions are made (Doern 2012).

One final key point about seeing the Energy-Environment Regime through the evolution of the NEB is to point out two major policy events where the NEB was essentially a non-player. In the National Energy Program era from 1980 to 1983, it was effectively shut out of any of the discussions centred in EMR. It is also fair to say that the NEB was largely disconnected from the climate change debate and Canada's abject failures in meeting its international commitments under the Kyoto Protocol regarding reductions in greenhouse gas emissions.

1966 TO PRESENT: FEDERAL ENERGY DEPARTMENTS AS LEAD POLICY PLAYERS – FROM EMR TO NRCAN

Previous sections have already brought out some features of both EMR and NRCan as lead players in the Energy-Environment Regime. Here we develop a clearer overview of their origins and evolution. Federal energy policy's home departmental base was EMR from 1966 to 1992 and NRCan from 1993 to the present.

EMR was established to help develop more integrated energy policies; however, for most of its first decade it functioned more like two departments. Its larger traditional technical base was centred in entities such as the Geological Survey of Canada, whereas its newer energy policy and economic components were emerging but were not initially very strongly or aggressively asserted vis-à-vis the rest of the government (Doern 1981). Indeed, EMR seemed almost bewildered by the energy supply and price shocks of the 1970s referred to in chapter 2.

The department published two energy policy/strategy documents, one in 1973 and the other in 1976 (EMR 1973, 1976). These spoke of the need for better policies and actions on Canada's energy supply, more secure sources of supply, and also some early environmental concerns. Environmental issues also were accelerated by the work of the Berger Inquiry. Berger reported in 1977 after holding major hearings and conducting extensive research on to two pipeline proposals to bring massive US natural gas supplies found in Prudhoe Bay, Alaska, to American markets via an overland route through Canada, including one route through the Mackenzie Delta. Berger recommended a ten-year delay and opposed the Delta route for economic and environmental reasons as well as concerns over the rights of Aboriginal peoples in the North. Not for the first time were pipelines a focal point for national energy policy, for Aboriginal peoples, and for environmental debate (Doern and Toner 1985). We see these further below in the current multi-pipeline development and safety and environment regulatory context of Harper-era policy.

EMR's tentative early roles were massively changed in 1979–80 following the second OPEC-centred energy crisis. EMR became a de facto central federal agency. It was the chief architect of the highly interventionist National Energy Program of the 1980–83 Trudeau Liberal government. The NEP has been discussed above and in previous chapters, but suffice it to say that this period was EMR's heyday and the NEP became and remains massively controversial in Canada's current energy-policy memory and discourse, including conversations to be avoided (Gattinger 2013).

The election of the Mulroney Conservative government in 1984 brought fundamental changes to the energy regulatory regime. As we have seen in chapter 2, the Conservatives embraced market-based ideas and concomitant policies on the assumption that as much as possible, markets, not government intervention and regulation, should determine energy development, prices, output, and allocation. The first step taken in 1985 was to deregulate crude oil marketing and pricing as well as the licensing of exports. This was followed by deregulation of gas pricing and substitution of direct buy–sell relationships and negotiations between gas producers and users (Toner 1986; Doern 1999). The Mulroney era's later signature Canada-US Free Trade Agreement in 1988 also consolidated liberalized energy markets in large part because of a desire led by Alberta to prevent any future NEP-like policy interventions and adventures (Doern and Tomlin 1991).

NRCan as the lead energy department began in 1993. It emerged out of the late Mulroney and early Liberal major restructuring of the federal government (Doern 1993a) and also the Chrétien Liberals' mandate Red Book proposals that advocated the combined ideas of sustainable development and the innovation economy (Doern and Gattinger 2001). Energy and mining were key resource industries, but NRCan was also especially created to generate greater support for Canada's forestry industry in the context of an integrated natural resources policy. Some of the flavour of this newly expressed Liberal NRCan mandate was found in personally crafted writing of the NRCan vision statement by its second minister, Ralph Goodale: "As we enter the millennium, Canada must become and remain the world's 'smartest' natural resources steward, developer, user, and exporter – the most high tech, the most environmentally friendly, the most socially responsible, the most productive and competitive – leading the world as a living model of sustainable development" (Natural Resources Canada 2000, 1).

With aspirations of this kind, NRCan was seeking to avoid the label of its industries belonging to the "old economy" and to assert its determination to be a key part of the new innovation economy (Persaud, Kumar, and Kumar 2007). We of course are looking here at NRCan mainly in relation to energy policy and thus have surveyed its overall statutory base at the beginning of this chapter. NRCan's other resource sectors and their natural resource-environment regime features are the focal point of chapter 6.

However, with respect to energy-environment per se, as the Chrétien-Martin Liberal era ended in 2005, it is fair to say that sustainable development found a greater presence as a policy goal and aspiration, but it was nonetheless a struggle for, rather than any obvious or provable achievement of, sustainable development. Thus, not for the first time in this book's historical account, it was greenlite in many ways regarding boundary realities and also "means-ends" calculus. In part this was also due profoundly to the failure of Liberal-era climate-change and Kyoto Protocol implementation, which, as previous chapters have highlighted, saw Canada's GHG emissions increase by 24 per cent (relative to a 1990 baseline), not decrease by 6 per cent, as stipulated by Canada's Kyoto Protocol commitment.

A further development in which Ottawa overall had a role centred on electricity markets and how at the provincial level and in the United States they were being transformed in the 1990s from hierarchically regulated markets into amore competitive market system, albeit of a still essential service industry (Dewees 2009). The core of this system in several provinces, but particularly Ontario and Alberta, targeted municipally owned electricity companies with the intent of permitting different kinds of competing energy sources to supply the electricity grid and, hence, to obtain a better mix of pricing and energy supply characteristics for different types of power, even at different times of day in the supply and demand system.

The new system involved a mixture of deregulation and continued regulation, particularly on the challenges of grid management. In Canada, the grid was still essentially provincial but also much more Canada–United States in nature rather than interprovincial. The federal role emerged periodically, such as in a major Canada-US 2003 electricity blackout in the northeastern United States but extended into Canada as well. This raised issues about complex connected grids, their reliability, and the need for new forms of balanced cross-border "smart grid" governance (Minkel 2008). However, electricity markets and their regulation were mainly provincial. The regulatory systems for electricity all encountered problems in their initial design and the setting of prices to consumers. Difficulties also emerged over the entrance of new renewable sources of supply into electricity grids (Feehan 2012).

This is not to suggest that Ottawa had no regulatory roles affecting the electricity industry. The NEB mandate included electricity exports and imports. However, the Canadian Electricity Association, the main industry lobby, stresses further that eight federal laws affect "its efforts to meet demand while simultaneously replacing aging infrastructure and achieving continuous improvements in emission reduction efforts and overall environmental performance" (Canadian Electricity Association 2013b, 1). These included major environmental laws as noted in chapter 4, including the Fisheries Act, the Species at Risk Act, and the Navigable Waters Protection Act.

The electricity industry, especially in its Quebec and British Columbia hydro systems, but also in other provinces as well, saw itself as a vital energy and socio-economic player. But it also cast itself as being environmentally superior to the oil and gas industry. In the context of the Harper-era export and multiple pipeline dynamics (see more in the next section), it saw itself as the "backbone on any strategy to confront and leverage the new energy landscape" in that such a strategy had to involve "an enhanced North American electricity system" (Canadian Electricity Association 2013a, 2). An enhanced Canada-US grid would maximize environmental sustainability and, among other things, support "existing measures that are proven to cost-effectively deliver emission reductions and help enable intermittent renewables technologies" (3). The Canadian electricity industry also sees the Canadian electricity grid as being "stretched thin" by the combined dynamics of rising demand and aging infrastructure (McCarthy and Kerr 2013).

While business lobbies such as the Canadian Chamber of Commerce support this broad logic and argument regarding electricity, they also support the need for more serious study and action on electricity connections between provinces. Such concerns include dealing with some regulatory barriers and complexity that are associated with the absence of an energy chapter in the Internal Trade Agreement (ITA) (Canadian Chamber of Commerce 2012, 23–4). Academic and related professional association research has also advocated the development of a pan-Canadian electricity market (Pineau 2012; Canadian Academy of Engineering 2012).

ENERGY-ENVIRONMENT IN THE HARPER ERA: BIOFUELS, CARBON CAPTURE AND STORAGE, SHALE GAS, PIPELINES, AND RESPONSIBLE RESOURCE DEVELOPMENT

Previous chapters have already dealt with key aspects of Harper-era energy policy and the muted support under the Conservatives for related environmental policy since 2006 and also the apparent unwillingness to even use the discourse of the "environment" per se, except in regard to some of its early Budget Speeches when specific tax measures were being announced. The account in these earlier chapters has included climate change failure and withdrawal from the Kyoto Protocol, the use of inflated discourse of Canada as an energy superpower in the oil sands era and a trusted source of "ethical oil" for the US market, and some discussion of pipelines and its natural resources export strategy and focus since 2011. But before returning to recent developments and to its energy-focused responsible resource development strategy, we also need to examine the Conservatives' technology-centred Energy-Environment Regime developments centred in order on biofuels, carbon capture and storage, and shale gas produced by hydraulic fracturing "fracking" technology. Each is globally driven but with immediate Canadian manifestations and policies and contentious Energy-Environment Regime trade-offs and green-lite features and policy complexities. These are more recent features of a larger Canadian renewables story that certainly predates the Harper government, including in the sense that provincial hydro development (big hydro and small hydro) and hydro exports to the United States have always been cast as an environmental renewable energy advantage for Canada and for key hydro provinces.

Biofuels refer to liquid renewable fuels such as ethanol (an alcohol fermented from plant materials) and bio-diesel (a fuel made from vegetable oils or animal fats) that can substitute for petroleum-based fuels (International Institute for Sustainable Development 2009). Early on, the Harper government was a strong advocate of such renewable fuel development as a non-carbon fuel initiative (Canadian Renewable Fuels Association 2013). But it was also motivated strongly by pressure from western Canadian agricultural interests, in the heartland of Tory support. Such support was central to the 2006 Federal Renewable Fuels strategy (O'Connor 2011), the drivers of which, in order of importance, were "creating new economic opportunities for our farmers and agricultural sector; advancing the bio-based economy; and reducing GHG emissions" (10). In the wake of this policy, several western Canadian provinces announced their own initiatives to complement other forms of support that they had begun much earlier.

While the federal biofuels initiative has received early positive assessments of its fiscal and regulatory design, the environmental impacts are deemed not to be "well understood, anticipated, and routinely evaluated or integrated into policy structure" (International Institute for Sustainable Development 2009, 4). In global studies, particularly of the US biofuel industry, the adverse environmental impacts include water depletion, land conversion and habitat loss, and nitrogen runoff. Indeed, recent accounts of the US ethanol-led biofuels industry have pronounced it to be in considerable disarray in energy and environmental terms (Meyer 2013). Regarding the less robust Canadian biofuels industry, the IISD report stressed that "the broader suite of environmental impacts that might arise from accelerated biofuels production is not currently taken into account in Canadian policies" (IISD 2009, 4). If biofuels policies are not even evaluating environmental impacts, then this is certainly a good example of green-lite realities of the means-ends calculus and conflict kind. There have also been concerns about bioethics in the research and development phases of biofuels (Phillips 2010).

Carbon capture and storage (CCS) as a technology and policy realm has also been of considerable interest to the Harper Conservatives and to the Alberta-centred oil sands, oil and gas industry, and the Alberta government. NRCan does not particularly draw attention to it but clearly sees CCS as potentially significant regarding the oil sands and the industry's need to significantly reduce GHG emissions. CCS is defined by NRCan as "a clean energy technology that aims to capture emissions of carbon dioxide (CO_2) ... from industrial facilities – before they are released into the atmosphere. The CO_2 is then compressed, and transported by pipeline or tanker truck to a storage site and injected between one and five kilometres ... underground in deep geological formations, where it will be safely stored for the long term. Many of the formations chosen as potential sites have already had fluids (such as oil) or gases (such as natural gas) trapped within them for tens of millions of years" (Natural Resources Canada 2013a, 8).

The International Energy Agency also sees CCS as a major potential technology to significantly reduce GHG emissions from large-scale, fuel-based emitters (International Energy Agency 2013a). With CCS projects underway in several countries, the federal government has launched a number of initiatives. One was the process of the Canada-Alberta ecoEnergy Carbon Capture and Storage Task Force, whose 2008 report estimated that 75 per cent of oil sands CO_2 emissions are "capturable." The federal government has helped fund projects to work towards the commercialization of CCS. Two large-scale CCS demonstration projects are underway, and some $6 billion is being invested, one-third from the federal and provincial governments and two-thirds from the private sector.

The potential of CCS is just that, "potential." Demonstrable progress at the global level has been stalled (Cryderman and McCarthy 2013). But the Alberta government, under ever-greater pressure in the United States to demonstrate environmental progress on the oil sands, is determined to make CCS progress with well over $1 billion of provincial money now invested in CCS but also knowing that the oil sands is the most costly locale for the deployment of CCS compared to other kinds of facilities such as coal-fired plants. The IEA has stressed, however, that regarding the quality and pace of CCS technology and its adoption, "the quality of the policy matters," nationally and via close international cooperation (IEA 2013a).

The CCS developmental and political-environmental trajectory is now at least of fifteen years' duration, depending on when one starts the story. But its evolution and its future shape and contours also involve what Meadowcroft and Hellin (2010) refer to as a technological transition versus an enhanced "carbon lock-in." They point to still daunting cost and related environmental concerns and uncertainties about the capture phase, as storage sites are identified and operationalized but also regulated and monitored on a massively long-term basis. In our terms, CCS is replete with green-lite features of the temporal kind but also of the multi-scalar kinds regarding storage sites. Though such emission hazards are different from those of storing long-term nuclear wastes, they face similar temporal challenges in even contemplating multi-century systems of monitoring and regulatory trust. Drawing on other related research, Meadowcroft and Hellin also point to the concept of "carbon lock-in" and how it occurs as societies become bound to a carbon-intensive energy trajectory under which "early competition over the purposes and orientation of new technologies typically settles down after the emergence of a 'dominant design'" (239–40).

Related kinds of carbon lock-in may also be well underway in *shale gas and related fracking technologies* (Prud'Homme 2014). Fracking refers to the hydraulic fracturing of rock formations, such as shale, that has already begun to produce a shale gas revolution, particularly in the United States, and initially in North Dakota (Brooks 2013; Levi 2013; Dobb 2013), but also with early Canadian shale gas development underway in British Columbia (Horne and Campbell 2011). Fracking-related technologies have also developed for "tight light oil" or "tight shale oil" (Natural Resources Canada 2013d).

With regard to shale gas, NRCan describes its role as that of providing "geoscience information used in making exploration, resource management and environmental protection decisions" (Natural Resources Canada 2013d, 1). Partly given the primacy of provincial jurisdiction, the Harper government has not been an open advocate or promoter of shale gas, but it is certainly having to think through how to deal with its already major impacts in the United States, which, as we have seen in earlier chapters, has massively increased domestic gas and oil production and hence reduced the need by the Americans for foreign oil and gas, from the Middle East and from Canada. This already feeds into the larger federal resource-development strategy, since it relates to pipeline development battles and where to export the oil and gas – now, and, even more so, if Canada's shale gas industry takes off in more substantial ways.

A useful way of understanding the federal perspective on shale gas is through NRCan's presentation of the key facts about shale gas.

• Shale gas is emerging as the new low-cost source of natural gas in North America.
• In Canada potential and producing shale gas resources are found in [all provinces except Newfoundland and Prince Edward Island], with most of the current drilling and production activities occurring in Northern British Columbia ...
• Natural gas is an important transition fuel for a low carbon economy because it is cleaner burning than any other fossil fuel and is in abundant supply. Current research estimates that the natural gas supply in North America, largely in the form of shale gas, will last more than 100 years.
• Natural gas offers the potential to replace fuels that produce more greenhouse gases and that are currently used for power generation, heating and transportation.
• Hydraulic fracturing has been used by the industry to safely stimulate oil and gas production in North American conventional reservoirs for more than 60 years.
• Although shale gas development is a relatively mature industry in the United States (with more than 40,000 producing wells) shale gas is still in its nascent stages in Canada. (Natural Resources Canada 2013d, 1).

The environmental issues related to shale gas and fracking are partly acknowledged but mainly ignored in these early NRCan presentations. The department's life-cycle analysis suggests that "shale gas in Canada produces on average 4 percent higher life cycle greenhouse gas emissions than average conventional Canadian gas"

(Natural Resources Canada 2013d, 5). Though not emphasized, there is some mention of the fact that each shale-gas drilling exploration site will often be unique because of the relative permeability of diverse rock formations involved. This means that on-site environmental risks and remediation approaches will be numerous and even unique to specific sites. The concerns about possible methane emissions from drilling and hydraulic fracturing are mentioned but basically dismissed on the basis of Canada's current regulatory and exploration practices. Not mentioned are risks to water resources, as discussed in a Pembina Institute study of shale gas in British Columbia (Horne and Campbell 2011) and as examined in relation to US developments (Brooks 2013).

Concerns are also expressed in some commentaries about interacting longer-term effects if shale gas production takes off and affects the price and use of competing fuels and their relative price structures in different markets. As Reguly (2013, 22) argues,

> Before we declare the shale gas revolution a net positive for the planet, consider that gas is still a carbon-intensive fuel. If the market works as it normally does, the enormous supplies and falling prices will make the fuel irresistible to the electricity-generation and transportation industries in the regions where shale gas is plentiful. Conservation would go out the window. So might the use of renewable energy such as wind, solar and biomass power and emission-free nuclear reactors. At the same time, regions without cheap gas, such as China, will continue to rely on coal. The shale gas surge could easily translate into greater overall carbon emissions in spite of gas's lower carbon content.

The three energy-environment realms and sub-realms are driven partly by technological developments but also by diverse and different interests federally, regionally, and provincially within and across biofuels, oil sands and carbon capture and storage, and shale gas. Each is being recognized in different degrees through federal spending, partnership-building and regulatory discussion, and some policy change. But meanwhile, the Harper government is concerned mainly with pipelines and exports, and responsible resource development as its overriding energy agenda.

At time of writing, several pipelines, planned and possible, are at the heart of the Harper energy policy and related environment agenda (Canadian Energy Research Institute 2012; Doucet 2012; Mowat Centre 2013). The first is the Keystone xL Pipeline to ship oil sands bitumen to the US Gulf Coast. The Obama administration rejected the initial proposal because of pollution concerns in the Nebraska Ogallala Aquifer route planned. TransCanada then submitted a revised proposal, which is still being considered, and regarding which the federal and Alberta government are lobbying actively in the United States. Support emerged for Keystone following the 2014 Congressional election when the Republican party won control of both houses but President Obama announced early in 2015 that he would veto the Keystone project.

The second planned project is the $6.5 billion Northern Gateway Pipeline by Enbridge (Vanderkliffe 2013). It would build the first crude oil pipeline link between the Edmonton area and the British Columbia coastal community of Kitimat. It is planned as a two-pipeline system, with the western pipeline carrying "dilbit blend" (heavy crudes and/or bitumen-related products) "to Kitimat where it can be transferred to tankers and shipped to markets throughout the Pacific Rim" (Canadian Energy Research Institute 2012, 2).

This project was subject to a Joint Review Panel (JRP) process involving over 4,000 participants at community hearings across Alberta and BC, including numerous Aboriginal groups (National Energy Board and Canadian Environmental Assessment Agency 2013). A key development here centres on the fact that the BC Liberal government headed by Premier Christy Clark formally rejected the Enbridge proposal, by setting out several weaknesses, many of them related to safety and environment (Fowlie, Simpson, and Lee 2013). The Clark government surprisingly won a subsequent provincial election, so BC holds considerable political and jurisdictional leverage.

The Joint Panel report was published in December 2013, in which it recommended that "the federal government approve the project, subject to 209 required conditions" (National Energy Board and Canadian Environmental Assessment Agency 2013, 1). "Based on a scientific and precautionary approach" carried out in its complex review, the panel concluded that the project "would be in the public interest" (1). However, the conditions for the pipeline's approval were strongly criticized by environmental and Aboriginal groups, with the federal government having to deal with numerous lawsuits (Cryderman and Jang 2013).

Two further pipeline projects also figure in the energy and political-economic calculus. One is the $5.4 billion Kinder Morgan project proposal to expand its TMX pipeline, which since the 1950s has been shipping hydrocarbons to the West Coast (Moore 2013). The TMX expansion application to the NEB is also centred on securing new markets for Canadian oil producers, "which are currently selling their crude to US customers at heavy discounts" (Canadian Energy Research Institute 2012, 2). Kinder Morgan has expressed serious concern that some of the NEB's eventual conditions on the Northern Gateway project could have adverse impacts on the TMX expansion plans (Cryderman 2013).

And last but not least is the announcement in 2013 by Trans-Canada Corporation of the planned $12 billion Energy East pipeline to ship oil and bitumen to eastern Canada and to export markets. It has been planned in concert with the Irving Oil Corporation in New Brunswick (Cattaneo 2013; Mowat Centre 2013). Subject to regulatory approval, the pipeline will convert 3,000 kilometres of TransCanada's main natural gas pipeline into an oil pipeline. Another 1,400 kilometres of new pipelines will also be built in Alberta, Ontario, Quebec, and New Brunswick. The Energy East proposal has gained increased interest, in part because of the potential difficulties with both the Keystone XL and Northern Gateway projects, but also because of its national energy strategy appeal (Canada West Foundation 2013). Support for Energy East came from Alberta Premier Alison Redford, who later left office, the New Brunswick government, and from Prime Minister Stephen Harper (McLaughlin 2013). But it will by no means be a smooth path to obtaining regulatory approval and completion, given environmental and climate change lobbies, Aboriginal concerns en route, and also given some possible opposition from the natural gas industry (McCarthy and Jones 2013). The idea of a national energy strategy gained some renewed impetus following the election victories of Liberal parties in Quebec and Ontario, which led to the 2014 provisional agreement at the conference of the Council of the Federation (Benzie 2014). Supported by all provincial premiers, the strategy includes stronger climate change provisions and thus challenges the broad contours of the Harper approach.

These pipeline battles and configurations are big, important, complex, and rife with green-lite features. But they are by no means the only commercial factors at stake regarding possible transportation of oil supplies. One alternative already evident in the United States, and now actively proposed in Canada, is the greater use of railways to transport oil. Up to 500,000 barrels of oil are moved annually by railways in the United States, a twenty-five-fold increase since 2008 (Vanderklippe 2013). Canadian National railway (CN) started shipping crude oil by rail in 2010 and plans to expand. Not surprisingly, as with pipelines, there are concerns about accidents and spills on rail routes as well (Vanderklippe 2013d). Moreover, rail shipping would involve potential regulatory jurisdictional coordination with Transport Canada and transport regulators. These are added to a rail industry safety agenda in 2013–14 that started with the 2013 Lac-Mégantic train disaster that killed forty-seven people and destroyed the town centre. It involved an oil shipment by rail and thus in various possible ways may affect the rail-versus-pipeline transportation safety and environmental debates and options in Canada and in the United States.

Also emerging are proposals and plans for oil shipment via tankers in the Arctic Ocean as it is transformed into a year-round route created by the melting of the arctic ice due to climate change. Omnitrax Inc., a US company that owns both Manitoba's Hudson's Bay Railway and the port of Churchill, is developing plans that would see Alberta and Saskatchewan oil shipped east via Hudson's Bay to Europe but also west (Jones 2013).

Behind this set of core pipeline proposals are linked issues centred on three fast-converging energy political-economy dynamics. The first is the shrinking export opportunities to the US market because of the US fracking-driven oil and gas production boom and its falling domestic demand. The second is the massive increase in projected Alberta oil sands production and the need to reach markets through new pipeline capacity and routes. Finally, Western Canada has insufficient access to US markets outside of the US Midwest. One consequence of these dynamics is downward pressure on oil prices compared to overseas benchmark rates (Canada West Foundation 2013b).

Interwoven with these developments is the previously discussed Harper responsible resource development strategy that has led to its 2012 efficiency driven changes to the environmental assessment process and also to its often belligerent attack politics approach to environmental groups (Toner and McKee 2014). But by 2013 and the mid-way point in the Harper majority government some second sober thoughts may potentially be emerging. A June 2013 NEB forum discussion with the major pipeline companies reported a growing recognition that "public trust has been eroded" (Graveland 2013) because of recent oil spills and the clash between inflated federal "energy superpower" and "ethical oil" rhetoric and the practical day-to-day and project-to-project development practicalities and divergent views about pipeline routes and environmental and safety concerns, including those involving Aboriginal peoples and land. Aboriginal issues, participation, and protests have increased in most new pipeline proposals simultaneously at play.

Decisions by the Supreme Court of Canada have also been a factor, including the 2014 unanimous ruling that expanded Aboriginal rights to claim possession of ancestral lands and control of those lands permanently (Fine 2014; Blaze Carlson 2014).

The recent oil spills related not only to the Keystone XL pipeline in the United States but also to a serious toxic spill in northern Alberta (Vanderkliffe 2013a). In addition, media analysis was beginning to reveal more details of the Harper government's 2012 changes to the Fisheries Act associated with their agenda of promoting responsible resource development (Toner and McKee 2014). This analysis showed how the provisions that weakened the act were the result of energy-and-resource business lobbies being given support that overrode the strong environmental concerns of both Fisheries and Oceans Canada and environmental groups (Galloway 2013). Local environmental concerns are also being forcefully expressed in Alberta to its regulators on the oil sands "steaming process" that became an issue following a spill in Cold Lake (Pratt 2013).

THE THREE REGIME ELEMENTS

Environmental Policy and Related Green Ideas, Discourse, and Agendas

As highlighted in table 5.2, this first element of the book's analytical framework, the main policies and ideas in the Energy-Environment Regime, are very focused on energy. This is true in the statutory base of the regime and in related discourse about agenda development across fifty years and more of the story conveyed above.

Nuclear energy policy is anchored in values regarding the peaceful use of nuclear power as a source of electricity, mainly in Ontario, but with federal support via AECL and its Chalk River research capacities. The NEB-focused story reveals a strong energy development and export set of policy ideas, initially muted in the statutory utility-regulation language, including "public convenience and necessity," but then shifting to an overt goal of energy promotion. Later ideas and discourse spoke of the NEB's "enabling" role and its central task of being a responsible energy-development regulator. The EMR- and NRCan-focused prism for capturing the regime's essence has revealed an impetus for their establishment and a central mandate centred on an "integrated energy policy" under EMR and then a broader expressed and stressed goal of integrated natural resources policy with the formation of NRCan. Energy policy in the Harper era has been expressed in terms of responsible resource development in a booming oil sands era and in terms of Canada as an energy superpower and as an exporter of ethical oil.

The hyphenated environmental policy ideas of the Energy-Environment Regime show up in a small number of its core statutes, but also in other expressions of mandates, in websites and in continuous reporting, as environmental pressure and ideas emerged. In the nuclear energy sphere, safety was paramount in regulating reactors and in international concerns about controlling nuclear proliferation for weapons. Global reactor accidents were also a constant reminder of the core safety issues in Canada and in Canadian public opinion. Other ideas and environmental values to appear from the outset relate to the long-term storage of nuclear reactor wastes but also regarding uranium mining. Nuclear liability reflected safety policy and values in who should pay when things go wrong.

In the EMR- and NRCan-focused story of the Energy-Environment Regime, overall energy pipeline safety was present from the outset and was strengthened by explicit environmental assessment policy. The Berger Inquiry in the mid-1970s, and later developments, also brought out environmental concerns about northern pipelines and ecosystems and related concerns about Aboriginal peoples. Offshore energy development evoked ideas about fisheries conservation and common property resources. Ideas and discourse about the innovation economy also contained links to environmental industries and more broadly to sustainable development and energy. Later environmental aspects and concerns emerged on alternative energy in areas such a biofuels, carbon capture and storage as its long-term handling of carbon emissions in the name of climate change policy. Ideas such

Table 5.2: The Energy-Environment Regime and the three regime elements: Selected summary highlights periods examined

The three analytical elements

PERIODS EXAMINED	POLICIES, IDEAS, DISCOURSE, AND AGENDAS	POWER STRUCTURES, DEMOCRACY, AND GOVERNANCE	SCIENCE, EVIDENCE, KNOWLEDGE, AND PRECAUTION
• 1950s to present: nuclear energy and environment	• Peaceful nuclear power reactor development • Control of global nuclear proliferation • Reactor safety • Impact of global nuclear accidents, and safety lessons drawn • Long-term storage of nuclear wastes • Climate-change claims/ideas about nuclear as zero or low-GHG emitter • Uranium mining safety • Radio isotopes as beneficial health diagnostic • Nuclear as ideal for baseload electrical power • Privatization of some AECL assets • Nuclear liability policy • CANDU exports as "precarious opportunity"	• Federal role central via AECL as producer and research entity and CNSC as safety regulator • Core federal-Ontario partnership, with Ontario as dominant nuclear power user • CANDU reactors also in Quebec and New Brunswick • Tentative interest in CANDU use in western Canada in climate-change context • Canada is minor reactor exporter but a globally dominant and essential radio-isotopes producer • Anti-nuclear lobby exists but weaker than in some other countries • Saskatchewan uranium industry a global player • Ontario Hydro and now OPG a key power player • NWMO is focal point for long-delayed effort in credible long-term waste storage • Harper-era support for nuclear but in context of partial privatization of AECL to SNC-Lavalin	• CANDU as technologically unique, Canadian-developed reactor in global market • Radio-isotopes research and product development • Science and technology base of CNSC and of NWMO is central and recognized as such • Debate over extent to which nuclear industry claims re: zero or low GHG emissions are valid • Constant debates about the knowledge and technical base of long-term storage of wastes • Second-generation CANDUs developed • Extensive links with IAEA as global nuclear regulator and also vis-à-vis other national regulators (US)

Table 5.2: (*continued*)

PERIODS EXAMINED	The three analytical elements		
	POLICIES, IDEAS, DISCOURSE, AND AGENDAS	POWER STRUCTURES, DEMOCRACY, AND GOVERNANCE	SCIENCE, EVIDENCE, KNOWLEDGE, AND PRECAUTION
• 1959 to present: National Energy Board	• 1959 regulatory powers only as utility regulator but included criteria such as "public convenience and necessity"; implicit national energy policy role, but declined and delayed • Adopted promoting role of exports of oil and gas to United States • 1970s oil price and supply shocks • Left out of 1980 NEP as Liberal interventionist policy and creation of new regulators • Mulroney-era support for stronger NEB safety and environmental assessment role • Reinvented government ethos in NE • SD added to mandate via NRCan but finessed by NEB into "sustainable energy" development; • Harper-era NEB goals expressed as pipelines, energy development, and trade: "protect and enable" discourse in NEB reports • Responsible energy development law in Alberta with emulation in Harper-era similar discourse	• NEB independence but with some Cabinet oversight in early period • Functioned as closed shop with links only to the immediately regulated • Greater criticism and demands for participation from consumer and environmental groups, and electricity producers and interests • Left out of NEP discussions centred in EMR • NEB moved to Calgary in Mulroney era and thus close to oil and gas heartland • Offshore Petroleum Boards established to deal with offshore energy development but also fisheries in Atlantic Canada • Growing power of land-owner opposition in Alberta and effects on NEB and later approaches • NEB as non-player in climate-change and Kyoto Protocol policy • NEB consultation processes strengthened but very managerial as the result of growing concern about pipeline development and speed of approvals and decisions as oil sands boomed	• Technical knowledge is dominant in pipeline regulation • Economic knowledge of markets and pricing increasingly drawn on; focus on regulatory management capacities • complex new evidence mixes in recent multiple pipeline contexts

- 1966 to present: EMR and NRCan as lead players

- Integrated energy policy
- Early reports focus on energy supply and security after first OPEC oil-price and supply crisis
- Berger Inquiry brings environmental and Aboriginal ideas to forefront on northern gas pipeline
- EMR as author of 1980 NEP nationalist and interventionist energy policy
- Establishment earlier of Petro Canada
- Mulroney-era deregulation and market-based energy policy
- Energy free trade as part of Canada–US free trade agreement
- NRCan emerges from Liberal Red Book SD and innovation ideas/agenda
- Integrated resource development
- Ideas and discourse about resources in terms of "old" economy versus "new economy"
- competitive electricity ideas about electricity as essential service industry
- Electricity blackout and grid reliability and ideas about smart grids

- Statutory structure for federal energy policy gradually established
- Early EMR functioned almost as two departments (its technical branches versus newer economic and policy ones)
- OPEC power regarding 1973 and 1979–80 price and supply shocks and crises
- EMR and federal power asserted in NEP
- Growing environmental and Aboriginal peoples influence during and after Berger Inquiry
- Mulroney era that abolished the NEP and asserted need for market-based power and approaches
- Offshore regulatory boards established in Atlantic Canada
- Forestry interests increase influence and presence federally
- SD advanced and introduced but weak or difficult-to-assess adoption and implementation

- Traditional geo-science capacity in EMR and NRCan eras
- Electricity SD core expertise based in provinces and electricity utilities
- Economic and industry market analysis of growing importance
- Aboriginal knowledge and input increasing but very episodically
- Knowledge and analysis of aging pipeline and electricity infrastructure and need for smart and reliable grids

Table 5.2: (continued)

| | The three analytical elements | |
PERIODS EXAMINED	POLICIES, IDEAS, DISCOURSE, AND AGENDAS	POWER STRUCTURES, DEMOCRACY, AND GOVERNANCE	SCIENCE, EVIDENCE, KNOWLEDGE, AND PRECAUTION
• 2006 to present: Harper era	• Environment discourse avoided and recast as clean energy and as responsible energy and resource development • Canada as "energy superpower" and supplier of "ethical oil" • Speedier regulation and red-tape reduction • Carbon capture and storage in relation to long-term safe and secure storage • Alternative energy ideas focus on biofuels • Fracking and shale gas ideas mentioned but not as yet strongly advocated federally • West to east national pipeline ideas emerge and for electricity grids, but only tentatively • Oil transport plans and ideas in US and by CN Rail in Canada	• Harper direct power as prime minister exerted, centred on his Alberta political base and oil sands boom • Agricultural industry influence significant on biofuels, especially in Western Canada • IEA support for carbon capture in Canada and globally, as part of GHG-reduction solutions • Shale gas development in northern BC and consideration in other provinces • Political-economic duelling and complex claims for new or extended pipelines to move oil sands and oil to US and East Asian markets • US power/veto over Keystone XL pipeline • BC and Aboriginal power strong on Northern Gateway pipeline • Public opinion affects recent pipeline oil spills	• Hydraulic fracturing technology related to shale gas and thin oil • Carbon-capture and storage R&D support programs, especially with Alberta • Knowledge and impacts of biofuels on adverse impacts on grain and food production, as intended and unintended effects, nationally and globally • Complexity of cost-benefit advocacy and knowledge of multiple pipeline proposals • Knowledge of US energy market and supply changes

as speedier and more efficient regulation and reduction of red tape also had implications for environmental discourse. So also do assertions about competitive electricity regulation and management in an essential-service industry, including concerns about electricity-grid reliability and smart grids.

Environmental Power Structures,
Democracy, and Governance

Table 5.2 conveys a complex and changing element in environmental power structures, democracy, and governance. This is a regime where energy corporations and developers had the most consistent political and economic power base. But in nuclear energy the political-economy power structure was government centred and federal-Ontario centred, anchored in AECL but also crucially in Ontario Hydro and later OPG. Saskatchewan is also a major player in the related uranium supply industry. SNC-Lavalin now has private ownership of key AECL reactor industry assets, but overall the public and private nuclear reactor industry does not have great political leverage because of its small role in global reactor sales. The anti-nuclear lobby has been present throughout but is not as robust as in other countries.

The NEB has been a central player in regulating Canada's mainly privately owned oil and gas industry and indeed in the 1990s was relocated from Ottawa to Calgary, where it functions in close proximity to the power centre of the energy industry in Alberta and vis-à-vis the Alberta government. Power politics and policy in energy have also been changed and affected by offshore governance approaches regarding Atlantic Canada, and within Alberta by strong lobbying by property owners battling for property rights vis-à-vis energy companies and their exploration and development.

Energy power within the federal government has had periods of dormancy and also political power surges. EMR lay low for many years, including during the oil pricing and supply crisis in the early 1970s and then was the dominant force in the Liberal NEP era of the early 1980s. Political and governance changes surged in a different direction under Mulroney-era energy deregulation and free trade. Later, as NRCan was formed, forestry industry interests were given a stronger base in the new department. This period also brought in the greater presence of sustainable development ideas in the NRCan mandate, linked to ideas about the innovation economy.

In the Harper era, the Energy-Environment Regime has seen a resurgence of the political and governance power of energy centred in the oil sands boom in Alberta and in the Harper Conservatives' own electoral base as both a minority and majority federal government. Political power and governance has also been affected by the sudden shale gas boom in the United States and the search for oil sands markets in a shrinking US market, and in the search by Canadian governments and the energy industry for new export markets to Asia. All of this converged in the current major battle over multiple pipeline proposals.

Science, Evidence, Knowledge, and Precaution

This third and final analytical element reveals the different degrees to which science, evidence, knowledge, and precaution emerge as characteristics of the regime. The precautionary principle is not an overt part of any Canadian energy policy. De facto precaution, however, can be seen in the politics, science, and practice of solving the problem of the long-term storage of nuclear wastes. Such long-term storage has nowhere been successfully put into practice.

The nuclear energy field reflects a strong science base that was essential to Canada researching and developing the CANDU reactor. A strong nuclear science capacity is critical to the functioning of both AECL and the CNSC, in concert with the IAEA as the key international body. The Canadian nuclear industry's ability more recently to mount credible evidence for its pro–climate change stance depended on the broader international and national efforts to assemble data on the GHG emissions of competing fuel sources.

The NEB, in contrast, depends on its own and others' credible technical knowledge on oil and gas pipelines and their regulation. As an energy-development promoter/enabler, it also depends on economic knowledge of markets and projects. It also draws on its own and industry managerial knowledge in part through the public hearings it conducts. Regarding the closely related EMR and NRCan stories surveyed, one sees levels of relative knowledge. EMR and then NRCan still contain strong geo-science knowledge, traceable back to the Geological Survey of Canada. Both departments, in different eras and different policy advice contexts, had to develop and improve economic knowledge. It remains weaker in energy realms such as electricity, where the core expertise is with provincial regulators and mainly public utility electricity suppliers. This is true also on current issues such as aging electricity infrastructure (and also for aging pipelines). And its knowledge of Aboriginal peoples and their energy needs, concerns, and options is very episodic at best.

In the Harper era, federally but mainly in Alberta, the science and technical evidence needed to support carbon capture and storage is underway. Biofuels development has received considerable industrial and public research funding but arguably less on the unintended or unexamined environmental effects on food systems and agriculture. At some basic level, Canadian agencies, federal and provincial, had some working knowledge of hydraulic fracturing and the shale gas revolution but much less so on the impact it is having and is likely to have on the American market and hence on Canada's North American energy export prospects. The environmental effects on the potentially hundreds of different unique shale gas sites is also almost by definition minimalist at present.

CONCLUSIONS

This chapter has traced the evolution and current characteristics of the federal Energy-Environment Regime through an examination of four policy and governance histories and their related historical time frames: nuclear energy policy, the National Energy Board, energy policy via the origins and trajectories of EMR and NRCan as lead departments and ministries, and energy policy in the Harper era from 2006 to the present. Not surprisingly it has been mainly an energy policy and statutory story driven by energy-development firms and industrial structures related cumulatively to different energy fuels and sources nationally, provincially, and regionally, particularly in relation to Canada-US energy trade and relations.

The story overall covers some energy fuels such as nuclear that begins in the 1950s and extends to the present as varied accounts of oil and gas policy and governance, the current oil sands pinnacle, provincial-centred hydroelectricity development, and related fuels and technologies such as biofuels and shale gas, but also a constant energy infrastructure story related to pipelines and electricity grids. And of course, although we are proceeding with a federal government focus, we have seen in fundamental ways how energy and its multiple fuel sources are anchored in provincial jurisdiction and in the light of diverse energy and resource endowments. Though provincial jurisdiction in energy is pivotal overall, the federal government has considerable room for its own involvement in international trade, interprovincial energy matters, and the North, as well as Aboriginal peoples.

The analysis has shown the continuous but largely secondary presence of environmental values and concerns from the outset, certainly in nuclear power but also in slower and somewhat more episodic and uneven ways regarding other fuels and of course the interactions among fuels on both the producer and consumer side of the market equation. The Energy-Environment Regime has been influenced by the concurrent development of the Environment Canada–Centred Regime and by the presence within its own ambit of mandated, legislated, and expressed environmental values and ideas, including those expressed as safety, clean energy, and cleaner energy; GHG emission reductions and climate change; and sustainable development, sustainable energy, renewable energy and low carbon policies, some meaningful and some more rhetorical or whose impacts are difficult to discern.

This chapter, in concert with earlier chapters, has shown that energy policies and power centres at their highest agenda peaks are not very friendly to overall environmental matters, nor do they demonstrate much inclination to even address them. This was true in the earliest NEB years, the early 1980s heyday of the NEP, the Chrétien and Harper Kyoto Protocol era, and the current Harper-era oil sands boom, where the search for markets has shifted sharply and relatively suddenly, and the battle over competing pipelines are the private and public weapons of choice.

In relation to our green-lite analytical and empirical features, the Energy-Environment Regime reveals several examples. These include in profound green-lite temporal terms the unsolved issues regarding the storage of nuclear wastes over hundreds of years, where legitimacy and trust is massively difficult if not impossible to garner. The overall policy and consultation processes involve multi-scalar levels and realms, communities, and Aboriginal peoples but have failed to deal with ethical and social issues. There are also temporal features centred on periodic nuclear accident–driven crises. These disasters immediately affect markets and nuclear regulatory safety approaches, including those at the Canadian Nuclear Safety Commission. They also become linked to ideas, policies, and practices regarding nuclear safety liability.

The NEB policy history shows how the NEB finessed Mulroney- and Chrétien-era sustainable development policy pressure in a green-lite "ends-means calculus and conflict" type of policy and governance pattern. It was very reluctant to see its statutory mandate contain SD obligations, but it did argue in its annual reports that it did in fact practise it in the "triple bottom line" sense of the concept. In later annual reports in both Liberal and Harper eras, the NEB also argued that its goal was *sustainable energy development*, which may or may not mean sustainable development.

The policy and governance history of NRCan as an energy depart-ment in Liberal and Conservative eras has shown different kinds and complexities of risk, centred on the oceans and the fisheries as a com-mon property resource. This still reflects green-lite features centred on the tragedy of the commons and complex multi-scalar coordina-tion problems but also of a temporal kind. As we have suggested, they were not even close to being solved in the more pro-environmental Mulroney era, and they have been harmed further by Harper-era weakening of the Fisheries Act in the name of responsible resource development.

The brief look at policies that support a Canadian biofuels indus-try is certainly a relevant example of green-lite features of the means-ends calculus and conflict kind. Federal policy has certainly been cast in terms of agricultural and Western Canadian farm interests. But, as shown above, an IISD report stressed that environmental impacts that might arise from accelerated biofuels production are not even being evaluated.

Finally, the chapter's discussion of carbon capture and storage CCS as a Harper-era technology-focused solution to climate change shows that CCS is replete with green-lite features of the temporal kind but also of the multi-scalar kinds regarding storage sites. Though such emission hazards are different from those in storing long-term nuclear wastes, they face similar temporal challenges in even contemplating multi-century systems of monitoring and regula-tory trust.

The chapter's discussion of NRCan has brought out briefly the greater political and institutional presence federally of the forestry industry and of forestry as a natural resource and also to some extent of offshore oil governance in relation to oceans and fisheries. But we have barely scratched the surface of these issues, hence the need to proceed in chapter 6 to an analysis and understanding of the Natural Resources–Environment Regime.

6

The Natural
Resources–Environment Regime

INTRODUCTION

Canada's resource wealth has long been the fulcrum for political and policy debate over how to use these resources for the betterment of Canadians, now and in the future. Complicating matters is the discord created by the separation of powers between the federal and provincial governments over natural resources and the regional concentration of particular resources. More recently, significant changes have occurred within Canada and the global economy to affect resource policy decisions at all levels of government.

In this chapter, we explore the Natural Resources–Environment Regime. To get traction on the complicated terrain that this regime presents, we contrast three natural resources: forests, fisheries, and minerals. Energy is treated alone in chapter 5. We recognize that this focused approach leaves out certain resources that have gained considerable attention, especially water and species at risk. When particularly important, we mention these other resources; however, we retain the focused comparative perspective, as it allows us to trace the regime from the vantage point of resources that experience quite different jurisdictional divisions between the levels of government in Canadian federalism. From this we observe two general patterns.

The first involves the often-noted ebb and flow of federal involvement in natural resource governance, which has frequently coincided with shocks from the global economy or other downturns in the fortunes of a given resource sector. For instance, the federal government has cyclically taken greater interest in the forest sector when the industry is ailing (Howlett 1989); the status of many ocean fisheries have gone through several high and low production years driven by overfishing and other causes (Gough 2007). Mining, too, has seen cycles of good and bad times that motivate government action.

The second pattern is a more notable shift, wherein the issues to be considered in decisions to govern natural resources have broadened. These shifts included the increasing importance of Aboriginal peoples, as a product of more proactive legal action and as a consequence of provisions in the Constitution Act of 1982. Also relevant here is the increased liberalization of trade, such as through the North America Free Trade Agreement (NAFTA), the World Trade Organization (WTO), and foreign investment protection agreements, as well as through disputes specifically with the United States over softwood lumber; this trade liberalization has particular implications for Canada as a major exporter of resources. Finally, after the 1992 Rio Earth Summit, attempts were made to have environmental concerns more deeply woven into the fabric of Canada's natural resource policies, in part but by no means exclusively through the creation of Natural Resources Canada in 1993 as a broader natural resource focal point in the federal government and with a nascent sustainable development mandate.

However, the last several years have brought overt retrenchment. Just as with fish, minerals, and timber in previous eras, oil and gas has become the staple of choice for the Harper government, and, incrementally at first, the recent direction has been an accelerated rethinking of the ideas of sustainable development, with "responsible" resource development taking centre stage (Toner and McKee 2014).

This chapter reviews forty years of environment and natural resource policy in Canada, with an emphasis on the federal government's role. It begins with crucial details of the original division of powers between the provinces and the federal government, dating back to 1867, as central to the tenor and focus of conflict over natural resource policy up to the 1970s. The 1980s marked a significant shift owing to the changes contained in section 92A of the Constitution Act of 1982, though we highlight how the federal government continued to episodically take on greater roles on a resource-by-resource basis. In the post-1992 period, the federal role embraced, sometimes half-heartedly, the aims of sustainable development. The final period highlights the Harper government's shift in focus to responsible resource development. To conclude, the chapter uses the historical review and the authors' three regime elements to trace change and inertia in the natural resource–environment regime, elucidating the specific green-lite realities that the empirics reveal.

RESOURCE PROMOTER (AND REGULATOR?): 1867 TO 1970S

We begin late in the history of Canada's resource exploitation. Since colonial times, minerals, wildlife, forest products, and agricultural production have been central to Canada's existence. Much of this resource wealth was found on Crown lands, for which responsibility was given to the provinces. In BC, for instance, 94 per cent of the province is Crown land. More easterly provinces have a greater share of private ownership, as a result of the history of land deeds in the early period of colonization. In New Brunswick, as an example, only 48 per cent of lands are provincially owned.

Since Confederation, natural resources have involved a complicated division of overlapping provincial and federal powers. The original jurisdictional divisions were set out in the 1867 British North America (BNA) Act. Under section 109, the BNA Act gave provinces (at the time Ontario, Quebec, New Brunswick, and Nova Scotia) ownership of land and resources; similar provisions were extended to British Columbia, Prince Edward Island, and Newfoundland (now Newfoundland and Labrador) when each joined Confederation (Hessing, Howlett, and Summerville 2005; Howlett 1991). The situation was different for Manitoba, Alberta, and Saskatchewan, each of which was established from lands purchased by the federal government from the Hudson's Bay Company in 1889; these three provinces were granted control over Crown land from the federal government in 1930 (Hessing, Howlett, and Summerville 2005). The BNA Act also gave provinces jurisdiction to make laws affecting the management and sale of provincially owned public lands and any timber resources these lands supplied (section 92(5)) (Department of Justice 2013). The federal government was given more exclusive rights to make laws concerning fisheries resources (through sections 91(10) on navigation and shipping, and 91(12) on sea coast and inland fisheries). It also gained some sway over natural resources through its powers to regulate trade and commerce (section 91(2)) and its powers to raise "Money by any Mode or System of Taxation" (section 91(3)). The provinces, by contrast, were given power only for direct taxation within their respective provincial territories (section 92(2)) (Department of Justice 2013).

Not surprisingly, the overlapping jurisdiction over natural resources has greatly affected the development of this hyphenated regime. Although, as time progressed, the breadth of issues at stake in resource-governance decisions has expanded, provincial ownership of land and legal jurisdiction over resources featured as an ongoing point of conflict between the levels of government. By the time of Confederation, Hessing, Howlett, and Summerville (2005) explain that resource royalties were the largest source of provincial revenues and that this period involved considerable struggle between the federal and provincial governments over access to and control of these rents.

Through this period, questions of jurisdiction were still handled by the Judicial Committee of the Privy Council (JCPC) in the United Kingdom; the Supreme Court became the highest court only in 1949. Observers have noted, moreover, how most challenges were decided by the JCPC in favour of greater provincial powers, such as by limiting the interpreted strength and scope of the federal Parliament's trade and commerce powers while weighing more heavily the province's ownership of land and resources (Bushnell 1980; MacIvor 2006).

The general pattern that followed involved the federal government overseeing its own lands, and seeking to influence provincial policies through "reason and persuasion" (Hessing, Howlett, and Summerville 2005). Also, beginning in 1972, the federal government started work on a process for assessing the environmental impact of projects over which the federal government had some decision-making authority; this work represents an initial instance of green-lite features in agenda setting for the hyphenated resources regime. The decision-making authority increased in formality in the coming years via a Cabinet directive, termed the Guidelines Order, created in 1974 (refined in 1977) and formally established in 1984 as a consequence of the Government Organization Act of 1979 (Hanebury 1990). Through this period, the federal government did, however, also seek greater influence episodically. It exerted control over resource production and prices during the two world wars (Hessing, Howlett, and Summerville 2005), and it has since sought to influence resource policy generally on a resource-by-resource basis in a reoccurring manner.

With fisheries, the pattern has been more consistent, though concerns for provincial interests have also been pivotal. Federal parliamentary powers over the sea coast and inland fisheries, in part, were the basis for the establishment of the Department of Marine and Fisheries back in 1867 (Department of Marine and Fisheries 1869). Fisheries remained the explicit focus until 1969, when the department's name changed to the Department of Fisheries and Forestry, as the Forestry Branch of the former federal Department of Forestry and Rural Development was added to its remit (Department of Fisheries and Forestry 1970).

In spite of the clearer constitutional powers, there remained federal-provincial tensions over fisheries policy. A central point of friction was trade-offs between local and regional development concerns and the broader, national economic benefits from resource exploitation. As Schrank (1995, 291) notes in reflection on the precursors to the cod fishery collapse, "Perhaps the fundamental administrative problem is that the Department of Fisheries and Oceans (DFO) has suffered from a policy schizophrenia, never being able to determine whether its chief goal is to set and implement policy for the fishery as a viable industry or whether it is to maximize employment and save non-viable communities." This DFO dilemma itself illustrates the complex boundary and temporal features of our green-lite concept.

Moreover, this tension, as Schrank details, was evident in the provincial-federal relations surrounding the move by the federal government to extend Canada's coastal jurisdiction. In the 1970s, Canada was part of international negotiations on oceans and the law of the sea. Since the Second World War, there had been growing pressure on fisheries resources and increasing calls for international action to better manage oceans. Three UN Conferences on the Law of the Sea were held in 1958, 1960, and 1973, with the aim of generating agreement on a new regime for the oceans. The first of these negotiated the Convention on Fishing and Conservation of the Living Resources of the High Seas that came into force in 1966 (Garcia 1992). The subsequent negotiations led to, among other things, a framework for extending territorial sovereignty from 3 to 12 nautical miles and by providing coastal states with a 200-nautical-mile Exclusive Economic Zone (EEZ), where they would control fishing and mining rights (deFontaubert 1995). Unilateral implementation of these provisions happened during the 1970s, and then, in 1982, the UN Convention on the Law of the

Sea (UNCLOS) was formally opened for signatures, a culmination of nine years of negotiations (United Nations 1998).

These discussions were highly relevant to domestic politics and policy of fisheries resources, as the result of an understanding of an impending problem of overcapacity and overfishing on the East Coast. Schrank (1995) explains that, since 1970, the federal Department of Fisheries and Forestry had been aware of the problem of overcapacity in the Canadian East Coast fishery and had proposed measures to rationalize the industry to ensure better returns for individual fishing operators and more sustainable annual catches. Recognizing that this would have substantial effects for the region, the extension of Canada's coastal economic jurisdiction via the 200-nautical-mile EEZ was a welcome option, as it provided a short-term, less-painful solution to address the tension between incumbent interests in the fisheries sector and the long-run sustainability of the fishery; rather than having to rationalize, Canadian fishing operators could seemingly displace foreign fleets to increase the Canadian share of the total East Coast fishery (Schrank 1995). We return to this below in discussing the subsequent collapse of the cod fishery. Here, it is relevant, however, for illustrating that even where the federal government had greater jurisdiction over fisheries resources, provincial interests were still a critical consideration, particularly those focused on economic development and competitiveness in their region. Still, in 1977 an amendment to the Fisheries Act set requirements for habitat loss, in response to growing concerns over spawning grounds for salmon in BC; the new requirements, guided by the "polluter-pays" principle, included penalties for activities that negatively affected habitat (Gough 2007, 307).

Provincial officials were also keenly interested in the negotiations leading to UNCLOS as the result of proposals on seabed mining in areas beyond national jurisdiction; Ontario had representatives advising the federal negotiators on nickel mining, as any agreement might have created competition for a critical mineral sector of the province's economy (Riddell-Dixon 1989, 96–104). Previous disputes over seabed resources had also occurred between the provincial and federal governments. In the mid-1960s, the federal government sent a reference case to the Supreme Court of Canada asking the justices to rule on the federal and provincial jurisdiction over the seabed beneath the territorial waters and beneath the waters extending beyond the territorial waters to the limit of the Continental

Shelf (Head 1966; the reference case was limited to waters off the coast of BC). At the time, provinces were issuing offshore exploration permits, as was the federal government. Both claimed authority, leading to a complicated conflict over rights and responsibilities (Fitzgerald 1991). Even though the court sided with Canada, the federal government negotiated a settlement that gave some extractive rights to coastal provinces, and it agreed to share with the provinces any revenues from mineral extraction that accrued from seabed resources it would control. Still, Quebec continued to claim jurisdiction over the seabed along its coasts, and Newfoundland took a similar position a few years later with the aim of securing control of coastal oil and gas resources (Swan 1975).

For other resources, the 1960s and 1970s involved events that increased tensions over possible greater centralized federal control. Two separate processes played out. First, the increased planning and administrative capacity of the provinces made joint federalism – "sharing of decision-making powers and financial responsibility for particular programs or projects between the two levels of government" (Smiley 1964, 373) – less tenable. Up to the 1960s, much of the intergovernmental relations were managed by professionalized bureaucrats who brought shared language, expertise, and training to negotiations over how to handle overlapping federal and provincial powers. As provinces sought greater control over longer-term planning of their financial and programmatic affairs, it became increasingly apparent that unilateral action by either level of government was problematic; this created a perceived need for mechanisms that would facilitate greater ongoing federal-provincial consultations on a range of policy matters (Smiley 1964).

For resource policy in general, these developments were most clearly articulated in the lead up to and during a 1961 conference – "Resources for Tomorrow" – held in Montreal. The conference was supported by all provinces but driven by the Diefenbaker government (Best 1960). Three years of research and planning had gone into the conference, and perceptions at the time were that it offered an opportunity to cast a problem-oriented perspective on the role and potential of resource policy in Canada (Miller 1961). Indeed, for some time, Canadian professional foresters had voiced concerns over the state of forest resources, and these concerns received specific attention at the 1961 conference (Fellows 1986); Diefenbaker had also established the first federal Department of Forests in 1960

to exert more influence over the sector (Howlett 1989). After the
Montreal conference, a commentator explained a key issue: "It
was Ottawa's hope that the conference would demonstrate to the
provinces that co-operation between themselves and the federal
Government could be achieved despite political differences. The
conference proved the point, but it also accentuated the fact that
the provinces jealously guard their constitutional rights to their
own resources, and look with much suspicion at any attempt by
Ottawa to concern itself with resource problems outside its jurisdiction" (Gray 1962). In recognition of the need to explore new
means for cooperation between the levels of government and among
the provinces (ibid.), one outcome of the conference was the formal
establishment in 1963 of the Canadian Council of Resource Ministers
(CCRM), which later became the Canadian Council of Resource
and Environment Ministers (CCREM) in 1971 (Sproule-Jones, Johns,
and Heinmiller 2008, 79).

The second process that emerged at this time involved a shift in
constitutional jurisprudence on the division of provincial and federal powers. It occurred as the Supreme Court of Canada took its
role as the highest Canadian court from 1949 forward. A series of
cases in this period – particularly two in 1977 and 1978 involving
policies the Saskatchewan government had put in place to regulate
the potash industry – began to reverse the positions established
by decisions of the JCPC. An analysis of case law on provincial and
federal jurisdiction over resource policy by Bushnell (1980, 317)
concluded, "The present trend of the interpretation of the trade and
commerce power by the Supreme Court towards restriction of provincial power over matters which have economic ramifications outside the province leads to the conclusion that control over natural
resources is passing or indeed has passed to the Dominion [federal
Parliament] through the trade and commerce power." These rulings
put the provinces on notice. As Howlett (1991, 129) explains in relation to the potash cases, "The impact of the decision was to put into
doubt the validity of all existing and future provincial tax and roy-
alty schemes in the resource sector. This was due to the fact that
most resources are exported from their province of origins. As
such, according to the Court's reasoning, any provincial tax or roy-
alty could be interpreted as affecting export prices and, therefore,
interfering with the federal trade and commerce power" (see also
Cairns 1992).

This second trend fuelled disquiet among the provinces that had been building over the 1970s concerning their respective control over resources. During meetings of the provincial premiers at the time, it was agreed that natural resources were a salient issue to be discussed with the federal government. Chandler (1986) details the attention this issue received at the First Ministers' Constitutional Conference in 1978, which presaged the negotiations of a resource amendment to the BNA Act. Indeed, the Continuing Committee of Ministers on the Constitution that was a product of the 1978 meeting gave particular attention, as Chandler (1986, 112–13) explains, to five issues: "the definition of natural resources; the definition of primary production; federal jurisdiction over trade and commerce in relation to natural resources; provincial access to indirect taxation in relation to natural resources and the use of the federal government's declaratory power regarding natural resources." We pick up on this critical issue below as we discuss the Constitution Act of 1982.

CHANGING TERMS OF THE RELATIONSHIP: 1980S

The 1980s brought several changes to the federal role on natural resources – some episodic, others more permanent. On the latter, the most notable shift came with the patriation of the BNA Act and the drafting of the Constitution Act of 1982. The episodic changes – each different for fisheries, forestry, and mining – came with the ebbing and flowing of ambitions in Ottawa to see more centralized control over Canadian natural resource policies. The period also ended, as we have seen in chapter 2, with what has been viewed as the second wave of public concern for the environment (the first occurring in the early 1970s) (Hoberg and Harrison 1994). We review these further as a crucial starting point in this period.

The Constitution Act of 1982 shifted federal-provincial relations. Building on earlier work, in the latter years of the 1970s, the federal government had been leading efforts to craft an agreement that culminated in Bill C-60, which was introduced to the House of Commons in June 1978. The provinces proposed an alternative termed the "Best Effort" draft, which was developed in 1978 and presented to the first ministers in February 1979 (Howlett 1991). Differences between the federal and provincial proposals hinged in part on attention to natural resources, including indirect taxation and resource regulation. While it appeared there was a large gap to bridge to reach a settlement, Howlett (1991) explains in detail that the federal government held the position that the provinces should be able to indirectly tax resources and that a clarification of the division of powers between the levels of government was necessary, particularly in light of the recent Supreme Court of Canada decisions in the potash cases. In this respect, the eventual resolution was not as hard to achieve as might have seemed.

A full discussion of the negotiations and outcomes is beyond the scope of this chapter; instead, we focus attention on two key provisions. First, the addition of section 92A to the original BNA Act clarified provincial versus federal jurisdiction over natural resources, particularly forestry, non-renewables, and electricity production. Within their territory, provinces were given the powers to make laws concerning exploration for non-renewables (92A(1)(a)) and concerning development, conservation, and management for the non-renewable and forestry resources (92A(1)(b)), as well as electric power generation (92A(1)(c)). The provinces were also given the ability to make laws on the interprovincial trade of the above resources, so long as such laws were not discriminatory in prices or exports (92A1(2)). The federal Parliament retained the power, through the provisions on trade and commerce, to make laws on these matters as well, and in the case of a conflict, the federal rules were to prevail (92A1(3)). With taxation, the provinces had their powers extended to include making laws to raise money by any means from primary production and electrical power generation (92A1(4)(a) and (b)), and a schedule was included that outlined the specific meaning of "primary production" (Department of Justice 2013).

Chandler (1986) explains that a key shift that this created involved the role provinces were given over interprovincial trade of primary products. Before 1982 the trade and commerce powers of the federal government had been justification for the Supreme Court of Canada to deem provincial laws ultra vires; after 1982 the federal government would have to actively develop rules to exert "paramountcy." In this way, section 92A (specifically section 92A1(3)) was a remedy for the shift in jurisprudence noted above and that Howlett (1991) explained was an unwelcome surprise to the federal and provincial governments alike. As Cairns (1992, 66) notes, "The amendment moves the discussion of what were essentially political matters away from the courts, which could give only all-or-nothing decisions, and into the political arena, where a multiplicity of interests must be balanced by the concurrent policymaking of the two orders of government."

Beyond the specific clarifications made to the federal and provincial roles in natural resources governance, a second consequence of the Constitution Act of 1982 was to afford greater opportunities for Aboriginal peoples to influence this hyphenated regime. Section 35 of the Constitution Act of 1982 recognized the rights of Aboriginal peoples in Canada, including in section 35(1) that "the existing aboriginal and treaty rights of the aboriginal peoples of Canada are hereby recognized and affirmed" (Department of Justice 2013). As Hessing, Howlett, and Summerville (2005, 70) note, "Although claims and rights of First Nations in Canada date back to the initial contacts with European colonizers and subsequent seventeenth-, eighteenth-, and nineteenth-century treaties and administrative arrangements, they began to receive continuous explicit constitutional status binding the actions of Canadian government only after 1982."

A particularly important case – the 1990 *Sparrow* case[*] – involved a dispute over the rights of a British Columbia (BC) First Nation – the Musqueam Nation – to fish for ceremonial purposes. The Musqueam argued that their right to fish was protected under section 35(1) of the Constitution Act of 1982 (Department of Justice 2013); they held that fishing was an existing right and should therefore be protected (Asch and Macklem 1991). The Supreme Court found that the management regime for Fraser River salmon had to give priority to these rights after conservation objectives and treaty allocations with the United States were met (Clancy 2008; Schwindt and Vining 2008). Nearly ten years later, the *Marshall* case[†] supported the Mi'kmaq's right to harvest and sell fish as part of their treaty rights in the Maritimes, again conditional on appropriate conservation measures being met (Clancy 2008; Hessing, Howlett, and Summerville 2005). Across natural resource sectors, court challenges by Aboriginal peoples of policy decisions affecting their traditional

[*] *Ronald Edward Sparrow v R* [1990] 1 SCR 1075, 70 DLR (4th) 385, 4 WWR 410, 56 CCC (3d) 263, 3 CNLR 160, 46 BCLR (2d) 1.

[†] *R v Marshall* (No. 1) [1999] 3 SCR 456 & *R v Marshall* (No. 2) [1999] 3 SCR 533.

territories or treaty rights have multiplied (McAllister 2007). And although the effects have been mixed, the opportunities afforded by the courts were generally enhanced from 1982 forward.

In addition to this more permanent shift in the separation of powers, the federal government continued its pattern of episodically giving attention to certain natural resources. As we discussed in chapter 5, the Trudeau Liberal government, through the Department of Energy, Mining and Resources, led the National Energy Program (NEP) from 1980 to 1983; concurrently, the Trudeau government also developed a forest strategy released in 1981 (Howlett 1989). With the election of the Mulroney Conservative government in 1984, centralizing as envisioned by the NEP was rescinded in favour of market-based approaches, such as the deregulation of crude marketing and pricing (Cairns 1992).

At the same time, however, the Mulroney government redoubled efforts to increase the federal role in forest management to assist the ailing sector (Mulgrew 1984). The initiative was multi-fold. Budget allocations for 1985–90 rose from $225 million to $1 billion, and a new Ministry of State for Forests, headed by Gerald Merrithew, was created (Howlett 1989). In 1985, the Canadian Council of Forest Ministers (CCFM) was also formed, and three years later, the CCREM became the CCME once again (Sproule-Jones, Johns, and Heinmiller 2008, 79).

Also in 1985, the federal government convened a series of regional workshops to discuss different challenges facing the forest sector; these culminated in the National Forest Congress held in Ottawa in April 1986 (Waddell 1985). The result of the workshops and the Ottawa meeting was a National Forest Sector Strategy, which was drafted by a task force of deputy ministers, industry representatives, environmental groups, labour, academia, and professional foresters; the strategy was released in 1987 and detailed recommendations on a series of issues, including market access and market development, investment, forest management, employment, research and development, and public awareness (Canadian Council of Forest Ministers 1987). Although Howlett (1989) notes the limited role given to the federal government in the strategy, the process itself was an uptick in federal attention, and the federal government did announce the initiation of a federal Department of Forestry in 1988. The new department was given the mandate "to promote the sustainable development and competitiveness of the Canadian forest sector for the well-being of present and future generations of Canadians" (qtd in Auditor General of Canada 1993).

This period was also punctuated by a dispute with the United States over Canadian exports of softwood lumber to the US market. The dispute centred on whether Canadian policies in some way subsidized forest operators harvesting timber from public lands, because they were allegedly charged below-market prices for the right to cut public timber (known as the stumpage rate). Subsequent rounds also focused on whether other policies, such as those regulating forest practices, were potential additional sources of advantage for Canadian producers. A 1982 petition from the US Coalition for Fair Lumber Imports to the US Department of Commerce was unsuccessful; a second petition in 1986 after a change in US law led to a successful determination that Canadian producers were unfairly subsidized, which justified a countervailing duty of 15 per cent on imports. In 1986, Canada and the United States signed a memorandum of understanding that saw the Canadian government impose a 15 per cent tariff on the value of softwood lumber to the United States in lieu of the US-imposed duty (Hessing, Howlette, and Summerville 2005). This disagreement and resolution was also pivotal in the dynamics that led to the signing of the 1988 Canada-US Free Trade Agreement (Doern and Tomlin 1991). And as we further discuss below, it set in motion a sequence of ongoing disputes with the US timber industry continually seeking redress for the purported unfair support offered by government to Canadian producers.

With mining, there were similar economic challenges in the 1980s, as mine closures outpaced mine openings (McAllister and Alexander 1997, 6). Annual exploration expenditures were up in the first two years of the 1980s and down and flat from 1982 to 1986; they peaked in 1987 at over $1 billion, and then dropped to half this by 1990 (McAllister 2007; McAllister and Alexander 1997, 6, 21–3).

The 1980s also involved some continued negotiations between the federal government and certain Atlantic provinces over offshore resources. We noted above that Newfoundland claimed powers over offshore resources. Though the Supreme Court of Canada had ruled that Canada held these offshore rights, in the early to mid-1980s the federal government negotiated the Nova Scotia Accord and the Atlantic Accord with Newfoundland. These agreements delegated authority to the provinces to collect royalties from offshore resource development as well as giving them a role in the management (Cairns 1992).

On the other coast, the powers over the seabed were complicated by a reference case that addressed the jurisdiction over Georgia
Strait (the body of water between the mainland of BC and Vancouver
Island). The BC Court of Appeal ruled that, as inland waters (not
part of the territorial seas or the continental shelf), the seabed should
be considered under BC's jurisdiction; on appeal, the Supreme Court
agreed (Fitzgerald 1991).

With fisheries, the 1980s involved the ending of some long-
standing support programs. As Gough (2007, 382) explains, "Since
the war, the department had subsidized construction of many new
fishing vessels. In the 1970s numbers could run to several hundred a
year. Now, with fleet over-capacity widely recognized, the department in 1986 ended its boatbuilding subsidies. The Department of
Industry, Trade and Commerce had also given a separate subsidy for
vessels over 65 feet long, including many large trawlers. This program ended by 1985." Not all supports were removed, however;
vessel insurance programs continued, for instance (Gough 2007).
New policies were also introduced in an attempt to move from a
focus on maximizing the volume of fisheries to increasing their
value. As in other jurisdictions, individual fishing quotas or individual transferable quotas were used for certain fisheries, with mixed
response. Over time, however, they became an increasingly important instrument that covered a rising share of the total landed value
of fisheries (Gough 2007, 380; Hilborn, Orensanz, and Parma 2005;
McCay et al. 1995).

At the close of the 1980s, there were two important developments.
First, as discussed in chapter 4, the federal government's approach to
environmental impact assessment faced two court challenges that
created the impetus for legislative changes. Both cases – one concerning the Rafferty Dam project in Saskatchewan and the other the
Oldman River Dam in southern Alberta – involved whether the environmental impact assessment process in place at the time created
binding legal requirements for federal departments to pursue assessments of projects that came under their remit. With both cases, the
Federal Court of Appeal ruled against the federal government. As
Hanebury (1990, 96) explained, "These Court decisions established
the Guidelines Order as a far reaching process which had to be relied
upon whenever a federal decision was made if that decision might
have an environmental effect on an area of federal responsibility."
Not unlike concerns over importing US-style adversarial legalism in

the discussion of species at risk that would commence in the 1990s (Illical and Harrison 2007), the federal government was wary of the implications of these court rulings for ministerial discretion over policy implementation; this became one motivation for the enactment of the Canadian Environmental Assessment Act of 1992.

Second, the end of the 1980s witnessed a second wave of public concern over the environment (the first occurred in the early 1970s). As Hoberg and Harrison (1994, 122) note, "Gallup reported that the percentage of Canadians who perceived the dangers of pollution to be 'very serious,' which had declined between the early 1970s and the mid-1980s to a low of 51 per cent, began to increase again in 1985, reaching an all-time high of 77 per cent by 1990." The polls at the time also asked Canadians the level of government they felt should address environmental concerns; the majority indicated that it ought to be the federal government (Hoberg and Harrison 1994). Although the Mulroney government had been advancing a cost-cutting agenda in the latter years of the 1980s, this second major uptick in public support for environmental protection was heeded (see chapter 2).

Under the lead of Lucien Bouchard, as environment minister, a process began in 1989 to develop an environmental plan. The initiative faced resistance from within the government due to turf battles among departments but also the cost. Public consultations followed, as requested by Cabinet, and were run by Bouchard's successor, Robert de Cotret, who facilitated extensive public engagement comprising information sessions and two-day consultations across the country; the process culminated with a session in Ottawa attended by 400 stakeholders (Hoberg and Harrison 1994). The Green Plan, announced in December 1990, was the product; it involved a $3 billion program focused on eight broad categories of actions, including a category on sustaining renewable resources (Doern 1993a; Gale 1997; Hoberg and Harrison 1994).

Much like other initiatives, however, the ambition of the Green Plan was constrained, in part, by federal-provincial relations. As Howlett (1989) found with the 1987 Forest Strategy, Hoberg and Harrison (1994) provide an assessment of the Green Plan's initiatives that indicates the bulk (56 per cent) could be categorized as focusing on information, including instruments addressing research, public participation, and technology development and demonstration projects, among others. Only twenty-eight initiatives (12 per cent) were classified as regulatory. To relate this to our ideas of agenda-setting features of green-lite, the Green Plan showed an initial high that was quickly followed by slippage back to a less ambitious green agenda.

THE SUSTAINABLE DEVELOPMENT AGENDA: 1992–2006

The rise of the sustainable development agenda, and Canada's role as an early proponent, had its roots in the 1980s (see chapter 3). Early articulations of the ideas of sustainable development appeared in the World Conservation Strategy released by the International Union for the Conservation of Nature (1980) (IUCN). The ideas then gained greatest attention in *Our Common Future*, the report of the World Commission on Environment and Development, commonly termed the Brundtland Report, that was released in 1987 (World Commission on Environment and Development 1987). Canada took a prominent role in the lead up to the UN Conference on Environment and Development (UNCED, or the Rio Earth Summit); resource policies were a central component of the agenda.

Beyond the ideational shift that proponents of sustainable development envisioned, this period marked a growing set of international pressures on Canada's resource policies. Though the conflicts surrounding provincial-federal control over resources did not vanish, they were now placed beside an increasing array of external pressures, most notably those coming from international rules, market pressures, global norms, and organizational networks (Bernstein and Cashore 2000). A product of these pressures is the emergence of the NGO, markets, and business–environment regime we discuss in chapter 9.

Another early sign came in the form of the continuation of softwood lumber disputes with the United States. The dispute reignited just before the Rio Earth Summit. In 1991, the US Department of Commerce and the US trade representative assessed Canadian supports for the timber industry following Canada's announcement that it would stop imposing the 15 per cent tariff on exports to the United States. Both US assessments found that Canada was indeed unfairly supporting its industry through below-market stumpage rates and log-export bans. Canada challenged the decisions through GATT and the US-Canada Free Trade Agreement, and it received favourable rulings from both. In spite of the successful rulings, and after much delay and considerable resistance from the US administration, Canada acquiesced by signing the 1996 Softwood Lumber Agreement, which set a series of rising export taxes on softwood lumber dependent on the level of exports flowing from Canada to the United States (Hessing, Howett, and Summerville 2005).

Wrangling over softwood lumber through the US-Canada FTA and GATT were a high-profile example of a broader shift occurring towards formalized regional and bilateral trade and investment agreements (see chapter 3). Indeed, chapter 11 of NAFTA became an important template for subsequent bilateral investment agreements Canada signed with trading partners (Gordon and Webber 2008; Mann 2008). The first of these, negotiated with Poland, entered force in 1990; one with the Russian Federation entered force in 1991, and another fifteen were brought into force in the 1990s, particularly with countries in Latin America (e.g., Argentina in 1993), Asia (e.g., the Philippines in 1996), and the former Soviet States (e.g., Hungary in 1993). Canada has now ratified twenty-seven such agreements, it has signed an additional three, negotiations are complete on another eleven, and negotiations are ongoing with another twelve.‡

Though the provisions of the agreements vary, those developed after the Rio Earth Summit typically include some mention of sustainable development as a significant priority. However, more importantly, they provide protection to investors to ensure host governments do not directly, or indirectly through changes in policies, expropriate the investments, and they have established private arbitration processes to allow investors to seek remedy when they feel their rights have been violated (Mann 2008). While it is beyond the scope of this chapter to examine the consequences of these agreements, they have been found to play an important role in increasing foreign direct investment to developing countries (Büthe and Milner 2008), while also raising grave concerns about the human rights and environmental abuses that companies, particularly Canadian mining companies (Gordon and Webber 2008), have perpetrated while protected by the agreements' provisions. That is, these agreements are argued

‡ See Foreign Affairs, Trade and Development Canada (2013) for a list of all the ratified and signed agreements, as well as those agreements still under negotiation.

to tie the hands of host countries in ways that ensure they cannot effectively regulate the operations of foreign companies, such as mining companies, and the agreements place no specific obligations on the home country (in this case, Canada) or its investors (e.g., a mining company) to perform in line with human rights or environmental norms.

More generally, and returning to domestic policy, the period marked some important new directions for public policy decisions taken by the federal and provincial governments alike in several specific ways. First, new and competing ideas about the character of the problem gained traction. There was a growing concern for the cumulative effects of economic development at geographic scales greater than individual projects. Two strands of policy action followed: one focused on species and another on protected areas. With the former, the adoption of the UN Convention on Biological Diversity (see chapter 3) was an important impetus for the federal government to consider new legislation geared specifically for protecting endangered species (Westell 1994). Although some officials at the Canadian Wildlife Service felt that existing statutory law provided sufficient powers to manage species, the absence of a single and focused law on endangered species became the focus of criticism from NGOs and a rallying cry for action. Indeed, Elizabeth May, then executive director of the Sierra Club of Canada, penned a letter to the *Globe and Mail* underscoring the importance of a federal statute, given the perilous state of species in Canada and the existence of only four provincial laws on the issue (May 1994). A task force was struck to examine the issue, which proposed the first of a series of bills that navigated the tricky balance between the interests of NGOs and business and the jurisdictional powers of the provinces. The Species at Risk Act (SARA) then took until late 2002 to receive Senate and Commons approval, along with royal assent (Illical and Harrison 2007).

With the latter, the rising interest in protected areas was associated with international soft law norms that were promoting greater attention to protection of representative areas of biological diversity (Dearden, Bennett, and Johnston 2005; Dearden and Dempsey 2004). These were first articulated in the 1960s by the IUCN, and they gathered growing support at both the UN Conference on the Human Environment held in Stockholm in 1972 and then at the UNCED in 1992. In each instance, governments made commitments to protecting representative areas to conserve the diversity of eco-systems found within their jurisdiction. At the provincial level, concerns over wilderness protection had been growing in salience, particularly in certain areas that conservation advocates felt were under imminent threat from some proposed extractive use. In BC, for instance, the NDP government in the 1970s had begun to develop a plan for wilderness protection, which included imposing a moratorium on proposed harvesting in candidate areas until proper planning and consultations could occur (Wilson 1998, 117). Even though wilderness areas grew during this period – the provincial NDP government increased the area of protection in BC by 55 per cent, from 2.9 million to 4.5 million hectares – a retrenchment occurred under the Social Credit government that followed; this helped stoke concerns, particularly over certain highly disputed forested areas, such as the Stein Valley and the Valhalla (185–209).

In the late 1980s, similar concerns were expressed over forest protection in Ontario, particularly over logging activities in Temagami, which involved even Bob Rae, the NDP leader in Ontario at the time, who got arrested for blockading a logging road (Duffy 1990; Kelly 1989). In 1989, the WWF and Canadian Parks and Wilderness Society (CPAWS) launched the Endangered Spaces campaign that pushed federal, provincial, and territorial governments to work cooperatively to complete a protected areas network by 2000 for terrestrial systems (and 2010 for marine systems) (Dearden and Dempsey 2004).

In 1990, this issue was directly addressed in the federal Green Plan, noted above (and in chapter 2). Following a general proposal in the Brundtland Report for the need to triple global protection (at the time it stood at about 4 per cent),§ the government established a goal of protecting 12 per cent of the country's territory. Additionally, the government sought to establish five new parks by 1996 and finalize agreements on thirteen more, with the aim of completing the terrestrial system by 2000 (Auditor General of Canada 1996). In 1992, territorial, provincial, and federal ministers of parks, environment, and wildlife committed jointly to completing Canada's network of protected areas (NRTEE 2003). This confirmed Canada's commitment to establish a network of national protected areas rep-

§ See Bernstein and Cashore (2000) for discussion of this as an example of the influence of global norms on domestic policy-making.

resenting each of Canada's thirty-nine ecological regions (Auditor General of Canada 1996).

It was well understood that this would have specific and direct consequences for natural resource sectors. These concerns in relation to mining, and in how they intersect with Aboriginal interests, were made explicit in Canada's national submission to the UNCED:

> An emerging and significant environmental issue involving the mining industry relates to land use. Many new mining developments are being proposed in wilderness lands located in the northern parts of some provinces and in the territories. Others are in lands that are claimed by aboriginal peoples. Some believe that the best use for these lands is to remain wilderness, and that mineral development should be curtailed. Aboriginal peoples believe that they should be full partners in development decisions on claimed lands. Mining companies, on the other hand, believe they have legitimate claims to the resources. Any further land preservation in mineral-rich areas removes land from the industry's resource base and reduces commercial opportunities. (Environment Canada 1991, 42)

The Windy Craggy mine proposal, discussed in chapter 9, is a clear illustration of the consequences this new policy concern created for the mining sector. In that instance, resistance to a proposed mine in the northwestern corner of BC led to the area being designated as a protected area (i.e., the Tatshenshini-Alsek Provincial Park). As McAllister and Alexander (1997) explained, this case generated a perceived threat to the mining industry, since access to land for exploration and development is critical for the industry to maintain a long-term mineral supply. Similar concerns also existed over the protection of productive forested areas in BC and Ontario; they have become salient concerns more recently in relation to marine protected areas as well.

A second part was associated with contested models of how management of natural resources ought to take place. In BC, for instance, there had been a long-standing commitment to an overall model that considered areas of old forests as over-mature and unproductive. Because many of BC's forests followed a sigmoidal growth curve, the annual volume increment that older forests were producing could be quite small; sometimes it might even be negative, as more timber biomass decayed than grew annually. With the intention of transforming the overall forest estate to a more productive source of timber, the official policy was to liquidate the older cohorts to create faster-growing second-growth forests that could serve as the basis of a longer-term, regulated, and stable timber supply. This conception of the management problem became the central focus of contestation, as groups articulated concerns that older forests were integral habitat for many forest-dependent species (e.g., the spotted owl or the marble murrelet) (Cashore et al. 2001; Marchak 1983; Wilson 1998).

As others have observed (Hessing, Howett, and Summerville 2005), these changes meant increased contestation within Canada as well as growing international pressures to consider. And as we discussed in chapter 5, the Department of Energy, Mining and Resources was replaced by Natural Resources Canada (NRCan) in 1993, partly as an outcome of the late Mulroney and early Chrétien governments' major restructuring of the federal government. NRCan was not only to consolidate the federal view of natural resources as a more integrated policy field, it was also to create new synergies out of some of the earlier separate resource fiefdoms, especially that of forestry (Doern 1993). Among the synergies expected was greater applied attention to the ideas of sustainable development. Meanwhile DFO continued to oversee fisheries.

In this same year, the auditor general's report assessed the performance of the Department of Forestry. Generally, the report noted the valuable contributions the department had made in influencing the stewardship of forests within Canada and abroad. Since being created, and following limited action of the 1987 Forest Strategy, the department helped facilitate, with the CCFM, a process that led to the signing of the Canada Forest Accord and a revised National Forest Strategy culminating in 1992 (Auditor General of Canada 1993). But in the report, the auditor general highlighted the central discussions that were occurring over the transition from a sustained yield model of forest management to one that sought to embrace and apply sustainable development.

Even though the federal government was lauded for its work internationally and domestically in advancing discussions on sustainable forest management, most of the concrete policy changes and debates were playing out at the provincial level, as a back-and-forth began between industry attempting to get ahead of government with self-regulation and provincial governments responding to domestic and international pressure for stronger rules governing forest practices (see chapter 9). The Ontario Forest Industries Association (OFIA), for instance, undertook to assuage public unease.[¶] OFIA established a task force to develop a code of forest practices for its members. Released in 1992, the code was meant to illustrate the industry's commitment to "sustainable development and progressive forest management" (Ontario Forest Industries Association 1998). A year later, a third-party review of the code, commissioned by the association, indicated it needed revising to better reflect changing societal expectations. Meeting this revised code became a requirement for association members. "By applying this Code across the forest landscape," the OFIA explained, "members hope to demonstrate leadership through their forest management practices" (2).

Members were eager to regain "the public's trust by adhering to a strict set of rules that [went] beyond their legal requirements" ("Forestry Compaines Meet Compliance Deadline" 2000) claimed the OFIA president, R. Marie Rauter. At this time, efforts such as those of the OFIA were partly attempts to fend off increased government regulations. Indeed, Ontario's provincial government revised its forest legislation in response to two public consultation processes, which had highlighted limitations in the existing regulatory regime (Environmental Assessment Board 1994; Ontario Forest Policy Panel 1993). In 1994, the government enacted the Crown Forest Sustainability Act, which took effect in 1995, replacing the Crown Timber Act (Willick 2001). This was the same year that BC introduced a new Forest Practices Code with similar interests in assuaging public disquiet with the status quo forest operations in the province (Wilson 1998). However, in addition to these regulatory concerns, as we show in chapter 9, pressure from the market via NGO campaigns also began to matter.

In mining, the Whitehorse Mining Initiative (WMI), discussed in chapter 9, brought together stakeholders in the mining sector to foster a similar national discussion on mining as had occurred to develop the Canada Forest Accord (McAllister and Alexander 1997).

¶ Similar efforts were underway in other Canadian provinces. For instance, the Alberta forest industry had launched "Forest Care," a code of practices for its members (Lachance 1993). Likewise, the Forest Alliance of BC had developed a code of conduct, releasing it in 1992 (Forest Alliance of British Columbia 1992).

It paved the way for the federal government to develop a new policy – Minerals and Metals Policy of the Government of Canada: Partnerships for Sustainable Development – released in November 1996. This set a federal framework for mining in Canada through a focus on six objectives: decision-making based on sustainable development; business-friendly investment conditions; products, markets, and stewardship promotion; Aboriginal involvement in mining; science and technological innovation; and international leadership (Hilson 2000; Shinya 1998). Assessments of the new policy noted that it marked an important attempt by the federal government to integrate the ideas of sustainable development into policy in a comprehensive manner. However, as Hilson (2000, 203) explained, "The Policy fails to explain in great detail how each of these goals can be achieved, or, more specifically, by what means the government plans to go about 'operationalizing' each objective."

Similar to its involvement in forestry, the federal government was also active on international fisheries issues, having participated in a number of negotiations in the early 1990s on fisheries agreements and soft law instruments, such as the 1995 FAO Code of Conduct for Responsible Fishing, which served as a template for an industry code developed in 1998 (Gough 2007, 384). Domestically, DFO began to modify its policies in reaction to the court decisions concerning Aboriginal fishing rights that we noted above. The department released an Aboriginal Fisheries Strategy in 1992 that was designed to facilitate and manage a move towards greater Aboriginal involvement in fisheries. Part of the strategy involved transferring catch allocation to Aboriginal peoples, which started in 1994–95 and operated in BC and Atlantic Canada (386).

A second defining feature of this period was a cycle of problems with various fisheries that began with the significant and dramatic collapse of the East Coast cod fishery. The fishery fell under a two-year fishing ban that came into effect in 1992. In the next year, with the fishery making no signs of recovery, the ban was extended indefinitely and expanded to include recreational and subsistence fisheries (Schrank 1995). The implications were huge. The groundfish catch had been as high as 2 million tons in the 1960s and had represented as much as 40 per cent of the landed value of the Atlantic fishery's catch; in 1993, the groundfish catch was a mere 120,000 tons (Auditor General of Canada 1997a). Though a full diagnostic of the causes of the collapse are beyond the scope of this chapter (for one account, see Finlayson 1994), it was quite clear in the years following that the harvest levels were being set too high, and that chronic over-capacity in the region's fishery did not help. As a 1997 auditor general report noted,

> The deep cultural attachment to the groundfish fishery has been reinforced by several decades of government subsidies. This has resulted in substantial pressure on government to maintain the status quo; that is, to use the fish as a basis for providing income support. Successive governments have provided increasing income support for the people living in the remote coastal communities in Atlantic Canada. This reaction to social pressures has not resulted in an economically viable fishery. In fact, the absence of the fishery has revealed, more clearly than ever before, the substantial reliance on income support by a significant portion of the Atlantic fishing industry. This reliance makes dealing with already complex problems of overcapacity and fisheries management more difficult. (Auditor General of Canada 1997a, 2)

On the West Coast, similar concerns were ascendant. In 1997, the auditor general dedicated an assessment to the Pacific salmon resources, noting some serious challenges for certain stocks. In this case, the major issue involved the protection of habitat. The report explained that the 1986 Habitat Policy – which had been the regulatory regime implementing the provisions of the Fisheries Act for a decade – was not being adequately advanced, particularly on proactive measures such as through integrated resource management (Auditor General of Canada 1997b). A year before the auditor general's report, the Ocean Act was enacted and committed the government to the establishment of – in collaboration with stakeholders – a "national strategy for the management of estuarine, coastal and maritime ecosystems in the water that form part of Canada or in which Canada has sovereign rights under international law" (Government of Canada 2013). The plan was also to be based on the principle of sustainable development, integrated management, and the precautionary approach (ibid.), and it built directly from calls within the coastal and ocean management community for action on oceans (Ricketts and Harrison 2007).

In 1998, DFO also responded to the challenges noted by the auditor general with the release of a new policy – *A New Direction for Canada's Pacific Salmon Fisheries* – which laid out broad principles to guide the federal government's new approach to the salmon fisheries (Fisheries and Oceans Canada 1998); in the same year, it released *Toward Canada's Oceans Strategy* (Ricketts and Harrison 2007). The principles in the new directions document were to guide a discussion with stakeholders and BC on operational policies for salmon management. With a commitment of $400 million, the aim was to protect and rebuild habitat, move the industry toward selective methods of fishing, reduce the fleet size, increase diversification, and support communities and people through the transition seen as necessary in the sector (Fisheries and Oceans Canada 1998).

In 1999, the auditor general released a follow-up analysis of DFO's work on the Pacific salmon fishery. By this time, DFO was implementing provisions of the New Direction plan. Still, the auditor general noted many persistent problems, including the continuation of habitat loss and the problem of incomplete data on 8,000 individual salmon stocks (pink, sockeye, chinook, coho, and chum) (Auditor General of Canada 1999). Indeed, the commercial catch continued to decline; it had been 40 million fish in 1991 but was only 10 million in 1998. The report also noted the limited coordination between the regional and national offices of DFO, and that there appeared to be a lack of attention to how fisheries management issues would fit within the new Oceans Strategy. The auditor general followed with a third report on fisheries in 2000, which focused on salmon farming as a growing BC industry with potential impacts on ocean stocks of Pacific salmon. Aquaculture had risen markedly in BC and globally since the 1970s (Rayner and Howlett 2007). Despite this rising importance, the federal government – through DFO and Environment Canada – had been insufficiently applying the habitat provisions of the Fisheries Act to assess and regulate the possible harms of fish farms.

The final fisheries and oceans development came at the international level. In 2003, Canada ratified UNCLOS, which formalized a series of obligations and opportunities for Canada in maritime and fisheries affairs. For one, it started the clock on the ten-year window Canada had available to submit its research findings to the Commission on the Limits of the Continental Shelf to make a case for extending its EEZ to beyond 200 nautical miles to the lesser of the edge of the Continental Shelf or 350 nautical miles (United Nations 1998). This had understandably great significance for possible mineral, oil, and gas mining opportunities on the East, West, and Northern Coasts, as we discussed in chapter 3 (Ricketts and Harrison 2007).

In the background to these domestic and international developments, ongoing assessments of federal attempts to institutionalize sustainable development in the practices of the government were raising concerns. These were not out of line with the sector-specific challenges being articulated about the gap between aspiration and implementation. In 1997, the CESD – a position created in the Office of the Auditor General through an amendment to the Auditor General Act in 1995 – released a first report. In it, the CESD noted, "Previous work by the Office of the Auditor General has identified key weaknesses in the federal government's management of sustainable development: the gap between commitments and concrete action; a lack of co-ordination among departments and across jurisdictions; and inadequate review of performance and provision of information to Parliament" (CESD 1997, 2). The report drew these conclusions based on forty-two reports from the auditor general over the course of a decade that focused on environmental and sustainable development. This compilation of years of the auditor general's work on environment by the CESD supports our arguments about "ends-means" issues, key boundary and coordination matters, and issues to do with the weaknesses among departments, all of which fall under the umbrella of our green-lite thesis. From 1997 forward, the CESD reports became an important source of critical review of what was occurring in the government's efforts to address sustainable development in its own operations and in specific files, such as natural resources. Indeed, as we noted above, this was in step with the challenges articulated at the UN World Summit on Sustainable Development in Johannesburg. Goals had been set, but implementation was challenging. As noted in chapter 4, the CESD continued to report green-lite action by the government in the period since 1997.

FROM SUSTAINABLE TO RESPONSIBLE RESOURCE DEVELOPMENT: 2006–2014

The final period we review was not immediately marked by a landmark shift such as a constitutional change or a high-level world conference on the environment. Rather, it signified the start of an incremental acceleration towards what is now an explicit focus of the Harper government – responsible resource development. Chapter 5 has already set out some of implications of this policy on the energy sector, especially in relation to multiple new pipelines linked to oil sands and other exports. And although energy has been the defining resource of this period, the focus on responsible resource development has proven to have implications for a wide range of government policies. It undergirded a rethinking of Canada's development policies that led to the merger of the Canadian International Development Agency (CIDA) into the Department of Foreign Affairs and International Trade and motivated a wholesale revamping of legislative provisions relating to environmental impacts, such as the Fisheries Act and the Canadian Environmental Assessment Act (CEAA). The former of these has been criticized alongside the active promotion of Canadian mining companies abroad that CIDA has been involved with for some time, but has been institutionalized more formerly under the Harper government (Blackwell and Stewart 2012).

The latter changes have had different implications for the resources examined in this chapter. Though one important crosscutting shift involved changes to the CEAA. We noted above that the CEAA was enacted in 1992 in part as a reaction to the Federal Court's rulings on two dam projects where the federal government had not followed its own Guidelines Order. In 2012, the CEAA was revamped as part of the government's omnibus budget implementation bill, or Bill C-38, The Jobs, Growth and Long-term Prosperity Act, with the government arguing that this was a critical part of its agenda promoting responsible resource development (McLeod 2013). The 1992 CEAA was not without flaws. However, the 2012 reworking made dramatic alterations to the assessment process. Gibson (2012) details the myriad changes, including a reduced role of the federal government in the review process, greater delegation to the provinces and territories, the likely reduction in the number of federal assessments (from thousands to hundreds per year), greater ministerial discretion in determining which projects to review, and later timing of the assessments in the planning process of a given project. Procedurally, the changes were controversial too, as they had been brought in with little or no opportunity for debate within Parliamentary committees or in public, a stark contrast to the process that led to the 1995 enactment of the CEAA (ibid.). On related procedural issues, concerns have also be raised about the shift in language on who is eligible to participate in an environmental assessment; the new language states that only those "directly affected" by the proposal may participate, as compared the broader language of "interested parties" having a stake (Salomons and Hoberg 2013).

These changes, though unclear yet in their full implications and by no means a full accounting of the changes included in Bill C-38, do alter key aspects of the regulatory regime for natural resource management in Canada. An added component relates specifically to fisheries but will also have consequences for mining and forestry, which we turn to below. In fisheries, among the seventy statutes affected by Bill C-38, the Fisheries Act was modified. Section 35(1) adopted in 1976 that stated "No person shall carry on any work or undertaking that results in the harmful alteration, disruption or destruction of fish habitat" was removed; it was replaced by "No person shall carry on any work, undertaking or activity that results in serious harm to fish that are part of a commercial, recreational or Aboriginal fishery, or to fish that support such a fishery"** (Hutchings and Post 2013). The move has been widely criticized. Similar to the concerns about process for the changes to the CEAA, the lack of consultation was viewed as worrying. Four former fisheries ministers wrote an open letter to Prime Minister Harper, published in the *Globe and Mail*, detailing their grave concerns over the amendments (Siddon et al. 2012). A central thrust of the alarm centred on the lack of scientific input from DFO itself; as Hutchings and Post (2013, 497) note, "There is no evidence to suggest that the revisions themselves were based on consultation with, or advice received from, DFO science directors, fisheries scientists, or habitat biologists. Among other limitations, this lack of scientific engagement is in direct contravention of DFO and government of Canada policies concerning the use of science in decision making."

The context for these changes illustrates the manner in which they signify the shift in thinking on resources. Two considerations are important. First, in the lead up to the debates over Bill C-38, the CESD released a report in 2009 that had a chapter dedicated to protecting fish habitat. The report concluded,

Fisheries and Oceans Canada and Environment Canada cannot demonstrate that fish habitat is being adequately protected as the

** See the Government of Canada (2015) for specifics of the changes.

Fisheries Act requires. In the 23 years since the Habitat Policy was adopted, many parts of the Policy have been implemented only partially by Fisheries and Oceans Canada or not at all. The Department does not measure habitat loss or gain. It has limited information on the state of fish habitat across Canada – that is, on fish stocks, the amount and quality of fish habitat, contaminants in fish, and overall water quality. Fisheries and Oceans Canada still cannot determine the extent to which it is progressing toward the Policy's long-term objective of a net gain in fish habitat. (CESD 2009, 12)

Given this report and the expressions of the scientific community concerning the importance of moving toward an ecosystem-based approach (Hutchings and Post 2013), it is not surprising that the changes were viewed as an erosion of environmental laws, in terms of our argument, "ends-means" conflicts that are central to our green-lite thesis. This perspective was supported still further by an analysis that found environmental reviews under the Fisheries Act from 2001 to 2012 were completed within the timeframe the government offered as one of its justifications for legislative change; similar results were evident for assessments under the CEAA from an earlier time period (de Kerckhove, Minns, and Shuter 2013). Put differently, the evidence from the experience of most assessments did not support the government's argument that the process currently took too long and was having detrimental effects for economic growth.

A second relevant development illustrating the changing thinking on resources occurred on the West Coast. With worrying parallels to the cod fishery collapse on the East Coast, 2009 marked a year when the Fraser River sockeye fishery had a dismal run, and it was the third year of a commercial fishery closure. The situation led the government to set up a commission of inquiry led by Justice Bruce Cohen, who was mandated to determine the cause. Holding hearings over the proceeding two years, the third volume of the final report provided recommendations based on the findings. While stressing that there was no single cause but rather multiple stressors throughout the complicated sockeye life cycle were implicated in the unprecedented decline, the recommendations underscored the need for more thorough implementation of existing policies, including the 1986 Habitat Policy and a 2005 policy developed for wild salmon. Referring directly to the changes to the Fisheries Act in Bill C-38, Cohen opined,

> In my view, DFO does not need a new habitat policy; rather, it needs to complete implementation of the 1986 Habitat Policy. Although the policy may need updating to address changes in case law and legislation, including the changes to the Fisheries Act contained in Bill C-38 ..., its goals and No Net Loss principle are sound and should be retained. The 1986 Habitat Policy recognizes that the cumulative impact of development projects (due to the collective effect of habitat degradation and loss arising from multiple projects in an area) is a serious concern, but DFO considers proposed projects only on a project-by-project basis. On the evidence, I find that cumulative impact is one of the key factors that negatively affect fish habitat. DFO needs to manage this cumulative incremental harm, which, over time, could have a substantial effect on Fraser River sockeye habitat. The habitat management system DFO has in place does not address these harms adequately. (Cohen Commission 2012, 43–4)

The important thing about these two events are that in spite of the calls for redoubling efforts to effectively address habitat loss, the government's legislative agenda took the policy regime in an entirely different direction. One can think of this as an institutional case of cognitive dissonance. The government of Canada had long had a policy on the books that explicitly laid out a commitment to protecting habitat; in practice, this was hard to accomplish and implementation had fallen short for some time. Thus, instead of reaffirming the commitment – maintaining the aim of protecting fisheries habitat – the new direction of the Harper government, in essence, changed the laws to accord more closely with the longstanding behaviour of neglected implementation. No more dissonance.

The forestry sector offers an illustration of this method in practice. The inland spawning grounds for salmon fisheries had had implications for forestry practices since the 1986 Habitat Policy (Tripp 1998). However, as the Cohen Commission explained under the Forest and Range Practices Act of 2004, the provincial forest minister stopped forwarding the main operational plans of forest operators to DFO for consideration in relation to the Fisheries Act regulations; he also explained the reduced regional staffing given to fish-forestry activities within DFO (Cohen Commission 2012). In other words, the neglect for the fisheries provisions had been occurring for several years, as was also evident in the auditor general's reports we noted above.

This approach affected Canada's international agenda on resources as well. In March 2013, the Harper government announced it would withdraw from the UN Convention to Combat Desertification (UNCCD), one agreement that was a product of the 1992 Rio Earth Summit. Calling the UNCCD "too bureaucratic" and an ineffective use of taxpayers' money, Canada withdrew, saving roughly $300,000 in annual contributions and becoming the only country in the world not party to the UNCCD (Zililo 2013). Two months earlier, Canada had also withdrawn from the International Tropical Timber Organization, rescinding its adoption of the 2006 International Tropical Timber Agreement (Shane 2013). Referencing the earlier withdrawal from the Kyoto Protocol, the journal of *Biodiversity* and its publisher Biodiversity Conservancy International published an editorial on Canada's decision to leave UNCCD. Underscoring their concern, the piece noted, "We feel that Canada has lost its commitment to all three Rio treaties [UNFCCC, CBD, and UNCCD], in complete contrast to 20 years ago when Canada competed successfully for the privilege of hosting the CBD Secretariat. At the time Canada had a firm commitment to international environmental law and a respectable domestic environmental record. This is no longer the case and our global reputation is at stake" (Hendrickson and Aitken 2013, 131).

The final significant shift in Canada's international efforts on resources surrounded its approach to global mining practices. Attention has focused on the extent to which Canada should be working to advance better mining practices in countries where Canadian registered and owned companies are operating. Proponents for more aggressive Canadian action would like to see legislation setting certain mandatory requirements for overseas operations. Opponents, which have won the day, advocate for support of what companies are already committed to various voluntary initiatives. This approach has included the establishment of a CSR commissioner and a mining and development initiative led by CIDA (Dagher 2014). Paralleling these developments was the decision to have CIDA subsumed within the DFAIT.

THE THREE REGIME ELEMENTS

To close this chapter, we review the natural resource–environment regime as it relates to the three regime elements. Table 6.2 offers an overview of the key points from the review. We elaborate on them below.

Ideas, Discourse, and Agendas

Two ideational changes were occurring over the course of our study that had bearing on the kinds of policy actions Canada took on natural resources. First, there was an expansion of the values associated with resources. In forests and fisheries, this involved a move from managing forests for timber to managing forest ecosystems through an ecosystem-based approach. Though many within the forestry profession would note that there had been long-standing attention to multiple uses of forests, the focus on sustained yield of timber – as illustrated by the liquidation focus of the BC government's forest policies – undercut the degree to which this perspective was seriously put into practice in management and operational decisions. Second, there was a broader move from the "polluter-pays" principle to the ideas of sustainable development where economic, environmental, and social goals were seen as possibly pursued in step in a win-win-win manner. As Hoberg and Harrison (1994, 125) note on this point in considering the Canadian Green Plan, "This conception has implications for instrument choice, since if profit-seeking and environmental protection are indeed compatible, one need only educate people and they will voluntarily change their behaviour, without need for coercive measures." This comment was made in relation to the convenience of the idea of sustainable development – the idea that there did not need to be a trade-off between environment and development; the two had to occur together and in step.

Another apparent facet of the sustainable development period was the challenge presented by implementation. In the forest, fisheries, and mining sectors, the 1990s saw the development of broad and ambitious policies that sought to integrate sustainable development into resource management. Yet these three sectors were plagued by green-lite implementation problems, as previously noted; put another way, translating the aspirations of sustainable development into

Table 6.2: The natural resource–environment regime and the three regime elements: Selected summary highlights

POLICY HISTORIES	The three analytical elements		
	POLICIES, IDEAS, DISCOURSE, AND AGENDAS	POWER STRUCTURE, DEMOCRACY, AND GOVERNANCE	SCIENCE, EVIDENCE, KNOWLEDGE, AND PRECAUTION
Resource promoter (and regulator?): 1867–1970s	• Exploitation of resources seen as a means to affect regional development and generate revenue with a focus on volume of production (not necessarily value), e.g., BC's explicit policy of liquidating over-mature forests in favour of fast-growing secondary forests • Some early federal policy follows "polluter-pays" principle (e.g., amendments to the Fisheries Act) • Federal financial support for certain industries (e.g., fisheries)	• Joint federalism begins to erode as provincial governments gain planning and managing capacity and seek to solidify stronger control over resources • Change in jurisprudence over separation of provincial-federal powers after Supreme Court replaces the JCPC; the changes were most salient with two cases involving the Saskatchewan government and the potash industry that annulled provincial laws for usurping federal trade and commerce powers	• Technocratic approach focused on using resources as a means for economic and social development • Professional and technical knowledge a key input into policy decisions and means for coordination
Changing terms of the relationship: 1980s	• Resource exploitation remains central paradigm, but some concerns over biodiversity and ecosystem sustainability emerge to vie for agenda, e.g., in the late 1980s, calls for wilderness protection emerged as a national campaign led by WWF and CPAWS • Beginnings of idea of promoting economically valuable extraction over volume of extraction (e.g., move towards ITQs in fisheries)	• Executive federalism gains increasing role in shaping provincial-federal relations • Constitution reverses shift in jurisprudence, giving provinces formal powers to regulate interprovincial trade and raise money from resources by any means • Constitution affords First Nations power in resource policy decision-making	• Scientific documentation of natural resource depletion begins to gain salience, such as concerns over the loss of tropical and temperate rain-forests and the associated loss of biodiversity

Table 6.2: (continued)

	The three analytical elements		
POLICY HISTORIES	POLICIES, IDEAS, DISCOURSE, AND AGENDAS	POWER STRUCTURE, DEMOCRACY, AND GOVERNANCE	SCIENCE, EVIDENCE, KNOWLEDGE, AND PRECAUTION
• The sustainable development agenda: 1992–2006	• Sustainable development embraced in formulation of national policy statements and strategies; implementation problems then became pervasive • Liberalization of trade and increased trade disputes over resource policies (e.g., softwood lumber dispute with the US)	• Multi-stakeholder roundtables and coordination through council of first ministers and resource/environment ministers, e.g., the government supported the WMI in the mining sector and led renewed efforts to develop a national forestry strategy • Increasing importance of trade agreements and international rules as considerations of the specific design of policies	• Limits of managerial science in guiding decisions on complex resource management questions (cod fishery collapse) • Rising attention to precautionary approach in goals; harder to put into practice
• From sustainable to responsible resource development: 2006–13	• Government as partner of industry in facilitating international development (mining) • Narrowed view of legitimate interests in resources management concerns to those with commercial interests or those directly affected (those near the project) • Return to resource-focused economy as a positive thing, not as a trap (as envisioned by discourses such as Dutch disease and staples trap)	• Centralized control through PMO and executive • Alignment between elected officials and a pro-development coalition of provinces, broadcast networks (the *Sun*), and conservative pundits and strategists	• Efforts to control science produced within the government and outside

operational actions to be taken by federal departments proved to be the biggest obstacle. Indeed, perhaps not surprisingly, this issue of implementation shortfalls was to be the central theme of the UN World Summit on Sustainable Development in Johannesburg, South Africa (Wapner 2003).

By the end of the period, the tension between the aspiration of sustainable development and the realities of implementation tipped the scales away from continued commitment to the challenges of integrating social, environmental, and economic considerations. Indeed, the most salient considerations for Canada's resource-development policies concerned market access in the United States and elsewhere.

Environmental Power Structures, Democracy, and Governance

The most salient facet of this regime element concerned the shifting federal-provincial powers over resources. Our analysis began as the jurisprudence had begun to move after the Supreme Court took on the role as the highest court. While the JCPC had ruled in favour of provincial powers, the Supreme Court placed greater emphasis on federal powers over trade and commerce. This initial swing was then countered by the resource amendment in the Constitution Act of 1982 that explicitly expanded provincial powers to set rules affecting resource trade.

The Constitution Act also transferred greater power to Canadian First Nations; having their treaty rights and title noted facilitated a series of court decisions that have meant First Nations concerns are now much more central in resource policy decisions. For instance, in catch allocations for the Fraser River sockeye, the First Nation fishery is superseded only by conservation considerations and treaty obligations with the United States (Schwindt and Vining 2008).

The 1980s forward also marked the beginning of greater executive control over policy dealings with the provinces – a shift from joint or cooperative to executive federalism. Relations that had been influenced by professional ties and common bureaucratic language and expertise were more tightly controlled by central agencies at the respective levels of government. This also came with the increased formalization of coordination mechanisms through the Canadian Council of Resource and Environment Ministers, and subsequent offshoots (e.g., the Canadian Council of Forest Ministers). Efforts to create broader stakeholder involvement were attempted in the early 1990s, and greater international sources of pressure also grew during this time, but in the final period the pendulum has swung back towards a more tightly controlled executive focused on the interests of resource development.

Science, Evidence, Knowledge, and Precaution

With the final regime element, the most significant developments involved the changing centrality of science and evidence in the decision-making on resource policies. Initially, Canada's resource policies were largely a technocratic area where professionals trained in forest science, geology, or fisheries science played an important role in defining the problem and devising policy.

By the 1980s and 1990s, this technocratic vision was questioned both within the scientific community and by other groups that brought competing knowledge systems to policy discussions. Within the scientific community, the emerging field of conservation biology served as a counterweight to the dominance of the ideas forwarded by professional foresters, as an example. Similarly, ecosystem-based approaches were promoted in fisheries that questioned the single-stock assessment methodologies that were important tools used to establish management regimes for Canadian fisheries.

With the return to resource development as the central agenda, the concerns and ideas of ecosystem approaches to resource policy became more marginalized. And as we discussed in other chapters, government scientists were being controlled to ensure that they did not speak against or at odds with government policy. These concerns were made explicit, for instance, in the Cohen Commission report and in the assessments conducted of the Fisheries Act revisions included in Bill C-38.

CONCLUSIONS

Our mapping and analysis of the Natural Resources–Environment Regime shows that resources are in many ways the bedrock of the Canadian economy and the Canadian identity. In this chapter, we have traced federal attention to resources and the environment by exploring differences and similarities across fisheries, mining, and forestry. Although federal constitutional powers provided greater central control over fisheries policy, there remained important pro-vincial-federal interactions that affected the kinds of resource-environment policies adopted and their ultimate effects. In relation to our discussion of green-lite policy and governance patterns, a key feature centres on multi-scalar and multi-level governance chal-lenges throughout. These are compounded in agenda-setting con-texts by the tendency of the federal government to focus on one resource sector over key periods. For instance, DFO was challenged by its dual role as regulator of fisheries and as promoter of the industry as a means for rural development in Canada's maritime provinces.

Beyond the general and ever-present challenges of constitutional skirmishes, we also underlined the changing emphasis of federal poli-cies, as different governments chose varied levels and ways of seeking to influence the management of Canadian resources. At high points, we documented federal efforts to develop a national approach to for-est management. At lower points, the federal government played a background, albeit sometimes fundamental, role, such as moving Canada towards greater open trading relations with the United States and other countries. In essence, the arch of this hyphenated regime has been a simple one: from an early period where resources were seen simply as a regional tool to facilitate economic development, to a middle period where the environment and the economy were to be integrated under the rubric of sustainable development, to a final period where resources exploitation has again returned to domi-nance, under the moniker of "responsible" development. This shows overall green-lite features across all three time periods.

Underlying this overall arch, however, are important patterns of policy attention that highlight a constant policy and political chal-lenge of how and whether government can effectively use Canada's extensive resource endowments to advance short-term and long-term Canadian instruments and interests. And within this, what is the role that environmental policies might and can play. We docu-mented the frequent attempts made to think strategically about resources at a national level – such as from the early efforts in the Trudeau era through to attempts in the 1990s to develop and sustain support for a national forest strategy. And thus, while the current government has swung in one direction in its view on the role of resources in Canada's national economy, history instructs that other ideas are just as likely to rise to prominence in the future.

7

The Federal–Cities and Urban
Sustainability Regime

In this chapter we examine the Federal–Cities Urban Sustainability Regime. Despite limited constitutional capacity to control cities, the federal government has attempted to influence this hyphenated regime with varying intensity, by various means, and to advance a variety of ends over several decades. Sustainability is part of this complex mix, albeit an uncertain and episodic one, that has tended to favour economic and social sustainability over environmental objectives and outcomes in urban centres and related policy ideas and discourse. The evolution of this regime illustrates too the central importance of assessing the increasingly multi-level and spatially fragmented characteristics of environmental governance. Green-lite complexity of our environmental policy and governance patterns is evident in this regime, as noted throughout and as summarized in the chapter conclusions. Some infrastructure issues are noted in this chapter, but chapter 8 is the focal point for a needed separate mapping and analysis of the related infrastructure-based environment regime.

In spite of provincial responsibility for municipalities, it was the government of Canada that committed the nation to endorse and implement the principles outlined in Agenda 21, which emerged as a result of the Brundtland Commission findings, along with other global initiatives such as the International Council for Local Environmental Initiatives (ICLEI). As well as offering an analysis of the federal government's changing role in cities, and also the forces of inertia, the chapter samples key international, provincial, and local approaches that have sought to promote better environmental stewardship under the discourse of urban sustainability and sustainable development overall.

If sustainability is defined as "living within the Earth's limits," then it could be argued that the term *sustainable cities* is an oxymoron. As models of human settlement, cities can be inherently unsustainable black holes of consumption and waste production, with an ecological footprint that far surpasses their geographic parameters. In Canada and around the globe, human settlement patterns are following a powerful trend: for the first time in history those who live in urban centres outnumber rural dwellers. Urban living is rapidly becoming the norm for human habitation, with this trend forecast to continue.

When the Brundtland report *Our Common Future* was written, a little over twenty-five years ago, the effects caused by what it termed "the urban revolution" were very apparent: "The future will be predominantly urban, and the most immediate environmental concerns of most people will be urban ones" (Brundtland Commission 1987, 9.61). Urban regions were already seen as the locus of rapid population and economic growth that was responsible for generating increasing levels of air and water pollution that spread far beyond their geographic boundaries. Agricultural land was being converted to suburbia, transformed to accommodate the housing needs of city workers. With increased demands on the highways and roads from commuting citizens and growth in commercial traffic, snarled transportation systems contributed to increased levels of greenhouse gases and diminished air quality. Solid waste was being transported to neighbouring communities whose land was transformed into "urban dumps" – landfills that became toxic sources polluting groundwater and the air. Urban regions were consuming ever-increasing quantities of fossil fuels, particularly in order to support transportation and energy generation.

While Brundtland was able to put sustainable development on the political map – championing the idea of a collective or shared search for a sustainable development path based on multilateralism and the interdependence of nations – its messages were delivered in broad principles rather than specifics. As the authors admitted, "We do not offer a detailed blueprint for action, but instead a pathway by which the peoples of the world may enlarge their spheres of cooperation" (Brundtland Commission 1987, Intro, 4). However, as previewed in chapter 3, the Brundtland report was a catalyst that launched a wide range of further international initiatives that called for actions beyond the endorsement of broad principles, including the 1992 UN "Earth Summit" – the Conference on Environment and Development – held in Rio de Janeiro. The conference launched the Framework Convention on Climate Change, which led to the subsequent Kyoto Protocol on Climate Change. The Rio Summit also created an agenda for the twenty-first century that was endorsed by 179 nations. Agenda 21 was the UN's blueprint for global transformation that would put nations on the path towards sustainable development, focusing on explicit courses of action needed to cut emissions, limit environmental degradation, and transform societies in pursuit of more sustainable development.

As well, the ICLEI, launched in 1990 at the World Congress of Local Governments for a Sustainable Future, focused on the role of local governments in taking action at the municipal level, including reducing greenhouse gases and mitigating environmental damage that contributes to climate change. It was through initiatives such as these, rather than Brundtland per se, that concrete actions from nation-states were sought to move towards more sustainable cities.

In this chapter we begin by discussing the basic intent of the Brundtland agenda for urban sustainability and review briefly the international initiatives and agreements that have followed since. The second section sets out the constitutional context within which the federal government operates and the significant challenges this poses for coherent multi-level governance of Canadian cities in broader environmental aims and international agreements and obligations. This includes the key stakeholders that have attempted to enact urban sustainability in Canada. Although it is beyond the scope of this chapter to catalogue the myriad provincial and municipal initiatives, we do draw on examples, particularly those that have involved the federal government in multi-level initiatives. The third and empirical core of the chapter then examines four periods of federal-cities and urban sustainability policy and governance history since the 1960s. This is followed by an overall look at the federal role on sustainability in cities and urban communities. The fifth section provides a summary view of the four policy history periods in relation to the authors' analytical discussion of our three policy and governance elements. Conclusions then follow.

Overall the analysis shows that there have been four distinct eras over the last fifty to sixty years: the "pre-sustainability era" of the 1960s to late 1970s; the "early sustainable development and environmental era" of the 1980s dominated by Brundtland and Agenda

21; the 1993–2006 period focusing on "green" infrastructure and culminating in the New Deal for Cities and Communities; and the most recent period that has marked a return to "open federalism" and fiscal austerity under Harper and the demise of an explicit cities or environmental agenda. During these periods the federal government engagement with cities and the promotion of an environmental and later sustainable development agenda has ebbed and flowed as a result changing political and ideological commitment, economic and fiscal cycles, and intergovernmental politics and relations. Consequently, in spite of considerable rhetoric from the federal government and some notable examples of policy innovation and legislation such as the Federal Sustainability Act (2008), Canada has struggled to develop and sustain a coherent and credible framework to engage effectively with cities in pursuit of a sustainable urban agenda.

Each of our five green-lite policy and governance patterns emerge strongly in the overall analytical and empirical story.

THE INTENT OF BRUNDTLAND: URBAN SUSTAINABILITY THROUGH MULTI-LEVEL GOVERNANCE

In its proposals to address the environmental and developmental challenges found in "the natural evolution of the network of settlements," Brundtland outlined five general lessons learned about spatial strategies for urban development (Brundtland Commission 1987, 9.25). However, the report was cautious about imposing a standardized approach: "Urban development cannot be based on standardized models, imported or indigenous. Development possibilities are particular to each city and must be assessed with the context of its own region. What works in one city may be totally inappropriate in another" (9.36).

This observation is important in light of the above-mentioned different policy-field entry points where sustainable development might emerge in this regime. Here, as in other regimes examined, we are entering a very eclectic environmental regime. However, Brundtland did call for efforts to strengthen the capacity of local governments to deal with the forces of development: "To become key agents of development, city governments need enhanced political, institutional, and financial capacity, notably access to more of the wealth generated in the city. Only in this way can cities adapt and deploy some of the vast array of tools available to address urban problems"

(Brundtland Commission 1987, 9.36, 9.39). In addition to calling for a greater empowerment of local governments, Brundtland recognized that national governments had a role in developing "an explicit national settlements strategy and policies within which innovative and effective local solutions to urban problems can evolve and flourish" (9.31). While acknowledging that governments usually have some form of "implied urban strategy" – described as "implicit in a range of macroeconomic, fiscal, budget energy and agricultural policies" – Brundtland observed that these policies tended to be reactive rather than proactive, often conflicting with each other. Brundtland called for the development of "a national urban strategy [in order to] provide an explicit set of goals and priorities for the development of a nation's urban system and the large, intermediate, and small centres within it" (ibid.). Brundtland also cautioned that "such a strategy must go beyond physical or spatial planning [and that] it requires that governments take a much broader view of urban policy than has been traditional" (ibid.).

Agenda 21

Shortly after Brundtland, the Rio Earth Summit in 1992 created an agenda for sustainable development for the twenty-first century. Agenda 21 was the UN's blueprint for global transformation, a plan to put nations on the path towards sustainable development. Going beyond the broad concepts presented in the Brundtland report, it introduced detailed expectations of what was involved, "address[ing] the pressing problems of today and also aim[ing] at preparing the world for the challenges of the next century" (United Nations 1992, 1.3). While the stark economic and social disparities between "have" and "have not" nations was a common theme in its developmental and environmental objectives (à la Brundtland), Agenda 21 pointed out that industrialized countries and those in the developing world both faced environmental challenges, although from different perspectives (Hilton and Stoney 2008).

The consumption patterns of cities in industrialized countries were placing severe stress on the global ecosystem, whereas settlements in the developing world needed more raw material, energy, and economic development simply to overcome basic economic and social problems. Accordingly, Agenda 21 called on *all countries* to identify the environmental implications of urban development and to address them in a "multi-tiered" fashion that integrated international, national, and local efforts (United Nations 1992, 1.1).

While Agenda 21 reflected "a global consensus and political commitment at the highest level on development and environment cooperation" (United Nations 1992, 1.3), it recognized that successful implementation was "first and foremost the responsibility of Governments" (1.3). As a global contract meant to bind governments around the world to make fundamental changes to follow sustainable development paths, as with the Brundtland aims, it depended on the signatories to follow through with the required actions to put in place "national strategies, plans, policies and processes" (ibid.).

Agenda 21 also recognized the significant role played by local authorities in making sustainable development happen. In particular it recognized that national plans, strategies, and processes relied on both the willingness and the capacity of local governments to implement them and "as the level of governance closest to the people, they play a vital role in educating, mobilizing and responding to the public to promote sustainable development" (United Nations 1992, 28.1–28.3).

All cities were asked to "develop and strengthen programmes aimed at ... guiding their development along a sustainable path" (United Nations 1992, 7.20). The steps needed to follow a sustainable path at the local level were outlined in the chapter "Promoting Sustainable Human Settlement Development" (7). The human settlement objective called for improvement "to the social, economic and environmental quality of human settlements and the living and working environments of all people, in particular the urban and rural poor" (7.4). It recommended improvements based on "technical cooperation activities, partnerships among the public, private and community sectors and participation in the decision-making process by community groups and special interest groups" (ibid.).

Thus the deployment of human settlement discourse within Agenda 21, while broadly desirable, was itself also replete with green-lite policy and governance patterns of the complex boundary type, as well as means-ends conflict and ambiguity, not to mention diverse multi-scalar features.

The specific areas to be addressed in promoting sustainable human settlement development included a number of infrastructure-related issues: the provision of adequate shelter; sustainable land-use planning and management; integrated provision of environmental infrastructure (water, sanitation, drainage, and solid-waste management); sustainable energy and transport systems; sustainable construction industry activities; and human resource development and capacity-building for human settlement development.

Towards the aim of making improvements in urban areas, Agenda 21 called on all countries to improve the management of human settlement by "adopting and applying urban management guidelines in the areas of land management, urban environmental management, infrastructure management and municipal finance and administration" (United Nations 1992, 7.16a). All countries were encouraged to "adopt innovative city planning strategies to address environmental and social issues ... developing local strategies for improving the quality of life and the environment, integrating decisions on land use and land management, investing in the public and private sectors and mobilizing human and material resources, thereby promoting employment generation that is environmentally sound and protective of human health" (7.16d).

The steps required to promote sustainable human settlement development were a significant challenge for local governments. Accordingly, Agenda 21 called on all countries to "*strengthen the capacities of their local governing bodies* to deal more effectively with the broad range of developmental and environmental challenges associated with rapid and sound urban growth through comprehensive approaches to planning that recognize the individual needs of cities and are based on ecologically sound urban design practices" (United Nations 1992, 7.20c, emphasis added).

In addition, countries were asked to assess the environmental suitability of infrastructure in human settlements and to "develop national goals for sustainable management of waste, and implement environmentally sound technology to ensure that the environment, human health and quality of life are protected" (United Nations 1992, 7.39). It was explicitly acknowledged that each country's ability to make the necessary changes was "determined to a large extent by the capacity of its people and its institutions as well as by its ecological and geographical conditions" (37.1). Therefore, the need to increase human, scientific, technological, organizational, institutional and resource capabilities featured prominently as the underpinning of efforts to make sustainable development happen (Hilton and Stoney 2008).

As a signatory to Agenda 21, Canada had committed to implementing national policies that were needed to support sustainable development. It was expected "to complete, as soon as practicable, if possible by 1994, a review of capacity- and capability-building requirements for devising national sustainable development strategies, including those for generating and implementing its own Agenda 21 action programme" (United Nations 1992, 37.4). As will be evident in the next section, while the federal government provided some funding for environmental issues, there was a noticeable absence of an overall policy framework to guide it.

International initiatives have nevertheless continued to push for stronger action on urban responses to climate change, but in light of frustration with top-down approaches they have tended to focus more on bilateral collaboration between cities. In addition to these developments, the establishment of the C40 initiative represented a relatively new institutional form on the international stage. Founded in October 2005 as part of the Clinton Climate Initiative (CCI), C40 is an organization of forty (now sixty-nine) of the world's largest cities that have come together to deal specifically with the challenge of climate change. Significantly their membership comprises cities or local governments (not states or national governments), with an emphasis on empowerment, action, and measurement. Since 2005, the C40 has hosted several cities climate summits, including London (2005), New York City (2007), Toronto (2008), and Seoul (2009), bringing together mayors, senior staff, and business leaders from major cities to exchange information and work towards common projects. Often working in partnership with other climate-change partners such as ICLEI, universities, banks, and business, the C40 aims to develop awareness of urban sustainability projects and products, share best practices, and provide measurable goals for cities to meet. While the overall impact is still limited, they have garnered significant media attention and have launched "the Purchasing Alliance" to pool the purchasing power of the cities and beyond, "enabling more than 1,100 cities to have access to affordable energy-efficient products" (CCI 2009). Its development also provides further recognition of the importance of local governance and place-based initiatives for climate change.

The UN-HABITAT's Cities in Climate Change Initiative (CCCI), a component of Sustainable Urban Development Network (SUD-Net), targets environmental planning and management in developing countries in particular and also emphasizes the need for good governance, responsibility, leadership, and practical initiatives for communities and their citizens. Tools as well as financial and technical support are available for city leaders and practitioners addressing the impact of climate change and reducing greenhouse gas emissions. The support measures are intended to help establish global, regional, national, and city-to-city networks; localize the implementation of national adaptation and mitigation strategies; strengthen the capacities of local authorities to integrate climate-change concerns in local and city-wide planning and budgeting for cost-effective policy responses; and produce training institutes to provide climate-change training for local governments (CCCI 2010). These aims again reflect UN-HABITAT's ongoing attempts to build national, regional, and local awareness on the paramount role cities and local governments have in addressing climate change.

In recognition of the crucial role urbanization will continue to play in the mitigation of and adaptation to climate change, another international authority, the Convention on Biological Diversity Secretariat (see chapter 3), has been established to work with other research centres on the implications that rapidly expanding cities hold for biodiversity and ecosystems. Drawing on contributions from over 120 scientists worldwide, the CBD's *Cities and Biodiversity Outlook* (2012) estimates that over 60 per cent of the land projected to become urban by 2030 has yet to be built. This in turn is seen to present a "major opportunity" to greatly improve global sustainability by promoting low-carbon, resource-efficient urban development that can reduce adverse effects on biodiversity and improve quality of life (ibid.).

The CBDs task of exploring ways in which urban biodiversity and ecosystems could be "used, restored, and created in innovative ways to reduce vulnerability and enhance resilience" and how cities could move from being "just consumers to also generate ecosystem services and reduce footprints" is crucial but also daunting. It includes diverse concepts, knowledge, and initiatives in areas such as urban agriculture and food security, renewable energy, district heating and water-treatment systems, urban planning, and transportation. In addition to technological changes, conceiving of cities and building in new ways also requires social, cultural, and political transformations, including reform of local and regional governance and the values, rights, and duties being articulated through concepts such as "eco-citizenship." While a detailed analysis of the impact of such initiatives is beyond the aims and objective of this chapter, we would point readers to the work of Robinson (2009), which examines urban sustainability efforts in Canada and, in particular, their link to many of the international agencies and frameworks outlined here.

Our intention in this chapter is to provide an overview of the broader international context and the many agreements and initiatives affecting Canada. While these encourage national governments to provide financial and technical support, it is clear they have also been charged with providing an overall framework and strategy for guiding sustainable urban development. This role is expected to go beyond top-down programs and anticipates that national governments will enable local initiatives and facilitate place-based solutions and adaptation. In the following section we turn to the federal government's record in this multi-level governance context and, in particular, examine the barriers and challenges that have restricted Canada's progress towards these aims over several decades.

THE CANADIAN REALITY:
CONSTRAINTS, BARRIERS, IMPROVISATION,
AND ADHOCRACY

As Richard and Susan Tindal point out, making a community sustainable involves a significant change in management process to reduce the community's impact on the bioregion, "shrinking the size of [its] ecological footprint" (2004, 81). Towards this aim, the national government needs to "deploy a host of policy instruments and fiscal incentives to embed ecological factors into the decision making processes of citizens and governments" (ibid.). In Canada this was always going to be a difficult task, as many of the issues dealing with the implementation of sustainable development touch on the responsibilities of local governments, which in Canada fall under provincial/territorial jurisdiction.

Section 92 of the Constitution Act (1867) sets out the exclusive powers of provincial legislatures in sixteen areas, with section 92 (8) giving the legislature of each province total responsibility for making laws relating to that province's municipal institutions. Local governments are not recognized under the Constitution as a separate order of government and are often referred to as creatures of the provinces, legally subordinate to them and dependent on provincial legislation for defining the parameters.

As Berdahl concludes, constitutional constraints have been hugely significant in restricting a multi-level approach to urban sustainability with Canadian cities. "Federal engagement in urban affairs is unavoidable, a fact of political life, but, as with all aspects of Canadian politics, it is impossible to understand federal-municipal machinery without locating it within the broader context of the Constitution, federal-provincial relations, and the fiscal and power imbalance they create for municipalities." Nevertheless, this did not stop Lithwick (1970) from criticizing the federal government for avoiding an urban role: "The federal government has used the constitution as an excuse to abstain from playing a responsible urban role, despite overwhelming evidence that it is the principal actor in the urban political reality" (ibid., 577). Lithwick's comment reveals the basic paradox at the heart of federal-municipal relations in Canada: though it has been given no formal powers over local government, the reality for the federal government is that almost everything it does and spends has a direct or indirect impact on municipalities, and cities in particular.

Federal involvement in municipal and urban affairs carries several risks, not least of which is the political wrath of the provinces, which guard their powers jealously. As a result, federal interventions and spending in cities and communities tend to be mercurial and unstable, summary adjectives that when environmental issues are appended to federal-cities agendas become green-lite in many ways. The absence of constitutional authority also makes it difficult for the federal government to enforce conditions on provincial and municipal funding. Consequently, when other levels of government spend federal money, it becomes increasingly difficult to have federal coordination, evaluation, and accountability for results. The federal government also runs the risk that credit for investing in cities will be shared by provincial and municipal governments while its own role and contribution and will go unrecognized by the electorate.

In spite of the significant disincentives and constitutional limits, there is a strong history of federal involvement in urban affairs, an appreciation of which is at the heart of this chapter. As Tindal and Tindal observe, "While local government doesn't have any direct link with the federal government according to the constitution, nothing could be further from the truth" (2004, 207). The reason is that federal governments are acutely aware of the significant opportunities to develop a stronger policy handle and maximize political capital by investing in urban programs and projects. Issues such as declining competitiveness, urban sprawl, the environment, crime, and so on may have urban epicentres, but the political fallout is national, and this has helped to galvanize arguments for a more collaborative and consistent multi-level approach.

Because of the many challenges, federal involvement in urban and municipal affairs is not a linear progression; it ebbs and flows over time in response to a number of contingent factors and policy entry points. Wolfe (2003), for example, suggests that the concept of a national urban policy has emerged forcefully over the course of the twentieth century, particularly at times of urban crises in areas such as poverty, housing, and infrastructure. Connected to this role, federal spending in Canadian cities and communities can be seen as part of its role in nation-building, with resources being reallocated from affluent parts of Canada to relatively less well-off provinces, cities, and regions.

Two other factors also help to determine the degree of federal involvement in municipal affairs. The first is related to the finances of the federal government and the amount of money it has to spend on urban issues and programs. The second is the state of relations between federal and provincial levels of government and, more specifically, the political climate with regard to federal powers and the Constitution. The greater the tension and conflict between the two levels of government, politically and in partisan party terms, the less likely and able the federal government is to become directly involved in urban and municipal affairs. Stoney and Graham (2009) also concluded that the nature and extent of federal-municipal machinery is closely collated with the dynamics of constitutional politics and, in particular, the cycle of conflict and cooperation that characterizes different "eras" in federal-provincial relations.

Young has argued that other contingent factors also play a part in driving and shaping federal-municipal governance and investment. He highlights the nature of the municipality, the policy field, the position and policy capacity of the federal government, and the role of the province in mediating the relationship (2003, 5). For example, Prime Minister Martin's personal interest in urban issues was clearly a factor in driving the New Deal for cities and other tripartite initiatives across Canada. As Dunn states, "In 2003 the urban file was not as central to the federal vision, in part because the cities' champion Martin had been banished from cabinet ... The years 2004 and 2005 saw the rebirth of the urban file with the advent of Martin as Prime Minister" (2005, 59).

FOUR ERAS AND POLICY HISTORIES
IN FEDERAL-CITY RELATIONS:
URBAN SUSTAINABILITY POLICY AND GOVERNANCE

In their historical overview and analysis, Stoney and Graham (2009) identified three distinct periods in urban policy development and federal-local governance "machinery" between the 1960s and 2006, and in this book we also suggest a fourth from 2006 to the present.

Late 1960s to 1978: A Pre-Sustainability Era

With hindsight, we can in one sense cast this period as a pre-sustainability era but need to leave open the extent to which the policies and programs initiated in the name of urban policy have important quality of urban (and community) life impacts. Several are noted briefly.

Established in 1946, the Canada Mortgage and Housing Corporation (CMHC) was a central component in dealing with Canada's postwar housing problems and during the period 1950 to 1970 formed an important part of the story of this regime. Several important programs were introduced by the CMHC, including the Community Planning Association of Canada (CPAC). Based on the concept of community engagement in planning and land-use decisions, the program was formed in the 1950s, before cuts in grants during the 1970s led to its demise.

In 1967, the Federal-Provincial Conference on Housing and Urban Development was held in Ottawa, and Prime Minister Pearson spoke about the federal role in addressing urbanization. The following year, the Liberals, under Trudeau, came to power promising a strong federalist agenda and subsequently appointed the Federal Task Force on Housing and Urban Development (1968). Led by Paul Hellyer, minister of transport, the task force report recommended a "greatly expanded federal role" (Axworthy 1971) and the establishment of a Ministry of State for Urban Affairs (MSUA) (cited in Tindal and Tindal 2004, 208). The establishment of MSUA is seen as a landmark and is undoubtedly the machinery that dominates reflection on this period. When the MSUA was established in 1971, its official mandate was to effect a beneficial federal government influence on the process of urbanization, integrate the federal government's urban policies with its other policies, and foster cooperation on urban affairs with the provinces and municipalities.

In 1969, the federal government also created the Department of Regional Economic Expansion (DREE). The early 1960s saw a wide variety of specially focused economic development programs that were perceived to be overlapping and untidy. A major policy review from 1972 to 1974 led DREE to develop a series of ten-year general development agreements, which were generally well received and required the full cooperation of the provinces. While regions are the focus here, contained within them are concerns about communities, including in particular "one-industry towns" linked to hinterland natural resource development.

Perhaps conscious of the centralizing top-down potential of MSUA, the federal government introduced a number of mechanisms for enhancing citizen and local engagement during this period. Starting in 1973, for example, it initiated annual Federation of Canadian Municipalities (FCM) briefs to the federal Cabinet in order that Cabinet members could be made aware of the municipal perspective. Furthermore, in the same year, it introduced the Neighbourhood Improvement Program and the Residential Rehabilitation Assistance Program. These initiatives required that residents be involved in the planning and implementation of local policies, and so gained some control over what happened to their community in the new environment.

This period in federal-municipal machinery was also characterized by several tri-level meetings and conferences aimed at integrating federal, provincial, and municipal responses to urban issues. The first tri-level meeting, in Winnipeg in April 1971, helped to set up a national tri-level conference. A second national tri-level conference, held in Edmonton in October 1973, addressed the management of growth, housing and land-use strategy, transportation, and public financing and explored a possible three-way approach to managing growth. A third national tri-level conference, to discuss task force findings, was scheduled for the autumn of 1976 in Montebello, Quebec. However, faced with growing demands for constitutional recognition for municipal government by the FCM, the event was

eventually cancelled when provincial ministers of urban and municipal affairs announced they wouldn't be attending, and no further
national tri-level conferences were held.

Along with the demise of the MSUA, the cancellation of the tri-
level conference symbolized the end of an era that saw attempts at
building a comprehensive multi-level governance approach on a
national scale replaced by more opportunistic and ad hoc tri-lateral
arrangements geared to specific cities and regions.

1979–1993: Early SD and Environmental Concerns

By 1981, a number of specific tri-lateral agreements had evolved,
which brought together federal, provincial, and municipal levels of
government to address complex and spatially concentrated social
and economic problems. For example, Urban Development Agreement collaborations (UDAS), pioneered in Winnipeg and later
Vancouver, brought together the problem-solving resources of different levels of government, the community, and business sectors in
an integrated strategy for community-driven revitalization. The
best-known examples during this period include the Winnipeg Core
Area Initiative and the Winnipeg Development Agreement. As the
era of cooperative federalism was replaced with contested federalism, other federal-municipal machinery began to take on a more
regional dimension. For example, by the early 1980s, General Development Agreements were being replaced with new agreements
labelled Economic and Regional Development Agreements, and, in
January 1982, the federal government created the Ministry of State
for Economic and Regional Development and the Department of
Regional Industrial Expansion (DRIE). Two significant regional organizations, the Federal Economic Development Initiative of Northern
Ontario and the Atlantic Canada Opportunities Agency, emerged as
means for targeting programs for regional economic stimulation but
with considerable community-level issues involved. These varied
parent policy fields and their regional agency funding sources meant
that when small environmental features were built in as partial add-
ons, then green-lite policy and governance patterns of both the
multi-scalar and agenda-setting kind were inherent in this period
and in later ones.

With visibility and responsiveness, two of the key criteria in
federal-municipal relations, Ottawa dispatched bureaucrats to the

regions to gauge needs and establish a presence: 1982, for example, saw the creation of Regional Councils for Senior Federal Officials and the deployment of federal economic development coordinators. During this period, importance was also placed on community development partnerships. Also based on the principle of greater local autonomy, the partnerships were intended to cultivate financial and human resources at the grassroots level, so local communities could develop capacity and deliver government policy. Emphasis was on replacing centralized, homogenized policy responses with ones that were community sensitive and innovative – what today might be called place-based or place-sensitive solutions.

1993–2006: Cities and Communities: A Liberal New Deal

The late 1980s and early 1990s saw repeated calls for a tri-level approach to infrastructure investment in Canada's urban centres and communities. In 1993, growing pressure, fuelled by a sense of deepening crisis, led the Liberals to announce the Canada Infrastructure Works Program, launched the following year with an initial two-year $6-billion infrastructure program to upgrade transportation and local services and improve traditional and modern infrastructure such as the "Information Highway." By 2002, the various infrastructure programs were brought together by the creation of Infrastructure Canada. The establishment of Infrastructure Canada, led by Minister of State John Godfrey (Infrastructure and Communities), coordinated federal efforts to build the New Deal for Cities and Communities. The department was also established to make strategic investments in sustainable infrastructure projects through partnerships that meet local community needs, and these programs are outlined and discussed in chapter 8.

In February 2004, federal commitments to GST rebates for municipalities were announced, along with acceleration in infrastructure funding and the exploration of gas tax–sharing arrangements proposed for innovative policies for urban social economy and aboriginal peoples in cities. The creation of a new minister for urban affairs was one of the proposals made by the Prime Minister's Caucus Task Force on Urban Issues. Inaugurated in 2001 and chaired by Liberal MP Judy Sgro, the final report (2002) stopped short of proposing a national urban strategy but recommended more autonomy for municipalities and more collaboration among all levels of government.

As part of its attempt to address urban homelessness, the federal government had already established the National Homelessness Initiative. Launched in 1999, the three-year plan was designed to help ensure community access to those programs and services aimed at alleviating homelessness in communities across all provinces and territories. The centrepiece was the Supporting Communities Partnership Initiative, which supported local partnerships to establish comprehensive local strategies. The federal role was to encourage and enable community partners to lead development and implementation through the designated "community entity" of a municipal government or network of agencies.

The National Research Council established research centres in regions and provided $110 million to help forge links with private-sector partners and the Community Development Partnerships, which received $135 million from the federal government over five years and was formed to support local economic planning and finance small businesses in Canada's rural Atlantic communities. Disappointing general election results in 2000 and 2004 in western Canada made it a high Liberal priority for regional investment. Senior ministers and the prime minister were seen spending much more time in the west, stressing the federal government's commitment to western economic diversification. Consequently, western Urban Development Agreements continue to be prominent. For example, the Canada-Manitoba Agreement for Community and Economic Development (2004–9) built on twenty years of community-based experience in Urban Development Agreements and networks in Winnipeg to set out new strategic policies. These emphasized aboriginal participation in community and economic life, sustainable neighbourhoods, and knowledge-based cluster development.

Tripartite urban development models are also used to address specific urban initiatives. One of the best known is the Vancouver Agreement, a tripartite Urban Development Agreement between the governments of Canada, British Columbia, and the City of Vancouver. The agreement, signed in March 2000, committed these government partners to come together and work with local communities and business interests to develop a coordinated strategy for sustainable economic, social, and community development. The first focus of the Vancouver Agreement is the city's infamous "downtown eastside" area. The Vancouver Agreement was one of several initiatives to be assessed by the Office of the Auditor General, in 2005, and judged to be a fine example of horizontal management and accountable government (Auditor General of Canda 2005, chap. 4, exhibit 4.5).

The auditor general's report drew particular attention to the fact that the Vancouver Agreement governance model facilitated provincial, municipal, and federal governments working together to meet the needs of the community and found that the Western Economic Diversification Canada "provided leadership as the federal representative" (Auditor General of Canda 2005, chap. 4, exhibit 4.5). There was also some coordination between the activities of the Vancouver Agreement and the National Homelessness Initiative: "The Vancouver Agreement's task team on homelessness and housing met monthly leading to increased co-ordination between Human Resources and Skill Development and the British Columbia and Yukon office of the Canada Mortgage and Housing Corporation" (exhibit 4.5).

A related and targeted example of regional federal-municipal machinery in this period is the Urban Aboriginal Strategy, which decentralized federal funding to local committees in order to facilitate improved responses to community priorities and integrate funding streams from different departments. Created in 1998, with $25 million in funding over three years, the agreement was intended to coordinate federal services for the growing number of aboriginal peoples living in cities.

2007–2013: The Demise of Explicit Cities Agenda in Recession and a New Era of "Open Federalism"

Although the Liberals' New Deal for Cities waned quickly, following their loss of power in the 2006 and the economic crisis that followed, the legacy has been the extension of the Gas Tax Fund under the Conservative government, eventually made permanent in 2012. The Harper Action Plan stimulus program can also be seen to build on this experience, as the Harper government worked with provincial governments and territories to deliver funding to municipalities for much-needed infrastructure projects (discussed further in chapter 8). However, it also appears to provide further evidence of the shift from institution-building to "buying influence" through funding that has characterized the changing federal role over recent decades (Stoney and Graham 2009). This shift is also consistent with the Harper government's stated philosophy of "open federalism."

Regarded as a federal commitment to stay out of provincial affairs, open federalism, combined with skepticism about fossil-fuel-driven climate change, suggests that the federal government is unlikely to pursue multi-level approaches to urban sustainability in the near future.

Transportation and expanding markets appear to be the main sectors where the Harper government is willing to support a multi-level approach in order to advance its strategic priorities of trade and innovation through the competitive "gateways" and other initiatives. In establishing the gateways, the federal government is partnering with provincial governments, private-sector transportation leaders, and other stakeholders to put in place an "integrated package of investment and policy measures" aimed at advancing the capacity and efficiency of Canada's transportation network, with a view to "improving competitiveness" across the entire supply chain and facilitating trade with major international markets (Canada's Gateways 2013).

THE FEDERAL ROLE IN URBAN SUSTAINABILITY: ART OF THE POSSIBLE OR LACK OF VISION?

As outlined earlier in the chapter, Agenda 21 called for action in several areas of responsibility that are specific to local government and to certain sectors of business (such as manufacturing) that have a significant impact on the environment. These responsibilities include: promoting sustainable human-settlement development; integrating environment and development in decision-making; integrating the planning and management of land resources; protecting the quality and supply of freshwater resources (applying integrated approaches to the development, management, and use of water resources); promoting environmentally sound management of solid wastes and sewage-related issues; protecting the atmosphere; strengthening the role of non-governmental organizations (partners for sustainable development); and strengthening the role of business and industry.

To achieve improvements in all of these areas, the federal government needed to create appropriate policy instruments as well as the right financial incentives. When Agenda 21 was signed in June 1992, however, in addition to the ongoing constitutional challenges, the fiscal capacity of the federal government was under severe pressure and, as the Canadian economy slid into a recession, the federal deficit started to balloon out of control. Thus, at this juncture, green-lite features of both a means-ends conflict kind and an agenda-setting kind were evident. The Agenda 21 purposes were endorsed, but the expenditure means were eventually unavailable, and s D did not feature in budget speeches when deficit fighting and spending cuts were the norm.

Following the election of the Liberals in 1993, the immediate focus of the government was to stimulate the economy, and thus some initial supportive spending emerged. The FCM had lobbied diligently for federal government funding for municipal infrastructure, and the Liberals added this to their election platform. They delivered on the commitment shortly after they assumed power. In 1994 $2 billion in new federal spending (increased by another $400 million in 1997) was allocated to the provinces and territories as contributions to help "modernize" municipal infrastructure. The federal government usually shared one-third of the cost of infrastructure projects that created jobs in the construction sector. As this suggests, the principal driver for investments in municipal infrastructure was founded on Keynesian economics – stimulating the economy in communities across the country – rather than focusing on investments needed to support Agenda 21 (Hilton and Stoney 2008).

While the Canadian government made a commitment in the Speech from the Throne in 1994 to "promote sustainable development as an integral component of decision making at all levels of our society," this was largely rhetoric: it emerged that sustainable development was not really a priority issue for the federal government (Hilton and Stoney 2008). By the end of 1994, it began to initiate several expenditure reductions resulting from its program review to address the deficit of more than $40 billion. As the minister of finance admitted in his Budget Speech, the red ink had to be stanched: it was "crucial that government get its own house in order" (Canada 1995a, 7). Major budget reductions severely curbed Canada's capacity to meet its domestic and international commitments, including those related to the implementation of sustainable development.

As Gilles Paquet and Robert Shepherd note in their critique of the federal government's belt-tightening exercise, "What was originally envisaged as a rethinking and reforming of the role of the state within Canada's governance system and the role of the federal government within it was already dwarfed by the end of 1994 to an exercise of federal expenditure reduction, and by the end of 1995 to an efficiency-seeking exercise" (Paquet and Shepherd 1996, 32).

In the mid-1990s, the federal government launched its foreign policy review – "Canada in the World" – which called for the promotion of such "Canadian values" as "respect for democracy, the rule of law, human rights and the environment" (Foreign Affairs and International Trade Canada 1995, s. 2). The new foreign policy trumpeted the need to export or "project" these values abroad as a means of achieving "prosperity within Canada and ... the protection of global security" (s. 5). The federal government presented sustainable development as "a global concern ... [to which] Canada is committed [including] its interdependent objectives: protecting the environment, social development and economic well-being" (ibid.). Sustainable development was touted as "a *central component of the Canadian value system* ... a matter of both common security and good economics" (ibid., emphasis added). As part of its effort to "brand" Canada through its new foreign policy, the federal government marketed sustainable development not as a goal, but as distinctly *Canadian* value. Again in this foreign policy sense, sD was put into an even larger mix of values, creating valuable rhetoric but, in "ends-means" conflict terms, its green-lite limbo was obvious.

However, while the federal government was making pronouncements that sustainable development was "a central component of the Canadian value system," new capital spending was anathema to the "small is better government" mantra. Consequently, as Hilton and Stoney (2008) observe, the federal commitment to sustainable development has often appeared to be an expression without substance – a promise bereft of required policy and funding.

Significantly, "sustainable development" was not part of the federal government's vocabulary in either its domestic policy or fiscal frameworks during the 1990s. The 1995–99 budgets tabled in Parliament made no reference to "sustainable development." References to the environment involved support for businesses involved in creating environmental technologies through government programs such as Technology Partnership Canada. Even the rationale for the creation of a new foundation – the Canada Foundation for Innovation (CFI), which had an initial contribution of $800 million – was focused on the need to support economic growth. CFI would support the efforts of post-secondary institutions and research hospitals in modernizing research infrastructure (Canada 1997, 15). CFI's activities focused on health, the environment, science, and engineering, but there was no mention of how these activities would address sustainable development. In the words of the minister of finance, the future was all about growing the economy: "The Canada Foundation for Innovation is about looking forward. It is about our children. It is about education. In short, it is about investing in the future growth of our economy, making a down payment today for much greater reward tomorrow" (16). The federal agenda on the environment changed significantly as a result of a wave of international pressure to address climate change. As shown in chapters 2, 3, and 5, the Kyoto Protocol on Climate Change required industrialized countries to reduce their collective emissions of greenhouse gases.[*] In the 1999 Speech from the Throne, the federal government committed to "place greater emphasis on sustainable development in government decision making" (Privy Council Office 1999, s. 6).

With the federal deficit eliminated, the purse strings were loosened in Budget 2000. In the minister of finance's speech to the House of Commons, he included nineteen references to the environment. He made the commitment that "protecting the environment is not an option – it is something that we simply must do. It is a fundamental value – beyond debate, beyond discussion" (Canada 2000, 13). The federal government's new-found interest and concern for the environment heralded a big spending spree.

Support for climate change saw the federal government commit $210 million over three years for the Climate Change Action Fund (CCAF) and other federal energy-efficiency and renewable-energy programs. As well, $60 million (subsequently increased by another $50 million in 2003) was used to create the Canadian Foundation for Climate and Atmospheric Sciences (CFCAS), which became the

---

[*] Under the Kyoto Protocol, Canada agreed to reduce annual emissions over the period 2008–12 to a level 6 per cent below actual emissions in 1990. As the minister of the environment, Stéphane Dion, admitted in 2005, however, "Canada is indeed far behind but Canada is not giving up" (Dion 2005).

main funding body for university-based research on climate, atmospheric, and related oceanic work in Canada.[†]

The Federation of Canadian Municipalities as well as La Coalition pour le renouvellement des infrastructures du Québec had again lobbied successfully for more funding from the federal government for municipal infrastructure. Budget 2000 committed over $2 billion to "strengthen the basic physical infrastructure which underpins so much of the economic activity of both rural and urban Canada" (Canada 2000, 16). Unlike the earlier Canada Infrastructure Works Program, however, there was now a call for a new focus on "green infrastructure." Program funding would result in the "enhancement of the quality of the environment, support long-term economic growth, improve community infrastructure, increase innovation and use of new approaches and best practices [and make] more efficient use of existing infrastructure." With regards to the last, $12.5 million in funding from the program was directed to create the National Guide to Sustainable Municipal Infrastructure: Innovations and Best Practices, involving a partnership between the federal government and the Federation of Canadian Municipalities. This unique initiative represented a step towards the community capacity-building called for by Agenda 21, although the federal government's rationale for committing the funding made no reference to that proposal. The project ran until 2006, when a request for further funding from the federal government was denied by the Harper Conservatives.

The federal government also committed $600 million from Budget 2000 for improvements to provincial highways. The objective of the new program – the Strategic Highways Infrastructure Program (SHIP) – was to "improve the quality of life of Canadians by promoting safer and more environmentally sustainable transportation ... [and] make the Canadian surface transportation system more reliable, efficient, competitive, integrated, and sustainable" (Transport Canada 2007). Transport Canada defined "sustainable transportation" as "one that is safe, efficient and environmentally friendly ... a transportation system that respects the natural

† Established as an autonomous foundation, the Canadian Foundation for Climate and Atmospheric Sciences is "a network of institutes which will link researchers from across the country in order, for instance, to further our understanding of the impact of climate change and air pollution on human health" (Budget Speech 2000).

environment" (19). However, beyond the broad principle that "governments, industry and individuals must work together to integrate economic, social and environmental considerations into decisions affecting transportation activity" (ibid.), Transport Canada does not have a policy framework to explain what this means, nor has it explained how miles of new asphalt can be "environmentally friendly." This is not surprising, given the auditor general's earlier criticism of the federal government for its failure to have a highway policy and for the practice of committing significant amounts of money to highway projects in a "vacuum" (Auditor General of Canada 1998; Hilton and Stoney 2009b).

While interest in the environment featured prominently in Budget 2000, the major reason driving this interest was based in economics. As the minister of finance observed, "Those nations which demonstrate how to truly integrate environmental and economic concerns will forge new tools and develop new technologies that others will have to adopt. Tremendous rewards await those nations that get there first, for those which do it best ... Technology is key" (Canada 2000, 13). Under Budget 2000, the federal government pursued this theme aggressively, providing an additional $900 million in funding for the Canada Foundation for Innovation (CFI). It identified CFI as "one of the cornerstones of our plan to support the new economy" (12). As an independent corporation, CFI operates at arm's length from the government under the guidance of an independent board of directors, much to the chagrin of the auditor general.‡ The federal government made further increases to CFI's operating capital, raising its total funding to $3.65 billion, which allowed it to expand financial support for the scientific and technological communities (CFI 2005). In Budget 2007, the Harper government added another $510 million to CFI.

CFI's mandate is to fund research infrastructure needed to carry out research that creates "the necessary conditions for sustainable, long-term economic growth – including the creation of spin-off ventures and the commercialization of discoveries" (CFI 2005, 1.F). The CFI recognizes the importance of research in creating a sustainable

‡ The auditor general has sharply criticized the federal government's practice of creating and funding entities outside the reach of her oversight. She has raised the issue in several reports (see Office of the Auditor General of Canada 2002, chap. 1, and 2005a, chap. 4).

environment, providing funding for research in areas such as solid waste, water supply, transport systems, renewable energy sources, recycling, rational utilization of energy, protection of soil and groundwater, pollution and protection of the environment, infrastructure, and general planning of land-use. These areas of research have a potentially significant impact on local governments, although this is not acknowledged in CFI's literature. The opportunity to tie this research to the aims of Brundtland and Agenda 21 would appear to have been lost to the pursuit of economic growth (Hilton and Stoney 2008, 2009b).

The mandate of CFI is clearly focused on building research capacity "to ensure our international competitiveness in those domains in which Canada is, or has the potential to be, the world leader ... [and] translating the knowledge and ideas being generated by the research enterprise into new products and services that will enhance prosperity and our quality of life" (CFI 2005, 3). While CFI claims that it has funded infrastructure projects in sixty-two municipalities across Canada that have "contributed to the development of community based technology clusters and to the transfer of new knowledge and ideas to industry" (ibid.), it remains unclear how these results have contributed to sustainable development in Canada. We know of no independent or government-led attempts to measure outcomes in these specific areas. Any such measurement would be difficult to undertake and would, ideally, require non-CFI-funded research.

In its 2004–5 annual report, CFI set an objective to "ensure benefits to Canada [by] promot[ing] networking, collaboration, and multidisciplinary approaches and collaborating with other funding agencies and provincial governments to optimize the impact of research investments, and identify longer-term needs" (CFI 2005, 25). As well, CFI intends to "demonstrate the value of investments [by] examin[ing] the impacts of CFI-funded projects in different parts of Canada ... [and to] partner with other funding agencies within the federal and provincial governments to ensure that good and relevant information is being collected in evaluation and outcome assessment of CFI-funded projects" (ibid.). While CFI's preoccupation with economic prosperity and ensuring that Canada is "internationally competitive in research and innovation" is important, so too is determining how past results have contributed to sustainable development.

As noted earlier, in the time leading up to Budget 2000, the FCM and La Coalition pour le renouvellement des infrastructures du Québec lobbied the federal government for funding to help local communities use innovative technology – "green infrastructure" – that would generate measurable environmental, economic, and social benefits in addressing their environmental challenges. The federal government agreed to provide $125 million as an endowment to the FCM to encourage local governments to apply new technologies in energy and water savings, urban transit, waste diversion, and renewable energy. The federal government doubled its funding for GMF in 2001 and increased it by another $300 million in 2005. This arrangement is significant, because it involves direct funding by the federal government for the FCM through the establishment of an endowment fund. By becoming involved in the delivery of a federal program, the FCM, a representative association of local governments, may run the risk of compromising its independent platform from which to assess and, if necessary, criticize federal policy. Nevertheless it demonstrates the growing importance and influence of the FCM in the cities' regime and provides the federal government with a useful body by which to devise and implement urban policies and deliver funding to municipalities.

Spending programs such as the CFI are indicative of federal policy on innovation, green industries, and the new economy but may or may not be easy to discern in impacts or involvement at the level of cities, communities, and so-called local-regional innovation clusters. But aimed at universities and public-private research establishments, which are in the main located in larger cities, they can readily confer some environmental benefits in particular program applications approved under them (Doern and Stoney 2009; Wolfe 2009). However, in other respects, federal programs and funding directed towards municipalities per se appear to target primary outcomes such as economic growth, job creation, regional regeneration, and political success. Improving urban transportation, infrastructure, livability, and competitiveness appear to be secondary and sometimes merely collateral beneficiaries of the spending process (Bradford 2004a). Although there are clear constraints on what federal governments can do to influence Canadian cities, the lack of a clear coordinated vision and national strategy, combined with a lack of sustained commitment to intervene in urban affairs, has also contributed to the federal government's approach that Hilton and Stoney (2008) have characterized as one of "benign neglect."

THE THREE REGIME ELEMENTS

Policy Ideas, Discourse, and Agendas

As highlighted in table 7.1, this first element of the book's analytical framework, the main policies, ideas, and discourse in the Federal–Cities Urban Sustainability Regime have shifted significantly over time. Initially sustainability did not figure at all in ideas and discourse. Rather, they reflected concerns over potential contagion of the social tensions, the flight of the middle class from downtown areas, and riots occurring in several US cities. Consequently, federal interventions focused on social investment and economic regeneration in Canada's larger cities, especially in housing (CMHC) and community development through programs such as the Neighbourhood Improvement Programs (NIPS). Protecting civil liberties and enshrining human rights were also seen as part of the federal strategy to maintain peace and order in Canada's increasingly mixed urban centres and neighbourhoods.

By the 1980s the focus had shifted to concern about the environment and the impact of urbanization, and urban sprawl in particular. As discussed, urban sustainability emerged out of the findings of the Brundtland Commission. Agenda 21 then underscored the fact that cities were key to dealing with the broader environmental challenge. Economic regeneration continued to be seen as a central piece in the federal government's urban and regional policy-making, especially in cities such as Winnipeg, where tri-level urban development agreements (UDAS) were implemented. The neo-liberalization of markets also generated opportunities for private sector investments, and public-private partnerships were increasingly prominent in regeneration efforts. The election of successive Liberal governments in the 1990s provided the federal government a greater foothold in Canada's major cities and, along with reducing the fiscal deficit, the so-called infrastructure deficit provided a clearer agenda for investment and renewal. The New Deal for cities was made easier by the fact that the federal-provincial chill caused by constitutional wrangling had begun to thaw, and, with the rising costs of health and education, the provinces were more amenable to federal investment and collaboration in cities. In addition, the rise of place-based, multi-level approaches to "wicked problems" provided a number of policy options. Discourse such as on the "new urbanism" and "smart growth" also provided rationales for federal investment in green infrastructure.

The election of a Conservative government in 2006 coincided with rising gas prices and concerns about the economy, which had already appeared to make carbon taxes and green policies such as the Liberals' "green shift" less popular with the Canadian electorate. As well as being ideologically opposed to a multi-level governance approach, the Conservatives were much more dedicated to their Alberta base and much less committed to "green" programs. Investment in infrastructure continued and actually increased through this period, but the emphasis shifted away from the environment and sustainability to job creation and economic stimulus.

The changing discourse and ideas also began to emphasize increasing competitiveness, productivity, and innovation as a reason to invest in cities. Even so, the current government has shown little interest or inclination for developing an urban agenda or national transportation policy, and fewer funding programs are directed towards addressing an environmental or sustainability agenda. The market and individual preferences about where to live and how to commute ("the right to choose") appear to be ideologically preferable to state intervention, even if that produces negative externalities such as urban sprawl and rising emissions.

Also noticeable has been the government's reluctance to engage in emerging discourse and corresponding policy debates on urban agriculture and food security, urban biodiversity, and ecosystems and eco-citizenship. In many countries such debates have become mainstream, while in Canada they remain very much on the fringe of politics, often dismissed as eccentric or demonized as part of a radical "left-wing" environmental agenda. Eco-citizenship is premised on the belief that as citizens all individuals have ecological rights but also duties towards the natural environment. By establishing them as basic human rights and responsibilities it is hoped that individuals and organizations will be increasingly inclined to analyze and calculate their use of resources and subsequently reduce their individual and collective ecological footprints. Urban agriculture involves the practice of cultivating, processing, and distributing food in or close to a village, town, or city. When food is grown, processed, and distributed locally, it is regarded as a safer, more secure, and ultimately more sustainable process. These benefits can be reinforced by collecting and reusing food waste and rainwater and by educating, organizing, and employing local residents in production and recycling. To be transformative, urban agriculture also needs to be integrated with the ways that cities function and are managed, including municipal policies, plans, and budgets. In addition to being integrated into local town planning, these networks also require formal institutional support in order to overcome significant green-lite tendencies. In Canada, support for such initiatives has been localized within governments and civil society with little federal support, engagement, or leadership.

Environmental Power Structures, Democracy, and Governance

The record of federal intervention in the urban environment can be understood only in the context of Canadian federalism more broadly, and the relationship with the provinces in particular. The constitutional limits on the federal role in municipal affairs have been the main barrier to establishing a more coherent regime in pursuit of urban sustainability. Municipalities are, for the most part, dependent upon property taxes for revenues they generate themselves, and this has no doubt contributed to urban sprawl and the relative power of local pro-growth regimes that make city councils especially dependent upon local developers. National governments are normally seen to be less dependent on and less accessible to local developers, so the de facto absence of the federal government from urban affairs has been crucial in explaining their influence and role in local regimes.

As we have reviewed, the federal government has attempted to influence Canadian cities through a variety of measures. Institution-building marked the postwar period, with the 1960s MSUA marking the apogee of this approach. In spite of some success, the experience of the MSUA led to its demise in 1978. Its attempt to coordinate federal thinking and policies toward cities through an "urban lens" had irritated many senior departments, and the constitutional wrangling of the late 1970s and 1980s put an end to ambitious and overt interventions. Since the demise of MSUA, federal interventions have been more regional and targeted through tri-level agreements and projects located in urban cores. The trend has also shifted from "building" influence to "buying" influence, as noted by Stoney and Graham (2009). This has been most evident through the New Deal era and the stimulus spending that followed the financial crisis of 2007. During this period, Infrastructure Canada and the FCM have emerged as important institutions in federal-local relations, as the focus has shifted towards infrastructure investment and renewal.

SCIENCE, EVIDENCE, KNOWLEDGE, AND PRECAUTION

Politics, ideology, and the economy have always appeared to play a greater role in federal-municipal relations than science per se. However, social science and a number of influential task forces and reports have shaped federal interventions and provided the policy agenda through which it is administered. In the postwar period, CMHC generated an enormous amount of data and evidence justifying investment in housing and homelessness. Though short-lived, the MSUA also helped to put urban issues on the agenda, but a lack of resources and considerable resentment from the provinces and from within the federal bureaucracy seriously undermined its impact and influence on urban affairs. In addition to the irritation that some departments felt towards the MSUA and their perceived "meddling" in policy-making, federal governments have also been cautious about trying to address the "wicked problems" that cities generate and the financial "black holes," like infrastructure and housing, into which they could easily be drawn.

Other important conferences, commissions, and reports have continued to explore and propose possible roles for the federal government in urban matters. For example, in 1967, the Federal-Provincial Conference on Housing and Urban Development was held in Ottawa, and Prime Minister Pearson spoke about the federal role in addressing urbanization. The following year, the Liberals came to power promising a strong federalist agenda and subsequently appointed the Federal Task Force on Housing and Urban Development (1968). Led by Paul Hellyer, minister of transport, the task force recommended a "greatly expanded federal role" that led to the establishment of the Ministry of State for Urban Affairs (Tindal and Tindal 2004, 208). This was followed by a major policy review and led DREE to develop a series of ten-year General Development Agreements between 1972 and 1974.

Starting in 1973, FCM briefs were made available to all federal Cabinet members to make them aware of the municipal issues and concerns and the potential impact of their departmental policies. This period was also characterized by a number of tri-level meetings

Table 7.1: The Federal–Cities Urban Sustainability Regime and the three regime elements: Selected summary highlights

The three analytical elements

POLICY HISTORIES	POLICIES, IDEAS, DISCOURSE, AND AGENDAS	POWER STRUCTURES, DEMOCRACY, AND GOVERNANCE	SCIENCE, EVIDENCE, KNOWLEDGE, AND PRECAUTION
A pre-sustainability era: late 1960s to 1978	• Housing and social renewal • Environmentalism, local activism, and human rights • Community capacity-building (e.g., neighbourhood improvement programs • Federal centralization and intervention in a pan-Canadian approach • Keynesian social welfare and redistribution • Paternalistic and technocratic planning solutions to urban problems	• Federal-municipal machinery became increasingly institutionalized • CMHC • MSUA to coordinate federal role in cities • Liberal-dominated era	• Inner cities seen to be under pressure from immigration, growth, and economic decline; social tensions, including race riots, in United States • Federal funding, institutions, and policies seen in part as response to some of these challenges, particularly the "hollowing out" that was undermining the sustainability of cities south of the border • Urban aboriginal policies needed as shift to the cities gathered pace
Early SD and environmental concerns: 1979–93	• Sustainable development in late 1980s after Brundtland Commission • Devolved decision-making reflects subsidiary and enabling discourse • Partnerships and tri-level agreements seen as the way to bridge federal-local divide • Urban renewal and redevelopment seen as key priorities	• MSUA seen as failed intervention by federal government in provincial and urban affairs • Emphasis switches from national to regional and local agreements • Regional federal agencies (DREE, DRIE, federal economic development coordinators, etc.) are established to redistribute federal spending and outreach • Conservative era dominated by free-trade and constitutional wrangling (contested federalism) • Deficits, inflation, and high interest rates put pressure on the federal purse	• Environmental concerns were added to social concerns; acid rain and urban sprawl seen as the major challenges to the quality of life in Canadian centres • Brundtland and Agenda 21, ICLEA, and other international initiatives call for serious response to global warming • Cities seen as the largest producers of GHG emissions

| Cities and communities Liberal New Deal era: 1993–2006 | • Place-based policy-making advocates greater autonomy for local decision-making (subsidiarity and "glocalization") and a more enabling role for senior-level governments in helping municipal governments address local matters
• Multi-level governance dominates the discourse for a more coherent and collaborative approach to urban affairs and sustainable development
• Greater revenue sharing called for, as federal and provincial downloading increase financial pressures on municipalities
• Smart growth, new urbanism, a "green" infrastructure, and the ideas of Jane Jacobs dominate thinking about ways to tackle urban sprawl and land-use planning challenges
• Infrastructure deficit becomes very effective tool as FCM and business lobby lead call for infrastructure investment
• Growing political calls for action in Canadian cities | • Liberal-dominated era that allows for some continuity in policy development and institutions
• Urban Task Force (Sgro commission) calls for a "New Deal" for cities and communities
• Infrastructure Canada created to oversee programs and funding for municipal infrastructure
• Federation of Canadian Municipalities plays influential lobbying role for municipalities
• Gas Tax Program implemented with strong emphasis on green infrastructure and Integrated Community Sustainability Plans (ICSPS); program eventually made permanent | • Amalgamations across many of Canada's urban centres create metropolitan areas and "mega-cities"; increasing importance brings calls for a "multi-level" approach, including a rethink of city-region governance
• City-regions increasingly seen as the basis of international competitiveness
• Federal government urged to invest in infrastructure by think tanks such as the Conference Board and consultants KPMG; calls for city-states, increased local autonomy, and new forms of revenue sharing
• Richard Florida's creative class thesis fuels interest in urban centres as cultural centres with emphasis on "world class" cities and attracting global talent; international tables begin to measure and rank such factors, including competitiveness and productivity |

Table 7.1: (continued)

The three analytical elements

POLICY HISTORIES	POLICIES, IDEAS, AND AGENDAS	POWER STRUCTURES, DEMOCRACY, AND GOVERNANCE	SCIENCE, EVIDENCE, KNOWLEDGE, AND PRECAUTION
Demise of explicit cities agenda in recession and open federalism era: 2006–14	• Embrace of "open federalism" signals "lite" role for federal government in urban affairs (shallow federalism) • "Ethical" oil from Canada portrayed as better choice for US than foreign oil from Middle East • New discourse and policy debates emerge around urban bio-diversity and ecosystems, urban agriculture, food security and eco-citizens • Environmentalists demonized as "radicals" by some Conservatives • Economy, growth, and jobs become the Conservative mantra • (Renewable) energy competes with sustainable development as key environmental discourse • Federal infrastructure spending increases, but economic stimulus (jobs and growth) is the primary goal, urban renewal a secondary aspect • Innovation economy and smart regulation emerge in the discourse on competitive cities	• P3 Canada established to promote public-private partnerships • Think tanks, especially those based in western, oil-rich Canada, increase prominence • Effective lobbying from FCM helps ensure continued funding for infrastructure gas tax made permanent • stimulus funding (EAP/ISF) dominates infrastructure investment, but jobs, growth, and political visibility replace green and sustainability criteria as central aim • Shovel-ready projects sought, but still no national policy for Canada's cities and transportation • Sustainable Development Act passed in 2008 to provide legal framework for developing and implementing a Federal Sustainable Development Strategy and integrate environmental, economic, and social factors in the making of all decisions by government; some indicators developed, but still not clear what this means in practice and little mention of the act in political circles or debates	• Evidence-based policy-making rejected (no evidence that stimulus created jobs or improved measures of sustainability) • Climate change seen as "junk science" by some and marginalized or rejected • Federal environmental assessment protections streamlined or cut altogether • Federal changes to Statistics Canada census data collection make comparisons and forecasts harder and reduce information needed to inform urban planning • Evidence of organized corruption emerging from the Charbonneau Commission, and other hearings raise questions about the governance of municipalities and leads to calls for an "ethical" infrastructure in local government – especially if they are to continue to receive significant federal funding and be afforded greater revenue-sharing powers

and conferences aimed at integrating federal, provincial, and municipal responses to urban issues. The creation of a new minister for urban affairs was one of the proposals made by the Prime Minister's Caucus Task Force on Urban Issues. Inaugurated in 2001 and chaired by Liberal MP Judy Sgro, the final report (2002) stopped short of proposing a national urban strategy but recommended more autonomy for municipalities and more collaboration among all levels of government.

As the federal government has largely abdicated urban affairs since 2006, conferences and commissioned reports have also waned. The policy and research vacuum has been filled partially by government agencies such as the federal Policy Horizons Canada, academic centres (e.g., Mowat Centre, Centre for Urban Research and Education), think tanks and institutes (the Canada Urban Institute, FCM, Institute for Public Policy Research, Pembina Institute), international bodies (e.g., OECD, World Bank) and consultancies and foundations (e.g., KPMG, IBM, Bill Gates Fund). Although such organizations produce excellent reports, it is difficult to know the extent to which their recommendations are internalized within the federal government, but the continued absence of an urban agenda or strategy and the growing concerns about the neglect of evidence in policy-making suggests that the influence is very limited.

CONCLUSIONS

This chapter has examined the Federal–Cities and Urban Sustainability Regime as a further important but also nascent and episodic environmental regime that the federal government has attempted to influence over several decades. A wide range of policy fields have entered the regime story over fifty years.

We traced four eras and policy histories in which the federal approach has been markedly different. Early on, there were no sustainability ideas present as federal attempts were made to build institutional machinery in the 1960s and 1970s. The "interregnum" period of the 1980s and early 1990s saw the federal government adopt a more low-key approach based on some sustainability ideas but mainly via establishing regional capacity and targeted programs. During the mid-1990s, the favoured approach shifted towards federal involvement in tri-level agreements, but under successive Chrétien and Martin liberal governments a more coherent and coordinated approach emerged and was tabled as a "New Deal" for Canadian cities but not necessarily regarding sustainability per se. The so-called urban agenda appeared to signal the emergence of a multi-level governance regime, with the federal government working closely with provincial and municipal partners to invest in municipal infrastructure and related programs. There were glimpses of environmental and sustainable agendas, even if they were often secondary to competing or conflicting goals.

The election of Stephen Harper's minority governments brought a more cautious federal approach consistent with the principles of "open" or "shallow" federalism and consisting largely of federal spending on municipal infrastructure as part of the fiscal crisis and recession-era stimulus package aimed primarily at economic regeneration rather than urban renewal. The New Deal inspired federal rhetoric on finding long-term solutions to urban issues has changed dramatically in the last decade. For example, when asked about the government's response to a new study claiming that urban infrastructure is "near collapse," Finance Minister Jim Flaherty responded, "We're not in the pothole business in the government of Canada" (Campion-Smith 2007, A1). His dismissive remarks appeared to confirm that the era of urban-focused multi-level governance is over, at least for the time being.

As the different policy history eras illustrate, city- and community-focused multi-level government in Canada is transient and subject to constitutional constraints. Still, we have shown that federal governments, when motivated to act, have the means by which to influence urban affairs, including a mix of institutional, financial, and enabling policy options.

Although there are important differences across the periods examined, two common threads emerge throughout: the scant attention given to the urban consequences of federal policies, environmentally related or not, by politicians and bureaucrats; and the continued lack of intergovernmental communication and coordination on the national and international stage. Not surprisingly, this largely uncoordinated approach has severely limited Canada's capacity to implement international initiatives such as Agenda 21 and other follow-up discourse about urban sustainability. While Brundtland called on nations to develop a national urban strategy, and Agenda 21 called on all countries to identify the environmental implications of urban development and to address these in an integrated fashion, federal investments in municipalities have focused over the fifty-year story on other goals such as growth, housing, job creation, and economic stimulation.

As Canada's larger cities morph into city regions, governance becomes increasingly difficult to coordinate, including where environmental and related goals may be directly or even indirectly involved. For example, no single level of government appears to have adequate powers to provide integrated thinking on issues such as transportation and pollution prevention. While there are valid concerns about "multiple-tier" governance and the risk of confused accountability (from the taxpayers' perspective), there needs to be a broader discussion about the governance of Canada's urban regions to ensure that decision-making better incorporates the principles of urban sustainability and planning. As we have seen, however, the lack of multi-level governance in Canada reflects "the art of the possible" as well as an absence of federal vision and commitment. Realistically there is little evidence that significant changes in multi-level collaboration are likely to change in the near future, in spite of continued international pressure; as ever, intergovernmental relations are determined nationally and by the economic and political realities of the day. These are key factors that help reveal complexity and explain why progress on the Federal–Cities and Urban Sustainability Regime can accurately be described as *green-lite*. Each of our five green-lite policy and governance patterns emerges strongly in the full analytical and empirical story. Overall, the multi-scalar aspects of green-lite loom, large both in constitutional terms and in the scope and complexity of the internal Canadian boundaries involved in multi-level spatial governance and defined jurisdictions involving cities and communities. More specifically, the deployment of human settlement discourse within Agenda 21, while broadly desirable, was itself also replete with green-lite features of the complex boundary type, as well as means-ends conflict and ambiguity. The later story of varied parent policy fields and their regional and innovation agency-funding sources meant that when small sustainability and environmental features were built in as partial add-ons, then green-lite features of both the multi-scalar and agenda-setting kind were rampant. Green-lite features of both a means-ends conflict kind and an agenda-setting kind were evident throughout in the ups and downs of intergovernmental funding, especially when federal deficit fighting and spending cuts were the norm.

8

The Federal–Municipal Infrastructure Sustainability Regime

The previous chapter set out the broad framework of federal-urban and local relations and identified the ways in which the federal government intervenes in municipal affairs and influences urban sustainability. Identified as a policy area, infrastructure renewal has been central in defining the shift from institution-building to financing, and in this chapter we examine this important regime in more depth. Not only has infrastructure emerged as a financial "superhighway" enabling billions of dollars to flow from federal to local government, it has also provided a policy window through which the federal government can provide incentives for urban sustainability and the greening of Canadian cities. Compared to regimes examined in chapters 4, 5, and 6, the Federal–Municipal Infrastructure Sustainability Regime, similar to chapter 7, is a newer hyphenated and only partly congealed environmental regime. Moreover, it reveals key green-lite complexity, particularly involving policy and governance patterns: policy "ends-means" calculus and conflict; diverse and conflicting temporal realities inherent in what infrastructure capital is; and the intricate nature of, and triggering points for, environmental agendas.

Municipal infrastructure covers many of the basic installations and essential services needed by modern societies, including clean water, sewage treatment, roads, highways, bridges, communications systems, and public transit. Strategic functions served by this infrastructure are clearly crucial components in the pursuit of building more sustainable cities. In addition to providing opportunities to reduce the ecological footprint of cities by introducing cleaner technology, improving energy efficiency, and limiting the growth of urban sprawl, infrastructure renewal is also fundamental to economic sustainability. It requires investment in the building, refurbishment, and renewal of physical capital assets over decades, linked intricately to environmental capital. The role of public infrastructure as an economic foundation underpinning business productivity is well established (Ratner 1983; Aschauer 1988, 1990). However, Brox (2008) estimates that public infrastructure expenditure has fallen since 1970 to just over half its average 1960–70 value, measured as a percentage of GDP. This rate of decline has been corroborated by analyses using Statistics Canada conducted by the Canada West Foundation, although there has been a significant reversal of this trend since the nadir of the mid- to late 1990s (Vander Ploeg and Holden 2013). Brox (2008) argues that this downward trend is one of the main reasons for the productivity slowdown that has occurred since the relatively stronger economic growth and productivity of the 1960s and 1970s.

Prior to the stimulus-led increase in public infrastructure investment beginning in 2007–8, estimates from the Federation of Canadian Municipalities (FCM), the Technology Road Map (TRM), and McGill University (led by Saeed Mirza) show that the "infrastructure gap" (the difference between investment needed and actual investment) has continued to grow since estimates began in the mid-1980s.

As the infrastructure gap has widened, the pressure for all levels of government to increase their investment has increased. However, this has proved difficult to sustain in the face of rising demand and costs, especially in health care and education, and a series of economic downturns, crises, and budgetary deficits. The gap is also the product of the way that such assets are handled in budgetary terms, in that they are treated as mere expenses rather than long-term assets that can be budgeted for over their lifetime through bond financing (Doern, Maslove, and Prince 2013). As Mackenzie (2013, 12) suggests, it would be difficult to design a context more likely to produce a shortfall in public capital investment than the current one: "We have an evolving federation, in which responsibilities for public capital have been shifting steadily from the federal government (with the most robust and flexible revenue system) to local level government (with the least flexible revenue system). We have a political atmosphere that is hostile to the deficit financing that commonly provides the funding for capital investment and to the taxation that is required to cover the carrying costs. Adding to the

Chart 8.1: Canada's municipal infrastructure deficit ($ billions)

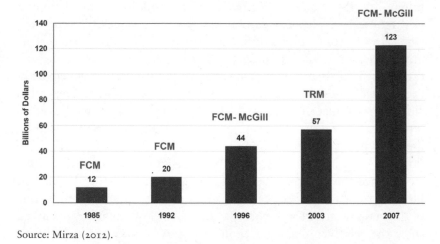

Source: Mirza (2012).

squeeze is the irresistible temptation faced by senior governments to export their fiscal problems by cutting transfer payments."

To examine how this affects municipal infrastructure, we present a historical overview that traces the evolution of federal transfers for municipal infrastructure in five historical periods, each defined by distinct characteristics. It outlines how these infrastructure-centred policy and financial arrangements have changed over time and to what extent environmental features emerge merely as "add-ons" or become more interwoven in the central policy aims and objectives of the various federal infrastructure programs.

FIVE PERIODS IN FEDERAL–MUNICIPAL INFRASTRUCTURE REGIME CHANGE

Infrastructure as Nation-Building: Post–First World War to 1960s

During this period, infrastructure was regarded principally as a key component of nation-building, particularly in transportation such as rail and highways but also energy, communication, water, ports, and navigation, and eventually airports, which were all crucial to settlement patterns across Canada. Although nation-building, immigration, and settlement have remained important drivers for federal involvement in national and interprovincial infrastructure projects, municipal infrastructure became increasingly important as urban centres grew rapidly.

The development and maintenance of local infrastructure in Canada is not a federal responsibility but falls solely under the jurisdiction of the provinces and their municipal governments, as detailed in chapter 7. Despite the parameters set out in the Constitution, during the decades after the First World War the federal government occasionally provided municipal governments with financial assistance that took the form of loans and grants for local public works projects. Ottawa's financial assistance was intended to be short term rather than ongoing, targeting economic and social problems resulting from high unemployment, housing shortages, urban decay, and environmental degradation.

As explained in chapter 7, the federal government often had very little institutional capacity for co-ordinating and delivering funding for municipal infrastructure during this period, and programs and loans were provided mostly on an ad hoc basis. There was little attempt to promote or enhance the federal role in providing municipal infrastructure and little either to distinguish Liberal from Conservative policies on local infrastructure spending. After a post–Second World War boom in investment, infrastructure began to wane as a percentage of GDP as federal, provincial, and municipal governments faced increasing fiscal pressures and service demands, particularly in housing and social services such as education and health.

Unsustainable Urban Growth: The Federal Government as Municipal Banker, 1960s to 1970s

In its response to crises and the growing need for infrastructure, the federal government acted very much like a bank, augmenting the financial resources available to provincial and municipal governments (Hilton 2007; Hilton and Stoney 2009a). Federal participation was temporary and arm's length, limited to creating programs that provided loans (requiring repayment), unconditional transfers of funds (grants), or alternatively, conditional payments (contributions using the federal spending power that provided a share of costs matched by the municipal and provincial government).

By the 1960s, the role and scope of the federal government role had begun to expand and included Keynesian stimulus programs and funding that allowed and enabled local governments and the provinces to take necessary action. For example, federal funding through the Sewer Treatment Program (1961–74) provided $979 million in loans and $131 million in grants to local governments to address the shortage of serviced land, which was a major impediment to expanding residential construction. The Municipal Winter Works Incentive (1958–68) provided $267 million to boost employment by supporting 50 per cent of direct payroll costs in municipalities. The Municipal Development and Loan Act established a $400 million fund during 1963–66 to stimulate employment by providing loans to local government that encouraged them to accelerate and expand their capital works. Programs such as these were designed to provide municipalities with temporary injections of cash, most of which were still on the basis of a repayable loan.

During this period there was rising concern and activism concerning rapid urban growth and the impact it was having on Canadian cities and the quality of life for the many millions who resided in and around sprawling city-regions such as Toronto, Montreal, and Vancouver. In 1961 Jane Jacobs published *The Death and Life of Great American Cities*, criticizing the urban renewal projects of the 1950s that prioritized the car and "destroyed communities," fuelling popular debate on city planning, public transit, and infrastructure. In Canada, public resistance in Toronto to the Spadina Expressway became a focal point of what would eventually grow into the "new urbanism" movement.

Broader environmental concerns were also emerging as urban sprawl became seen as a key contributor to acid rain and poor air quality. In 1979, Canada, the United States, and thirty-two European countries signed the Economic Commission of Europe (ECE) Convention on Long-range Trans-boundary Air Pollution. The Convention is a mechanism to deal with and manage "regional" trans-boundary air pollutants such as sulphur, nitrogen oxides, and volatile organic compounds, and air issues such as acid rain and ground-level ozone. Under pressure to take further measures, the government created the Department of the Environment in 1971 and also the Ministry of State for Urban Affairs (1971–79), both of which signalled a growing awareness of urban affairs and their national significance for the environment.

Following a merger in 1976, the Canadian Federation of Mayors and Municipalities was renamed the Federation of Canadian Municipalities (FCM), marking another important realignment in the municipal landscape. The FCM quickly established itself as a highly effective institution, lobbying federal and provincial governments for increased, predictable investment in municipal infrastructure and played an increasingly prominent role in advancing a progressive and sustainable environmental agenda for Canadian cities and communities. We discuss in chapter 9 how this period also saw the rise of certain environmental organizations concerned about local pollution issues, organizations such as Pollution Probe.

Responding to calls for predictable funding, the government introduced federal fuel taxes in the mid-1970s with a view to increasing and maintaining federal investment in municipal infrastructure over the long term. On 23 June 1975, John Turner, federal minister of finance, announced to the House of Commons that the government was introducing "a special excise tax on gasoline for personal use" (Department of Finance 1975, 35). The rate was set at ten cents per gallon and was expected to generate $350 million for the federal treasury during the first year. Together with increases in the price of domestic oil prices, the measures introduced in Budget 1975 were intended to "encourage motorists to make their driving habits more efficient in terms of saving gasoline ... [and] encourage the use of public transportation, thereby helping to relieve the growing congestion in our cities" (ibid.). Based on the cost-benefit principle of "user pays," fuel taxes were seen as a significant policy choice, as they aimed to capture the often hidden "price" of road infrastructure and discourage fuel consumption, while diverting funds into public transit infrastructure.

In spite of the new taxes and a greater focus on urban and environmental challenges, the infrastructure gap would continue to grow, as demands for public infrastructure from an expanding private sector, as well as individual citizens, increased rapidly during this period (Harchaoui, Tarkhani, and Warren 2004).

Early Sustainable Development and Environmental
Concerns, 1973–1993

During the 1980s "sustainable development" emerged in the environmental discourse and, as we have seen in earlier chapters, established zeitgeist status following the release of the Brundtland Commission report, *Our Common Future* (1987). The Brundtland Commission called for a serious response to global warming at different levels of government, with cities in particular being identified as the largest producers of GHG emissions. In response, the federal government played a prominent role at the Rio Earth Summit 1992 and initiated the creation of the Earth Council and the drafting of the global Earth Charter.

In spite of the government's willingness to sign onto international environmental commitments, free-trade and constitutional wrangling dominated the political agenda during the 1980s and 1990s, making concerted intergovernmental coordination difficult. In addition, as chapter 2 has shown, significant fiscal deficits, inflation, and high interest rates put pressure on the federal purse. Provincial governments' program spending, particularly in health and education, continued to dominate budgets and elections, and capital spending on infrastructure continued to decline as a percentage of GDP. Chronic under-investment in infrastructure characterized the 1980s and 1990s with dramatic consequences. Mackenzie (2013) calculates that the difference between a capital stock valued at 30 per cent of GDP in the early 1980s and 22 per cent in 2011 represents "missing" public capital stock with a current value of $145 billion. Research by the FCM, OECD, World Bank, and other national and international institutions began to measure and publicize the "infrastructure gap," and this figure became part of a strategy to convince governments to invest more in infrastructure.

The case for infrastructure investment was not simply for more of the same but for investment in transformative infrastructure that would use resources more efficiently and advance urban sustainability. An important part of this agenda was the emergence of New Urbanism, both as a body of knowledge and an urban design movement. Essentially it promotes walkable neighbourhoods containing a range of housing and job types and promotes transit-oriented development over roads and urban sprawl. It is closely associated with the broader concept of smart growth and Richard Florida's "creative class" thesis; it became increasingly prominent as an alternative to the "unsustainable" auto-dominated and anti-environmental development typical of many cities.

Green Infrastructure, Economic Growth, and the New Deal from Federal Banker to Partner and Promoter, 1993–2006

With the election of the Chrétien Liberal government in 1993, a new era in federal funding for municipal governments began. Despite the daunting $42 billion deficit in the federal treasury, a severe drop in federal revenues, and increased spending on employment insurance benefits caused by a severe recession, the Liberals sought to stimulate a recovering economy by adjusting monetary and fiscal policies that included new federal spending through a new infrastructure program. The Canada Infrastructure Works Program (CIWP) – with initial funding of $2 billion that was subsequently increased by an additional $400 million – was intended originally as a short-term means of stimulating the economy through job creation in the construction industry, much like those from previous decades. However, the CIWP, which ran over two phases during 1994–99, morphed into something quite different. It called for a "partnership" among the three levels of government to jointly deal with a variety of public policy needs that could be addressed through investment in local infrastructure. The federal government would now provide its own "share" of the costs of municipal infrastructure projects, up to a maximum of one-third.

The Liberals' election platform in 1993 (Red Book I) had outlined four objectives for a tripartite "shared cost, two-year $6 billion infrastructure program, to upgrade transportation and local services" (60). The new program was intended to help create employment rapidly over a two-year period, build infrastructure that "support[ed] economic growth," develop infrastructure that "enhance[d] community liveability," and demonstrate to the public that the federal government could work cooperatively with other levels of government. While spending to help spur job creation was again the main driver behind the policy, there was a much more significant and enduring legacy of the CIWP: it established the concept of a "tripartite shared cost" for municipal infrastructure that has helped to shape arguments calling for a realignment of the fiscal framework for the nation (Hilton 2007; Hilton and Stoney 2009a).

Following the CIWP, the federal government launched a series of other "partnership" infrastructure programs, notably the Canada Infrastructure Program ($2.05 billion), the Municipal-Rural Infrastructure Fund ($1.2 billion), and the Canada Strategic Infrastructure Fund ($6 billion). While the first two were "bottom-up," requiring local governments to apply for matched funding from their province and the federal government, the third appeared more susceptible to politically motivated spending. Unlike previous infrastructure programs, there was no application and vetting for the

Canada Strategic Infrastructure Fund (CSIF) (or for another program, the Border Infrastructure Fund). As Hilton observed, "Rather than basing [federal funding] decisions on public policy interests, the selection process became very much enmeshed in politics" (Hilton 2007, 91).

The potentially political distributive nature of CSIF was reinforced by the significant discretionary federal "investment" in infrastructure projects: the federal share of costs involved tens and, in some cases, hundreds of millions of dollars. As well, the allowed maximum federal funding had now risen significantly to 50 per cent of eligible project costs. Since spending in these programs was discretionary, there was considerable latitude in choosing recipients and the amount of funding they received.

The policy rationale underlying federal infrastructure programing also evolved. Projects receiving funding were intended to have a positive impact, improving the economy, the quality of life in communities, and the environment. Myriad similarly vague objectives for each program justified federal funding, providing the narrative for press releases and speeches announcing federal funding for local infrastructure projects. Even very small infrastructure projects were heralded by federal politicians for their contribution to "improving national, provincial and local economic competitiveness," "supporting long-term economic growth," "improving economic opportunities," "improving the quality of life," and "promoting improved environmental quality" (Hilton 2007; Hilton and Stoney 2009a).

The funding announcements and signage at construction sites were intended to provide the federal government with a visible presence in many rural and urban communities. Signage at construction sites large and small was, in effect, a means of trying to convince citizens that the federal government was relevant and played an active role in improving the quality of life in communities. The demand to promote "federal visibility" ramped up soon after the near-death referendum crisis in Québec in 1995 and the negative fallout across the country following announcements of severe reductions in federal programming in order to reduce the deficit. The federal presence in communities started to wane through resulting efforts to curb spending, which included significant reductions in social transfer programs to the provinces. Through its infrastructure programs, the federal government was endeavouring to "show the flag" in communities across the country. At the same time, it began to assume a far greater share of infrastructure costs and demanded – except in Quebec – a greater role in the administration of program spending (Hilton 2007; Hilton and Stoney 2009a).

Despite these efforts and the significant overhead costs associated with "communications" activities in infrastructure programs, a poll conducted by the federal government in 2004 revealed disappointing results: "This poll revealed that Canadians did not see the role of the federal government in communities. This finding heavily influenced the development of the communications annex of the GTF agreement [Infrastructure Canada] was to sign with each Province and Territory" (Infrastructure Canada 2007).

As a self-proclaimed "partner" in building local infrastructure, the federal government began to demand greater recognition for its involvement, requiring the recipients of federal funds to follow "communications protocols" outlining how media events and activities would ensure the participation of federal ministers and MPs. Particularly for the Canada Strategic Investment Fund (and the Border Infrastructure Fund), recipients were required to be accountable to Ottawa not only for how the funds were spent but also for progress reports at a project level. The federal government was now much more than a banker – it was becoming an active partner involved in project management. In order to garner political capital from its new role and increased funding, it continued to develop the branding and communication side of federal programs that would later culminate in the marketing and advertising of the Economic Action Plan (Hilton 2007; Hilton and Stoney 2009a; Stoney and Krawchenko 2012).

In 2000 the federal government endowed the FCM with $550 million to establish the Green Municipal Fund (GMF), designed to provide below-market loans and grants, education and training services to support municipal plans, studies and projects that improve air, water, and soil quality, and protect the climate. Through the GMF, the FCM endeavoured to promote sustainable development and infrastructure innovation, enhance environmental performance, generate new efficiencies, increase municipal tax revenues, create jobs, and bolster economic development. In particular, GMF funding and knowledge was aimed at helping municipalities build better transportation; construct more efficient and resilient buildings; divert waste from landfill; make previously unusable land available for development; and improve soil and water quality. The FCM continues to administer this fund.

In 2001, the federal government, through its Infrastructure Canada Program (IC) and the National Research Council (NRC), partnered with the FCM to create the *National Guide to Sustainable Infrastructure (InfraGuide)*. *InfraGuide* was both a new, national framework of people, and a growing collection of published best practice documents for use by decision-makers and technical personnel in the public and private sectors.

Based on Canadian empirical research and experience, the *InfraGuide* reports (2001–7) set out the best practices to support sustainable municipal infrastructure decisions and action in five key areas: municipal roads and sidewalks, potable water, storm and wastewater decision-making and investment planning, environmental protocols, and transit. The best practices were made available online and in hard copy. In spite of its innovative and forward-looking objectives, to build up and disseminate knowledge and enable better asset management, the program was ended in 2007 along with similar programs such as Infrastructure Canada's Knowledge and Outreach Awareness (KOA) program that funded research projects in sustainable infrastructure.

On the revenue side, fuel taxes continued to provide a crucial plank in the federal government's funding of municipal infrastructure. In addition to providing an important fiscal tool, they are also seen to have "green" credentials because of their potential to penalize auto use and transfer the revenues to public transit or other types of sustainable infrastructure. The federal excise tax remained unchanged at a flat rate of ten cents per litre, while the federal tax on diesel fuel (in effect since 1987) was also applied at a flat rate of four cents per litre. Although furnace oil, natural gas, and propane were exempt from this tax, the Goods and Services Tax (GST) or Harmonized Sales Tax (HST) was applied to all petroleum products. On gasoline, therefore, considerable government revenues were obtained from the flat tax rate and as the percentage of the retail price (*ad valorem*) when the GST/HST was applied (Hilton and Stoney 2009a).

Totalling $11.2 billion in 2005–6, road fuel taxes (including gasoline and diesel) became the most important component of federal, provincial, and territorial government tax revenues from transportation. Total fuel taxes made up 75 per cent of total revenues by transport users (Transport Canada 2006, 49). However, it was the introduction of the Gas Tax Fund (GTF), a crucial component in the

Liberal government's "New Deal" that explicitly linked gas tax revenues with municipal infrastructure needs, and "green" infrastructure in particular.

The Martin government's "New Deal for Cities and Communities" was ostensibly intended to address the need to enhance the fiscal capacities within cities and smaller communities and to address the infrastructure deficit in a meaningful and sustained fashion. In its first budget, the Martin government committed "to share with municipalities a portion of the revenue from the federal excise tax on gasoline to help fund local environmentally sustainable infrastructure." Under the heading of "A Greener, More Sustainable Canada," the 2005 Budget outlined further dimensions to the New Deal for Cities and Communities, most notably the requirement that "at least half of the new revenues to be transferred through the gas tax will be dedicated to sustainable infrastructure." The main project categories identified included public transit; local roads, bridges, and tunnels; active transportation infrastructure; community energy; solid waste; water/wastewater; and capacity-building/integrated community sustainability planning.

Unlike in previous programs, municipalities received federal funding via the gas tax in advance – not for specific projects – but for *intended* capital spending, and were audited after projects were completed. Any spending on ineligible projects would result in the suspension of the subsequent allocation (Hilton and Stoney 2009a). Consequently, the gas tax was classified as one "other transfer payment," because it did not conform to the federal Treasury Board's definition of previously existing transfer payments types. It was neither an unconditional transfer, where funds had no conditions attached and were not audited, nor was it a conditional transfer payment, where eligibility was tightly prescribed and individual projects had to be approved and a considerable application outlining the "business case" completed before funds were disbursed (Treasury Board 2008). As a "hybrid" instrument, the GTF was defined as a transfer payment "based on legislation or an arrangement which normally includes a formula or schedule as one element used to determine the expenditure amount; however, once payments are made, the recipient may redistribute the funds among the several approved categories of expenditure in the arrangement" (Treasury Board 2008). In addition, the annual funding could be spent or banked at the discretion of the municipality.

Another innovative aspect of the GTF was the proposed requirement that recipients of federal funding under the program develop a long-term plan for sustainability within the first five years of receiving gas tax funds. The Integrated Community Sustainability Plans (ICSPS) were intended to be a "long term plan, developed in consultation with community members, for the community to realize sustainability objectives it has for the environmental, cultural, social and economic dimensions of its identity [sic]" (Treasury Board 2008, 9).

Not surprisingly, given the nature of Canadian federalism, jurisdictional tensions have undermined the GTF's policy rationale in a number of ways and particularly the goal of "building environmentally sustainable infrastructure." In addition to the patchy and sometimes perfunctory development of ICSPS, the federal government has struggled to ensure that municipalities use the GTF monies for the intended purposes. Imposing conditions on Quebec municipalities proved particularly futile at times, but cities in other provinces also objected to the limitations being placed on their spending of the gas tax funds.

In describing the consultation process used with stakeholders during the development of the GTF, "Tracing the Development of the Gas Tax Fund" (Infrastructure Canada 2007), also reveals that "the Prime Minister told the big city mayors that he wanted them to limit their GTF spending to one or two of the eligible project categories" (21). Bureaucrats followed the prime minister's lead in this regard: "INFC placed restrictions on investments in roads and bridges. Municipalities with populations of over 500,000 were not allowed to invest in roads and bridges as such investments were not deemed to lead to positive environmental impacts" (14). This edict from bureaucrats did not go down well with some city governments:

The mayor of Winnipeg pushed strongly against the restrictions on the use of funds for roads and bridges, and this dispute received heavy media attention from the outset. The Government of Canada denied Winnipeg's demands to use the money on roads and bridges. The solution required multiple deputy minister–level meetings and heavy involvement from Minister Godfrey and his staff (Infrastructure Canada 2007, 24).

The arrival of the Harper Conservatives would eventually put an end to the bickering with the decision to allow Winnipeg to invest in roads with gas tax funding. Nevertheless, these examples illustrate that, in spite of the federal government's attempts to direct municipalities to be "green," "innovative," and "transformational," it has had to water down those conditions because of jurisdictional and enforcement challenges.

The GTF also illustrates the federal government's attempt to assume a more assertive role in decisions about what infrastructure is needed for local government. The federal government as "*dirigeant*" in decisions about municipal infrastructure marks a significant evolution in a role that began many decades ago when the federal government provided repayable loans and grants to local governments during crises.

Lastly, the allocation formula for the GTF appears to contradict the program's rhetoric about the need to focus on building environmentally sustainable infrastructure, helping to drive economic growth and productivity, and putting in place "world-class infrastructure." By deciding to spread federal funding around the country – a policy described by Martin as "no hamlet too small" – valid concerns remained about the program logic. As Infrastructure Canada acknowledged, "It was widely recognized that the larger city-regions had the greatest ability to affect environmental change and therefore their investments should be very focused." Gains in productivity and growth were also maximized through investment in urban infrastructure (Infrastructure Canada 2007, 12). The failure of the federal government to concentrate program funds on those areas of the country generating the greatest revenues from gasoline taxes – cities and city-regions – may have reflected another important focus of the GTF. As was evident in earlier infrastructure programs, the need to generate "visibility" and opportunities for federal politicians to engage in retail politics had become increasingly important in public policy design and implementation. This policy rationale appears to have been central to the Economic Action Plan (EAP), launched in 2008 as part of the Harper government's policy response to the economic crisis.

Changing Federal Agenda but ... "Green" Infrastructure Dollars Continue to Flow, 2006–2013

Soon after the gas tax agreements were launched, the Martin Liberals were defeated during a general election and replaced by the Harper Conservatives in 2006. During their first budget, the Conservatives committed to retain the GTF over five years; in Budget 2007, they extended the GTF by another four years with an additional $8 billion. The 2006 Speech from the Throne endorsed the GTF as part of a "historic investment of more than $16 billion over seven years in infrastructure – bringing federal support under a new long-term plan for infrastructure to a total of $33 billion, including the funding provided in Budget 2006" (Department of Finance 2007b).

In Budget 2008, the government committed to launching a "permanent" transfer of gas tax revenues to municipal governments: $2 billion annually. The Conservative government's rationale for making permanent a Liberal policy initiative was that "the Government recognizes the need for long-term funding for infrastructure to help drive economic growth and productivity, to achieve our environmental goals, and to build strong, competitive communities ... In response to ongoing requests for stable, long-term funding, the Government announces that the Gas Tax Fund will be extended at $2 billion per year beyond 2013–14 and become a permanent measure. This will allow all municipalities, both large and small, to better plan and finance their long-term infrastructure needs" (Department of Finance 2008).

Even if the Harper government had not wanted to extend the GTF, it had already proved so popular with municipalities that terminating it would have been politically very damaging.

The Liberals meanwhile were planning their way back to power on an environmental platform marketed as the "green shift." However, Stéphane Dion's plan to introduce a carbon tax at the federal level following the 2008 election never materialized. Significantly, it was seen by many as a key factor in the defeat of the Liberal party. The carbon "green shift" plan was designed to levy up to $15 billion in new taxes on carbon-intensive Canadian industries; the proceeds would then be used to cut income and other taxes for people facing higher energy costs and other rising prices. Although Dion's carbon plan would not have included new taxes on gasoline for cars, trucks, and buses (unlike the Green Party proposal, which hoped to raise up to $40 billion), the new tax on energy was still widely criticized by opponents, including some within the Liberal ranks.

Aided by a looming economic crisis and Dion's own difficulties framing and explaining the carbon taxes to Canadians, critics were successful in demonizing the "green shift." Harper likened it to the National Energy Program and described it as a "tax grab" that would "recklessly harm the economy," penalize industry, and ultimately "screw everyone" ("PM" 2008). Following the 2008 Liberal defeat, leading members of the Liberal party criticized the "green shift" as "too confusing, expensive and politically risky." Michael Ignatieff, the new Liberal leader, expanded on why he believed it to be a "vote loser": "You can't win elections if you're adding to the input costs of a farmer putting diesel into his tractor, or you're adding to the input costs of a fisherman putting diesel into his fishing boat, or a trucker transporting goods." Speaking of former leader Stéphane Dion's green shift plan, which would have sharply raised taxes on energy, Ignatieff told reporters, "You've got to work with the grain of Canadians and not against them. I think we learned a lesson in the last election" (Whittington 2009).

The 2008 defeat by the Conservatives was a chastening one for Liberals; environmentalists feared that lasting damage might have been done to policy initiatives targeting sustainable development. Even if this were not the case, the worsening economic situation quickly side-tracked the environment as an issue in the minds of politicians and the electorate alike.

As the Canadian economy entered into recession in 2009, the federal government tabled an early budget to address the building economic crisis. The 2009 Budget is significant, in part as the Canadian response to the historic global economic decline and the unprecedented Canadian deficit that the budget incurred as a result, but also for the level of fiscal transfers directed toward municipalities and the potential impact these transfers will have on multi-level governance in Canada.

The Government of Canada described the 2009 Budget as one of the largest infrastructure investments in Canada's history. The infrastructure-related components of federal stimulus measures in Canada were approximately $40 billion over two years. The largest portions of the infrastructure measures were tax credits for households – e.g., home renovation and energy efficiency tax credits administered through the Canada Revenue Agency.

Infrastructure stimulus funding was incorporated into the existing Building Canada Fund (BCF). The $8.8 billion BCF was established under the 2007 Building Canada plan to fund projects until 2014. The fund is intended to address national, regional, and local infrastructure priorities, and supports projects designed to deliver results in three areas of national importance: a stronger economy, a cleaner environment, and strong and prosperous communities. The fund makes investments in public infrastructure owned by provincial, territorial, and municipal governments, and in certain cases, private-sector and non-profit organizations. Funding is allocated to each province and territory on the basis of population. All projects funded through the Building Canada Fund are cost shared, with the maximum federal contribution to any single project being 50 per cent, with municipal projects normally cost shared on a one-third basis – the maximum federal share is limited to one-third, with matching contributions from the province and municipality.

The BCF is made up of two components: the Major Infrastructure Component and the Communities Component. Funding for research, knowledge, planning, and feasibility studies was also available for projects financed under these components. The Major Infrastructure Component (MIC) of the BCF targets "larger, strategic projects of national and regional significance" (Government of Canada 2009). Under the MIC, at least two-thirds of funding supports projects that address national priorities and improve the lives of Canadians; these include projects related to drinking water, wastewater, public transit, the core national highway system, and green energy.

The Communities Component of the Building Canada Fund targets projects in communities with populations of fewer than 100,000. The fund "recognizes the unique infrastructure needs of Canada's smaller communities and focuses on projects that meet environmental, economic and quality of life objectives" (Government of Canada 2009). Canada's Economic Action Plan expanded the Communities Component fund (originally $1 billion) with a top-up of $500 million. By January 2014, the program had funded more than 1,400 smaller-scale projects that improve water, wastewater, public transit, local roads, and other types of community infrastructure (ibid.).

Through Canada's Economic Action Plan, the Government of Canada also established the $1 billion Green Infrastructure Fund (2009–14), which targeted projects that would "improve the quality of the environment and lead to a more sustainable economy over the long term" (Government of Canada 2009). Specifically, the Green Infrastructure Fund (GIF) was intended to support projects that "promote cleaner air, reduced greenhouse gas emissions and cleaner water" (ibid.). This included new or rehabilitation infrastructure projects in wastewater infrastructure, green energy generation and transmission, and solid waste carbon transmission and storage (ibid.).

The GIF was provided on a cost-shared basis to provinces, territories, local or regional governments, public sector bodies, and other eligible non-profit organizations and private sector companies, either alone or in partnership with a province, territory, or a government body (Government of Canada 2009). The fund, which ended in 2011, focused on a few, large scale, strategic infrastructure projects (ibid.).

As noted earlier, the Building Canada Fund was part of the Building Canada Plan, which remains even though the EAP stimulus funding has been wound down. The Building Canada Plan is directed towards "building a stronger, safer and better Canada through modern world-class public infrastructure." Launched in 2007, this seven-year plan was established to support projects that contribute to "cleaner air and water, safer roads, shorter commutes, and better communities" (Government of Canada 2009). The plan is providing $33 billion in stable, flexible, and predictable funding to provinces, territories, and municipalities, allowing them to plan for the longer term and address their ongoing infrastructure needs, and it combines a number of funds and institutions, including the Public-Private Partnerships Fund, as well as the establishment of P3 Canada.

Following the launch of the Building Canada Plan, the federal government signed infrastructure framework agreements with provincial and territorial governments. The aim of these agreements was to align the two levels of government to advance common goals – economic growth, environmental performance, and community interests – in the value of infrastructure projects. Canada's Economic Action Plan also focused on the Building Canada program, with the intent of speeding up and streamlining approvals for projects in small communities and projects that were shovel ready (Government of Canada 2009).

The updated Building Canada Plan is the largest and longest federal investment in provincial, territorial, and municipal infrastructure projects in Canadian history – over $53 billion in investments, including over $47 billion in new funding over ten years, starting in 2014–15 (Infrastructure Canada 2014). If it actually continues for ten years, this funding will be delivered through three key funds:

1 The Community Improvement Fund, consisting of the Gas Tax Fund and the incremental Goods and Services Tax Rebate for Municipalities, will provide over $32 billion to municipalities for

Table 8.1: Building Canada Plan programs and funds

Program	Amount ($ billions)
Municipal GST rebate	5.8
Gas Tax Fund	11.8
Building Canada Fund	8.8
Public-Private Partnerships Fund	1.25
Gateways and Border Crossings Fund	2.1
Asia-Pacific Gateway and Corridor Initiative	1.0
Provincial-Territorial Base Funding	2.3
Total	$33.0

Source: Government of Canada, Building Canada website 2014.

   projects such as roads, public transit, and recreational facilities,
   and other community infrastructure. Gas Tax Fund payments
   will be indexed at 2 per cent per year starting in 2014–15, with
   increases to be applied in $100-million increments.
2 The new Building Canada Fund will provide $14 billion to
   support major economic projects of national, regional, and local
   significance across the country.
3 The renewed P3 Canada Fund will provide $1.25 billion to
   continue to support innovative ways to build infrastructure
   projects faster and provide better value for Canadian taxpayers
   through public-private partnerships.

   An additional $6 billion will be provided to provinces, territories,
and municipalities under current infrastructure programs in 2014–
15 and beyond. In addition, the government will make significant
investments in First Nations infrastructure and in federal infrastructure assets. Overall federal infrastructure funding will total $70 bil-
lion over ten years (Government of Canada 2014).
   In spite of the references to "green" infrastructure and the environment, the government states that funding "will ensure that
Canada's public infrastructure is world-class and a contributor to
job creation, economic growth and productivity for years to come"
(Government of Canada 2014). Curiously, the motivation for investing in infrastructure appears to have come full circle, with jobs and
economic growth again at the heart of the government's agenda.

Of the billions of dollars earmarked for infrastructure in the EAP, it was the $4 billion Infrastructure Stimulus Fund (ISF) that emerged as the most high-profile and contested aspect of the 2009–10 stimulus measures. The ISF sparked a media furor over the decision-making process to select projects and accountability for the funds spent. The ISF was also the component of stimulus spending that had the greatest financial bearing on other levels of government, as it required joint contributions to infrastructure investments. Under the ISF program, the federal government contributed up to 50 per cent for provincial and territorial assets and not-for-profit private sector assets, up to 33 per cent for municipal assets, and 25 per cent of eligible costs for for-profit sector assets (Infrastructure Canada 2011).

The federal government intended the ISF to be "delivered in a flexible manner," with proposals having differing selection processes depending on each province and territory (Infrastructure Canada 2011). Eligible projects were put forward through provincial and territorial governments to Infrastructure Canada, where the final decisions on which projects to fund were made. In this way, the ISF, along with a number of other stimulus-related programs, gave the federal government discretion over the final selection of projects. ISF project eligibility was guided by three major requirements: that project construction was ready to begin, that the project would not otherwise have been constructed by 31 March 2011 without the federal funding requested, and that the project plan be completed with all permits and necessary approvals in place.

The emphasis on "timely" stimulus spending led to concerns that decisions were disproportionately advancing short-term, "shovel-ready" opportunities at the expense of longer-term plans and criteria such as sustainability and improved competitiveness. There were also concerns that the due process normally associated with government programs was being compromised in the rush to begin construction. For example, some projects circumvented environmental screening practices and public consultation processes – an issue that was raised in the fall report of the auditor general of Canada (2010). Specifically the report found that, as part of the Economic Action Plan, the government introduced Exclusion List Regulations under the Canadian Environmental Assessment Act in order to eliminate the need for environmental assessments for a wider range of projects. These regulatory amendments were expedited and were not released in draft form for public comment prior to taking effect (ibid.). Although the amendments were intended to be temporary and slated to expire on 31 March 2011, they represented the marked emphasis that the Canadian government placed on fast-tracking the flow of funding for infrastructure. In all, 93 per cent of the project proposals approved under the ISF were excluded from environmental assessment (ibid.).

In establishing the ISF, the federal government chose to use the application-based Building Canada Fund despite urging from a variety of municipal politicians to use the GTF mechanism to flow the money. In particular, the FCM lauded the gas tax mechanism as "highly efficient" and one that would deliver funding "quickly, fairly and accountably" (FCM 2009b). Municipal governments urged the federal government to use the GTF as the transfer vehicle to deliver the stimulus money. In an open letter issued before the budget, Carl Zehr, chair of the FCM's Large Cities Mayors Caucus, argued that "to counter a recession this year [2009] we need a program that gets money to projects in time for the spring construction season. A program based on the gas tax funding model is the best tool for the job." He further argued that the Building Canada mechanism would be "too slow to deliver the stimulus needed to fight the recession and create jobs" (FCM 2009a). Municipalities had been quick off the mark to show their willingness and ability to spend infrastructure money quickly, releasing a list of over 1,000 infrastructure projects. FCM members committed to undertake these projects starting in the spring of 2009 if the federal government made funding available in the budget. The FCM estimated that the funding would create over 150,000 new jobs (FCM 2009a). In spite of job creation being a central policy rationale, no effort was made to accurately track the number of jobs created through infrastructure stimulus programs, making it impossible to accurately evaluate one of the key stated objectives of the stimulus program (Raj 2009a, 2009b; Scoffield 2010). When questioned, Infrastructure Minister John Baird stated, "It is not the federal government's job to track the results of stimulus funding" (Raj 2009b). This was a curious assertion, given the government actively promoted the ISF as a highly successful program, based largely on its ability to generate jobs. Canada's parliamentary budget officer, Kevin Page, who provided a source of independent analysis on the usage and impact of the infrastructure stimulus funds, became a vocal critic of the federal government's own reporting on program results (Chase 2009). In a 2010 report on the infrastructure stimulus funds, the parliamentary budget officer concluded, "As we have indicated in previous reports on the ISF, parliamentarians have been poorly served with limited data architecture and information collection, especially when compared to the US practice. The lack of good data inhibits basic analysis let alone accountability" (Parliamentary Budget Officer 2010, 3).

The lack of reporting on job creation was also raised in the in the fall 2010 report of the auditor general. The information on project-level jobs was described by government officials as "anecdotal." There were no consistent measures or methodologies used to estimate the number of jobs created or maintained as a result of stimulus funding (Office of the Auditor General of Canada 2010, 63–4).

In a comparison of Australia, the United States, and Canadian stimulus spending, Stoney and Krawchenko (2012) concluded that the Canadian government stands out in its failure to implement measures to ensure accountability and transparency in decision-making and in reporting mechanisms that aid in communicating program results. The lack of transparency in the Canadian case has led to allegations that the process has been politicized with disproportionate funds going to Conservative ridings. For example, an analysis by the *Globe and Mail* of infrastructure stimulus projects awarded through the Recreational Infrastructure Canada program found disproportionate reward in Conservative ridings (Chase, Anderson, and Curry 2009). The lack of transparent reporting on funding commitments has made substantiation or denial of these claims difficult, and such analyses were beyond the mandate of the Office of the Auditor General in its review of the program. Nevertheless the significant increase in program advertising, promotion, and branding of the EAP has continued to fuel concern that the ISF and other infrastructure funding programs have been heavily influenced by short-term partisan interests.

THE THREE REGIME ELEMENTS

Policy Ideas, Discourse, and Agendas

The five periods examined reveal a developing and varied set of discourses, agendas, and policy ideas concerning infrastructure, the environment, and the role of the federal government. During the period following the First World War until the 1960s, infrastructure was regarded principally as a key component of nation-building, particularly in public transportation, but also housing, electricity, water, and navigation, and later airports, which were all crucial to settlement patterns across Canada as immigration continued apace. Although this has remained an important reason for federal involvement in infrastructure, other considerations have emerged as central at different times. During the 1950s and 1960s, infrastructure investment took on an important Keynesian economic role, putting people back to work and helping to stimulate the economy through counter-cyclical spending. During the 1960s and 1970s, environmental activists such as Jane Jacobs challenged the view that urban growth had to be dominated by automobile usage and infrastructure, and appealed to governments at all levels to invest in walkable, liveable cities that would eventually form the basis for new urbanism and smart growth policies. During the 1980s and 1990s, Canada experienced significant economic and political challenges in global recessions and confederation respectively.

While Keynesian logic called for greater federal spending in infrastructure, the political crisis meant the government required "visibility," especially in Quebec. This prompted well-publicized infrastructure spending as the government tried and tested means of stimulating the economy and nation-building. Consequently, federal money was directed largely into "new build" projects such as bridges, highways, and airports such as Mirabel. This did little to address the real issue of deteriorating infrastructure in urban centres and left provinces and municipalities with ever more assets to maintain, thereby worsening the growing infrastructure gap and doing little to address urban sustainability.

During the 1990s it became increasingly clear just how serious Canada's under-investment in maintaining and replacing infrastructure had become. With climate change predicted to shorten the life expectancy of Canadian infrastructure, and increasing recognition that modern urban infrastructure was central to national competitiveness and productivity, the federal government's New Deal for Cities and Communities was intended to address some of the long-term needs of municipalities with predictable funding. The Gas Tax Fund (GTF), an innovative and central component of the "deal," was also designed to provide an incentive to municipal investment in transformative "green infrastructure," placing greater emphasis on climate change mitigation and adaptation.

The Liberal defeat and a Harper victory in 2006 signalled the end of the New Deal. Although the GTF has been made permanent, it remains a fraction of what is required, especially as "visibility" and "political" considerations have resulted in it being sprinkled across cities and communities, undermining its impact on strategic infrastructure decisions within major Canadian urban centres. With municipal spending on roads and highways now also permissible under the GTF, its green credentials are also being challenged.

A further economic crisis followed the Conservative election victory of 2008 and with the announcement of the Economic Action Plan (EAP), which again prioritized Keynesian demand-management measures to stimulate the economy and employment. The need to spend quickly meant that shovel-ready projects again took precedence over environmental or long-term strategic infrastructure needs. The EAP also confirmed the increasing politicization of infrastructure spending, with signage, advertising, and branding taken to levels never seen in Canada before, with the EAP forming a central theme in the Conservative party's election strategy.

As well as infrastructure's role in furthering distributive "retail politics," it is also increasingly viewed as a way to create opportunities for the private sector to deliver core public infrastructure. New institutions such as P3 Canada have been established to promote and facilitate P3s. In addition to providing a new source of capital and expertise, P3s also clearly open up new markets for the private sector companies and finance. The next phase could well see the federal government encourage domestic and international pension funds to invest in Canadian infrastructure.

The federal role in investing and influencing municipal infrastructure has also evolved. Following the First World War, the federal role was essentially to provide ad hoc short-term loans to municipalities with few long-term programs established. During the 1960s and 1970s the federal government began to play the role of banker by providing capital for specific provincial and municipal infrastructure programs, particularly those that created regional employment and visibility. In 1975, the federal government introduced the first of many gasoline taxes to help fund and grow its infrastructure programs. In spite of diverting significant funding to municipal infrastructure, the federal government avoided taking a strong role in influencing local priorities, as was particularly evident during the 1980s and early 1990s, when constitutional issues continued to dominate intergovernmental relations.

By the late 1980s early 1990s, however, in addition to a growing infrastructure crisis, environmental concerns were increasing pressure on the federal government to assume national leadership. This period would culminate in the New Deal and the GTF, which enabled the federal government to play a more active role by stipulating that the funds be targeted toward more sustainable "green infrastructure" projects. While the current federal government appears to be stepping back from promoting an interventionist role, it was directly involved in the selection of municipal infrastructure projects funded through its stimulus, and it continues to make funds available through the Building Canada Plan, some of which are conditional on meeting green and sustainability criteria, although these were secondary factors in the overall policy aims.

Environmental Power Structures, Democracy, and Governance

Perhaps nowhere have the constitutional limits placed on the federal government jurisdiction been more evident than in its inability and unwillingness to establish a national infrastructure strategy. Its importance to competitiveness, productivity, quality of life, health, well-being, and urban sustainability are well established, but the institutions and governance structures required to identify and invest in transformative and strategic infrastructure are patchwork at best.

Prior to the establishment of the MSUA in 1971, there was really no formal institutional framework that established municipal government and urban infrastructure as federal priorities. Its demise in 1979 made further attempts to locate urban issues within the federal government less likely and far more difficult to achieve. The establishment of the Department of the Environment in 1971 and the passing of subsequent legislation did provide the federal government with some policy capacity and regulatory powers in water and air quality and so on, but this often took the form of monitoring and enforcement, as opposed to innovation and investment.

The establishment of an amalgamated FCM in 1976 provided municipal affairs with a greater political voice, and the federal government has at times worked with them closely to influence and support municipal investment in infrastructure, particularly "green" infrastructure. In 2000, for example, the federal government endowed the FCM with $550 million to establish the Green Municipal Fund (GMF), designed to provide below-market loans

Table 8.3: The Federal–Municipal Infrastructure Sustainability Regime histories and the three regime elements: Selected summary highlights

PERIODS EXAMINED	The three analytical elements		
	POLICIES, IDEAS, DISCOURSE, AND AGENDAS	POWER STRUCTURES, DEMOCRACY, AND GOVERNANCE	SCIENCE, EVIDENCE, KNOWLEDGE, AND PRECAUTION
Infrastructure as nation-building, post–First World War to 1960s	• Short-term federal grants and repayable loans • Infrastructure not regarded as an environmental tool but as key in nation-building • Federal government continues to prioritize investments in railways, communication, ports, airports, highways, etc., rather than municipal infrastructure per se	• No specific institutional relations for delivering or funding municipal infrastructure • Urban infrastructure regarded as a municipal-provincial concern, unless interprovincial component • Little to distinguish Liberal and Conservative policies on infrastructure	• Core public infrastructure identified as bridges, roads, water, wastewater, transit, as well as cultural and recreational facilities, all seen as central to the development of Canada • After postwar boom, investment in infrastructure began to wane as a percentage of GDP, as provinces and municipalities faced increasing fiscal pressures and service demands
Unsustainable urban growth: federal government as municipal banker, 1960s–1970s	• Jane Jacobs published *The Death and Life of Great American Cities* (1961) criticizing the urban renewal projects of the 1950s that prioritized the car and "destroyed communities," fuelling popular debate on city planning, sprawl, public transit, and infrastructure • Specific programs, targeted and providing temporary injections of cash for municipal investment in public works (e.g., Sewer Treatment	• Ministry of State for Urban Affairs established 1971–79 by federal government signals growing awareness of urban affairs and national significance of regional and local agreements • In order to improve environmental management and protect water quality, the federal government passed the Canada Water Act in 1970 and created the Department of the Environment in 1971	• Environmental concerns emerged as acid rain and urban sprawl seen as major challenges to the quality of life in Canadian centres • In 1979, Canada, the United States, and 32 European countries sign the Economic Commission of Europe Convention on Long-Range Trans-Boundary Air Pollution, to deal with and manage "regional" trans-boundary air pollutants like sulphur, nitrogen oxides, and volatile organic

Table 8.3: (continued)

PERIODS EXAMINED	The three analytical elements		
	POLICIES, IDEAS, DISCOURSE, AND AGENDAS	POWER STRUCTURES, DEMOCRACY, AND GOVERNANCE	SCIENCE, EVIDENCE, KNOWLEDGE, AND PRECAUTION
	Program [1961–74]; Municipal Winter Works Incentive [1958–68]; Municipal Development and Loan Act) • Federal fuel taxes introduced in mid-1970s with view to increasing and maintaining federal investment in municipal infrastructure	• In 1976 the Canadian Federation of Mayors and Municipalities is renamed the Federation of Canadian Municipalities, which proves to be highly effective, lobbying federal and provincial governments for increased and predictable investment in municipal infrastructure	compounds, and air issues like acid rain and ground-level ozone • The infrastructure gap continued to grow as demands for public infrastructure from private sector and individual citizens increase, rapidly diminishing the ratio of public infrastructure capital in comparison to the overall needed and produced
Early sustainable development and environmental concerns, 1979–93	• "Sustainable development" provides new discourse in late 1980s following Brundtland Commission Report • New Urbanism, an urban design movement that promotes walkable neighbourhoods containing a range of housing and job types becomes increasingly prominent as an alternative narrative and discourse to the automobile-led development of postwar cities • Chronic under-investment in infrastructure continues through 1980s	• Free-trade and constitutional wrangling dominates the political agenda; deficits, inflation, and high interest rates put pressure on the federal purse • Provincial governments' program spending, particularly in health and education, continues to dominate, and capital spending on infrastructure begins to decline as a percentage of GDP • Federal government consults each level of government and private sector during the 1984–85 Inquiry on Federal Water Policy; guided by the findings	• Brundtland and Agenda 21, ICLEA, and other international initiatives call for a serious response to global warming; cities seen as the largest producers of GHG emissions • Federal government plays prominent role at the Rio Earth Summit 1992 and initiates the creation of the Earth Council and the drafting of the global Earth Charter • New Urbanism develops into a coherent and influential body of knowledge and social science, promoting transit-

and 1990s with damaging long-term consequences.

Green infrastructure and the New Deal, from federal banker to partner and promoter, 1993–2006

of the inquiry, the government releases its federal water policy in 1987, which serves as a framework for the water-related activities of all federal departments

- The concept of "green infrastructure" emerges in the mid-1990s and highlights the importance of the natural environment in decisions about land-use planning, including storm-water management, climate adaptation, and stressing mixed-use activities on the same piece of land
- In 2000, federal government endows FCM with $550m to establish the Green Municipal Fund, through which the FCM aims to promote sustainable development and infrastructure innovation
- Gas Tax Program implemented with strong emphasis on green infrastructure and Integrated Community Sustainability Plans; program eventually made permanent

- Amalgamations across many of Canada's urban centres create "mega-cities," force rethink of infrastructure and service delivery
- Federal and provincial downloading increases financial pressures on municipalities
- "Infrastructure deficit" becomes effective tool as FCM and business lobby lead call for infrastructure investment
- FCM instrumental in negotiating the federal government's 2005 New Deal for Cities program under which Canadian federal gasoline taxes are remitted to municipalities
- As part of the "New Deal" for Cities and Communities, Infrastructure Canada created to oversee programs and funding for municipal infrastructure, including the GTF
- In 2001, the federal government, through its Infrastructure Canada Program and the National Research Council, partnered with the

oriented development over roads and urban sprawl and is closely associated with environmentalism and the broader concept of smart growth

- City-regions increasingly identified as the basis of international competitiveness by academics, international reports, and independent studies; infrastructure identified as key, and public transit in particular
- Richard Florida's "creative class" thesis fuels interest in urban centres as cultural centres with emphasis on "world-class" cities and attracting global talent; infrastructure and smart growth policies seen as key factors
- International bodies such as the WHO and OECD, Canadian think tanks such as the Conference Board, academics, and consultants, including KPMG, disseminate reports and evidence on the need for public investment in public infrastructure
- Infrastructure Canada makes case that investments in infrastructure can be a powerful tool for achieving environmental goals; better infrastructure planning and construction can "re-

Table 8.3: (*continued*)

PERIODS EXAMINED	POLICIES, IDEAS, DISCOURSE, AND AGENDAS	POWER STRUCTURES, DEMOCRACY, AND GOVERNANCE	SCIENCE, EVIDENCE, KNOWLEDGE, AND PRECAUTION
			duce the impact of human activity, and help protect and improve the environment" • Based on empirical research and experience, the *InfraGuide* reports (2001–7) set out the best practices to support sustainable municipal infrastructure decisions
		Federation of Canadian Municipalities to create the *National Guide to Sustainable Infrastructure* (*InfraGuide*) • 1995 Quebec referendum intensifies federal desire for "visible" spending, and infrastructure seen as the primary vehicle for achieving it	
Changing agenda but ... "green" infrastructure dollars continue to flow, 2007–13	• Economy, growth, and jobs become the Conservative mantra and infrastructure investment driven by Keynesian stimulus rationale • Funding for "green" infrastructure initiatives stays largely intact over this period, although programs such as *InfraGuide* and KOA are terminated • Renewable energy competes with sustainable development as key environmental discourse • FCM successfully advocates for significant federal funding towards the	• Stéphane Dion's 2008 election defeat thwarts plans to introduce a federal carbon tax seen by many as a key factor in the defeat of the Liberal party • Private sector and governments see P3s as potential "solution" to address the infrastructure gap, drive the economy • P3 Canada established to promote public-private partnerships; funding is annual and priority is given to proposals that are "essential infrastructure projects that promote jobs and	• Smart growth emphasizes long-range, regional considerations of "sustainable development"; in addition to dominating debates about sustainable urban planning and infrastructure it quickly gains traction in academic, practitioner, consulting, and some political circles • Evidence-based policy-making increasingly rejected by the government, and no serious attempts made to assess the claims that stimulus created jobs or contributed to "sustainability"

The three analytical elements

- $123 billion municipal infrastructure deficit
- Federal government commits to $2 billion each year to municipalities from a permanent federal Gas Tax Fund, including provisions for sustainable "green" infrastructure, but also with provisions to invest in road infrastructure; over the next 20 years, this gas tax transfer will be worth $40 billion to cities and communities
- The seven-year Building Canada plan, launched in 2007, is intended to support projects that contribute to cleaner air and water, safer roads, shorter commutes, and better communities
- Heavy advertising and branding of the EAP dominates through TV and media and takes government "propaganda" to levels not seen in Canada before, renewing concerns that infrastructure spending has become an exercise in distributive "retail politics" rather than long-term strategic renewal

- economic growth"; it also has a number of categories including "green infrastructure"
- Think tanks, especially those in the west, become increasingly prominent with the government in policy formation
- Federal government declines calls for it to play a national leadership role in urban transit and transformational infrastructure renewal; Conservative desire to balance the budget for 2015 election and commitment to "open federalism" make this unlikely
- In 2011, NDP introduced Bill C-305, a National Public Transit Strategy; the first of its kind in Canada, intended to address "the growing problem of a fragmented and inconsistent approach to public transit planning across the country"; in 2012 Bill C-305 was defeated by the Conservative government, suggesting that one-off funding and short-term planning will continue.
- Increasing number of fatal and serious train disasters, including Lac-Mégantic in 2013, has increased focus on public infrastructure, safety, regulation, and modes of transportation and environment

- The termination of *InfraGuide* in 2007 ends the research and evidenced-based gathering and dissemination of best practices development of a "National Guide to Sustainable Infrastructure"; INFC's KOA research program is also terminated
- Federal environmental assessment protections streamlined or cut completely; estimated that under the stimulus infrastructure plan 93 per cent of projects went ahead without full environmental assessments
- Federal changes to Statistics Canada census data collection make comparisons and forecasts harder and reduce information needed to inform urban planning
- Evidence of organized corruption emerging from the Charbonneau Commission and other hearings raise questions about infrastructure funding, and federal transfers in particular
- Infrastructure Canada states that the federal government has "set the protection and promotion of a clean environment as a paramount national objective"; however, the definition of a "clean environment" becomes increasingly contentious as Kyoto targets become unreachable and Canada's commitment is finally scrapped

and grants, education, and training services to support municipal plans, studies, and projects that improve air, water, and soil quality, and protect the climate. In 2001, the federal government, through its Infrastructure Canada Program and the National Research Council (NRC), again partnered with the FCM to create the *National Guide to Sustainable Infrastructure (InfraGuide)*, which was both a new, national framework of people, and a growing collection of published best-practice documents for use by decision-makers and technical personnel in the public and private sectors.

The FCM was also pivotal in bringing the burgeoning infrastructure deficit and increasing financial pressures on municipalities to the attention of federal and provincial governments and pointing out this was partly the result of senior government downloading services to municipalities. The FCM and a strong business lobby used the infrastructure deficit as an effective tool to call for infrastructure investment in municipal infrastructure. In this context, the FCM was instrumental in negotiating the federal government's 2005 New Deal for Cities program under which Canadian federal gasoline taxes are remitted to municipalities. The FCM and other municipal associations have continued to work with and advise the government on the design and administration of the Building Canada Plan.

Within the federal government, Infrastructure Canada continues to play a key role in designing and administering funds. Since it was established in 2002 it has overseen billions of dollars in funding for provincial, territorial, and municipal infrastructure through programs such as the Gas Tax Fund and the Building Canada Fund. It has to try to balance regional and local needs with national priorities and efficiency with oversight and accountability, but in a little over a decade it has also institutionalized infrastructure and sustainable development as key issues within government. Part of its mandate has also been to enable and foster partnerships between different levels of government and also between sectors.

As the private sector and governments look increasingly towards P3s as a potential "solution" to address the infrastructure gap, P3 Canada was established to facilitate and promote public-private partnerships. The P3 Canada Fund was created in 2009 to "improve the delivery of public infrastructure and provide better value, timeliness and accountability by increasing the effective use of P3s" (PPP Canada 2014). Funding is annual and priority is given to proposals that are "essential infrastructure projects that promote jobs and economic growth" (ibid.). Specifically, P3 Canada prioritizes public infrastructure projects in transportation, water/waste-water, solid waste disposal, and brownfield redevelopment. It also has a number of other categories including "green infrastructure" (ibid.).

Think tanks, especially those in the west, appear to have gained influence with the current government, particularly on energy policy, but infrastructure and public transportation in particular are returning to the political agenda in light of climate change, urban sprawl, and traffic congestion, and a number of serious human and environmental tragedies, such as Lac-Mégantic, examined in earlier chapters. In 2011, NDP Transport Critic Olivia Chow introduced Bill C-305, a National Public Transit Strategy (NPTS). The first of its kind in Canada, it was intended to address "the growing problem of a fragmented and inconsistent approach to public transit planning across the country" (National Transit Strategy 2014). In 2012 Bill C-305 was defeated by the Conservative government, suggesting that one-off funding and short-term planning will continue for the time being, but this could develop into a significant issue in future elections. Because of the massive economic, safety, and environmental implications of investments in infrastructure, and transportation in particular, it could be that new networks and alliances emerge in support of increased investment in urban sustainability, including environmentalists, business, and trade unions.

Science, Evidence, Knowledge, and Precaution

Until the 1960s, infrastructure was seen mainly through a functional lens, but also as an opportunity in nation-building. Roads, rail, highways, airports, potable drinking water, and communication were seen as crucial components of a large and rapidly developing and "modern" economy looking to attract people and investment and exploit its vast natural resources. In the 1960s and 1970s, concerns grew as pollution, acid rain, and urban sprawl came to be seen as threats to the quality of urban life and the broader environment. As Canada quickly urbanized, it became clear that cities provided the main source of pollutants and would require action on a national scale. The federal response was to establish Environment Canada and sign a number of international conventions to establish limits on air pollutants. In 1975, Prime Minister John Turner also established a federal fuel tax, which would be used to invest in municipal infra-structure, as it became clear from demographic projections and technical reports in asset management that demand for infrastructure, particularly in urban centres, would rapidly outstrip municipal resources and make the existing model increasingly unsustainable.

The 1980s saw an increase in scientific research on the environmental, health, and social impacts of unsustainable growth, and the Brundtland and other international initiatives call for serious response to global warming. Cities were again identified as the biggest producers of GHG emissions, and with urbanization accelerating, urban sustainability emerged as the discourse around which knowledge and theory would build. The federal government played a prominent role at the Rio Earth Summit 1992 and initiated the creation of the Earth Council and the drafting of the global Earth Charter.

At the local level, New Urbanism was developing into a coherent and influential body of knowledge and social science, particularly within urban geography and municipally focused political science. It promotes transit-oriented development over roads and urban sprawl, and is closely associated with environmentalism and the broader concept of smart growth that would also become discursively and intellectually influential in developing more sustainable urban forms.

In addition to the environmental and ecological cases for pursuing sustainable urban growth, increasing national and international research demonstrated that smart growth, and investment in green infrastructure, was necessary to ensure economic sustainability. Better public transit moves people and goods around and across cities and regions more efficiently, and in doing so could also help to attract knowledge workers, the "creative class," to move and stay in greener, more compact, and livable cities with relatively easy access to work, leisure, culture, shopping, and the arts. Because place matters more in a globalized world, cities with more sustainable urban lifestyles would, according to this thesis, be better placed to attract investors, innovators, and wealth creators. Clearly transformative public infrastructure and progressive planning would underpin a virtuous and sustainable cycle as envisioned by Richard Florida and others.

International bodies such as the WHO and OECD, Canadian think tanks such as the Conference Board, academics and consultants, including KPMG, have all disseminated research and evidence on the need for public investment in public infrastructure, based on similar arguments. International tables and indices have also begun to measure and rank sustainability factors such as competitiveness, quality of life, safety, air quality, commute times, and so on.

More practical and technically focused, the federal government partnered with the FCM and municipalities to produce the *InfraGuide* reports. They drew on research and experience to set out the best practices to support sustainable municipal decisions and actions. The best practices were made available online and in print and were considered highly successful and innovative by many, because they attempted to build and share knowledge about sustainable infrastructure at all levels of government, within and between sectors, and establish communities of practice across Canada.

Also during the early to mid-2000s Infrastructure Canada added to this public stock of knowledge by funding major research projects into infrastructure and sustainable development and communities through its Knowledge-Building Outreach and Awareness programs (KOA), but, like the *InfraGuide,* its funding was not renewed after 2007. It is difficult not to see the closure of such programs as part of the Harper government's much criticized reluctance to fund scientific research that addresses environmental concerns and impacts, or advance the case for sustainable development. If this is the case, it is a short-sighted and potentially dangerous strategy.

As Quebec, and specifically Montreal, has demonstrated recently, deteriorating public infrastructure can have tragic human consequences as well as serious commercial implications as business relocates or withholds further investment. A strong case can be made that the precautionary principle should apply to critical and major infrastructure such as bridges, highways, water, and communication. This is compounded when we consider the broader health implications, which Infrastructure Canada acknowledges explicitly: "Maintaining a healthy and sustainable environment is directly related to the health and prosperity of Canadians" (Infrastructure Canada 2014). The website also states that the federal government has "set the protection and promotion of a clean environment as a paramount national objective." This may be so, but it is difficult to see consistent patterns of federal action, policy, and funding in the pursuit of urban sustainability.

CONCLUSIONS

Until recently, in spite of the fundamental importance of infrastructure to the economy, safety, quality of life, environment, and longer-term sustainability of Canada's urban centres, successive federal governments have allowed investment to decline steadily as a percentage of GDP since the 1960s. Increasing pressure to fund growing social programs, combined with fiscal crises and austerity measures, political shifts, and short-term planning cycles, have all contributed to this trend. In addition, investment in basic infrastructure is ongoing, the results of which are often unseen and unrecognized by the electorate over the course of a four-year election cycle. Whether for the national interest, as with the Quebec sovereignty issue, or for partisan interests, governments seek "visibility" and political returns in exchange for their spending, and these are often easier to find by investing in social programs such as health and education.

For these reasons, governments prefer to invest in "shiny" new infrastructure projects such as bridges, highways, sport stadiums, and other flagship projects than fund asset-management responsibilities for sewers, roads, energy, communications, and other largely unseen but nonetheless crucial infrastructures. Environmental concerns and issues can and do emerge in debates about infrastructure, but, as we have seen in our examination of five periods, they are seldom the prime driver or policy concern.

There are already disturbing signs of Canada's decades of underinvestment in infrastructure, including recent fatalities in Montreal as bridges and overhead passes visibly crumble, and sinkholes open up on major highways. However, the full magnitude of the problem is difficult to know, but recent estimates have suggested the "infrastructure gap" could be in the region of $150 billion. In addition to the financial, health and safety, productivity, and social problems caused by aging and underfunded infrastructure, there are also the foregone opportunities to invest in transformative or "green" infrastructure and smart-growth planning that can reduce a city's geographical and carbon footprint, contributing significantly to reductions in GHGs omissions and their longer-term sustainability.

As we have seen, the federal government, with at best a tenuous mandate for intervening in urban affairs, has been slow to respond to the challenge of urban sustainability. Until the 1960s it acted primarily as banker, extending loans to municipalities for specific projects. Since then, federal government investment has waxed and waned according to the economic and political circumstances of the period. However, since the mid- to late 1990s, a series of significant programs were established to help fund municipal infrastructure, culminating in the New Deal–inspired Gas Tax Fund and the recently announced Building Canada Fund. These funding programs, while welcomed by municipalities, barely scratch the surface of what is required, however, and Canada still lags well behind other G8 and developed nations on its per capita investment in infrastructure.

In addition to municipal concerns about the overall amounts invested, when, how, and why the federal government invests also pose major challenges. In recent decades the government has invested in municipal infrastructure in order to stimulate the economy and create jobs, address provincial unrest, and gain political profile, to name but a few reasons. While these may be justifiable reasons, they do not constitute the basis for a predictable, strategic planning to address urban infrastructure needs or promote sustainable development.

How the government invests also affects these issues. Transfers raise questions of accountability and oversight, and in trying to strike a balance between local autonomy and central control they raise efficiency and jurisdictional issues. In particular, federal attempts to impose "green" or "sustainability" conditions on infrastructure spending are open to creative interpretation and legal challenge. Although the federal government may wish to encourage sustainable infrastructure projects, it has to avoid being seen to subvert or distort local priorities and decision-making. Joint funding of specific municipal projects such as light rail transit, bridges, or sports stadiums addresses some of these issues but constitutes policy by project rather than a coherent national strategy.

Recent initiatives such as the Building Canada Plan suggest that the government will continue to fund infrastructure through specific programs and encourage private-sector opportunities through P3s. The Building Canada Plan is a step in the right direction and provides a significant source of long-term funding over the next ten years. In spite of the Harper government's skepticism on climate change and the environment, the Building Canada Fund earmarks specific programs for green and sustainable infrastructure projects. However, it is difficult to see how transformative these limited funds will be in the absence of a broader strategy, that might have included

InfraGuide, the Green Municipal Fund, and some of the other promising federally funded research programs discussed earlier, and with a leader and a party that appears reluctant to champion the urban sustainability cause in the way the Martin and Dion Liberals were prepared to do. Nevertheless, the time, effort, and money that have gone into advertising, promoting, and branding federal investment in infrastructure and a cleaner environment in recent years suggest that the opportunities for political capital are not lost on the Harper government. The challenge for the Canadian electorate will be to make the reality of the government's claims match the "world-class" rhetoric and promotion.

The analysis has demonstrated overall key green-lite complexity features, particularly involving policy and governance patterns in policy "ends-means" calculus and conflict over numerous sets of normative visions for infrastructure. Federal-cities infrastructure and stimulus programs had some environmental aspirations, but it remains difficult to know and determine if they are real or manifested in literally tens of thousands project locations. Diverse and conflicting temporal realities have been shown to be inherent in what infrastructure as a long-term capital asset is and what renewing it means over different periods, not to mention who pays. And the intricate nature of, and diverse triggering points for, environmental agendas have been shown in part to result from the combined nature of federal, provincial, and city/local budget cycles.

9

The NGO, Market, and Business–
Environment Regime

INTRODUCTION

The centre of gravity of governance and regulation in many environmental domains has become notably diffuse in recent decades. In part, this has been an explicit and intentional move associated with a deregulatory agenda commonly associated with neo-liberalism and New Public Management. Yet other factors have contributed in ways that are important to understand, as we assess the trajectory of Canada's environmental policy agenda and practice as a whole since the 1970s.

In this chapter, we turn to examining the manner in which non-governmental organizations (NGOs), markets, and businesses, and their associations have become central players in a set of governance processes and venues not directly controlled by public policy. We begin with the roots of discontent that directed much attention to Canada's federal and provincial policies that were seen as falling short on aspiration and performance. In this period, Canada's position in the global economy began to serve as a central source of political power, as those groups unhappy with domestic practices took their concerns to international audiences – the governments of other countries, the international forums of the United Nations, and the markets for Canadian products. Starting with early activism that engaged Canada's international markets to vilify practices such as seal hunting, the role of market pressure has risen. In the past two decades, private governance processes have been added as a further venue affecting the practices of Canadian operators and the content of Canadian environmental policy.

Together, we term this area of activity the NGO, market, and business–environment regime. It is different from many of the other hyphenated environmental policy regimes we have examined in that, as just noted, its authority is not solely, or even, at times, entirely, associated with government. There are exceptions. In some cases, the federal government actively encouraged these processes under the rubric of voluntary environmental programs (Webb 2004). In others they followed. Organic agriculture, for instance, began as a form of private regulation developed by organic farming associations and organic agricultural enthusiasts. Now organic production is regulated by the Canadian Food Inspection Agency through authorities created in the Canadian Agricultural Products Act. The mining sector's Whitehorse Mining Initiative (WMI) in the early 1990s aimed, among other things, to inform government policy. These cases are best characterized as forms of explicit and intentional co-governance or co-regulation. In other cases, private governance continues to operate without the implicit or explicit sanction of government authority. In fisheries and forestry there are certification programs that set standards and monitor compliance for a considerable number of Canadian operators.

In this chapter, we trace the origins and implications of a handful of these initiatives as they have permeated the practices of Canadian environmental policy-making. Our analysis spans initiatives from natural resources to industrial processes. We start with a chronology of these developments. We then review how they fit within the three strands of our regime concept identified and reviewed in chapter 1: ideas, discourse, and agendas; power, democracy, and governance; and science, evidence, knowledge, and precaution. We also show the ways in which this regime exhibits several of the green-lite complexity features in several of the environmental policy and governance patterns.

PHASES OF REGIME CHANGE

Roots of Discontent: 1960s–1970s

Conservation organizations were active in Canada well before the 1970s. Ducks Unlimited Canada, for instance, formed in 1938 to advance efforts to protect waterfowl through conservation initiatives in important areas of habitat. The now well-known Nature

Conservancy of Canada formed in 1962 with a focus on conserving specific properties of ecological significance; the first project was a wetland area – Cavan Swamp and Bog – in Ontario that included twenty-two species of orchids (Nature Conservancy of Canada 2013). As well, at the time, urban centres served as the focal point for political debates over the appropriate restrictions on sources of air pollutants; Temby (2013), for instance, documents the role that those with real estate interests in Toronto pushed for effective pollution control in the 1950s, as the salience of ground-level air pollution grew. (We discuss more on urban policy issues in chapter 7).

By the 1970s, a few additional groups had been added to the Canadian list (see table 9.1), including the Canadian Wildlife Federation (established 1962), the Sierra Club of Canada (as a chapter of the US organization, established in 1963), Canadian Parks and Wilderness Society (established 1963), World Wildlife Fund (WWF) (Canadian office established in 1967), and Pollution Probe (established 1969). Some of these organizations were founded on concerns over conservation, but others began to focus on the pollution made particularly salient in the public mind in North America by Rachel Carson's book *Silent Spring* (1962). These groups also began to professionalize with increased capacity to include scientific arguments in their appeals for policy action. Pollution Probe, for instance, began as a student movement at the University of Toronto with a focus on local issues, including the cleanup of the Don River in Toronto, litter and garbage, and waste management (Ogilvie 2006). Other local organizations – such as Ecology Action Centre Halifax and the Society Promoting Environmental Conservation in Vancouver – established around the same time and had a similar focus on local pollution and waste concerns (Paehlke 2010). Pollution Probe has since evolved to address many other issues, and it has developed partnerships and collaborations directly with businesses to address various environmental challenges (Ogilvie and Everhardus 2004).

Another key facet of this period was the groundwork laid in relationships between Canadian groups and their US and international counterparts. The WWF was a national office of a larger international network. Ducks Unlimited, the Sierra Club, and the Nature Conservancy had ties to US organizations. As well, the early 1970s saw the birth of Greenpeace. A group founded in Vancouver to protest nuclear testing in the Aleutian Islands, Greenpeace quickly became active on environmental issues. It formalized its first anti-whaling campaign in April 1975, which solidified its reputation for direct action protests that sought to disrupt business practices and to bear witness to the environmental consequences of human activities (Weyler 2004).

Greenpeace's actions against the whaling sector were also part of an important early international environmental campaign. After Japan and the Soviet Union blocked efforts to impose a moratorium through the International Whaling Commission (IWC), groups in the United States, including the National Wildlife Federation, Fund for Animals, Friends of the Earth, and Animal Welfare Institute, were calling for consumer boycotts of Japanese products ("Japanese and Soviet Whaling" 1974). In the later 1970s and through the 1980s, whaling captured media attention around the world; this early concern helped facilitate the 1982 decision of the IWC to place a moratorium on commercial whaling (Skodvin and Andresen 2003).

This was also when Greenpeace and other groups voiced outrage over the long-practised commercial hunt of baby harp seals (Raloff 1979). Harter (2004) documents how the campaigns moved from an initial attempt to work with small-scale seal hunters to oppose the larger, industrial sealing operators – some of which were foreign – to an attempt to draw international attention to the Canadian industry, vilifying the sealers and their communities. He explains, "Greenpeace had traded in its alliance with workers for an alliance with [US] senators and movie stars." And the tactic worked. By 1982, the European Commission initiated a voluntary boycott on seal products, and the Government of Canada followed with a ban on the large offshore vessels in 1987 (ibid.).

Other groups founded during this period built from Greenpeace's direct-intervention tactics to champion the defence of marine life. The Sea Shepherd Conservation Society, commonly known as Sea Shepherd, formed in 1977 (officially incorporating in 1981) and used direct action tactics akin to those of Greenpeace to end the seal-pup hunt and expose and stop illegal whaling (Sea Shepherd Conservation Society 2008). Greenpeace and Sea Shepherd actions against Japan and then later Norway and Iceland occurred throughout the late 1980s and even into the 1990s (Wapner 1996). Boycotts and blaming-and-shaming tactics were used, and operated in concert with continued threats of US economic sanctions against Iceland and Norway (Andresen and Skodvin 2008, 137).

The story of the seal hunt serves as an important ideational precursor to dynamics that would develop in Canada at the end of the 1980s. Before turning to these dynamics, the next section reviews the development of the NGO community as a foundation for the market campaigns that subsequently formed.

Trying to Gain Influence at Home: 1960s–1980s

The efforts of environmental groups to gain access to the policy process in Canada have been myriad. Considerable research has examined the specific and varied opportunities for influence at the municipal, provincial, and federal levels. Table 9.1 provides a snapshot of the environmental groups that have developed in Canada over nearly a hundred-year period. It is far from a comprehensive list, but it provides some insights into the shifting sources of concern and strategies for seeking influence that groups have adopted. We review both of these shifts as they have played out over the past forty years.

First, the character of problems has been broadening. Although centred more prominently in the United States, the conservation movement was an important force early in the twentieth century pushing for the preservation of nature, often in the form of parks (Gottlieb 1993; Paehlke 2010). Paehlke (2010, 4) explains that the 1970s then brought new concerns to light: "The new focus was on urban concerns, the possible limits that might arise given the way our economy functioned and how we lived our lives – all of which struck a popular chord. The newer environmental activists were still concerned with protecting nature and wilderness, but their first concern was with protecting human health and well-being. For a time, protecting nature seemed passé compared to what was painted as a fundamental crisis of industrial society itself and a direct threat to human survival."

These concerns coincided with the 1970s energy shocks, which as we have seen in chapter 2 helped propel an agenda to reduce reliance on costly fossil fuels, but which subsequently waned during the economic down turn of the early 1980s. Still, the expanded problem focus would remain.

Second, the strategies for seeking influence began to broaden and diversify. A source for this diversification increasingly came from international sources, particularly the United States. A Canadian

chapter of the US group the Sierra Club formed in 1963, and the
WWF set up an office in Canada in 1967. A decade later, in 1978,
Friends of the Earth established a Canadian office. Then, in the early
1970s, a number of groups formed with a focus on environmental
law, including the Canadian Environmental Law Association, the
Canadian Institute for Environmental Law and Policy, and West
Coast Environmental Law. As Paul Emond – a lawyer who studied
at York University at the time and who became a part of a legal
movement on the environment – recently noted in reflection on this
period, "Much of the impetus came from the USA and in particular
the passage of the *National Environmental Protection Act* (NEPA)
in 1969, from 'radical' new environmental legislation in Michigan,
the 1970 *Michigan Environmental Protection Act* (MEPA) in 1970,
and from the prospect of similar legislation being enacted at both
the federal and provincial levels across Canada" (Emond 2008, 222).

As we detailed in chapters 2 and 4, there were few environmental
statutes in Canada at that time that focused on pollution control as
the main objective (with some exceptions such as the Fisheries Act).
The actions in the United States were, therefore, a source of inspiration for a generation of lawyers who saw the judicial system as a
potential avenue through which to affect environmental outcomes.
The effects of these initiatives were mixed in the short run but did
help facilitate some changes in the longer run, as legislation was
changed to accommodate the critiques issued by these environmental groups with legal expertise. For instance, Emond (2008, 226–7)
explains the long-standing push in Ontario for an environmental bill
of rights that would include three provisions: the "legal right to a
clean environment, the ability to participate fully in the regulatory
process, and legal tools ... to enforce that right." Groups were also
successful in importing certain US legal ideas in the debates over
endangered species that eventually led to the passage of the Species
at Risk Act (Illical and Harrison 2007).

A third development involved the ostensible opening up of previously closed policy networks where business and government dominated decision-making (McAllister and Alexander 1997; Wilson
1998). This change, aligning with the ideas of sustainable development in the 1987 Brundtland report, saw the rise of numerous
roundtables and multi-stakeholder processes that sought to address
tensions between economic growth and social and environmental

Table 9.1: Establishment of environmental groups in Canada

Organization	Year established	Mission
Ducks Unlimited	1938	"Conserves, restores, and manages wetlands and associated habitats for North America's waterfowl"
Nature Canada	1939	"Protect and conserve wildlife and habitats in Canada by engaging people and advocating on behalf of nature"
Conservation Council of Ontario	1952	"Provincial association of organizations, businesses, municipalities, and individuals working individually and cooperatively to promote and apply conserver values across Ontario"
WWF	1961 (international) 1967 (Canada)	"Stop the degradation of the planet's natural environment and to build a future in which humans live in harmony with nature"
Canadian Wildlife Federation	1962	"Dedicated to ensuring an appreciation of our natural world and a lasting legacy of healthy wildlife and habitat"
Nature Conservancy of Canada	1962	"Lead, innovate, and use creativity in the conservation of Canada's natural heritage" "Secure important natural areas through their purchase, donation, or other mechanisms, and then manage these properties for the long term"
Canadian Parks and Wilderness Society	1963	"Envisages a healthy ecosphere where people experience and respect natural ecosystems"
Sierra Club	1963 (chapter of US org) 1989 (national office)	"Empowers people to protect, restore, and enjoy a healthy and safe planet"
Environmental Defence Canada	1968 (US) 1984 (Canada)	"Challenge, and inspire change in government, business, and people to ensure a greener, healthier, and prosperous life for all"
Pollution Probe	1969	"Exists to improve the health and well-being of Canadians, by advancing policy that achieves positive, tangible environmental change"
Canadian Environmental Law Association	1970	"Specialty community legal clinic providing services to low-income individuals and disadvantaged communities across Ontario in environmental law matters"

Organization	Year established	Mission
Canadian Institute for Environmental Law and Policy	1970	"Inform legislative, policy, and regulatory outcomes for sustainability at the national and provincial/territorial levels of government in Canada"
Friends of the Earth Canada	1971 (international) 1978 (Canada)	"Voice for the environment, nationally and internationally, working with others to inspire the renewal of our communities and the earth, through research, education, and advocacy"
Greenpeace	1971	"Acts to change attitudes and behaviour, to protect and conserve the environment, and to promote peace"
West Coast Environmental Law	1974	"Through legal advice, education and advocacy, West Coast provides citizens and organizations with the knowledge, tools, and innovative solutions needed to protect our environment and build sustainability locally, nationally, and internationally"
Sea Shepherd Society	1977	"End the destruction of habitat and slaughter of wildlife in the world's oceans in order to conserve and protect ecosystems and species"
Friends of Clayoquot Sound	1979	"Peaceful, courageous advocates in protecting the ancient temperate rainforest, ocean, rivers, and biodiversity of Clayoquot Sound"
Wilderness Committee (Western Canada Wilderness Committee)	1980	"Protect Canada's life-giving biological diversity through strategic research and grassroots public education"
Pembina Institute	1984	"Advance clean energy solutions through innovative research, education, consulting, and advocacy"
Wildlife Habitat Canada	1984	"Deliver habitat conservation projects on all land and seascapes and all provinces and territories in Canada"
Rainforest Action Network	1985	"Campaigns for the forests, their inhabitants, and the natural systems that sustain life by transforming the global marketplace through education, grassroots organizing, and non-violent direct action"

David Suzuki Foundation	1990	"Protect the diversity of nature and our quality of life, now and for the future"
Ecojustice (formerly Sierra Legal Defence Fund)	1990	"Ensure the long-term protection and health of our rich and diverse environment"
Ecotrust	1991 (US) 1995 (Canada)	"Enterprising non-profit whose purpose is to build the conservation economy in coastal BC and beyond"
Land Stewardship Centre	1996	"Enabling people and organizations to become better stewards"
Land Conservancy of BC	1997	"Protects important habitat for plants, animals, and natural communities as well as properties with historical, cultural, scientific, scenic, or compatible recreational value"
Living Ocean Society	1998	"Advocate for oceans that are managed for the common good, according to science-based policies that consider ecosystems in their entirety"
Watershed Watch Salmon Society	1998	"Catalyze efforts to protect and restore BC's precious wild salmon"
Mining Watch Canada	1999	"Address the need for a co-ordinated public interest response to the threats to public health, water and air quality, fish and wildlife habitat, and community interests posed by irresponsible mineral policies and practices in Canada and around the world"
ForestEthics	2000	"To protect endangered forests, wildlife, and human well-being"
Climate Action Network Canada	2002	"Combat climate change, particularly by pressing for comprehensive climate change action plans by all levels of government, based on the best available science, with specific policies, targets, timetables, and reporting, and to work with Canada's governments, First Nations, Inuit and Metis, private sector, labour, and civil society for the effective implementation of these plans"
Canadian Boreal Initiative	2003	"National convener for conservation in Canada's Boreal Forest"

Table 9.1: (*continued*)

Organization	Year established	Mission
Canadian Land Trust Alliance	2005	"Promote private land conservation and strengthen the land trust movement nationally through communication, education, and the development of partnerships"
Ancient Forest Alliance	2010	"Protect the endangered old-growth forests of BC and ensure sustainable forestry jobs in the province"

Source: Information gathered by authors from the websites of the listed organizations

outcomes (Paehlke 2010). We pick up on this development with specific details of the mining and forestry cases below.

A final aspect of the shifting strategies concerned the move towards the market. The ties to US and other international groups were important in facilitating this shift. In a number of sectors, US groups began to take an interest in Canadian environmental policy (see chapter 3). This was not without precedent. The Canada-US Boundary Waters Treaty, which formed the International Joint Commission, was established in 1909, and the Migratory Bird Convention, which entered into force in 1916, were both earlier examples of a recognition that problems in Canada spilled over to the United States, and vice versa (Paehlke 2010). However, as time progressed, the extent of this recognition on a range of environmental issue began to deepen.

Two cases illustrate this shift and connection among scales. A first case involves the internationalization of disputes over the protection of forests in BC. For many decades, the forest policy community in the province had involved close relationships between business, the provincial government, and labour unions. Policy decisions over forests were taken on the basis of a compromise among these three groups for how rents from the exploitation of BC's forests would be divided among provincial revenue, profits for firms, and well-paid jobs for forest workers (Cashore et al. 2001; Wilson 1998). As we have seen in detail in chapter 6, provincial control over natural resources partly facilitated this historical pattern of policy development. Here, in the context of the NGO, Market, and Business–Environment Regime, the important aspect of this period was the motivations it created for environmental groups to seek out other avenues of influence.

In several cases, NGOs and First Nations formed coalitions to protest companies with logging licences for the province's forests. In 1980, for example, the Nuu-chah-nulth Tribal Council submitted a formal land claim for an area of Vancouver Island's west coast, and asked that no logging occur on Meares Island during settlement negotiations (Wilson 1998, 195). Just before this, MacMillan Bloedel had announced logging plans for the island, which set the stage for a period of conflict. With the creation of Friends of Clayoquot Sound – a local group of residents opposing logging – an environmental–First Nations alliance was formed that eventually, with the help of a favourable decision by the BC Court of Appeals, temporarily stopped logging on the island. The BC government sought to respond to these concerns with a range of new policy initiatives, including roundtable discussions among stakeholders to designate land-use plans for large areas of the province. The most important such project was the 1992 Commission on Resources and Environment (CORE). Yet, at the time, environmental groups were also beginning to take their claims to international audiences; this was the beginning of a widely followed international conflict over forestry practices in Clayoquot Sound, and in BC more generally (Bernstein 2000).

These disputes over forest practices soon intermingled with disquiet over the effluents released by pulp and paper facilitates. In 1986, Greenpeace launched an international campaign targeting the release of dioxins and furans by these facilitates that resulted from their use of chlorine-bleaching processes (Harrison 2002). Federal and provincial governments responded with stronger rules on pulp-mill effluent ("Dioxin Testing Ordered" 1988; Harrison 2002; Noble 1989); however, implementation shortfalls were a problem that spurred an internationalization of the issue (Gibbens 1991). At this point, the frame of concern encompassed both forestry and pollution. Starting around May 1991, Greenpeace and Sierra Club organized a tour of BC for European journalists, politicians, and scientists to expose them to existing forest practices (Stanbury 2000). Before this, Greenpeace Germany had published *Das Plagiat,* a takeoff on *Der Spiegel,* a widely read German newsmagazine, as a way to highlight to Europeans the problems with BC forestry.

The venue shift proved quite advantageous for environmental groups. As Pralle (2003, 246) explains,

Power in the international arena on this issue was tied less to political and material resources and more to cultural resources. This gave environmentalists an advantage over their opponents, who had relied on traditional political resources (such as lobbying, political ties, administrative access, etc.) when they competed in venues at the provincial level ... For example, Clayoquot activists used international treaties and norms to shame Canada, a country proud of its "green" reputation abroad, into changing their forestry policies and practices. While devoid of any real enforcement power, international treaties such as the 1992 Biodiversity Treaty provided a rich array of symbols and arguments to environmental groups, adding legitimacy to their claims.

Pralle's analysis offers useful insights into the shifts that were occurring at this time. Although it might appear that decisions made by activists were highly calculated, Pralle documents that the strategic shift was due, at least in part, to learning and experimentation. This move to the market, as we shall see below, was a critical foundation for the rise of private governance.

A second illustration comes from the mining sector. Much like in forestry at the time, Day and Affum (1995) described the mining sector in BC as having close relations with regulators at the exclusion of other interests. In the 1980s, one mine project galvanized considerable attention both in Canada and the United States. It was a mine site proposed for an area in the northwest corner of BC, on the borders of the Yukon and Alaska, in a region referred to as the Haines Triangle. The ore deposit was first discovered in 1958, and then optioned by Geddes Resources in 1981; through further exploration, Geddes forecast that the deposit would yield 297 million tonnes of copper ore over twenty years (Hood 1995).

The BC government responded to the Windy Craggy mine proposal with the same policy instrument it used to assuage conflict in the forest sector. It charged CORE with evaluating the situation, as it had for Clayoquot Sound. Ultimately, the decision, taken in 1993, was to reject the project and to designate the Tatshenshini-Alsek area as a provincial wilderness park. Day and Affum (1995) provide some evidence that the Windy Craggy decision was made to win back support from groups' disappointment over the government's approach to Clayoquot Sound. But the important point to note in this process was that links between Canadian and US environmental groups were solidified through the process. As Hood (1995, 17) explains, "In 1989, a coalition of environmental interest-groups calling itself Tatshenshini Wild formed. A year later the coalition, now called Tatshenshini International, had grown and encompassed over 50 conservation organizations intent on halting the Geddes proposal." A key aspect of the tactics was to put pressure on the US administration, which led to, among other things, a joint resolution in the US Congress and Senate calling the secretary of interior to seek an agreement with Canada to protect the region where the mine was proposed (Hood 1995; McAllister and Alexander 1997).

The outcomes of the mining and forestry cases were different; however, in both cases, the internationalization of protests was an important source of leverage for influence. In the next section, we build on this point by examining the rise of private governance, and how Canada's place in the global economy has partially shaped the manner in which this key component of the NGO, Market, and Business–Environment regime has gained traction. Our analysis of the emergence and cross-border origins and links among the increasingly complex structure of environmental groups and alliances is important in green-lite terms. It reveals the multi-scalar and environmental governance and democracy coordination and conflict dynamics, as suggested in our green-lite complexity framework. More aspects of this also emerge later in the chapter.

The Rise of Private Governance and Co-Governance: 1990–2014

Paralleling the move to markets as a venue for leveraging policy change in Canada – what Bernstein and Cashore (2000) term "the markets pathway" – various groups began to develop rule-setting and rule-enforcing processes, commonly termed "private governance." These initiatives are sometimes referred to as "partnerships," a term used to encompass a broad range of policy initiatives (Bendell 2000). Partnerships are separate from the certification systems we discuss below, mainly because of their more limited institutionalized governance (Auld, Bernstein, and Cashore 2008; Rondinelli and London 2003). This has been a huge area of growth for governance in general, and it has had specific implications for Canadian environmental policy. To map the rise of private governance and co-governance, we explore five separate cases. Each provides a different perspective on the origins, evolution, interactions with government, and possible consequences. These cases are organic agriculture, the chemical industry, mining, forestry, and fisheries. Each provides insights into the changing and complex boundaries of environmental policy in Canada, realities captured by our green-lite analytical lens.

ORGANIC AGRICULTURE

First, organic agriculture had roots as far back as the 1900s. Early experiments with biodynamic approaches to agriculture in Germany, the United States, and other countries helped generate a community of farmers keen to see alternative forms of agriculture gain a place in the market. These groups formalized information sharing through the International Federation of Organic Agriculture Movements (IFOAM) in 1972 (Langman 1992). Since then, organic certification has become a central space in which there are overlapping public and private rules, from state and provincial levels to national, supranational, and international levels. By the early 1990s, BC, Manitoba, and the federal government were developing rules for the definition and certification of organic farming (Hill and MacRae 1992). This was in step with developments in the United States and the EU (Auld 2014; Guthman 2004). By the end of the decade, there were increasing calls for a greater role of government, particularly as, at the time, forty certification bodies were operating in Canada and often used different standards. In 1999, the federal government took a first step towards fully regulating organics by introducing a national standard for organic agriculture (Forge 2001). Currently, through the Organic Product Regulations (Department of Justice 2009), the federal government also oversees the accreditation of organic certifiers and requirements for the use of organic claims and labels.

CHEMICAL INDUSTRY

A second case of private governance came from the chemical industry. In 1985, the Canadian Chemical Producers Association (CCPA), now the Chemical Industry Association of Canada (CIAC), launched Responsible Care as an industry self-regulatory initiative. Dow-Canada was important in developing the ideas behind the initiative, following an accident at its Sarnia, Ontario, facility; it then helped promote and initiate the program within the United States, where a Responsible Care program was launched in 1988 (Prakash 2000).

By the fall of 2013, Responsible Care was operational in sixty countries, as a product of the work of fifty-four industry associations. Scholars have pointed to the key role the chemical industry's collective reputation played in leading to the launch of this initiative. Gunningham (1995), for instance, details the accident rates of the chemical industry in the late 1970s and 1980s, how the public perceived the industry in a negative light, and the view of management of major chemical companies that they faced a serious problem with public trust. In Canada, the first moves towards the initiative formed in 1979, when the CCPA issued a Statement of Policy on Responsible Care; it subsequently made this a condition of membership in 1984 in light of the Bhopal disaster and the associated drop in public trust for the industry (Moffet, Bregha, and MiddelKoop 2004).

This early version of Responsible Care consisted of six codes of practice that followed from the policy statement members had committed to. It also included continuous improvement, which has meant the requirements have evolved considerably over time. Moffet, Bregha, and MiddelKoop (2004) detail some of the changes in Canada: in 1993, members were required to record and publish data on emission and waste and to conduct internal audits against the code; in 1994, external verification was added; and in 1992, members were to report on greenhouse gas emissions voluntarily.

Considerable interest has surrounded Responsible Care and whether the program has had measureable effects on environmental performance. Moffet, Bregha, and MiddelKoop (2004) document reductions in emissions from 1992 to 1999: of heavy metals to water (down by 74 per cent); of chlorofluorocarbons (down by 94 per cent); of sulphuric acid to water (down by 100 per cent) and to air (down by 31 per cent); of volatile organic compounds (down by 43 per cent); of stratospheric ozone-depleting chemicals (down by 50 per cent); and of known carcinogens (down by 72 per cent). However, these authors are careful to note that other factors, including government regulations, may have contributed to these reductions, making the evaluation of Responsible Care challenging. Indeed, studies in the United States have paid extensive attention to the effectiveness of Responsible Care (and other similar self-regulatory and voluntary initiatives), and the results have found mixed evidence of improvements. For instance, King and Lenox (2000) reported finding limited evidence for improvement; they even indicated that there was some evidence that members reduced their emissions less quickly than non-members. Still, since the inception of Responsible Care, they did find that the chemical industry had improved its performance overall.

Other work on self-regulation has pointed to the clear need for external monitoring and sanctions to ensure performance (Potoski and Prakash 2005). This is one reason why there was early pressure on Responsible Care to require third party monitoring (Gunningham 1995).

MINING

The rise of private governance in mining has some parallels to the developments in the chemical·industry. In both sectors, companies led efforts to raise standards of practice within the industry in response to negative public perceptions and potential regulatory threats. By contrast, there are parallels as well to the fisheries sector; the diversity of private governance initiatives in the mining sector has been extensive. This characteristic sets it apart from the chemical industry and the forestry sector, which we turn to next.

Similar to the chemical industry, the Canadian mining industry moved quickly in an effort to respond to concerns about its activities. Indeed, Dashwood (2007) identifies domestic concerns as the more significant impetus for the adoption of corporate social responsibility practices among particular lead companies than rising global norms. Yet, as we noted above, many of the pressures within Canada were already forming international ties, as the coalition of actors opposing the Windy Craggy mine illustrated.

The Mining Association of Canada (MAC) was a leader in beginning to address the collective practices of its sector. In the early 1980s, the association introduced an environmental policy that its members were required to follow (Fitzpatrick, Fonseca, and McAllister 2011). The late 1980s were a tough period for the Canadian industry, as new investments shifted to Latin America and Southeast Asia, and public pressure constraining access to land appeared to be mounting (see chapter 6). Indeed, the process surrounding the Windy Craggy mine brought home the realty of the constraints mining in Canada might face. As McAllister and Alexander (1997, 34) explain, "Calls for designating land solely to be used as wilderness preserves pose a particular concern to the mineral industry because of its unique requirement to explore large areas in order to discover very few new mineral deposits ... Land access, then, is the key to long-term sustainable mining in Canada. If the industry cannot renew its depleting mineral reserves through new exploration, the mining sector will inevitably decline."

Not coincidentally, as the Windy Craggy mine proposal faced mounting resistance, the Canadian industry took action. In 1991, on the international front, the Canadian industry helped establish the International Council of Metals and the Environment (ICME), with some observers noting that inspiration came in part from Responsible Care. The ICME's first initiative was the launch of an environmental code of practices similar to the environmental policy developed by MAC in the early 1980s (Sánchez 1998).

Domestically, MAC also took action by initiating and participating in the Whitehorse Mining Initiative (WMI), a multi-stakeholder process focused on Canadian mining. Unlike the other initiative discussed in this section, WMI involved a greater role of government. Indeed, the industry felt that the initiative was necessary to set a new course for mining in Canada on issues such as compensation for cancelled mineral rights, reforms to the tax regime, complex and overlapping environmental regulations, and uncertainty over land title and environmental liability (McAllister and Alexander 1997, 41). The WMI was proposed in September 1992 at an annual meeting of the Mines Ministers' Conference, by MAC; with the support of provincial, territorial, and federal governments, planning for the initiative then commenced (Hood 1995; McAllister and Alexander 1997; McAllister and Milioli 2000). The first meeting occurred in February 1993, and a series of discussions then ensued on how to structure the process. An operating structure was eventually determined that involved a secretariat, leadership council, working group, and four issue groups. Five thematic areas had been identified for discussion, including Aboriginal issues; land access, land use, and land allocation; workforce, workplace, and community issues; financial performance and taxation issues; and environmental issues. However, the WMI adopted four working groups, as representatives for Aboriginal peoples stressed that their concerns and interests should be addressed in all the other issue groups as a crosscutting theme (McAllister and Alexander 1997, 84).

After more than a year of work, the Whitehorse Mining Accord was signed in 1994 and set out a vision for the sector, along with more specific principles and goals and an associated statement of commitment. McAllister and Alexander (1997, 116–17) listed six challenges the accord detailed: concerns with the needs of business, environmental protection, Aboriginal concerns, decision-making, resolution of land-use issues, and meeting needs of workers and communities. Both government and the industry took cues from the accord. A number of provinces developed policies drawing on the accord (McAllister and Alexander 1997, 124–57). Manitoba's Sustainable Development Mineral Policy Applications served as a guide for operators in the province to practise in line with the accord (Hilson 2000).

As discussed in chapter 6, at the federal level, the WMI paved the way for the development of a new policy – Minerals and Metals Policy of the Government of Canada: Partnerships for Sustainable Development – released in November 1996, which set a federal framework for mining in Canada through a focus on six objectives: decision-making based on sustainable development; business-friendly investment conditions; products, markets, and stewardship promotion; Aboriginal involvement in mining; science and technological innovation; and international leadership (Hilson 2000; Shinya 1998).

Since the WMI, the mining sector has developed a series of initiatives within Canada and abroad. In Canada, the mining sector made a commitment to the Accelerated Reduction/Elimination of Toxics program, which involved companies reducing certain pollutant discharges, including copper, arsenic, lead, cyanide, and mercury (Hilson 2000). More recently, the Towards Sustainable Mining initiative – launched in May 2004 – has become a key plan that includes guiding principles and performance indicators for crisis management, energy use and greenhouse gas emission, external relations, and tailings management (Fitzpatrick, Fonseca, and McAllister 2011). Unlike the WMI, these more recent initiatives are more focused on the specific activities of companies (ibid.); in this respect, they mirror more closely the private governance initiatives of the other sectors reviewed in this chapter.

Further developments internationally were occurring alongside those in Canada. ICME, which then became the International Council on Mining and Metals (ICMM), oversaw a number of initiatives to advance the sustainability of the global mining sector. The Global Mining Initiative (GMI) was launched in 1998 to address global concerns over practices in the sector. Led by the three largest mining companies at the time – Rio Tinto, Western Mining Corporation, and Phelps Dodge Corporation – the initiative played a key role in launching the Mining, Minerals, and Sustainable Development (MMSD) project in April 2000 (Sethi and Emelianova 2011), which was informed by a commissioned scoping report by the International Institute for Environment and Development (IIED) started in May 1999 and finished in October 1999 (International Institute for Environment and Development 2013). The IIED then was contracted to conduct the full-scale project that GMI envisioned for MMSD that occurred from April 2000 to the publication of the final report in May 2002, and it involved extensive research, workshops, and regionally focused discussions on specific topics (International Institute for Environment and Development 2002). ICMM took over from ICME in 2001 and became the institutional home for moving forward with the MMSD project; it has since led on a series of initiatives to do with the environmental and social performance of the mining sector, including a statement, released in 2003, on mining and protected areas that committed members, *inter alia,* to not conduct exploration or mining in World Heritage areas; a position on climate change reporting released in 2006 that followed the standards of the Global Reporting Initiative; and a statement on transparency of mineral revenues released in 2009 (Dashwood 2005; Sethi and Emelianova 2011).

Finally, the sector has also seen a number of more issue-specific initiatives. Initiatives have developed around concerns over conflict minerals, such as the Kimberley Process for conflict diamonds (Grant and Taylor 2004) and the Responsible Jewellery Council that has established a certification program for gold and diamond supply chains (Fleury and Davies 2012). The Canadian group, Partnership Africa Canada, played an important role in establishing the Kimberley Process; Ian Smilie, who worked with the group at the time, released a report in 2000 that detailed links between the diamond trade and the conflict in countries such as Sierra Leone. When combined with the campaign pressures from Global Witness and other NGOs, along with government and UN enquiries, the industry felt compelled to act (Grant and Taylor 2004; Haufler 2010). In a three-year period that followed, the diamond industry took steps to address the problem, initially through a voluntary certification program, and eventually in collaboration with governments that were seen as integral for adequate enforcement. Following a meeting in Kimberley, South Africa, in 2000, which included the World Diamond Council (an industry group set up to tackle the conflict diamond issue), consuming and producing states, and civil society groups, two years of work produced the Kimberley Process Certification Scheme (Grant and Taylor 2004; Haufler 2010).

These certification initiatives make mining comparable to developments in forestry and fisheries; however, their focus has often been different – concerning the relationship between resource extraction and conflict and corruption. Moreover, private and co-governance for mining has remained much more fragmented, with varied initiatives across scales and problems. In green-lite terms, complex boundary dilemmas and multi-scalar realities are in evidence in mining, encompassing environmental and sustainability issues but also international conflict and corruption. This is quite in contrast to the forest sector, to which we now turn.

FORESTRY

In forestry, the 1992 Rio Earth Summit was a turning point for groups pushing for change in global forest practices. The late 1980s had witnessed, as we discussed above, growing pressure for change through boycott calls against tropical forest products at first, but then later Canadian forest products too. Early attention had focused on the possibility that the International Tropical Timber Organization and the Tropical Forest Action Plans of the Food and Agriculture Organization of the United Nations would help advance sustainable forest management in tropical forests (Humphreys 1996; Poore 2003). As well, in the lead up to the Rio Earth Summit, Canada was part of a group of countries pushing for a forest convention. In the end, all of these processes fell short of expectations. In addition, there was growing opposition to boycotts based on the logic that they could make things worse for forests rather than better; a boycott might lead forest operators to opt to convert forestland to agriculture, if forest markets were closed to access (Cabarle et al. 1995).

Waning success in intergovernmental efforts and questions about the efficacy of boycotts were important in laying the foundation for the establishment of the Forest Stewardship Council (FSC). The FSC came about through the work of a coalition of NGOs concerned about the social and environmental impacts of status quo forestry (e.g., Cultural Survival, Greenpeace, Friends of the Earth, WWF) and businesses that were seeking to move towards more responsible sources of wood and paper products (e.g., the Ecological Trading Company, B&Q). Officially launched at a founding meeting held in

Toronto in 1993, the FSC incorporated in 1994. In that year, it approved nine of ten global Principles and Criteria (P&C); the tenth principle on plantations was approved in 1996. The final set of P&C required local working groups to develop standards governing legal compliance and adherence to FSC rules; long-term tenure and use rights; indigenous people's rights; community relations and workers' rights; benefits from the forest; environmental impacts; management planning; monitoring and assessment; the maintenance, conservation, and restoration of high conversation value forests; and plantation management (Forest Stewardship Council 1996).

FSC served as the standards-setter, and it worked to accredit certification bodies (first doing so in-house and now having this done by a separate organization, Accreditation Services International) that would conduct the local assessments of operations against the P&C and chain-of-custody rules to ensure the authenticity of certified products was not compromised along a global supply chain. It also endorsed national offices to coordinate development of (sub)national interpretations of the global P&C. Canada's first national contact person was endorsed in January 1997, with a national working group receiving endorsement in May 1998 (Forest Stewardship Council 1999). Standards development occurred in British Columbia, the boreal forest region, the Great Lakes Saint Lawrence region, and the Maritimes. The FSC was also established as a membership organization comprising three interest-based chambers – environmental, social, and economic – that held equal shares of the voting rights. Within each chamber, votes were also weighted evenly between interests from the global North and South (Meidinger 1997).§ FSC Canada chose to add a fourth chamber for First Nations in recognition of their particular significance to natural resource governance in Canada (Tollefson, Gale, and Haley 2008).

The Canadian forest industry, in step with industry in other countries, did not react with enthusiasm to the launch of the FSC. Just as the FSC held its Toronto meeting, the Canadian Pulp and Paper Association (now the Forest Products Association of Canada, or FPAC) announced that it would create its own forest certification

§   The initial chamber structure gave 25 per cent of the voting rights to
    economic interests and the remaining 75 per cent to environmental
    and social interests. This was changed at the first General Assembly
    meeting in 1996.

program. Within a year, industry had created a coalition of twenty-two associations to form the Canadian Sustainable Forestry Certification Coalition; this group approached the Canadian Standards Association (CSA), asking it to develop a standard for certification in Canada. The first standard was released in 1996 (Cashore, Auld, and Newsom 2004). Industry also sought to have the CSA standard serve as a forestry-specific version of the generic ISO 14001 environmental management systems standard, which had been supported by the World Business Council for Sustainable Development following the Rio Earth Summit (Elliott 2000, 13). Starting in 1995, Canadian officials proposed using their CSA-sponsored program as a starting point (Zarocostas 1995), and, in June 1996, a meeting of the Technical Committee 207 (the group working on the ISO 14000 series of standards) voted in support of having a forestry working group examine the feasibility of applying the generic ISO 14001 standard to forestry ("Falling Off a Logo" 1997). WWF International initially supported this work and participated in the talks ("Agreement Reached" 1995). This soon changed, however, with the group – and other NGOS – expressing concern that ISO was being used to legitimize a less-credible form of certification (Auld 2014). Eventually, the discussions ended, yet ISO 14001 still served as an early alternative for the FSC that Canadian companies pursued (Cashore et al. 2005).

The CSA would eventually receive endorsement from the Program for the Endorsement of Forest Certification (PEFC), an initiative formed by European forest landowners in the late 1990s, which subsequently remodelled itself as a global program in 2005 (Auld 2014). And as of 2000, the CSA program has had a mutual recognition agreement with the US program, the Sustainable Forestry Initiative (SFI), which was formed by the American Forest and Paper Association (Cashore, Auld, and Newsom 2004). The SFI began as a code of conduct for the Association's members, but in 1997 it added voluntary third party certification in the hopes of competing with the FSC in the US market (Cashore, Auld, and Newsom 2003; Overdevest 2004).

The rise of forest certification intersected with the market campaigns noted above. Canadian officials from industry and government were concerned about losing market access as environmental groups in Europe convinced many of the country's large forest-products customers to demand reforms in pulp and paper manufacturing processes and, later, changes in where and how forestry practices occurred

(Gunningham, Robert, and Thornton 2003; Stanbury 2000). As Hogarth (1991) explained at the time, "Greenpeace has crossed the Atlantic to persuade European businesses and consumer to stop buying forest products from Canadian companies that fail to heed the environmental group's standards. The European market accounts for 16% of Canada's forest exports, with almost two-thirds of that originating in B.C." Thus, in green-lite complexity terms, these dynamics reveal the diverse nature of, and triggering points for, environmental agendas, not only for companies but also for governments and environmental groups, as international leverage points are sought out or have been monitored and followed.

These market pressures slightly preceded the development of forest certification, but they would soon envelope certification and propel it forward. At the time, the government and industry began reacting. In 1992, the Canadian provincial forest ministers and representatives of leading industry associations, among others, signed Canada's first Forest Accord that set out the country's broad commitment to maintaining and enhancing the environmental health and integrity of its forests. As we discussed in chapter 6, provincial action on forests was critical, and this was a busy period for policy reform, as governments sought to help industry head off pressures from international buyers.

These market campaigns soon made explicit mention of certification. In Europe, groups such as Friends of the Earth continued with boycott calls. These efforts were then joined by WWF's efforts to encourage and support European buyers to make commitments to sourcing sustainable timber products. The first WWF buyer group was launched in the United Kingdom in 1991; others quickly followed. By 1996, the UK group had nearly ninety members that held a reported 15–25 per cent share of the British forest products market. Across Europe, there were over 700 companies involved in national buyer groups (Auld 2009; Cashore, Auld, and Newsom 2004). The United States followed by the later 1990s, after the campaign against and subsequent purchasing commitment of Home Depot. Though the campaign had deeper historic roots, several NGOs, including Greenpeace, the Coastal Rainforest Coalition (now ForestEthics), the Natural Resources Defense Council (NRDC), and the Rainforest Action Network (RAN), increased pressure around 1997, with support from a network of US foundations (Bartley 2007). Two years later, in August 1999, Home Depot announced that it would end sales of "wood from endangered areas" by the end of 2002 if these products were not from independently certified forests, and that it would give a general preference to products from forests independently certified as "well managed" (Cashore, Auld, and Newsom 2004). At the time, Home Depot was estimated to buy and sell 10 per cent of the world's lumber market (Howard and Stead 2001), meaning its commitment would have implications for many suppliers. Similar commitments made by Wickes and IKEA further strengthened the pressure for certification in the wood product supply chain (Auld 2006).

The pressure from the US market was particularly challenging, given a higher reliance on it as an export destination. And the pressure did not end with the solid wood sector. The environmental groups then took the same tactics to target the office supply sector. In September 2001, the RAN, ForestEthics, and the Dogwood Alliance launched a paper campaign. They targeted Staples, staging over 600 protests outside the company's outlets and using a host of other tactics to tarnish the company's public image. This campaign also targeted the catalogue industry, such as Victoria's Secret and L.L. Bean, that promote and sell products via mail catalogues. A series of campaigns were used in this instance, too, to convince these companies to change their paper-purchasing practices (Auld 2006).

This outside pressure – exploiting Canada's position in the global economy – has played a critical role in creating motivations for the forest sector in Canada to become certified. Other factors have mediated the pressure, which itself has not determined the choice of certification programs companies have adopted (Auld 2006; Auld and Cashore 2013; Cashore, Auld, and Newsom 2004). Still, the extent to which certification has taken root in the Canadian forest sector illustrates the critical role private governance now plays in Canada. Canada is a leading country in certified forestlands accounting for, in 2010, 42 per cent of the world's certified area, roughly 150 million hectares (Forest Products Association of Canada 2011). This represents 58.4 per cent of Canada's 256.7 million hectares of forests defined to have commercial potential (Natural Resources Canada 2006).¶ The majority of forestlands are certified with the CSA system

¶ When Natural Resources Canada (NRCan) last reported the area under forest management in 2006, it totaled 143.7 million hectares (Natural Resources Canada 2006). This implies that virtually all forests under management in Canada have been certified.

and the S F I program. Together, these two P E F C-endorsed programs had certified 112.7 million hectares, while F S C-certified forests covered 40.6 million hectares, or about 30 per cent of the F S C's global total of 134.2 million hectares (Forest Products Association of Canada 2011).

In parallel to the rise of certification, two other multi-stakeholder collaborations formed, more linked to the regional land-use planning processes we introduced above. Yet, here N G O s and businesses initiated these processes and largely controlled the policy formulation and decision-making; governments became involved more during the crucial implementation. The green-lite features involving means-ends conflict are especially germane here.

The first initiative focused on the Great Bear Rainforest, or the B C North and Central Coast, a region spanning coastal watersheds from the northern tip of Vancouver Island to the Alaska panhandle. As groups mounted pressure against the buyers of B C forest products to call for certification, their aims were actually more complicated. Indeed, once companies such as Western Forest Products announced they would seek certification with the F S C, N G O s noted that protection was actually the more salient, top-ranked goal, particularly in B C's coastal forest where there remained many unlogged valleys (Auld and Cashore 2013). Thus, although companies began to seek certification, a broader set of talks were underway between companies (initially Western Forest Products, Canfor, International Forest Products, Weyerhaeuser, West Fraser Timber, and Fletcher Challenge Canada) and Greenpeace, the Sierra Club of B C, and the Coastal Rainforest Coalition on how to resolve the dispute over forest protection in the region (Gibbon 2000). In April 2001, the talks generated an accord supported by both sides that proposed setting aside 600,000 hectares of forest from harvesting in the region and designating another 536,000 hectares as requiring study to determine the location of further necessary protection.

With this agreement in hand, the N G O s ceased their market pressure, and companies were assured returned access to customers, though at a cost of reduced harvesting rights and with consequences for forest industry jobs in certain communities on the B C coast (Mickleburgh 2001). This agreement fed into Land and Resource Management Planning for the Central Coast that in 2003 supported a plan for the region building from the initial 2001 accord. A similar process was also undertaken for the North Coast. Both processes recommended increased protection over the original 2001 accord and they supported the implementation of ecosystem-based management as a guide for development (Coast Forest Conservation Initiative 2014).

The second initiative is a more complicated version of the first. It sought to develop a similar consensus on the balance of forest harvesting, the rights of Aboriginal peoples, and forest conservation in a process that initially sidestepped government. In commentary on the process unfolding in BC, skeptics and critics worried that the same NGO pressure tactics would move from BC to other parts of Canada. Indeed, as noted above, ForestEthics launched its campaign against the US office supply sector in 2001, just months after the BC accord had been reached. Attention, in other words, was shifting to the Boreal, a major source of fibre for paper products reaching the US market, including catalogue papers. Tzeporah Berman, from ForestEthics, began to court interest in a Boreal initiative, approaching companies that might be willing leaders, including Tembec (Hamilton 2003). It would become a long process, with shifting membership and a series of agreements (a first occurred back in 2003 among First Nations, companies, and NGOs creating the Boreal Forest Conservation Framework; see Beyer 2003) culminating in the Canadian Boreal Forest Agreement that was signed in 2010.

The agreement committed seven environmental groups (Forest-Ethics, CPAWS, Canadian Boreal Initiative, the David Suzuki Foundation, the Pew Charitable Trusts, the Nature Conservancy, and the Ivey Foundation), Kruger Forest Products, and eighteen member companies of the FPAC to work together to conserve the forest habitat while ensuring continued harvesting access and forest sector jobs (Reidr 2014). Notably, the boreal forest was a much more complex undertaking than the BC North and Central Coast initiative. Spanning multiple provinces with different forest sector economies and other demands on the boreal ecosystem (e.g., Alberta's tar sands development), the process of turning the agreement into regional implementation plans is complex. Its green-lite attributes thus centred on multi-scalar breadth and also complex agenda features to develop and keep plans on track. In addition, the group had made some tough decisions about the groups to have around the table (e.g., First Nations were not involved nor did they sign the agreement), which meant work would be necessary to expand acceptance of the plan.

By 2013, many of the anticipated challenges were becoming more apparent. Greenpeace withdrew from the agreement in late 2012, expressing disquiet with the lack of progress; then in May 2013, Canopy, another environmental group that had joined the agreement, decided to withdraw. A central tension embroiling the agreement involved Resolute Forest Products, which environmental groups charged was not negotiating in good faith to address caribou habitat issues on its licensed forest lands in Ontario and Quebec; the company countered that the demands were too high and would jeopardize jobs and production (Jang 2013).

Resolute has since sued Greenpeace for defamation for claims that the group made against the company's operations that it argues were unfounded, and challenging issues have arisen around the company's audits with the FSC, as the Grand Council of the Cree issued a complaint to Accreditation Services International (the group that accredits organizations that audit for the FSC) against Rainforest Alliance's assessment of Resolute Forest Products (Accreditation Services International 2014). Hence, a conflict that began within the Boreal Agreement has spilled over to entangle the Canadian courts and private complaint procedures of forest certification. And within the Boreal Agreement, groups have also expressed concern that progress has been insufficient in Alberta, particularly for protecting critical caribou habitat.

FISHERIES
In fisheries, similar sources of pressure for certification emerged. However, the politics surrounding these initiatives has been notably different: it has not formed around a competition between two different conceptions of certification – one backed by NGOs and another supported by industry – but instead it has been divided among programs certifying fisheries versus aquaculture and NGO-supported buyer guides and campaigns versus certification. Still, a common feature is that Canada's place in the global economy, as a major exporter of seafood products, has made private governance an important new governance mechanism affecting the operations of Canadian fisheries and fish farms.

The first significant development in the sector came with the launch of the Marine Stewardship Council (MSC); it was specifically modelled after the FSC, but with some important and notable design differences. Established by Unilever and the WWF in 1996, it became an independent organization in 1997. It formed as a foundation not a membership association, in an effort to avoid perceived inefficiencies in the multi-stakeholder governance model adopted by the FSC (Sutton and Whitfield 1996; Synnott 2005). The MSC was run initially by a board of trustees and a chair, as the public face of the organization, and a secretariat that facilitated the work of a standards council, advisory board, and national working groups (Fowler and Heap 2000, 141). Based on a 2001 review, the MSC made significant governance changes, including swapping in a technical advisory board for its standards council; this new body took charge of advice on standards, chain of custody, and logo licensing. A stakeholder council – including thirty to fifty members – also replaced the advisory board and took on the role of advising the trustees. Two members from the stakeholder council and one from the technical advisory board were also given seats on the board of trustees (Marine Stewardship Council 2001). Still, the trustees retain authority over rule-making. Although stakeholder engagement was increased through these reforms, the MSC still lacked the same multi-stakeholder quality emblematic of the FSC. This is important to note as it has affected the manner in which the politics of fisheries certification in Canada has played out.

Another important characteristic of the MSC is the focus of its standards. It was developed through a series of workshops around the world starting in September 1996. Initial discussions included the possibility of focusing on social and environmental aspects of fisheries management, but the eventual decision was taken to attend primarily to the latter. The MSC also chose to deal only with ocean-capture fisheries and not aquaculture (Auld 2014). The final standard includes three principles and associated criteria. The first principle deals with the sustainability of the fish stock. It requires that stocks be managed to avoid over-fishing or depletion; when a stock is depleted, the fishery must undertake steps towards recovery. The second principle deals with habitat integrity. It focuses on concerns such as avoiding trophic cascades and depletion of genetic, species, or population diversity, and negative impacts on vulnerable species. Principle three deals with the operation's management approach; the aim is to ensure the fishery is advancing responsible fishing practices. This principle focuses on issues such as having a transparent process for consulting with parties affected by the fisheries, balancing long-term, customary, and legal rights of people dependent on the fishery with ecological sustainability, and control measures and dispute-resolution procedures. It also includes operational criteria for gear specifications and ensuring minimal by-catch and waste.

Other programs have also formed in the fishery sector. The MSC's decision not to certify aquaculture had important effects for the growth of certification. Some programs already existed in this space, but others would soon follow. Organics was the first. In the early 1990s, the Soil Association, Naturland, and Bio-Gro each developed requirements for organic farmed fish operations; these then informed a 2005 global standard endorsed by IFOAM. The next initiatives were launched by industry in 1997. The Global Aquaculture Alliance (GAA) formed in response to controversy over shrimp-farming practices, but it has since broadened to cover other species. The global GAP initiative, or Global "Good Agricultural Practices" (formerly EurepGAP), was launched by European retailers to address concerns over food safety and quality in agricultural supply chains, with some attention to environmental and labour practices as well. It released, in 2004, an Integrated Aquaculture Assurance standard. Finally, in 2009, the WWF worked with the Dutch Sustainable Trade Initiative to establish the Aquaculture Stewardship Council (ASC), which uses standards from WWF aquaculture dialogues that had been underway for over a decade (Auld 2009; Kalfagianni and Pattberg 2013).

The Friend of the Sea is a final seafood certification program and is distinct in that it covers both aquaculture and ocean-capture fisheries. The program began preliminary assessments as early as 2001, but since officially launching in 2006, it has grown considerably and now claims to account for 10 per cent of world capture fisheries (or ten million metric tonnes) (Washington and Ababouch 2011).

The two-program competition that developed in the forest sector did not emerge in fisheries for several reasons. Still, the struggles over certification do share some characteristics with forestry. One major similarity is the role of market campaigns, particularly targeting the US market (Auld and Cashore 2013). Canadian fishing and aquaculture operations have faced varied corporate campaigns, and these, too, have been an important incentive for operators to seek certification. As it did in forestry, demand began in Europe – specifically the United Kingdom. When the MSC launched, Sainsbury and Tesco committed to sell MSC-labelled seafood when it became available, and Unilever committed to sell only MSC-labelled products by

2005. Market interest for MSC then continued expanding, with thirty-one processors and four distributors in the United States achieving chain-of-custody certifications in order to sell MSC-labelled salmon in the US market, while Whole Foods offered the first such products to end consumers. Unilever also reported having sourced 5 per cent of all its seafood products from MSC-certified producers by the end of 2001 (Auld 2009).

Notably, the WWF did not organize buyer groups similar to those it supported within the forestry sector. Support for MSC certification in the market was much less coordinated. Some of this interest in MSC can be attributed to Greenpeace's prior campaigns targeting Tesco, Unilever, and others for their purchase of sand eels from the North Sea (as noted above). In the United States, groups such as NRDC, the Pew Charitable Trusts, and SeaWeb were also focused on single species. In 1998, responding to worrying numbers about swordfish populations in the North Atlantic and the declining average catch size, the groups collaborated with several high-end restaurants that agreed to take swordfish off their menus for one year (Burros 1998). The other initiative was the formation of "buyer guides" that ranked the performance of fisheries for easy comprehension by end consumers. Various groups in Europe and North America established such lists (Roheim and Sutinen 2006). More than with forestry in the late 1990s, these efforts were largely detached from MSC's work.

The next stage came around 2005, when Greenpeace UK began targeting UK supermarkets, placing pressure on them to change and greatly improve their seafood procurement practices. Greenpeace released a series of reports on supermarket performance. In its first, *A Recipe for Disaster*, Marks & Spencer received the highest grades, whereas ASDA (the UK subsidiary of Walmart) faired the poorest (Greenpeace 2005). Just three months after the report was released, in January 2006, ASDA announced an ambitious commitment to MSC – it sought to sell only MSC-certified fisheries within five years – and it added efforts on depleted stocks, including removing North Sea cod from its shelves (Hickman 2006). ASDA's new commitments moved it from dead last to a respectable fifth, with a grade of "pass" in Greenpeace's second supermarket report (Greenpeace 2006). Success in the United Kingdom led to the spread of supermarket reviews among national Greenpeace offices. Even before the US Greenpeace office released its first review, Walmart announced its equivalent commitment to ASDA for sourcing MSC-certified fresh and frozen seafood for its 3,800 North American stores by 2011. This added to the commitment the company had made in late 2005 to sourcing farmed shrimp certified according to the GAA standard ("New Certification" 2005).

This market interest, spurred largely by pressure from groups such as Greenpeace, has been an important factor creating a drive for fisheries certification in Canada. Indeed, Canada's uptake of fisheries certification, both aquaculture and capture, has also been extensive. With the MSC, several fisheries have sought and received certification. In addition, several fisheries are currently in full assessments or pre-assessments with the MSC. The BC salmon industry has also been certified with Friend of the Sea since 2007 (Friend of the Sea 2012). With aquaculture, several salmon farm operations are GAA certified, including Marine Harvest Canada, Grieg Seafood BC, and Mainstream Canada, all based in BC; and Northern Harvest Sea Farms, based in New Brunswick and Newfoundland and Labrador (Best Aquaculture Practices 2013).

THE THREE REGIME ELEMENTS

To close this chapter, we discuss the NGO, Market, and Business–Environment Regime in relation to the three elements of our regime concept. Table 9.2 provides an overview of the key aspects as they relate to the three time periods discussed above.

Environmental Policy and Related Green Ideas, Discourse, and Agendas

A prominent interpretation of the rise of what we are terming the NGO, market, and business–environment regime turns to the powerful role of ideas in shaping how problems are understood and policy actions are designed and implemented. Significant scholarship notes that neo-liberal ideas were critical to facilitating the shift to greater roles for business, NGOs, and private governance in addressing environmental problems, across spatial scales. Indeed, at the global level, Bernstein (2002) characterizes this shift as a rise of liberal environmentalism, where the idea that markets can be used to solve the externalities produced by markets has become a dominant normative frame.

Table 9.2: The NGO, Market, and Business–Environment Regime and the three regime elements: Selected summary highlights

TIME PERIOD	POLICIES, IDEAS, DISCOURSE, AND AGENDAS	POWER STRUCTURE, DEMOCRACY, AND GOVERNANCE	SCIENCE, EVIDENCE, KNOWLEDGE AND PRECAUTION
Roots of discontent: 1960s–70s	• Conservation movement concerned with the protection of nature, such as through parks • Broadening of the agenda to include environmental concerns with pollution, particularly in urban settings • Particular concerns over local, urban pollution	• Policy networks dominated by business interests	• Growing understanding of ecology and the externalities produced by industrial society (e.g., via Rachel Carson's *Silent Spring*)
Trying to gain influence: 1960s–80s	• Further broadening of the agenda towards regional and global environmental problems • Rise of a legal environmental movement that sought to import US ideas on environmental law • Beginning of experiments with roundtables and multi-stakeholder processes as a tool to address growing conflict over environmental issues • Increasing attention to international processes and norms as guides and standards with which to cajole domestic action on the environment	• Canada's place in the global economy as a source of power for NGOs with limited access to domestic policy-making processes • Deepening ties between the US and Canadian environmental NGOs • Changing scales of collective action, with attention to the local as well as the global • Rise of transnational activist networks	• Growing epistemic community around environmental issues • Greater contestation between knowledge communities, including First Nations, industry technical experts, and environmental groups
Rise of private governance and co-governance: 1990–2014	• Building discourse around liberal environmentalism where markets are seen to be able to solve the environmental problems that markets create • Idea of consumers as political agents and the possibility of green industries	• Varied power of industry association systems across sectors • Institutionalizing new decision-making forums outside of government; NGOs no longer sources of pressure on agenda-setting, but increasingly playing roles in formulating, implementing, enforcing, and evaluating policy	• Science as a source of authority used rhetorically to support claims of interests • Changing nature of evidence as technology allows for greater surveillance of distant processes

On a discursive level, there are evident features of reframing that move the appropriate locus of attention in two directions – one to the global and one to the local. At times, they are in step and complementary; at others, they are discordant. For instance, the Canadian forest industry set up organizations following the international market pressure that sought to re-localize the debate about appropriate forest management. In the case of the FSC, standard-setting was meant to occur at a more localized level to accord with specific social, economic, and cultural conditions.

Aside from these bigger political ideas about the organization of the market, state, and society, the chapter also documented how private governance and co-governance served as an open space in which new ideas for how to manage resources could gain prominence. The most striking example is the introduction of ecosystem-based management through the North and Central Coast processes in BC. But these ideas have also found traction in the standards-setting processes of the FSC and to an extent the MSC. Moreover, the period represented a shift in understanding how the scale of an individual operation needed to be located within a larger landscape. Although the Boreal Agreement has been struggling lately to implement this idea, it appears that the rise of co-governance and private governance in Canada has opened up opportunities to push resource management in a different direction. These processes, thus, can be seen as a partial check on some of the green-lite realities we have identified in other chapters, although by no means an unproblematic or perfect check.

Environmental Power Structures,
Democracy, and Governance

This regime element is likely the most fascinating. Two broad trends are evident. First, the power of interests in the policy process underwent a notable shift in certain sectors over the course of the forty-year period. Whereas the issues we reviewed were typically business dominated in the early period, market campaigns and private governance challenged these network structures.

Second, Canada's place in the global economy was a key feature that affected the power balance between NGOs and business, particularly on forestry and fisheries, given these two sectors are significant net exporters. There are evident implications for democracy that result from this pattern of influence, which has been a long-standing preoccupation for Canadians concerned about US influence over Canadian domestic policy choices. But the chapter also highlighted that this factor did not fully determine the choices that companies or the government could make; rather, the field of private governance and co-governance offered choice among options. Moreover, the power of industry's associational system also mediated the pressure, with certain sectors – particularly the chemical industry and mining – having more success in getting ahead of NGOs in developing private governance.

Finally, the evolution of the regime highlights a changing capacity of NGOs to influence the policy process. Often environmental groups are considered to have greatest capacity to affect agenda-setting processes – as was illustrated by the analysis Pralle provided of the global framing of the forest problems in Canada that affected the course of policy-making in BC – and policy evaluation. However, the chapter highlighted how NGOs, through private governance and co-governance mechanisms, began playing an increasing role in policy formulation, implementation, and enforcement. Although this may appear as a form of new service delivery or public-private partnerships where the state delegates or contracts out roles and responsibilities, the picture we have provided highlights that the origins of these relations are much more complicated and nuanced than this perspective affords.

Science, Evidence, Knowledge, and Precaution

The role of science, evidence, knowledge, and precaution are less prominent in the details this chapter has reviewed. Still, three key developments arise. First, science played a critical role as a source of knowledge about the challenges industrial society posed for the environment and human health; these insights were critical for the early work of groups such as Pollution Probe, and they informed campaigns such as the one that Greenpeace launched against the pulp and paper industry for its release of dioxins and furans.

Second, the idea of earth systems sciences – which began to provide ideas about the interconnected nature of earth systems and the points of vulnerability that tied local activities to global outcomes – served as an important ideational basis for environmental groups that increasingly saw their issues as inherently global. This increased systems approach to conceptualizing planetary systems contrasted with the often focused, technical science that companies brought to the policy process.

Finally, contested knowledge claims first emerged as a clear issue in the development of roundtables focused on land-use across Canada. As we noted above, First Nations viewed their concerns differently from those of other groups involved in the WMI process; this was a reflection, in part, of a different world view and understanding of knowledge claims. Just as governments in Canada have had to grapple with this more diverse set of truth claims (Prince 2007), private governance programs faced similar challenges.

CONCLUSIONS

Our examination of the NGO, market, and business environmental regime has shown the extensive rise of private governance and co-governance as it has played out in Canada. We have not been able to cover all instances of this important developing trend, but the cases from various sectors provide sufficient evidence to underscore the manner in which a rescaling of governance has occurred in Canadian environmental policy. One common thread for the chapter has been the role that Canada's place in the global economy has played in providing opportunities for NGOs, on the one hand, to leverage external pressure to shape environmental policy and practice in Canada, and on the other hand, how this has forced industry to find new ways to collectively organize to respond. Indeed, the associational system serves as an important intermediary variable in understanding the power relations that have developed over policy struggles across sectors, as companies have faced increased pressures to address their environmental and social performance.

By reviewing different sectors in which private governance and co-governance have developed, the analysis has highlighted the quite different dynamics that have emerged even just within Canada. Whereas the forest sector experienced a competitive struggle between proponents of two different conceptions of private governance, with government mostly supporting the conception advanced by forest companies, in other sectors the field of private governance has been much more fragmented, and in still others, the eventual arrangements have involved a greater collaborative, or co-governance, approach with government.

Hence, to be able to understand the future trajectory of Canadian environmental policy, one needs to carefully consider the interactions between these different governance mechanisms. Put differently, understanding environmental policy in Canada no longer means looking at the rules set by the different levels of government; it also requires considering the rules set by business for their own operations and the rules set by the likes of the governance initiatives addressed in this chapter.

We also observed the ways in which this regime exhibits several green-lite environmental policy and governance patterns. The cross-border origins and links among the increasingly complex structure of environmental groups and alliances reveals the multi-scalar and environmental governance and democracy coordination and conflict dynamics. Also revealed are developments and cases showing complex and fragmented boundary realities regarding the content of certification and other agreements, not only in business and resource sectors but also in the sub-domains within and across them. Finally, we observed the now diverse nature of, and triggering points for, environmental agendas available for companies, governments, and environmental groups, as international leverage points are sought out or have been monitored and followed.

10

Green-lite: Complexity in Fifty Years of Canadian Environmental Policy, Governance, and Democracy

The core academic focus and contribution of the book has been to show the extent to which green-lite captures the evolution of Canadian environmental policy, governance, and democracy. This conclusion rests on our extended and in-depth mapping of six environmental regimes covering forty or fifty years, including the ebb and flow of prime ministerial eras and shifting international pressures. The analysis also underscores that further analysis of environmental policy, governance, and democracy ought to extend into the federal cities and infrastructure regimes and into the NGO, Market, and Business–Environment Regime, and thus overall into areas of provincial and territorial environmental policy and multi-scalar realities. These increasingly important regimes have been forged and developed in more recent decades. Attention to them is critical to understanding Canada's green-lite features and record, and for shedding light on the country's governance and democratic underpinnings. We have not, for reasons of space, been able to conduct a full comparative analysis of provinces or cities and their environmental policy histories. Still, by elucidating key and crucial parts of the provincial stories, we are confident that our conceptual conclusions about Canadian environmental policy and multi-scalar governance are well grounded empirically and can be built upon by others in future research.

To conclude, we present our findings in two overall ways. First, we offer a summary view of change and inertia in the six environmental regimes examined. Second, we detail our main arguments on the book's three research questions; we begin this synthesis with the core green-lite concept centred on complexity in policy and governance patterns.

THE SIX ENVIRONMENTAL REGIMES:
A FINAL LOOK

Our analysis of the six environmental regimes reveals a varied and complex picture and diverse ranges of environmental policy change, inertia, scope, and coverage. The chapters in Part Two of the book offered a detailed comparison of the regimes. We have seen that each regime has unique but also shared and linked features.

The Environment Canada–Centred Regime (chapter 4) offered a look at a department with initial – and in part continuing – aspirations to be at the centre of environmental policy and progress. However, from the outset, the department was buffeted and opposed directly or indirectly by other ministers and departments and their mainly industrial, natural resource, and sectoral interest groups. The regime contained the central environmental laws, giving it a de jure central role. Yet, the de facto environmental content of these laws was muted (and still is), because they were highly dependent on the co-administration and interpretation by other federal departments and their agencies, not to mention provincial and local governments as well.

The Energy-Environment Regime (chapter 5) presented a look at a regime hyphenated to the nth degree. It has environmental content and mandates, yet very few of its laws and regulatory systems were titled with environmental nomenclature. Throughout its history, it has mainly been about energy resources and resource promotion and use. When EMR was the lead ministry, oil and gas and nuclear were the focus. Its remit broadened to forestry and mining when NRCan was established and took the reigns; it also then flexibly deployed sustainable development as the triple bottom line encompassed by economic, social, and environmental criteria and processes.

The Natural Resources–Environment Regime (chapter 6) continued the story of NRCan as the lead department but with a more explicit focus on forestry and minerals policy as pan-Canadian natural resources and Canada's province-centred staples heartland. It also encompassed fisheries and oceans as a contrasting case to illustrate the role of constitutional divisions of powers between the provinces and the federal government as critical to the character and evolution of Canadian resource policies. Indeed, although the federal government held clearer powers to regulate fisheries resources, provincial interests remained paramount in navigating management decisions, given the concentrated economic and social impacts of federally driven regulatory initiatives.

The Federal–Cities Urban Sustainability Regime (chapter 7) reviewed the first of three "newer" regimes. Its history is structured not only in the sense of provincial jurisdictional imperatives in Canadian federalism and local government but also in complex spatial and multi-scalar realities and locales. With a provincial context as background, the chapter explored four periods of a federal-cities focus from the pre–sustainable development era in the 1960s and 1970s to the recent waning of federal interest in cities under the Harper Conservatives. In all of these periods, environmental policy issues and ideas fought for space and impact, often with dubious success, as they were subsumed under related policy influences and imperatives or undermined through periodic cycles in funding.

The analysis of the Federal–Municipal Infrastructure Sustainability Regime (chapter 8) mapped infrastructure renewal as the core of a newer hyphenated environmental regime. Infrastructure emerged as a financial "superhighway" enabling billions of dollars to flow from federal to local government, with associated affects for provincial funding. It also served as a policy window through which the federal government could steer urban sustainability and the greening of Canadian cities, to come extent, by promoting cleaner technology, improving energy efficiency, and limiting the growth of urban sprawl. Infrastructure renewal mattered too for economic sustainability. The chapter highlighted how infrastructure has been a critical public asset over several decades and also needs refurbishment and renewal. Consequently infrastructure needs to be treated as investment rather than just normal spending or political opportunism and will require innovative thinking and funding to make up lost ground.

The NGO, Market, and Business–Environment Regime (chapter 9) elucidated another newer and less generally known regime of rule-making where the state itself (federal, provincial, local) may be only an observer and facilitator of private networked governance, co-governance, or even enforcement. Canada's position in the global economy has been a central structural factor affecting the evolution of this regime. We showed how environmental groups unhappy with domestic practices and policy responses took their concerns to international audiences – the governments of other countries, the international forums of the United Nations, and the markets for Canadian products – to leverage market and normative pressure on the Canadian government and Canadian operators. Sectors and realms, such as organic agriculture, chemicals, mining, forestry, and fisheries, were examined, where ultimately N G O - and market-driven pressures and naming-and-shaming strategies facilitated varied outcomes, sometimes clear environmental improvements.

The regimes were assessed using our three regime elements: (1) environmental policy ideas, discourse, and agendas; (2) environmental power structures, democracy, and governance; and (3) science, evidence, knowledge, and precaution. Both inertia and change were revealed through these elements seen across the four to five decades of coverage and through the twenty-five illustrative policy histories across the six regimes examined. But they also help us see the variety of green-lite realities, as we see further below. Our contextual review of prime ministerial eras and agendas in chapter 2 and of Canada-US and international pressures and developments in chapter 3 provided additional and related aspects of the conceptual and empirical story. We also pointed out that some policy and governance dynamics show up and are best understood via reference to more than one element feature.

With regard to the element of environmental policy ideas, discourse, and agendas, the regime analyses revealed a wide range of environmental policy ideas, communication and expression of environmental values, and new or amended discourse. Conservation ideas emerged from the outset and were then joined by ideas regarding pollution control and "polluter-pays," cleanup, and related remedies.

Sustainable development produced a further layering of important ideas. These were softened in a green-lite manner in terms of actual practicality by discourse that included a balanced triple bottom line "consideration" of economic, environmental, and social factors. But what constitutes "consideration" and also what does the notion of "balanced" mean in practice? Does it mean, for example, that environmental ideas are at best one-third of the content and hence very much "green-lite"?

In the Energy-Environment and the Natural Resource–Environment Regimes, statutes and policy made mention of ideas from pipeline safety to "public convenience and necessity" and even the more recently expressed idea of the "social licence." The idea of export promotion has long been a mainstay; it has become increasingly salient in recent years alongside promotion of the idea of "responsible" resource development. Nuclear energy evoked genuine desires for both the peaceful use of nuclear power and the long-term storage of nuclear wastes and the non-proliferation of nuclear weapons. Alternative and renewable energy ideas and discourse also fought for attention and possible implementation, including biofuels, big versus small hydro, and even carbon capture and storage as a part of "clean energy." Climate change as a complex and deep problem emerges as well in diverse forms, arenas, and debates, as do related arguments about the melting of the Arctic.

In the federal-cities environmental regime, ideas and discourse initially concerned housing and the economic and social regeneration of Canada's larger cities. Sustainable development entered this regime as city and local governments embraced the idea of managing human settlements and fostering green infrastructure and urban and city centre–suburban sustainable transportation systems as solutions to congestion.

The analysis of the NGO, Market, and Business–Environment Regime saw an early focus on conservation values and protection, including urban and local pollution. These changed and broadened to include ideas about global environmental problems and about multi-stakeholder processes as being valued in themselves. Still later, explicit ideas and discourse that was centred on liberal environmentalism emerged where markets could solve problems that markets create. The infrastructure environmental regime centred on the nature of capital assets as an idea and how they can or cannot be supported and financed and also what they imply for concepts of natural environmental capital.

Environmental power structures, democracy, and governance as partial explanatory elements have shown diverse impacts on change and inertia. We have seen prime ministerial power and interest in variously defined environmental matters as both beneficial and harmful across the various regimes and across and within the four prime ministerial eras covered. Environment Canada's aspirations as a central agency and player has been shown to be subject to continuous pushback from other ministers and departments as overall agendas changed, including those centred on economic recessions and deficits, global free and fair trade, and Canada-US relations. Power structures, democracy, and governance also affected environmental policy when particular natural resource sectors gained ascendency in certain periods, including forestry, fisheries, and oceans. However, rarely did these resources trump the consistent base of power of the oil and gas and electricity industries or the massive Alberta-centred oil sands industry.

In the context of both the federal-cities and infrastructure regimes and also the NGO, Market, and Business–Environment Regime, new forms of governing structure, democracy, and power emerged, tied to an enhanced use of a particular central policy instrument. For cities, this emerged partly out of the Martin government's agenda but also because city and local governments lobbied nationally in several ways. Infrastructure developments arose from direct concerns about the under-investment in urban and community capital assets and also from interwoven periodic stimulus programs, especially in the 2008 to 2013–14 period. The initiatives discussed in chapter 9 emerged alongside direct NGO actions and corporate responses, either at the individual corporation level or via business interest groups. Motivations for business action varied. Some responses were attempts to fend off pressure or reluctantly acquiesce. Other businesses and their groups responded proactively, seeing themselves as progressive or virtuous practitioners of overall corporate responsibility.

Science, evidence, knowledge, and precaution, as the third element in our framework, also revealed some intriguing aspects of change and complexity. Natural and physical scientists, either in Canada or internationally, were of course often the first to identify and make known the existence of particular hazards, pollutants, or harms, ranging from particular chemicals and particular biotechnology products, to acid rain, the hole in the ozone layer, climate change, and lead in gasoline. The historical story has often stressed the primacy of science-based governance and regulation on these issues, with the related eras of science, evidence, knowledge, and precaution emerging later in the environmental age. Science-based centrality was a feature of free trade agreements, as we have seen, to ensure that environmental and health-protection rules were not or did not become a vehicle for disguised alternative forms of economic and trade protectionism.

However, our analysis revealed that notions of, and the need for, diverse kinds of combined science, evidence, and knowledge have been present from the very beginning of the environmental age. These include the social and economic sciences and knowledge transmitted and exchanged through related science activities as practised by front-line officials in related environmental and health fields. Such science is also present in the front-line review of projects being subject to environmental assessment requirements. The federal-cities and infrastructure regimes and also the NGO, Market, and Business–Environment Regime showed complex mixtures of social science, managerial science, law, and economics. These included economic ideas that advocated and built the arguments against command-and-control forms of environmental and health regulation and in favour of market approaches. Instances of front-line citizen science in environmental realms and programs – such as birdwatching and environmental monitoring of local pollution and biodiversity – have also become part of the story.

Concepts of precaution have been present in the regime analysis, particularly in some international agreements and related notions of scientific uncertainty. However, in most regimes, explicit statutory or mandate concepts of precaution have been absent. But some forms of precaution are, in fact, present in practice, as the result of the structured involvement of assessment processes on projects and products, and in more limited ways on policy and regulatory development itself. By not requiring environmental assessments for the vast majority of the infrastructure projects funded under the stimulus program, as discussed in chapter 8, some of these structured de facto precautionary processes have also clearly been weakened in recent years.

Last but not least, the analysis revealed the growing emergence of anti-science and anti-evidence forces and practices. They are apparent in the continuous attack politics among political parties and also in social media. Traditional media have also been practitioners of these dark arts, and governments, especially the current Harper Conservatives, have muzzled their scientists, especially environmental scientists, and have attacked their motives and mobilized their communications officials to reign in on what topics and where they can speak (see more below).

OUR ARGUMENTS IN THE CONTEXT OF THE MAIN RESEARCH QUESTIONS

Throughout our analysis, we advance several arguments, beginning with the core green-lite concept centred on complexity and policy

and governance patterns. We offer a concluding view of these in relation to the book's three research questions and their presence as
features of change and inertia within and across the environmental
regimes.

Our first two arguments supply linked but partly different answers
to the first research question: how, why, and to what extent has
Canadian environmental policy changed in the last forty to fifty
years? The green-lite argument suggests that specific agendas and
discourse have changed episodically. At the same time, overall features of complexity in environmental policy and governance patterns have been present from the outset of the Trudeau era. Increasing
centralization of executive and prime ministerial powers, for example, has continued during the Chrétien-Martin and Harper eras,
changing the political and governance landscape significantly in the
process. In spite of their increased powers, prime ministers in all four
eras have only periodically given explicit support to environmental
progress. In most years across these regimes, priorities resided decidedly and not surprisingly in other policy realms. But to see these
answers, we need to examine the arguments more closely as part of
our final summary.

Green-lite as an Empirical Feature of Complexity regarding Canadian Environmental Policy and Governance Patterns

Our central argument and conceptual contribution is that green-lite
captures overall the way in which environmental policy is being put
into practice in Canada over the entire forty years and more covered
since 1970.

Table 10.1 summarizes the numerous examples of each of the five
types of policy and governance patterns at play in green-lite complexity examined in previous chapters: (1) complex policy "ends-
means" calculus and conflict; (2) complex boundary realities and
therefore hyphenated environmentalism; (3) diverse and conflicting
temporal realities; (4) the diverse nature of, and triggering points for,
environmental agendas; and (5) complex multi-scalar and spatial
environmental, governance, and democracy coordination and conflict dynamics. We have drawn attention to these at various points in
the chapter analyses and show them here in summary to convey the
weight and depth of the green-lite evidence.

We stress again that green-lite as a concept does not imply that there has been no environmental policy progress. The regime chapters have shown that some environmental progress has occurred in Canada, including the establishment of Environment Canada, Canadian leadership in early environmental summits, and successes in the development of environmental assessment processes, national parks, the Great Lakes, migratory birds, acid rain, and the ozone layer. However, green-lite as an empirically grounded concept implies that environmental progress in Canada is still very much a struggle because of complexity in the overall Canadian environmental policy and governance system as examined in the book as a whole.

Environmental Policy and Governance in Growing Prime Ministerial–Dominated Executive Power

We contend that Canadian federal environmental policy was once briefly centred on Environment Canada; however, power and policy have increasingly been ceded to the prime minister in growing prime ministerial–dominated executive power. This has also related to other central agencies, particularly in the Chrétien-Martin and Harper eras. Prime ministers have always held pre-eminent power and control in Cabinet government, and thus at one level it should be no surprise that their interventions regarding their support for or non-interest in environmental policy can be pivotal. Chapter 2 showed this quite vividly but also diversely. Prime Minister Trudeau saw strong interventions and interest in the birth of Environment Canada in 1971 and earlier, but then not much concerted interest for the rest of his tenure to 1983 as overall priorities shifted.

The Mulroney era saw a prime minister who was pivotal in putting the 1990 Green Plan into place and also acid rain agreements with the United States. Yet for most years from 1984 until 1993 the environment was far from being front and centre in his agenda. The Chrétien-Martin era saw growing intellectual and policy support for sustainable development as an idea, especially when linked with the innovation economy and smart regulation. Environmental references were more frequent as discourse but were modest in practice, and abysmal regarding climate change and Kyoto performance, and also regarding severe cuts to environmental science and to Environment Canada during program review.

Table 10.1: Empirical summary evidence of green-lite complexity regarding five Canadian environmental policy and governance patterns

---

1 Complex policy "ends-means" calculus and conflict

- The co-administration and strategic interpretation of many environmental laws by two or more departments/agencies, as is the case with Environment Canada's main parent laws, but also those of several other departments and agencies; multi-level sets of normative visions, goals, principles, and strategies, partly in reports, statutes, and regulations, but also embellished in departmental and agency websites

- Efforts to establish "cap-and-trade" systems that are opposed by key interests (and parts of the government such as finance departments) by labelling them as just another "tax" when in fact they are not

- Sustainable development policies and mandates cast as the triple bottom line where environmental, economic, and social factors must be "considered" but not necessarily acted upon

- Policies with broad sustainability content but anchored mainly by de facto "name-and-shame" accountability information and diverse forms of co-governance and joint enforcement that are hard to evaluate

- The 1990 Green Plan as environmental policy highlight but followed quickly by slippage back to a less ambitious mix and instrument content

- Varied cities-communities federal funding by a mix of regional agencies when small environmental features were added on but not necessarily sustained or evaluated

- Canada's Kyoto GHG emission-reduction policy commitments not matched by any reductions but in fact by significant increases under the Chrétien Liberals and then targets severely weakened by the Harper Conservatives but still not met, and with implementation started so late that they could not possibly be achieved

- Trudeau-era commitment to environmental assessment policy but only on a de facto guideline non-statutory basis until the courts ruled it be law-like and it was later given a statutory basis but with the latter laden with considerable room for ministerial discretion

- Federal-cities infrastructure and stimulus programs with some environmental aspirations but difficult to know and determine if they are real in literally tens of thousands project locations

- Weakening of Fisheries Act and environmental assessment under the Harper-era Responsible Resource Development approach

- International and internal trade agreements signed with provisions allowing environmental policy as legitimate objectives, but then in the same agreements these are constrained by complex rules of proof that they are not "technical barriers to trade"

- Core environmental ideas do not tend to replace each other but rather are layered on top of each other or beside each other in debates and agency mandates across the decades

2 *Complex boundary realities: Hyphenated environmentalism*

- Environment Canada as a department with horizontal cross-governmental realities and aspirations but consistent pushback from other policy departments
- Environment-energy boundaries for particular energy sources and mixes of sources (oil, gas, nuclear, several types of renewables)
- Environment-natural resources boundaries for particular resources and mixes of resources (forestry, mining, agriculture), but also water (rivers, lakes, oceans) as most complex planetary resources of all
- Environment-cities and communities boundaries and dealing with overlapping pollutants and product impacts in diverse locations
- Great Lakes water quality versus water-quantity issues in hundreds of water areas
- Department of Fisheries and Oceans boundary and mandate conflicts on its chief goal of whether to develop the fishery as a viable industry or to maximize employment and save some non-viable communities
- Compilation in 1997 by CESD of forty-two auditor general reports showing the continuous gap in sustainable development policies between commitments and concrete action and also a lack of coordination across departments
- Diverse range and often conflicting values of mandates, such as that of Sustainable Development Technology Canada, which include SD technology, but also enhancing the competitive position of Canadian companies, supporting prosperity and growth, and respecting the values, culture, and human needs of communities
- Fragmented arrangements on boundary content of certification and other agreements, not only for business and resource sectors but also in the sub-domains within and across them

3 *Diverse and conflicting temporal realities*

- Cleanup and remediation time periods and lags regarding negotiated solutions, partial solutions, and which polluters and how much polluters should or will pay or will avoid paying
- Diverse preventive or sustainable development time frames
- Accidents and spills at the national, regional/local, and international scales
- Inability of Environment Canada to develop strategic science strategies to deal with medium- and longer-term research underpinnings for environmental policy
- Adequacy of speed or length of time needed for effective environmental assessment of projects and in whose interests
- Long-term (hundreds/thousands of years) storage of wastes and their monitoring (e.g., nuclear, uranium, carbon capture, and storage)

- Weak performance and follow-up in long-term mapping of Canadian biodiversity
- Nature of infrastructure and natural assets as long-term capital, including how they may be constrained by budgeting and financing cycles and theories of public budgeting
- Environmental issues buffeted by political-business cycles and electoral cycles
- Pre-market product assessment versus post-market life-cycle notions and aspirations that cover vastly extended time frames for complex monitoring
- The diverse performance outcomes and related time frames as seen in NGO, Market, and Business–Environment Regime regarding organic agriculture, chemicals, forestry, mining, and fisheries and their standard-setting and co-governance certification arrangements, agreements, and disputes
- Under-investment over decades in infrastructure renewal in the face of climate change, extreme weather conditions, and rapid urbanization, with green infrastructure only a subset of such investment, if any, and with short-term goals continuing to dominate long-term needs

4 *Diverse nature of, and triggering points for, environmental agendas*

- The episodic nature of prime ministerial support for, or non-interest in, environmental matters and priorities relative to others given bigger imperatives of fiscal policy, deficits, expenditures cuts, inflation, and price controls, etc.
- Early attention at international environmental summits, but also often sluggish medium- and long-term follow-up among diverse sets of nations for any particular potential convention or later protocols
- Political duplicity in Canada's overall climate change policy and GHG-reduction commitments under both Chrétien Liberal and Harper Conservative governments
- Environment as lower or non-existent priority as expressed in Speeches from the Throne, except for 1990 Green Plan by Mulroney government
- High turnover of federal environment ministers (every eighteen months on average since 1971)
- Relatively low ranking or recognition of environmental issues in public opinion surveys across most of the past forty years
- Triggering of agendas within particular regulatory agencies due to new hazards and harms (e.g., chemicals in general or particular new individual chemicals)
- Diverse cities and communities agendas where environmental and sustainable development ideas and policies are present or where environmental impacts (good, average, and harmful) are buried in other triggering ideas, including those on housing, transportation, fiscal revenue-sharing, and job creation
- Certification dynamics and complexity in agendas not only for companies but also for governments and environmental groups as international leverage points are sought out or have to be monitored and followed

5 *Complex multi-scalar and spatial environmental governance and democracy coordination and conflict dynamics*

- Early energy pipeline proposal debates and consultation in Canada's north regarding routes and markets and Aboriginal peoples (Berger Inquiry)

- Current multiple pipeline proposals, routes, and hearings (US and Canadian) for oil sands exports and cross-Canada transport by pipeline and rail

- Multi-scalar and multi-level constitutional governance challenges throughout the Natural Resources–Environment Regime, compounded by tendency of federal government to focus on one resource sector over key periods

- Aboriginal peoples' involvement in environment- and resource-related land claim rights and projects and interpretations and determination of economic and social benefits

- Multi-scalar features inherent in the human settlement discourse and content of Agenda 21

- Meetings and negotiations under the United Nations development of Framework Convention on Climate Change of 1992 to 2014 and their complex coalitions of support and opposition among and between developed and developing countries and also involving small, threatened, coastal island states/regions

- Multiple negotiations of several environmental or partial environmental agreements and protocols at the same time

- Complex multi-level, scalar, and spatial processes for Canada-US environmental cross-border agreements (Great Lakes, biodiversity, migratory birds, acid rain, water exports, forestry, ocean shipping, rail and air transport of dangerous goods)

- Arctic regional governance and democracy regarding melting arctic waters due to climate change via the multi-country Arctic Council but also bilateral and multilateral actions vis-à-vis the United States, Russia, and various conceptions of sovereignty and also of the North versus the South within member states

- Processes for conceptualizing and dealing with city and multi-city spatial and scalar domains involving diverse interacting pollutants and risk-benefit impacts on human settlements

- Regulatory governance and democracy when new technologies with environmental impacts emerge globally, nationally, and regionally, and in diverse sites (e.g., fracking, carbon-capture storage locales, new forms of nuclear reactor technology)

- The identification and handling of environmental disputes and remedies in global, regional, and bilateral trade agreements, including the WTO, NAFTA, and also internal trade agreements within Canada

- Emergence and cross-border origins and links among environmental groups and alliances

Interest in water and sustainability were apparent early in the Harper era. This dissipated quickly, however, as the prime ministerial focus turned unambiguously to exploiting natural resources and promoting pipelines to facilitate the flow of oil from Canada's and Alberta's oil sands and, in turn, secure more diverse global markets instead of just to the US market. Direct prime ministerial power was involved in attacks on environmental groups and on a considerable weakening of Canada's core environmental policy and regulatory governance.

With regard to our second research question – the influence of the multi-scalar nature and complex interaction of regimes upon our ability to assess environmental policy – our next three arguments are especially germane. First, multiple democratic criteria and venues make it more difficult to garner consensus and agreement even before we start discussing environmental policy. It is a more general political-institutional feature that then results in places for both environmental demands and stalemate to occur. Our regime analysis also suggests this especially when one adds evidence from the newer Federal–Cities, Federal–Municipal Infrastructure and N G O, Market, and Business–Environment Regimes. Our argument about the staying power of the staples base of the Canadian economy and Canadian capitalism, if anything, adds to both the multi-scalar realities and to the complexity and time scales of how to assess environmental performance and as seen by different interests and regions in Canada.

Environmental Governance and Multiple Democratic Criteria and Venues

We also argue that Canadian environmental democracy, defined broadly as criteria and venues of participation and consultation with groups, interests, and citizens, has become increasingly fragmented and diffuse. This may seem contradictory when seen against the above argument about strong prime ministerial executive dominance. But in other ways it is not. A primary driver of this change is the greater importance of Internet- centred and enabled networked relations and a proliferation of ways of understanding democratic practice in Canada, which includes the growing effort to also accept and promote the legitimacy of the five criteria and venues of Canadian democracy we introduced and reviewed in the regime analysis: Cabinet-parliamentary representative democracy; federalist democracy; interest group pluralist democracy; civil society democracy; and direct democracy, including social networks. It also involves conflicts and cooperation among such criteria and venues.

Cabinet-parliamentary representative democracy, as distinct from prime ministerial executive power, has certainly had its environmental moments and effects (adverse and beneficial), first in the structure of majority versus minority governments. These have produced the current Harper government with its political base in oil sands– and resource-rich Alberta, but also in Western Canada more generally. But the Trudeau era produced a government and Cabinet with very weak representation from Western Canada and hence a lesser interest in natural resources but a strong central-Canada, Ontario-Quebec power base. Parliamentary government has also been seen in the development of some environmental issues based on the work of particular parliamentary committees but also parliamentary watchdogs such as the auditor general and the commissioner of environment and sustainable development.

Federalist democracy and stalemate has been particularly apparent too in the overall story of Canadian environmental policy, partly through the concepts of multilateral and bilateral federalism, and more recent Harper-era practices of open federalism. It has clearly influenced energy, forestry, and mining aspects of the story; its influence is ostensible for inland waters, and the offshore fisheries and oceans as well. The democratic criteria and venues of interest group pluralism, civil society democracy, and direct democracy, including social media, have all been present, though often in very dispersed ways and often in competition with each other for basic democratic claim-making and legitimacy-staking. This was seen in the early battles over the nature and scope of environmental assessment laws and processes, and in the changing shape and contours of the National Energy Board and its sense of its core clientele interests. In both cases, business, environmental, consumer, and health interest groups had instances of strong and weak influence. Civil society forms of democracy had some ascendency in international environmental protocols and agreements to which Canada was a signatory. All such venues and criteria of democracy sought to advance environmental agendas, partly through the advocacy and use of changed discourse in concert with similar interests in other countries.

Continuing Natural Resource Staples
Imperatives and Power

The analysis has also shown how the pan-Canadian scope, importance, and power of Canada's natural resources continues to significantly influence, drive, and often weaken overall environmental
policy, particularly on the needed steps to develop green industries
and alternative green energy sources. Our literature review showed
initially the importance of the staples theory as a central historical
feature of the Canadian political economy and capitalism. Other
analysis in the regime chapters has shown the strong staying power
of varied natural resources and their political interests spread across
Canada's vast territory and regions and within national, provincial,
and territorial governments. The Macdonald Commission in the
1980s, the royal commission that advocated free trade with the
United States, had argued that Canada needed to wean itself off this
resource-driven economic habit and work towards a global and new
technology-driven innovation-oriented economy. Some of this took
hold when, as we have seen, NRCan was formed and then sought to
describe itself as a new innovation department rather than an entity
guiding and promoting the old economy.

But, if anything, the staples economy has reasserted itself in ways
that have made it politically difficult in Canada to foster alternative
energy sources and green industries. We have seen that some efforts
have been made to foster these, including efforts to promote biofuels
and some kinds of plant-based biotechnology. Invariably, however,
these have become bound up in resource-sector imperatives, regionally and otherwise, in ways that have produced technologies and
products skewed to deliver dubious total environmental or viable
innovation economy benefits.

This does not mean that staple resources carry no environmental
values. As we have seen with the political economic story of the
development of Canadian national parks, there are important conservation and preservation ethics that Canadians support and foster.
But overall, the resource sectors often provide a path of least resistance to some form of better economic future. The positive connections may be especially the case with forests, rivers, and ecosystems
that Canadians can see nearby or in classic and still present one-
industry resource towns. But it may not be as strong when it comes

to the more distant Canadian "norths" that few see or have visited, including the north of a fast-melting high Arctic.

The Rescaling of Environmental Governance

Fourth, we argue overall that Canada's environmental policy cannot be understood without examining an ongoing rescaling of environmental democracy, politics, and policy. Decisions have been down-scaled to the city and local government and community level with implications for what priorities are set, how decisions are made, how well or inadequately they are funded or regulated, and what outcomes ensue. Decisions have also been up-scaled to the supra-national level, to intergovernmental and non-governmental processes and actors. On the latter, for instance, Canada's position in the global economy as a major exporter of staples products such as fish, food, oil, minerals, and forest products, exposes Canada to new and old forms of international pressures. Most importantly, decisions being made through international supply chains by individual companies, collections of companies, and multi-stakeholder private regulatory initiatives are becoming critical venues shaping and sometimes surpassing the importance of Canada's public policy processes.

To understand the trajectories of environmental policy in Canada, we argue that a careful understanding of this rescaling and subsequent funding and regulatory shifts must be seen in relation to the ongoing transformation of Canada's federal environmental system. This rescaling is also prominent in the areas of green energy policies at the provincial level, regarding natural resources in particular, and in key urban sectors such as construction, waste and infrastructure, and public transit.

The Harper Era and the Muzzling of Public Environmental Science and Evidence

Last but certainly not least we argue that environmental science has always had to compete for access and attention with other forms of evidence, knowledge, and practice within Canada and internationally. However, we argue that there has been a significant worsening in the role of science and evidence in environmental policy and agendas in the current Harper era. We do not include in this view the use of related knowledge regarding economics and cost-benefit analysis or risk-benefit concepts and advocacy. But it does include the ascendancy of communications strategies and related central control and also the presence of permanent campaigning and attack politics and the explicit muzzling of federal scientists.

This muzzling and harassing has been evident in Canada's recent climate change and climate science criticism by federal environment and resource ministers in relation to proposed oil sands–centred pipelines. But the constant attack-politics mode of behaviour also weakens debate when they prevent open discussion from occurring and seem to enshrine debate centred on fabricated evidence, as some science groups have argued in public demonstrations about the death of evidence. While there is little doubt historically that the Harper government has been the worst practitioner of these dark arts of political warfare, other eras have also revealed other kinds of disdain for science, including environmental science, such as when the Liberal government slashed science budgets and staff under its program review. And of course, governments and political parties have also ignored some of the science and science advice they have received publically and privately under the norms of Cabinet secrecy.

We have posed the question of whether environmental and related science and evidence is declining as a factor and determinant in the conduct of environmental policy and in the development of environmental agendas. Our resounding answer for the Harper era is yes, in the sense of core attack politics. But our regime and interregime analysis has also pointed out that notions of, and the need for, diverse kinds of combined science, evidence, and knowledge have been present from the very beginning of the environmental age. They are not a recent phenomenon. This includes the social and economic sciences and knowledge transmitted and exchanged through related science activities (RSA) as practised by front-line officials in related environmental and health fields but also in the front-line review of projects being subject to environmental assessment requirements in diverse and different projects and project ecosystem locations.

Thus, in any number of ways Canada's environmental story, both its successes and its weaknesses, needs to be understood in a deeper historical context and in a series of political-economic and ecological settings and with the full array of environmental regimes fully appreciated and fully in view. This is what our green-lite approach and its focus on complexity has sought to do, and hopefully new forms of debate, coordination, and action will ensue as a result.

Glossary of Major Terms

AGENDA 21 The United Nations blueprint for global transformation that sought to put nations on the path towards sustainable development, focusing on explicit courses of action needed to cut emissions, limit environmental degradation, and transform societies in pursuit of more sustainable development. Agenda 21 also called on all countries to identify the environmental implications of urban development and to address them in an "integrated fashion." Agenda 21 recognized the significant role played by local authorities in making sustainable development happen. National plans, strategies, and processes relied on the willingness and the capacity of local governments to implement them. Each local authority should enter into a dialogue with its citizens, local organizations, and private enterprises and adopt a local Agenda 21 (United Nations 1992, 28.1–28.3. All cities were asked to "develop and strengthen programmes aimed at ... guiding their development along a sustainable path" (7.20).

BERGER INQUIRY Inquiry headed by Justice Thomas Berger. It reported in 1977 after holding major hearings and conducting extensive research on two pipeline proposals to bring massive US natural gas supplies found in Prudhoe Bay, Alaska, to American markets via an overland route through Canada, including one route through the Mackenzie Delta. Berger recommended a ten-year delay and opposed the Delta route, on both economic and environmental grounds, but also in relation to meeting the needs of Aboriginal peoples in the north.

BIODIVERSITY A contraction of *biological diversity*, where diversity refers to the range of variation or differences among a set of entities. Biological diversity is the variety in the living world and hence a descriptor of the number, variety, and variability of living organisms. It has become common practice to define biodiversity in terms of genes, species, and ecosystems.

BIOFUELS Liquid renewable fuels such as ethanol (an alcohol fermented from plant materials) and bio-diesel (a fuel made from vegetable oils or animal fats) that can substitute for petroleum-based fuels.

BRUNDTLAND COMMISSION Headed by Gro Harlem Brundtland (who later became the Norwegian prime minister), the World Commission on Environment and Development reported in 1987. It advocated sustainable development and put it on the global agenda after its visits and meetings in countries around the world. Canada's formal response to the commission's final report, *Our Common Future,* was positive and led to several federal policy and institutional changes in support of sustainable development.

CABINET DIRECTIVE ON REGULATORY MANAGEMENT (CDRM) is the overall federal policy directive on regulation making and the evaluation of regulatory programs. Announced in 2012 by the Harper Conservative government, the policy built on earlier overall policy documents, including the Cabinet Directive on Streamlining Regulation, adopted in 2006. It includes requirements for departments to submit regulatory plans and priorities and contains provisions for a more explicit life-cycle approach to regulation. The CDRM also complements statutes such as the Statutory Instruments Act.

CANDU REACTOR The unique Canadian deuterium uranium pressurized heavy water reactor developed in the late 1950s and 1960s by Atomic Energy of Canada Ltd, Ontario Hydro (now Ontario Power Generation), and Canadian General Electric.

CAP-AND-TRADE REGULATION An incentive-based approach to environmental and related kinds of regulation whereby a cap on a given type of emission is set by the government, but then good and efficient complying firms are allowed to trade/sell their assigned emission permits to firms that are not.

CARBON CAPTURE AND STORAGE An energy technology that aims to capture emissions of carbon dioxide (CO_2) from industrial facilities before they are released into the atmosphere. The CO_2 is then compressed, and transported by pipeline or tanker truck to a storage site and injected between one and five kilometres underground in deep geological formations, where it will be safely stored for the long term. Many of the formations chosen as potential sites have already had fluids (such as oil) or gases (such as natural gas) trapped within them for tens of millions of years.

CARBON SINK Anything that absorbs more carbon that it releases. Forests, soils, oceans, and the atmosphere all store carbon, and this carbon moves among them in a continuous cycle. This constant movement of carbon means, for example, that forests act as sources or sinks at different times. Climate change negotiations have included proposals for countries with significant carbon sinks to gain credit for them against their carbon emission record.

COMMAND AND CONTROL REGULATION A regulatory approach that involves detailed procedures and controls that are largely input-focused rather than output- or outcome-focused. It was and is criticized by those who advocate more flexible and incentive-based approaches to economic regulation in recognition of the different situations that regulated entities face where a one-size-fits-all approach simply does not work.

CONSERVATION Values and processes that seek to preserve nature in all its forms for current citizens and future generations. Conservation measures relate to land, forests, and water, but also to endangered species and areas of outstanding natural beauty. It is a value relating to sustainable development held long before the concept and discourse of sustainable development was articulated.

CONSTITUTIONAL AND QUASI-CONSTITUTIONAL PROVISIONS Systems that govern the substance and processes of environmental policy and regulation. Constitutional provisions govern the federal-provincial constitutional division of powers and the provisions of the Canadian Charter of Rights and Freedoms. Quasi-constitutional provisions are rules governing rule-making in free trade agreements such as NAFTA and also the federal-provincial agreements such as the Agreement on Internal Trade. The Canadian Human Rights Act is relevant as well.

CO-REGULATION A process whereby the state and businesses, interest groups, and NGOs make rules jointly and also assist in a coordinated system of monitoring and enforcement. Relates to ideas and practices of partnerships and networked governance arrangements. It is a key part of the concept of regulatory capitalism.

DEREGULATION Major steps being taken to eliminate rules so as to allow more competition. Deregulation is linked especially to a major era of deregulation in the late 1970s and in the 1980s in what were previously monopoly or oligopolistic utility industries such as telecommunications, energy, airlines, and railways. The purpose was to allow new entrants into the industry to compete on the basis of price and quality. Deregulation has been revived as a topic of debate in more recent years on the effects

of previous efforts and the moves toward new forms of deregulation in
areas such as environmental assessment.

ECO-POLITICS A way of viewing and analyzing environmental ecosystems, policy, politics, and governance at a planetary level, with the focus
on the survival of the planet and its vital natural capital functions for
humankind as a whole, and for biodiversity and all life forms.

END-OF-PIPE CLEANUP AND REMEDIATION Basic ideas and forms
of pollution control where harmful emissions and effluents have already
occurred but now need to be cleaned up and remediated to the maximum
extent possible. It is strongly linked as well to the "polluter-pays"
principle.

ENVIRONMENTAL DEMOCRACY All criteria and arenas of democracy
in the Canadian political system that deal with or affect environmental
policy and governance. These include elected representative Cabinet-
parliamentary democracy, federalist democracy, interest group pluralist
democracy, civil society democracy, and direct democracy, including burgeoning Internet-based social networks.

ENVIRONMENTAL FEDERALISM The diverse ways in which environmental policy, democracy, and governance are affected by, and in turn
shape, constitutional jurisdiction on environmental policy and the use of
policy instruments. The environmental area is a shared jurisdictional
realm overall and thus yields conflict, cooperation, and complexity in
Canada and in Canada's relations with other countries that are also
federal.

ENVIRONMENTAL GOVERNANCE A subset of the broader concept of
overall governance where governance can be expressed simply as an
effort to recognize more explicitly that governance was more than government, more than the state, and more than public policy pronounced
and implemented by the state and its bureaucracies. As such, environmental governance implies that the state plays an environmental role
characterized at times more by steering than rowing, by co-regulation
and joint funding, and by more explicit efforts to improve service delivery, but in addition it still implies the continued need for a strong state
and state-led capacities in environmental matters.

ENVIRONMENTAL POLICY Government statements, laws, and rules
intended to reduce and prevent pollution and related adverse impacts
on nature and natural capital. Such policy encompasses a widening set
of normative concerns and values. Environmental policy is made by
multiple levels of government, by private corporations and business

interest groups, and by environmental non-governmental organizations. Environmental policy can be direct as defined above, or it can consist of de facto indirect policies that emerge from other policy fields and policy-makers, such as those on energy, trade, innovation, fisheries and oceans, and agriculture.

ENVIRONMENTAL REGIMES Integrated systems of environmental ideas, organizations, interests, policies, and policy instruments. Environmental regimes include environmental policies that are both direct and indirect in their environmental impacts. Direct ones have environmental goals that are primary and explicit. Indirect policies are those from other departmental and policy fields where environmental impacts (good and bad) are secondary or tertiary and produce both intended and unintended outcomes, such as via policies on innovation and regulatory red-tape reduction. This book examines six such environmental regimes.

ENVIRONMENTAL RIGHTS AND JUSTICE Advocacy and analysis, as well as processes that seek to make environmental matters an issue of individual, human, and collective rights and that are justiciable in the courts, and in national and international law.

EVIDENCE-BASED REGULATION A broadening of the concept of science-based regulation by including more diverse kinds of knowledge and expertise, including the social sciences, the theory and practice of cost-benefit analysis, law, and the medical and health professions, but also certain kinds of front-line knowledge possessed by people such as bird-watchers functioning as citizen scientists. Increasingly, the concept and its advocates expressed increasing deep concerns about regulation based on little or no evidence, and knowledge where individuals and interests argued that their values and ideologies were reasons enough for taking regulatory action or denying the need for regulation.

EXTERNALITIES The costs or benefits resulting from a program (regulatory, spending, or tax) or project that accrue to third parties, which may or may not be addressed explicitly by public authorities.

FEDERAL SPENDING POWER The power of Parliament to make payments to people or institutions or governments for purposes on which Parliament does not necessarily have power to legislate. Under the authority of the spending power of Parliament, several federal-provincial programs have been funded by the federal government. Essentially, the spending power of the federal government has been used to institute conditional grant programs that are in effect spending with rules of eligibility.

G-20 The organization, meetings, and stated joint policies of the twenty leading economies of the world, through their first ministers, finance and trade ministers, and officials. It came into being because of the growth of Asian and other economies, and assumed a much greater and more visible role during the global recession, banking, and sovereign debt crisis since 2008. It is increasingly seen by many as a de facto or eventual replacement for the G-7 or G-8 in global governance.

GDP Gross domestic product shows the value of production of goods and services in the economy, of Canadians or of non-residents. It does not include returns from Canadian investment abroad.

GNP Gross national product includes the value of goods and services produced by Canadians, earned inside or outside Canada.

GOVERNANCE A conceptual construct to recognize more explicitly that governance is more than government, more than the state, and more than public policy pronounced and implemented by the state and its bureaucracies. It also implies the state playing a role characterized at times more by steering than rowing, and also employing softer instruments of governing rather than harder command-and-control regulatory ones. At its core, governance is a set of interacting policies, decisions, policy instruments, processes, laws, and values involving joint action by the state and its agencies, business interests, non-governmental organizations, and civil society interests and entities.

GREEN INDUSTRIES Industries focused on developing alternative energy and production processes that are environmentally progressive and effective in moving towards a low carbon economy and society. Such industries are often centred on firms created to profit and take advantage of environmental regulation by offering expertise and innovations that can be sold but also further developed by their client firms. Defined more broadly, green industries can be any firm that innovates to reduce emissions and create environmentally related production and distribution efficiencies.

HYDRAULIC FRACTURING A process, commonly known as "fracking," in which water, mixed with sand, is injected at high pressure into a wellbore to create fractures, which form conduits along which fluids such as gas, petroleum, and groundwater may migrate to the well. It has been associated particularly with the massive discovery in the United States of shale gas reserves and production.

INFRASTRUCTURE The physical assets and structures needed to support the economy and society. It includes capital assets such as roads, bridges, railways, airports, shipping ports, lands, schools, hospitals, water supply, electricity grids, sewers, and telecommunications. Privately owned infra-structure is treated in budgetary terms as a capital asset that is depreci-ated so that funds are being set aside for modernizing and renewal. Government-owned infrastructure is not treated this way, and hence public infrastructure can deteriorate without reinvestment being pro-vided for.

LAISSEZ-FAIRE An economic doctrine that asserts that the best way to achieve strong economic growth and a high standard of living is to strictly limit all government intervention in the economy to maintaining the value of the currency and to protecting private property. This includes regulatory intervention of some kinds. The doctrine is derived from the writings of Adam Smith.

LEGITIMATE OBJECTIVES A term in both international and internal trade agreements on policy rights such as those regarding health, safety, and environment which states can legitimately pursue in terms of national sovereignty and in the public interest. This, of course, is precisely how environmentalists believe such policies should be carried out. The quali-fier in trade agreements is that when legitimate objectives are pursued, they must be carried out in the least trade-distorting manner possible by adhering to rules and processes regarding technical barriers to trade. These processes in turn centre on differences of view on the role of sci-ence, evidence, and knowledge in decision-making, as well as concepts such as the precautionary principle.

LEVERED MONEY Spending where those seeking public funds receive such funding only if they bring other money (public or private) as well to the total funding of a given project or program. It involves funding with many kinds of rules about eligibility, co-funding, reporting, and account-ability requirements within and among participating and networked partners.

LIFE-CYCLE REGULATION An approach to regulation that advocates the need to regulate and monitor the complete cycle of behaviour in temporal and spatial terms. Such full cycles can include the later formal evaluation of regulatory programs; regulating the full life of a given physical asset such as a mine or energy facility from cradle to grave; and engaging in pre-market assessments of products prior to approval for use and then exten-sive post-market assessment of actual product use once on the market.

MANAGEMENT-BASED REGULATION An approach to regulation that more explicitly recognizes that regulation is increasingly a matter of de facto co-governance with private firms and related interests and orga-nizations. Thus it deploys regulatory authority in fields such as food and related supply-chain regulation in a way that utilizes the private sector's knowledge about its particular circumstances and engages with firms in developing their own internal procedures and monitoring practices to regulate and respond to risks.

MANAGEMENT OF HUMAN SETTLEMENTS A concept introduced in the UN's Agenda 21 program, which called for "promoting sustainable human settlement Development" (United Nations 1992, 7). The human settlement objective called for improvement "to the social, economic and environmental quality of human settlements and the living and working environments of all people, in particular the urban and rural poor" (7.4). The specific areas to be addressed in promoting sustainable human settlement development included a number of infrastructure-related issues: the provision of adequate shelter; sustainable land-use planning and management; integrated provision of environmental infrastructure (water, sanitation, drainage, and solid-waste management); sustainable energy and transport systems; sustainable construction industry activities; and human resource development and capacity-building for human settlement development.

MARGINAL BENEFIT The extra satisfaction or benefit that results from the production of an extra unit of a particular good or service.

MARGINAL COST The extra cost incurred in producing an additional unit of output. The concept is central to the determination of the optimal prices and quantities of goods and services.

MARKET-DRIVEN COMPETITIVE CERTIFICATION Processes of rule-making and standard-setting that are driven by market players, including firms and environmental NGOs, and that yields certification standards and joint monitoring and enforcement that are more non-governmental.

MULTI-LEVEL REGULATION refers to rule-making and compliance coordination and monitoring involving international, regional, national, sub-national (provinces, cities and local government) authorities. Such regulation can be cooperative and also conflictual in nature.

NATURAL CAPITAL The sum of all of the resources and free services provided by nature that is not normally accounted for in traditional economic GDP- or GNP-centred ways.

NEW DEAL FOR CITIES AND COMMUNITIES The establishment of Infrastructure Canada led to coordinated federal efforts to build a New Deal for Cities and Communities. The department was also established to make strategic investments in sustainable infrastructure projects through partnerships that met local community needs. It also led in 2004 to Martin-era federal commitments to GST rebates for municipalities, along with acceleration in infrastructure funding and the exploration of gas tax sharing arrangements proposed for innovative policies for urban social economy and Aboriginal peoples in cities.

OPEN FEDERALISM The Harper Conservative government's approach to federalism announced as it took office in 2006. As a concept, it meant (1) taking advantage of the experience and expertise that the provinces and territories can contribute to the national dialogue; (2) respecting areas of provincial jurisdiction: (3) keeping the federal government's spending power within bounds; and (4) full cooperation by the Government of Canada with all other levels of government, while clarifying the roles and responsibilities of each.

PERFORMANCE-BASED REGULATION A form of rule-making and compliance where the focus is on achieving and reporting on agreed stated performance outcomes / results without heavy prior prescriptive requirements on how they are achieved. This approach to regulation obviously contains many of the implicit features of flexibility and incentive-based regulation but is even more outcome-focused. It depends on complex accountability and transparency requirements for periodic reporting about performance claims and outcomes.

POLITICAL ECONOMY OF ENVIRONMENTAL REGULATION Literature that offers broad interpretations of stages in environmental regulatory development, with a focus on the macro relations of power between the state and capitalism and between the state and society.

POST-MARKET REGULATION More recent approaches to regulation that focus beyond the one-time pre-market notions of regulation to the longer and broader post-market uses of products and processes in diverse individual, sectoral, social, and spatial settings and networks. It involves a much larger set of actual and potential players, citizens, patients, and knowledge experts in the post-market monitoring process.

PRECAUTIONARY PRINCIPLE An environmental decision-making idea that allows policy-makers, regulators, and scientists to take provisional risk-management measures when an assessment points to the likelihood of harmful environmental and health effects and there is a lack of scientific certainty.

PRE-MARKET REGULATION Processes for the safety and risk assessment of products and production processes before they are allowed to be sold on the market. In areas such as drug regulation in the wake of the thalidomide crisis in the 1960s, pre-market safety regulation became the dominant model of safety regulation in many product realms.

PRIME MINISTERIAL ERAS The main federal prime ministerial and governing political party and partisan eras from the Trudeau Liberals from 1968 to the early 1980s, the Mulroney Conservatives in the 1984 to 1992 period, the Chrétien and then Martin Liberals in the 1993 to 2005 period, and the Harper Conservatives from 2006 to the present.

PUBLIC GOOD A good or service that is available to all, once produced; excluding some individuals from consuming the good is either impossible or exceptionally expensive. Markets cannot provide public goods; therefore they are usually financed by governments.

R&D Research and development comprises scientific, engineering, and design activities that result in new or improved products and production processes. Such spending is considered a significant indicator of a country's capacity for innovation and economic growth.

RED FLAGS A term and discourse where new health, safety, and environmental hazards, risks, and harms are flagged or brought to public attention and imply the need or potential need for more regulation or new kinds of regulation.

RED TAPE The term and discourse used to discuss excessive regulation, either in parent rules or in the procedures and paperwork involved. Red tape initially referred simply to the colour of the tape used to bind files and folders of statutes. This could simply mean that all rules are red tape. But in a contemporary sense, red-tape reduction involves identifying excessive red tape typically linked by business interests to concepts of unreasonable or undue compliance costs.

RED-TAPE ANALYSIS How red tape is thought about and examined empirically and who is doing the analysis and in whose interests. All red-tape analysis is caught up in the fact that many laws and rules produce good rules or aspects of good rule-making; nevertheless the focus, in practical terms, is on *excessive* red tape or undue compliance costs, which is built into the very definition of actual red tape. In short, on almost a daily regulation-making basis, there can be and is more red tape for some, less red tape for others.

REGULATION Rules of behaviour backed up by the sanctions of the state. Such rules include mainly delegated law or the "regs" but in a larger sense it refers also to rule-making in the parent statute. The Statutory Instruments Act defines regulation as a "statutory instrument made in the exercise of a legislative power conferred by or under an Act of Parliament, or for the contravention of which a penalty, fine or imprisonment is prescribed by or under an Act of Parliament."

REGULATION THEORY Emerged in France and was reflected and modified in other European countries, depending in part on particular systems of capitalism in different countries. Regulation in this theoretical tradition did not refer to the particular policy instrument notion of regulation (where regulation is just one instrument of governing) but rather something that, in today's terminology, is much more akin to broad governance structures. It concentrates on systemic features of power in systems of capitalism and at different stages of capitalism such as the Fordist and post-Fordist eras.

RE-REGULATION New rules and regulatory agencies established in the era of 1980s deregulation to meet new or changed public interest needs related to sectors such as telecommunications, transportation, and energy, but also trade law, which had been deregulated in significant ways. In countries such as the United Kingdom, re-regulation was also deemed essential because of the privatization of state-owned industries that were a part of liberalized market strategies.

REGULATORY AGENDA Processes whereby departments and agencies are required to indicate their regulatory priorities for a given period. Such agendas may be simply in the form of lists rather than explicit rankings whereby some proposed new regulations will proceed and others will not. Such agendas have not yet emerged or been required at a cross-government level.

REGULATORY CAPITALISM A characterization and era of regulation that seeks to differentiate it from the 1970s and 1980s era of neo-liberalism. It seeks to capture the fact that regulation is growing markedly but is less a feature of state rule and enforcement and much more a system of co-regulation and compliance between the state and business interests and firms but also other non-state interests and networks. It is thus a crucial feature needed to understand both regulation and modern capitalism.

REGULATORY CAPTURE A theory and set of frequently expressed views that regulatory agencies tend to be captured by the interests they are regulating. Such capture dynamics are said to occur gradually or that they are built in from the outset through political-industrial collusion.

REGULATORY GOVERNANCE A subset of the broader concept of overall governance (see glossary definition above) that emerged in the literature on politics, policy, and public administration over the past thirty years. Thus regulatory governance, including environmental regulation, refers to the deployment of softer instruments of governing such as guidelines and codes of behaviour, rather than just harder command-and-control direct regulatory ones, in part out of recognition of the need to regulate and serve difference kinds of entities being regulated, but also other clients who are the beneficiaries of regulation. But regulatory governance theory has always recognized to some significant extent that state-centred regulatory bodies almost always do more than regulate. They are typically multi-functional. In addition to regulation per se, they are planning entities, they exhort, persuade, and provide information, they adjudicate, negotiate, network, conduct research, and utilize different kinds of science, evidence, and knowledge, and the rules they deploy mandate large amounts of mainly private spending by businesses and citizens.

REGULATORY HARMONIZATION The process whereby nation-states or sub-national governments in federations agree to adopt rules that are virtually identical.

REGULATORY IMPACT ASSESSMENT SYSTEM The formal analytical process and methodology required under regulatory policy to identify regulatory impacts and to ensure, where appropriate, that new regulations proceed only where regulatory risk-management benefits exceed regulatory costs.

REGULATORY POLICY The overall policy of a government on its approach and processes for rule-making, especially for delegated law (the "regs").

REGULATORY STATE A particular way of theorizing and characterizing the state by identifying particular states or jurisdictions that had weaker or less-developed welfare states. Both the European Union and the United States have been cast in this way. In practice, of course all modern states are regulatory states in significant ways.

RELATED SCIENCE ACTIVITIES Actions that complement and extend R&D by contributing to the generation, dissemination, and application of scientific and technological knowledge. RSA is often crucially embodied in the education, training, and experience of scientific and technical personnel working on the front lines of regulatory monitoring activity and of regulatory product approvals in key federal regulatory departments and agencies.

RESOURCE RENTS The surplus value that is generated from the sale of the resource (such as oil and gas) beyond the normal profit needs of the industry and the wages paid to workers in the industry.

RESCALING A body of literature that argues that globalization is causing a rescaling of collective action problems such that they are no longer very well matched in the scale of the nation-state. As Cerny (1995, 597) explains, "The more that the scale of goods and assets produced, exchanged, and/or used in a particular economic sector or activity diverges from the structural scale of the national state – both from above (the global scale) and from below (the local scale) – and the more that those divergences feed back into each other in complex ways, then the more that the authority, legitimacy, policy making capacity, and policy implementation effectiveness of states will be challenged from both without and within."

RESPONSIBLE RESOURCE DEVELOPMENT The Harper-era name for its pro–natural resource development and export policy and approach, with the word "responsible" indicating some environmental concerns but under greatly weakened environmental policy and regulation. The term was also in common use in Alberta and among Western Canada–centred energy interest groups.

RISK-BENEFIT REGULATION Views and discourse that sought to draw more applied attention to the belief that most areas of safety regulation are rarely only about safety in some absolute sense but increasingly about complex kinds of risk-benefit regarding rule making, pre-market product and process approvals, and post-market monitoring.

SCIENCE-BASED DECISION-MAKING AND REGULATION The term applied to the need for decisions and regulation to be underpinned by independent science-based causal knowledge, especially science in the natural sciences and engineering. Related discourse also emerged in trade agreements where rules and product approvals had to be based on so-called sound science. Later and other regulatory mandates have extended these notions by referring to evidence-based regulation and knowledge-based regulation where knowledge expertise can include social sciences, including interdisciplinary science.

SELF-REGULATION Processes by which the state allowed key professions such as law and medicine to regulate themselves. Thus in exchange for their delegated control of entry to the profession and basic qualifications, these two dominant professions had to maintain core professional legal and medical values anchored as well on lawyer-client and doctor-patient privilege and confidentiality. Few if any later professions have matched the power structure won by doctors and lawyers historically, but many subsequent knowledge groups and occupations have sought and partially achieved similar but more limited powers. The notion of self-regulation has also been used as a descriptor where other particular kinds of partial self-regulation by business and NGOs emerge in concert with regulation by the state.

SHOVEL-READY PROJECTS The term frequently used by governments to describe projects that can be quickly mobilized and funded to generate construction-related jobs and growth and also produce needed infrastructure and community facilities.

SOCIAL LICENCE The term or public discourse used more recently to describe policy and regulatory values similar to earlier notions of the public interest and earned public support for environmental and related consumer values.

STAPLES THEORY Theory that argues that the export of natural resources, or staples (fish, fur, timber, grain, oil, etc.) from Canada to more advanced economies has a pervasive impact on the economy, as well as on the social and political systems. Developed initially in the 1920s by Harold Innis, the theory has continued resonance, including when policy analysts refer to Canada's current economic falling into a so-called staples trap.

STATUTORY PROGRAMS Types of spending approved under separate statutes or agreements and broadly speaking are more difficult (though not impossible) to change in a quick, annual, discretionary way. These are often said to be a characteristic of major social domain programs but they exist in other policy domains as well.

STEWARDSHIP AND RESPECT FOR LIFE A frequently expressed environmental idea that seeks to ensure actions and results that produce a duty of care and the practice of conservation over time of natural resources, ecosystems, and related biodiversity.

STIMULUS Short-term programs of increased spending and/or reduced taxation established by governments to respond to recessions caused by insufficient demand in the economy. Such policies are attributed to the theories of Keynes.

SUSTAINABLE DEVELOPMENT Policies anchored in preventive and intergenerational ideas about environmental harms and benefits. The former idea, articulated especially by the Brundtland Commission in the late 1980s, is an idea and paradigm whose intent is to ensure in any number of areas of governance that the environment and its ecosystems are left in at least as good a state for the next generation as they were for the current generation. Cast somewhat more loosely, such policies are often seen by governments as those that take into consideration the economic, social, and environmental effects of policies, the "triple bottom line."

TAX EXPENDITURES Revenue that the government gives up through special provisions in its corporate, personal income, and retail tax laws to provide an incentive for a particular action or to provide relief for a particular sector of society. Sometimes these are referred to as tax breaks.

Such expenditures can have direct and indirect, and adverse and favourable environmental effects and impacts.

URBAN DEVELOPMENT AGREEMENT A number of specific tri-lateral agreements in the early 1980s that brought together federal, provincial, and municipal levels of government to address complex and spatially concentrated social and economic problems. For example, urban development agreements, pioneered in Winnipeg and later Vancouver, brought together the problem-solving resources of different levels of government, the community, and business sectors in an integrated strategy for community-driven revitalization. The best-known examples during this period include the Winnipeg Core Area Initiative and the Winnipeg Development Agreement. As the era of cooperative federalism was replaced with contested federalism, other federal-municipal machinery began to take on a more regional dimension.

References

Abele, Frances. 2011. "Use It or Lose It? The Conservatives' Northern Strategy." In *How Ottawa Spends 2011–2012: Trimming Fat or Slicing Pork?*, edited by Christopher Stoney and Bruce Doern, 218–42. Montreal and Kingston: McGill-Queen's University Press.

Abele, Frances, and Michael J. Prince. 2006. "Four Pathways to Aboriginal Self-Government in Canada." *American Review of Canadian Studies* 36 (4): 568–95.

Accreditation Services International. 2014. Grand Council of the Crees (Eeyou Istchee)/Cree Regional Authority. Complaint against Rainforest Alliance's Decision to Close Major Nonconformance #25/12. At RA-FM/COC-005956. Bonn: Accreditation Services International.

Adkin, Laurie. 2010. *Environmental Conflict and Democracy in Canada*. Vancouver: UBC Press.

Agranoff, Robert. 2007. *Managing within Networks: Adding Value to Public Organizations*. Washington, DC: Georgetown University Press.

"Agreement Reached on International Forest Management Consultations." 1995. *Business Wire*, 1 July.

Air Quality Committee. 2012. *Canada–United States Air Quality Agreement Progress Report 2012*. Ottawa: International Joint Committee.

Alberta Energy. 2013. "Regulatory Enhancement Project." Alberta Energy. http://www.energy.alberta.ca/Initiatives/RegulatoryEnhancement.asp.

Alexander, J. 2009. *Pandora's Locks: The Opening of the Great Lakes–St Lawrence Seaway*. Ann Arbor: Michigan State University Press.

Alm, Leslie R. 2000. *Crossing Borders, Crossing Boundaries: The Role of Scientists in the US Acid Rain Debate*. Westport, CT: Praeger.

Andonova, L.B., and R.B. Mitchell. 2010. "The Rescaling of Global Environmental Politics." *Annual Review of Environment and Resources* 35:255–82.

Andresen, S., and T. Skodvin. 2008. "Non-State Influence in the International Whaling Commission, 1970 to 2006." In NGO Diplomacy: The Influence of Nongovernmental Organizations in International Environmental Negotiations, edited by Michele Merril Betsill and Elisabeth Corell, 119–47. Cambridge, MA: MIT Press.

Arctic Council. 2013. "About the Arctic Council." http://www.arctic-council.org/index.php/en/about.

"The Arctic: Tequila Sunset." 2013. Economist, 9 February.

Armstrong, C., and H.V. Nelles. 1986. Monopoly's Moment: The Organization and Regulation of Canadian Utilities, 1830–1930. Philadelphia: Temple University Press.

Aronczyk, Melissa, and Graeme Auld. 2013. "Tar, Ethics and Other Tactical Repertoires: The Co-Evolution of Movements for and against the Tar Sands." Paper presented at the International Studies Association meeting, San Francisco, 3–6 April.

Asch, M., and P. Macklem. 1991. "Aboriginal Rights and Canadian Sovereignty: An Essay on R. v. Sparrow." Alberta Law Review 29:482–98.

Aschauer, D.A. 1988. "Government Spending and the Falling Rate of Profit." Economic Perspectives 12:11–17.

– 1990. Public Investment and Private Sector Growth. Washington, DC: Economic Policy Institute.

Atomic Energy of Canada. 2008. AECL 2008 Annual Financial Report. Ottawa: AECL.

Aucoin, Peter. 1997. The New Public Management: Canada in Comparative Perspective. Montreal and Kingston: McGill-Queen's University Press.

– 2008. "New Public Management and New Public Governance: Finding the Balance." In Professionalism and Public Service: Essays in Honour of Kenneth Kernaghan, edited by David Siegel and Ken Rasmussen, 16–33. Toronto: University of Toronto Press.

Aucoin, Peter, Mark D. Jarvis, and Lori Turnbull. 2011. Democratizing the Constitution: Reforming Responsible Government. Toronto: Edmond Montgomery.

Auditor General of Canada. 1993. Chapter 16: Department of Forestry. In Report of the Auditor General of Canada. Ottawa: Office of the Auditor General of Canada.

– 1996. "Canada Heritage, Parks Canada: Preserving Canada's Natural Heritage." In 1996 Report of the Auditor General. Ottawa: Office of the Auditor General of Canada.

– 1997a. "Chapter 14: Fisheries and Oceans Canada – Sustainable Fisheries Framework: Atlantic Groundfish." In *Report of the Auditor General of Canada: October 1997*. Ottawa: Office of the Auditor General of Canada.

– 1997b. "Chapter 28: Fisheries and Oceans Canada – Pacific Salmon Sustainability of the Resource Base." In *Report of the Auditor General of Canada – December 1997*. Ottawa: Office of the Auditor General of Canada.

– 1998. "Chapter 25: Investment in Highways." In *Report, Transport Canada – December 1998*. Ottawa: Office of the Auditor General of Canada.

– 1999. "Chapter 20: Fisheries and Oceans – Pacific Salmon: Sustainability of the Fisheries." In *Report of the Auditor General of Canada – November 1999*. Ottawa: Office of the Auditor General of Canada.

– 2005. *Report of the Commissioner of the Environment and Sustainable Development to the House of Commons*. Prepared by T. Williams, Science and Technology Division.

– 2010. *Fall Report of the Auditor General of Canada*. Ottawa: Office of the Auditor General of Canada.

Auld, Douglas. 1985. *Budget Reform: Should There Be a Capital Budget for the Public Sector?* Toronto: C.D. Howe Institute.

Auld, G. 2006. "Choosing How to Be Green: An Examination of Domtar Inc.'s Approach to Forest Certification." *Journal of Strategic Management Education* 3:37–92.

– 2009. "Reversal of Fortune: How Early Choices Can Alter the Logic of Market-Based Authority." PhD diss., Yale University.

– 2014. *Constructing Private Governance: The Rise and Evolution of Forest, Coffee, and Fisheries Certification*. New Haven, CT: Yale University Press.

Auld, G., S. Bernstein, and B. Cashore. 2008. "The New Corporate Social Responsibility." *Annual Review of Environment and Resources* 33:413–35.

Auld, G., and B. Cashore. 2013. "Mixed Signals: NGO Campaigns and NSMD Governace in an Export-Oriented Country." *Canadian Public Policy/Analyse de politiques* 39 (S2):143–56.

Auld, G., I. Kurzydlo, and L. Steiner. 2013. "Oceans Apart: Why Marine Protection Lags Terrestrial Protection: The Case of Canada." Paper presented at the International Studies Association meeting, San Francisco, 3–7 April.

Axworthy, Lloyd. 1971. "The Housing Task Force: A Case Study." In *The Structures of Policy-Making in Canada*, edited by G. Bruce Doern and Peter Aucoin, 130–53. Toronto: Macmillan of Canada.

Bakenova, Saule. 2004. *Making a Policy Problem of Water Export in Canada: 1960–2002*. PhD diss., Carleton University.

Baker, Peter, and Coral Davenport. 2014. "Using Executive Powers, Obama Begins His Last Big Push on Climate Policy." *New York Times*, 31 May.

Barrett, Scott. 2002. *Environment and Statecraft: The Strategy of Environmental Treaty-Making*. Oxford. Oxford University Press.

Bartley, T. 2007. "How Foundations Shape Social Movements: The Construction of an Organizational Field and the Rise of Forest Certification." *Social Problems* 54 (3): 229–55.

Baumgartner, F.R., and B.D. Jones. 1993. *Agendas and Instability in American Politics*. Chicago: University of Chicago Press.

Bell, S., and Andrew Hindmoor. 2009. *Rethinking Governance: The Centrality of the State in Modern Society*. Cambridge: Cambridge University Press.

Bendell, J. 2000. *Terms of Endearment: Business, NGOs and Sustainable Development*. Sheffield, UK: Greenleaf Publishing.

Benkler, Yochai. 2006. *The Wealth of Networks*. New Haven, CT: Yale University Press.

Bennear, Lori S. 2007. "Are Management-Based Regulations Effective?" *Journal of Policy Analysis and Management* 26:327–48.

Bennett, Mia. 2013. "Pro-Development Arctic Council, Led by Canada, Begins to Take Shape." *Arctic News Wire*, 14 March.

Bennett, Scott. 2012. "Federal Infrastructure Program Impacts: Perceptions at the Community Level." In *How Ottawa Spends 2012–2013: The Harper Majority, Budget Cuts and the New Opposition*, edited by G. Bruce Doern and Christopher Stoney, 190–206. Montreal and Kingston: McGill-Queen's University Press.

Benzie, Robert. 2014. "Premiers Tout Their Own National Energy Strategy." *Toronto Star*, 29 August.

Berkman, Paul A. 2009. *Monitoring Surface Ship Movement in the Ice-Diminishing Arctic Ocean*. Project report paper presented at Cambridge University Judge Business School.

– 2010. *Environmental Security in the Arctic Ocean: Promoting Co-operation and Preventing Conflict*. Whitehall Paper Series, vol. 77. London: Royal United Services Institute for Defense and Security Services.

– 2013. "Preventing an Arctic Cold War." *New York Times*, 12 March.

Bernstein, Marver. 1955. *Regulating Business by Independent Commission*. Princeton, NJ: Princeton University Press.

Bernstein, S. 2000. "Ideas, Social Structure, and the Compromise of Liberal Environmentalism." *European Journal of International Relations* 6 (4): 464–512.

– 2002. *The Compromise of Liberal Environmentalism*. New York: Columbia University Press.

Bernstein, S., and Ben Cashore. 2000. "Globalization, Four Paths of Internationalization and Domestic Policy Change: The Case of Ecoforestry in British Columbia, Canada." *Canadian Journal of Political Science* 33 (1): 67–99.

– 2002. "Globalization, Internationalization, and Liberal Environmentalism: Exploring Non-Domestic Sources of Influence in Canadian Environmental Policy." In *Canadian Environmental Policy: Context and Cases*. 2nd ed., edited by Debora L. VanNijnatten and Robert Boardman, 212–32. Oxford: Oxford University Press.

Best, M. 1960. "Resources for Tomorrow." *Globe and Mail*, 3 March.

Best Aquaculture Practices. 2013. "Search BAP Plants, Feed-Mills, Farms, and Hatcheries." http://www.bestaquaculturepractices.org/index.php?option=com_content&task=view&id=126&Itemid=109.

Bickerton, James, and Alain-G. Gagnon. 2009. *Canadian Politics*. 5th ed. Toronto: University of Toronto Press.

Bickis, Liga, Margaret. 2008. "Improving Strategy for the Canadian Wildlife Service: A Comparative Study with the Parks Canada Agency and the Department of Fisheries and Oceans." PhD diss., University of Waterloo.

Biermann, Frank, and Steffan Bauer, eds. 2005. *A World Environmental Organization: Solutions or Threat for Effective International Environmental Governance?* Farnham, UK: Ashgate.

Biermann, Frank, and Bernd Siebenhuner, eds. 2009. *Managers of Global Change: The Influence of International Environmental Bureaucracies*. Cambridge, MA: MIT Press.

Birnie, Patricia, Alan Boyle, and Catherine Redgwell. 2009. *International Law and the Environment*. Oxford: Oxford University Press.

Bishop, Grant. 2013. "After Lac-Mégantic, How Should We Regulate Risk?" *Globe and Mail*, 16 July.

Blackwell, E., and V. Stewart. 2012. "CIDA and the Mining Sector: Extractive Industries as an Overseas Development Strategy." In *Struggling for Effectiveness: CIDA and Canadian Foreign Aid*, edited by S. Brown, 217–45. Montreal and Kingston: McGill-Queen's University Press.

Blasiger, Jorg, and Stacy D. VanDeveer, 2012. "Navigating Regional Environmental Governance." *Global Environmental Politics* 12 (3): 1–17.

Blaze Carlson, Kathryn. 2014. "Land Claims Court Ruling Reshapes Resource Sector Nationwide." *Globe and Mail*, 26 June.

Boardman, Robert, ed. 1992. *Canadian Environmental Policy: Ecosystems, Politics and Process*. Toronto. Oxford University Press.

– 2002. "Milk and Potatoes Environmentalism: Canada and the Turbulent World of International Law." In *Canadian Environmental Policy: Context and Cases*, edited by Debora L. VanNijnatten and Robert Boardman, 190–211. Toronto: Oxford University Press.

Borins, Sandford, and David Brown. 2008. "E-consultation: Technology at the Interface between Civil Society and Government." In *Professionalism and Public Service: Essays in Honour of Kenneth Kernaghan*, edited by David Siegel and Ken Rasmussen, 178–206. Toronto: University of Toronto Press.

Bothwell, R. 1988. *Nucleus: The History of Atomic Energy of Canada Ltd*. Toronto: University of Toronto Press.

Botts, Lee, and Paul Muldoon. 2005. *Evolution of the Great Lakes Water Quality Agreement*. Ann Arbor: Michigan State University Press.

Boutros, Serena, L. Hayward, Anique Montambault, Laura Smallword, and Glen Toner. 2010. "Growing the Children of Brundtland: The Creation and Evolution of NRTEE, IISD, CESD, and SDTC." In *Policy: From Ideas to Implementation*, edited by Glen Toner, Leslie A. Pal, and Michael J. Prince, 257–286. Montreal and Kingston: McGill-Queen's University Press.

Boyd, David R. 2011. *Unnatural Law: Rethinking Canadian Environmental Law and Policy*. Vancouver: UBC Press.

– 2012. *The Environmental Rights Revolution*. Vancouver: UBC Press.

Bradford, Neil. 2004a. "Global Flows and Local Places: The Cities Agenda." In *How Ottawa Spends 2004–2005: Mandate Change in the Martin Era*, edited by G. Bruce Doern, 70–88. Montreal and Kingston: McGill-Queen's University Press.

– 2004b. "Place Matters and Multi-level Governance: Perspectives on a New Urban Policy Paradigm." Canadian Policy Research Networks, 7 February.

Braithwaite, John. 2005. "Neoliberalism or Regulatory Capitalism." Occasional Paper 5. Australian National University, Regulatory Institutions Network.

– 2008. *Regulatory Capitalism*. London: Edward Elgar.

Braithwaite, John, and Peter Drahos. 2000. *Global Business Regulation.* Cambridge: Cambridge University Press.

Bratt, Duane. 2008. *Prairie Atoms: The Opportunities and Challenges of Nuclear Power in Alberta and Saskatchewan.* Calgary: Canada West Foundation.

– 2012. *Canada, the Provinces and the Global Nuclear Revival.* Montreal and Kingston: McGill-Queen's University Press.

Bregha, Francois. 2006. "The Federal Sustainable Development Strategy Process: Why Incrementalism Is Not Enough." In *Innovation, Science, Environment: Canadian Policies and Performance 2006–2007*, edited by Bruce Doern, 82–104. Montreal and Kingston: McGill-Queen's University Press.

– 2011. "How to Get Serious about the Strategic Environmental Assessment of Policies and Plans." In *How Ottawa Spends 2011–2012: Trimming Fat or Slicing Pork?*, edited by Christopher Stoney and Bruce Doern, 144–62. Montreal and Kingston: McGill-Queen's University Press.

Brenner, Neil. 2009. "Restructuring, Rescaling and the Urban Question." *Critical Planning* (Summer): 69–79.

"Brian Mulroney, Greenest PM." 2006. *Corporate Knights* 12:7–9.

Bridge, Gavin, and Philippe Le Billon. 2013. *Oil.* London: Polity.

Brooks, Michael. 2013. "Frack to the Future." *New Scientist,* 10 August.

Brousseau, Eric, T. Dedeurwaerdere, Pierre-Andre Jouvet, and Marc Willinger, eds. 2012. *Global Environmental Commons: Analytical and Political Challenges in Building Governance Mechanisms.* Oxford:Oxford University Press.

Brownsey, Keith. 2007. "Energy Shift: Canadian Energy Policy under the Harper Conservatives." In *How Ottawa Spends 2007–2008: The Harper Conservatives – Climate of Change*, edited by G. Bruce Doern. 143–60. Montreal and Kingston: McGill-Queen's University Press.

– 2013. "Energy Strategy under the Harper Government: Provinces and Industry Led." In *How Ottawa Spends 2013–2014: The Harper Government; Mid-Term Blues and Long-term Plans*, edited by Christopher Stoney and G. Bruce Doern, 127–44. Montreal and Kingston: McGill-Queen's University Press.

Brox, J. 2008. "Infrastructure Investment: The Foundation of Canadian Competitiveness." *IRPP Policy Matters* 9 (2): 1–47.

Brundtland Commission. 1987. *Our Common Future.* Oxford: World Commission on Environment and Development.

Bulkeley, H. 2010. "Cities and the Governing of Climate Change." *Annual Review of Environment and Resources* 35:229–53.

Burnett, J. Alexander. 2011. *A Passion for Wildlife: The History of the Canadian Wildlife Service*. Vancouver: UBC Press.

Burns, Tom. 2012. "Sustainability Revolution: A Social Paradigm Shift." In *The Meta Power Paradigm: Impacts and Transformations of Agents, Institutions and Social Systems – Capitalism, State and Democracy in a Global Context*, edited by Tom R. Burns and Peter M. Hall, 122–38. London: Peter Lang Publishers.

Burns, Tom R., and Peter M. Hall, eds. 2012. *The Meta Power Paradigm: Impacts and Transformations of Agents, Institutions and Social Systems – Capitalism, State and Democracy in a Global Context*, 501–18. London: Peter Lang Publishers.

Burros, M. 1998. "Eating Well: Serving No Swordfish." *New York Times*, 21 January.

Bushnell, S.I. 1980. "The Control of Natural Resources through the Trade and Commerce Power and Proprietary Rights." *Canadian Public Policy* 6 (2): 313–24.

Büthe, Tim. 2011. "Private Regulation in the Global Economy." *Business and Politics* 12 (1): 1–13.

Büthe, T., and H.V. Milner. 2008. "The Politics of Foreign Direct Investment into Developing Countries: Increasing FDI through International Trade Agreements." *American Journal of Political Science* 52:741–62.

Byers, Michael. 2009. *Who Owns the Arctic?* Vancouver: Douglas and McIntyre.

– 2014. "The North Pole Is a Distraction." *Globe and Mail*, 20 August.

Cabarle, B., R.J. Hrubes, C. Elliot, and T. Synnott. 1995. "Certification Accreditation the Need for Credible Claims." *Journal of Forestry* 93 (4): 12–16.

Cairns, R.D. 1992. "Natural Resources and Canadian Federalism: Decentralization, Recurring Conflict, and Resolution." *Publius: The Journal of Federalism* 22 (1): 55–70.

Calamai, Peter. 2007. "The Struggle over Canada's Role in the Post-Kyoto World." In *Innovation, Science, Environment*, edited by G. Bruce Doern, 32–54. Montreal and Kingston: McGill-Queen's University Press.

– 2008. "Chalk River Crisis Sired by AECL." *Toronto Star*, 19 January.

Canada. 1990. *The Green Plan*. Ottawa: Government of Canada.

– 1995a. "Budget Speech 1995." Ottawa: Department of Finance.

– 1995b. *Canadian Biodiversity Strategy: Canada's Response to the Convention on Biological Diversity*. Ottawa: Minister of Supply and Services.

– 1997. Budget Speech 1997. Ottawa: Department of Finance.

– 2000. Budget Speech 2000. Ottawa: Department of Finance.

– 2007. *Cabinet Directive on Streamlining Regulation (CDSR)*. Ottawa: Government of Canada.

Canada-Alberta EcoEnergy Carbon Capture and Storage Task Force. 2008. *Canada's Fossil Energy Future: The Way Forward on Carbon Capture and Storage*. Canada-Alberta ecoEnergy Carbon Capture and Storage Task Force.

Canada Foundation for Innovation. 2005. *"Results through Innovation" Annual Report of the CFI*. Ottawa: Canada Foundation for Innovation.

Canada's Gateways. 2013. "Advantages." http://www.canadasgateways. gc.ca/Advantages.html.

Canada West Foundation. 2010. *Western Leadership for a Canadian Energy Strategy*. Calgary: Canada West Foundation.

– 2013. *Pipe or Perish: Saving an Oil Industry at Risk*. Calgary: Canada West Foundation.

Canadian Academy of Engineering. 2012. *Canada: Winning as Sustainable Energy Superpower*, vols 1 and 2. Ottawa: Canadian Academy of Engineering.

Canadian Chamber of Commerce. 2012. *Electricity in Canada: Smart Investments to Power Future Competitiveness*. Ottawa: Canadian Chamber of Commerce.

Canadian Council of Forest Ministers. 1987. *A National Forest Sector Strategy for Canada*. Ottawa: Ministry of Supply and Service.

Canadian Electricity Association. 2013a. *The Integrated Electric Grid: Maximizing the Benefits in an Evolving Energy Landscape*. Ottawa: Canadian Electricity Association.

Canadian Electricity Association. 2013b. *Policy*. Toronto: Canadian Electricity Association.

Canadian Energy Research Institute. 2012. *Pacific Access: Part 1 – Linking Oil Sands Supply to New and Existing Markets*. Study no. 129. Calgary: Canadian Energy Research Institute.

Canadian Environmental Assessment Agency. 2007. *2006–2007 Report on Plans and Priorities*. Ottawa: Canadian Environmental Assessment Agency.

– 2013. *2013–14 Report on Plans and Priorities*. Ottawa: Canadian Environmental Assessment Agency.

Canadian Opinion Research Archive. 2013. *Trends*. Kingston: Canadian Opinion Research Archive, Queen's University.

Canadian Renewable Fuels Association. 2013. *Federal Renewable Fuels Programs*. Toronto: Canadian Renewable Fuels Association.

Canadian Wildlife Service. 2000. *Canadian Wildlife Service Strategic Plan 2000*. Ottawa: Environment Canada.

Cargnello, Davide, Mark Brunet, Matt Retallack, and Robert Slater. 2014. "The Unique Resource: Water Management in the Harper Era." In *How Ottawa Spends 2014–2015*, edited by G. Bruce Doern and Christopher Stoney, 152–64. Montreal and Kingston: McGill-Queen's University Press.

Carson, Rachel. 1962. *Silent Spring*. Boston: Houghton Mifflin.

Cashore, B., G. Auld, and D. Newsom. 2003. "The United States Race to Certify Sustainable Forestry: Non-State Environmental Governance and the Competition for Policy-Making Authority." *Business and Politics* 5 (3): 219–59.

– 2004. *Governing through Markets: Forest Certification and the Emergence of Non-State Authority*. New Haven, CT: Yale University Press.

Cashore, B., G. Hoberg, M. Howlett, J. Rayner, and J. Wilson. 2001. *In Search of Sustainability: British Columbia Forest Policy in the 1990s*. Vancouver: UBC Press.

Cashore, B., G.C. van Kooten, I. Vertinsky, G. Auld, and J. Affolderbach. 2005. "Private or Self-Regulation? A Comparative Study of Forest Certification Choices in Canada, the United States and Germany." *Forest Policy and Economics* 7 (1): 53–69.

Castree, Noel. 2014. *Making Sense of Nature*. London: Routledge.

Cattaneo, Claudia. 2013. "Why Canada Can and Must Pull Off Nation-Building Energy East Pipeline." *Financial Post*, 1 August.

Cerny, P. 1995. "Globalization and the Changing Logic of Collective Action." *International Organization* 49:595–625.

Chandler, M.A. 1986. "Constitutional Change and Public Policy: The Impact of the Resource Amendment (Section 92A)." *Canadian Journal of Political Science* 19 (1): 103–26.

Chase, Steven. 2009. "Ottawa's Reporting on Stimulus Spending Gets Poor Grade from Watchdog." *Globe and Mail*, 10 October.

– 2013a. "Harper Orders New Draft of Arctic Seabed Claim to Include North Pole." *Globe and Mail*, 4 December.

– 2013b. "Ottawa Seeking New Evidence to Bolster North Pole Seabed Claim." *Globe and Mail*, 6 December.

Chase, S., E. Anderssen, and Bill Curry. 2009. "Stimulus Program Favours Tory Ridings." *Globe and Mail*, 21 October.

Chu, Wayne, and Fred Fletcher. 2014. "Social Media and Agenda Setting." In *Canadian Democracy from the Ground Up: Perceptions and Performance*, edited by Elisabeth Gidengil and Heather Bastedo, 125–47. Vancouver: UBC Press.

Cities in Climate Change Initiative. 2010. The Cities in Climate Change Initiative. UN-HABITAT.org/aboutus/.

Clamen, M. 2013. "The IJC and Transboundary Water Disputes: Past, Present, Future." In *Water without Borders: Canada, the United States and Shared Waters*, edited by E.S. Norman, E.S. Cohen, and K. Bakker, 70–87. Toronto: University of Toronto Press.

Clancy, Peter. 2008. "Chasing Whose Fish? Atlantic Fisheries Conflicts and Institutions." In *Canadian Water Politics: Conflicts and Institutions*, edited by M. Sproule-Jones, C. Johns, and B. T. Heinmille. 261–85. Montreal and Kingston: McGill-Queen's University Press.

– 2011. *Offshore Petroleum Politics: Regulation and Risk in the Scotian Basin*. Vancouver: UBC Press.

– 2014. *Freshwater Politics in Canada*. Toronto: University of Toronto Press.

Clark, Pilita. 2013. "A Rising Power." *Financial Times*, 9 August.

Clarke, Tony, Diana Gibson, Brendan Haley, and Jim Stanford. 2013. *The Bitumen Cliff: Lessons and Challenges of Bitumen Mega-Developments for Canada's Economy in an Age of Climate Change*. Ottawa. Canadian Centre for Policy Alternatives.

Clarkson, Stephen. 2009. "The Governance of Energy in North America: The United States and Its Continental Periphery." In *Governing the Energy Challenge: Canada and Germany in a Multi-Level Regional and Global Context* (Toronto: University of Toronto Press, 2010), edited by Burkhard Eberlein and G. Bruce Doern, 99–121.

"Climate Change: In Praise of Second Best." 2014. *Economist*, 7 June.

Clinton Climate Initiative. 2009. "What We've Accomplished." http://www.clintonfoundation.org/what-we-do/clinton-climate-initiative/.

Coast Forest Conservation Initiative. 2014. *Coast Land Use Planning*. Vancouver: Coast Forest Conservation Initiative.

Coast Forest Conservation Initiative. 2014. *Coast Land Use Planning*. Vancouver: Coast Forest Conservation Initiative.

Coates, Ken S., P.W. Lackenbauer, William Morrison, and Greg Poelzer. 2008. *Arctic Front: Defending Canada in the Far North*. Markham, ON: Thomas Allen Publishers.

Coglianese, Cary. 2008. "The Rhetoric and Reality of Regulatory Reform." *Yale Journal of Regulation* 25:117–30.

– 2010. "Management-Based Regulation: Implications for Public Policy." In *Risk and Regulatory Policy: Improving the Governance of Risk*, ed. OECD, 159–84. Paris: OECD.

– 2012a. *Environment Canada's World Class Regulator Project: An Assessment*. Ottawa: Environment Canada.

– ed. 2012b. *Regulatory Breakdown: The Crisis of Confidence in US Regulation.* Philadelphia: University of Pennsylvania Press.

Cohen Commission. 2012. *The Uncertain Future of the Fraser River Sockeye.* Vol. 3, *Recommendations, Summary, Process.* Vancouver, BC: Commission of Inquiry into the Decline of Sockeye Salmon in the Fraser River.

Cohen, Mark A., and Don Fullerton, eds. 2013. *Distributional Aspects of Energy and Climate Policies.* London: Edward Elgar.

Coleman, Stephen, and Jay G. Blumler. 2009. *The Internet and Democratic Citizenship: Theory, Practice and Policy.* Cambridge: Cambridge University Press.

Coleman, William, and Grace Skogstad. 1990. *Policy Communities and Public Policy in Canada.* Toronto: Copp Clark Pitman.

Commissioner of the Environment and Sustainable Development. 1997. *Report of the Commissioner of the Environment and Sustainable Development.* Ottawa: Office of the Auditor General of Canada.

– 2000. "Chapter 3: Government Support for Energy Investments." In *May Report of the Commissioner of the Environment and Sustainable Development.* Ottawa: Commissioner of the Environment and Sustainable Development.

– 2009. "Chapter 1: Protecting Fish Habitat." In *Report of the Commissioner of the Environment and Sustainable Development to the House of Commons.* Ottawa: Office of the Auditor General of Canada.

– 2012. *Report of the Commissioner of the Environment and Sustainable Development.* Ottawa: Office of the Auditor General.

– 2013a. *Fall Report of the Commissioner of the Environment and Sustainable Development.* Ottawa: Office of the Auditor General.

– 2013b. *Publications.* http://www.ccc.org.

– 2013c. Reports. http://www.ccc.org.

Conference Board of Canada. 2010a. *Conflicting Forces for Canadian Prosperity: Examining the Interplay between Regulation and Innovation.* Ottawa: Conference Board of Canada.

– 2010b. *Intellectual Property in the 21st Century.* Ottawa: Conference Board of Canada.

Connor, Steve. 2013. "The $60 TRN Arctic Methane Time Bomb." *Independent,* 25 July.

– 2014. "UN Climate Deal in Peru Attacked by Activists as Weak and Ineffectual." *Independent,* 15 December.

Convention on Biodiversity. 1992. *Text of Convention.* Geneva: United Nations Environmental Program.

– 2012. *Cities and Biodiversity Outlook*. http://www.cbd.int/authorities/doc/cbo-1/cbd-cbo1-book-f.pdf.

Conway, Thomas. 1992. "The Marginalization of the Department of the Environment: Environmental Policy 1971–1978." PhD diss., Carleton University.

Couch, William, ed. 1988. *Environmental Assessment in Canada*. Ottawa: Canadian Council of Resource and Environment Ministers.

Craik, Neil, Isabel Struder, and Debora VanNijnatten. 2013. *Climate Change Policy in North America: Designing Integration in a Regional System*. Toronto: University of Toronto Press.

Cryderman, Kelly. 2013. "Energy Board's Northern Gateway Terms Could Hurt Other Projects, Kinder Morgan Warns." *Globe and Mail*, 10 June.

Cryderman, Kelly, and Brent Jang. 2013. "Conditions for Pipeline Approval Fail to Satisfy Critics." *Globe and Mail*, 20 December.

Cryderman, Kelly, and Shawn McCarthy. 2013. "Keeping the Faith in Carbon Capture and Storage." *Globe and Mail*, 7 May.

Curry, Bill, and Barrie McKenna. 2014. "Stimulus Gamble: How Ottawa Saved the Economy and Wasted Billions." *Globe and Mail*, 8 February.

Dagg, Anne Innis. 1974. *Canadian Wildlife and Man*. Toronto: McClelland and Stewart.

Dagher, Ruby. 2014. "CIDA, the Mining Sector and the Role of Economic Orthodoxy in Harper Decision Making." In *How Ottawa Spends: 2014–2015*, edited by G. Bruce Doern and Christopher Stoney, 192–204. Montreal and Kingston: McGill-Queen's University Press.

Dale, Anne, and Stuart B. Hill. 2011. "Biodiversity Conservation: A Decision-Making Context." In *Achieving Sustainable Development*, edited by Anne Dale and John B. Robinson, 97–118. Vancouver: UBC Press.

Dashwood, H.S. 2005. "Canadian Mining Companies – And the Shaping of Global Norms of Corporate Social Responsibility." *International Journal* 60 (4): 977–98. doi:10.2307/40204094.

– 2007. "Canadian Mining Companies and Corporate Social Responsibility: Weighing the Impact of Global Norms." *Canadian Journal of Political Science/Revue canadienne de science politique* 40 (1): 129–56. doi:10.1017/S0008423907070047.

Day, J.C., and J. Affum. 1995. "Windy Craggy Institutions and Stakeholders." *Resources Policy* 21 (1): 21–6. http://dx.doi.org/10.1016/0301-4207(95)92248-P.

Dearden, P., M. Bennett, and J. Johnston. 2005. "Trends in Global Protected Area Governance, 1992–2002." *Environmental Management* 36 (1): 89–100.

Dearden, P., and J. Dempsey. 2004. "Protected Areas in Canada: Decade of Change." *Canadian Geographer* 48 (2): 225–39.

deFontaubert, A.C. 1995. "The Politics of Negotiation at the United Nations Conference on Straddling Fish Stocks and Highly Migratory Fish Stocks." *Ocean and Coastal Management* 29 (1–3): 79–91.

de Kerckhove, D.T., C.K. Minns, and B.J. Shuter. 2013. "The Length of Environmental Review in Canada under the Fisheries Act." *Canadian Journal of Fisheries and Aquatic Sciences* 70 (4): 517–21.

Department of Finance. 2007a. *Budget Plan: Budget 2007*. Ottawa: Department of Finance Canada.

– 2007b. *Budget 2007: Aspire to a Stronger, Safer, Better Canada*. Ottawa: Department of Finance.

– 2008. *Budget Plan: Budget 2008*. Ottawa: Department of Finance Canada.

Department of Fisheries and Forestry. 1970. *Annual Report of the Department Fisheries and Forestry for Fiscal Year 1968–69*. Ottawa: Government of Canada.

Department of Justice. 2009. "Organic Products Regulations, 2009." http://laws-lois.justice.gc.ca/PDF/SOR-2009-176.pdf.

– 2013. *A Consolidation of the Constitution Acts 1867 to 1982*. Ottawa: Department of Justice. http://laws-lois.justice.gc.ca/PDF/CONST_E.pdf.

Department of Marine and Fisheries. 1869. *Annual Report of the Department of Marine and Fisheries for the Year 1868*. Ottawa: Government of Canada.

DeSombre, Elizabeth R. 2011. *The Global Environment and World Politics*. 2nd ed. London: Continuum.

De Souza, Mike. 2011. "Harper Should Heed Example of Brian Mulroney, Green Leader Says." *iPolitics*, 31 May.

– 2013. "Harper Government's Green Credentials on Display in Response to Obama Challenge: Analysis." *Post Media News*, 2 February.

Dewees, Donald. 2005. "Electricity Restructuring in Canada," In *Canadian Energy Policy and the Struggle for Sustainable Development*, edited by G. Bruce Doern, 128–50. Toronto: University of Toronto Press.

– 2009. "Electricity Restructuring in the Provinces: Pricing, Politics, Starting Points and Neighbours." In *Governing the Energy Challenge*, edited by Burkard Eberlein and G. Bruce Doern, 71–98. Toronto: University of Toronto Press.

Diduck, Alan, and Bruce Mitchell. 2003. "Learning, Public Involvement and Environmental Assessment: A Canadian Case Study." *Journal of Environmental Assessment Policy and Management* 5 (3): 339–50.

Dion, S. 2005. "Canada Falling Short on Kyoto Agreement." CTV News. http://www.ctv.ca/servlet/ArticleNews/story/CTVNews/20051128/climate_kyoto.

"Dioxin Testing Ordered at Canadian Pulp Mills." 1988. *Globe and Mail*, 26 January.

Djerf-Pierre, Monika. 2013. "Green Metacycles of Attention: Reassessing the Attention Cycles of Environmental News Reporting 1961–2010." *Public Understanding of Science* 22 (4): 495–512.

Dobb, Edwin. 2013. "America's New Oil." *National Geographic* 223 (3): 28–59.

Doern, G. Bruce. 1981. "Energy, Mines and Resources, the Energy Ministry and the National Energy Program." In *How Ottawa Spends Your Tax Dollars: Federal Priorities 1981*, edited by G. Bruce Doern, 56–89. Toronto: Lorimer.

– 1983. "The Mega-Project Episode and the Formulation of Canadian Economic Development Policy." *Canadian Public Administration* 26 (2): 219–38.

– 1993a. "From Sectoral to Macro Green Governance: The Canadian Department of the Environment as an Aspiring Central Agency." *Governance* 6 (2): 172–93.

– 1993b. *Green Diplomacy: How Environmental Policy Decisions Are Made*. Toronto. C.D. Howe Institute.

– 1995. *Institutional Aspects of R&D Tax Incentives: The SR&ED Tax Credit* Ottawa: Industry Canada.

– 1996. "Looking for the Core: Industry Canada and Program Review." In *How Ottawa Spends: 1996–97: Life under the Knife*, edited by Gene Swimmer, 73–98. Ottawa: Carleton University Press.

– 1999. "Moved Out and Moving On: The National Energy Board as a Reinvented Regulatory Agency." In *Changing the Rules: Canada's Changing Regulatory Regimes and Institutions*, edited by G. Bruce Doern, M. Hill, M. Prince, and R. Schultz, 82–98. Toronto: University of Toronto Press.

– 2000a. "The Contested International Regime for Biotechnology." In *The Economic and Social Dynamics of Biotechnology*, edited by John de la Mothe and Jorge Niosi, 143–60. Amseterdam: Kluwer Academic Publishers.

– 2000b. "Patient Science versus Science on Demand: The Stretching of Green Science at Environment Canada." In *Risky Business: Canada's Changing Science-Based Policy and Regulatory Regime*, edited by Bruce Doern and Ted Reed, 286–306. Toronto: University of Toronto Press.

– 2002. "Environment Canada as a Networked Institution." in *Canadian Environmental Policy: Context and Cases*, edited by Debora L. VanNijnatten and Robert Boardman, 107–122. Toronto: Oxford University Press.

– 2004a. "Martin in Power: From Coronation to Contest." In *How Ottawa Spends 2004–2005: Mandate Change in the Paul Martin Era*, edited by G. Bruce Doern, 5–24. Montreal and Kingston: McGill-Queen's University Press.

– ed. 2005. *Canadian Energy Policy and the Struggle for Sustainable Development*. Toronto: University of Toronto Press.

– 2007a. "Decision Processes for New Internal Trade Discussions: Models and Related Impacts on Canadian Federalism and National Unity." Paper prepared for Industry Canada. June.

– 2007b. *Red-Tape, Red-Flags: Regulation for the Innovation Age*. Ottawa: Conference Board of Canada.

– 2009. "Evolving Budgetary Policies and Experiments: 1980 to 2009–2010. In *How Ottawa Spends 2009–2010: Economic Upheaval and Political Dysfunction*, edited by Allan Maslove, 14–45. Montreal and Kingston: McGill-Queen's University Press.

– 2012. "Options on Alberta Energy Regulatory Governance: An Analysis and Commentary at the Pre-Legislative Stage." Paper prepared for Alberta Energy, April.

– 2013. "A New AIT Chapter on Technical Barriers to Trade: Gaps, Issues and Questions for Discussion." Paper prepared for Industry Canada, March.

Doern, G. Bruce, and Tom Conway. 1994. *The Greening of Canada*. Toronto: University of Toronto Press.

Doern, G. Bruce, Arslan Dorman, and Robert Morrison, eds. 2001. *Canadian Nuclear Energy Policy: Changing Ideas, Interests and Institutions*. Toronto: University of Toronto Press.

Doern, G. Bruce, and Monica Gattinger. 2001. "New Economy/Old Economy? Transforming Natural Resources Canada." In *How Ottawa Spends 2001–2002: Power in Transition*, edited by Leslie A. Pal, 223–46. Toronto: Oxford University Press.

– 2003. *Power Switch: Energy Regulatory Governance in the 21st Century*. Toronto: University of Toronto Press.

Doern, G. Bruce, M. Hill, M. Prince, and R. Schultz, eds. 1999. *Changing the Rules: Canada's Changing Regulatory Regimes and Institutions*. Toronto: University of Toronto Press.

Doern, Bruce, and Robert Johnson, eds. 2006. *Rules, Rules, Rules, Rules: Multilevel Regulatory Governance.* Toronto: University of Toronto Press.

Doern, Bruce, and Jeffrey Kinder. 2007. *Strategic Science in the Public Interest: Canada's Government Laboratories and Science-Based Agencies.* Toronto: University of Toronto Press.

Doern, G. Bruce, and Mark MacDonald. 1999. *Free Trade Federalism: Negotiating the Canadian Agreement on Internal Trade.* Toronto: University of Toronto Press.

Doern, G. Bruce, Allan Maslove, and Michael J. Prince. 2013. *Canadian Public Budgeting in the Age of Crises: Shifting Budgetary Domains and Temporal Budgeting.* Montreal and Kingston: McGill-Queen's University Press.

Doern, G. Bruce, and Robert Morrison, eds. 1980. *Canadian Nuclear Policies.* Montreal: Institute for Research on Public Policy.

– 2009. "Canada's Nuclear Crossroads: Steps to a Viable Nuclear Energy Industry." C.D. Howe Institute Commentary, no. 290.

Doern, G. Bruce, and Richard Phidd. 1983. *Canadian Public Policy: Ideas, Structure, Process.* Toronto: Methuen.

– 1992. *Canadian Public Policy: Ideas, Structure, Process.* Toronto: Nelson Canada.

Doern, G. Bruce, and Michael J. Prince. 2012. *Three Bio-Realms: Biotechnology and the Governance of Food, Health and Life in Canada.* Toronto: University of Toronto Press.

Doern, G. Bruce, Michael J. Prince, and Richard Schultz. 2014. *Rules and Unruliness: Canadian Regulatory Democracy, Governance, Capitalism and Welfarism.* Montreal and Kingston: McGill-Queen's University Press.

Doern, G. Bruce, and Ted Reed, eds. 2000. *Risky Business: Canada's Changing Science-Based Policy and Regulatory Regime.* Toronto: University of Toronto Press.

Doern, G. Bruce, and Chris Stoney, eds. 2009. *Research and Innovation Policy: Changing Federal Government–University Relations.* Toronto: University of Toronto Press.

– 2010. "Double Deficit: Fiscal and Democratic Challenges in the Harper Era." In *How Ottawa Spends 2010–2011: Recession, Realignment and the New Deficit Era*, 3–30. Montreal and Kingston: McGill-Queen's University Press.

Doern, G. Bruce, and Brian Tomlin. 1991. *Faith and Fear: The Free Trade Story.* Toronto: Stoddart.

Doern, G. Bruce, and Glen Toner. 1985. *The Politics of Energy*. Toronto: Methuen.

Doucet, Joseph. 2012. *Unplugging the Pipes: Pipeline Reviews and Energy Policy*. Toronto: C.D. Howe Institute.

Dryzek, John. 2013. *The Politics of the Earth: Environmental Discourses*. 3rd ed. Oxford: Oxford University Press.

Dryzek, John, and Patrick Dunleavy. 2009. *Theories of the Democratic State*. London: Palgrave.

Dryzek, John, Richard Norgaard, and David Schlosberg. 2013. *Climate-Challenged Society*. Oxford: Oxford University Press.

Duffy, A. 1990. "4,000 Rally for Peace, Environment." *Toronto Star*, 21 October.

Dunn, Christopher. 2005. "Fed Funding of Cities: That's All There Is." *Policy Options* 26 (8): 58–62.

Durant, Darrin, and Genevieve Fujii Johnson. 2010. *Nuclear Waste Management in Canada: Critical Issues, Critical Perspectives*. Vancouver: UBC Press.

Eberlein, Burkard, and Bruce Doern, eds. 2009. *Governing the Energy Challenge*. Toronto: University of Toronto Press.

Edelman, Murray. 1977. *Political Language: Words That Succeed and Policies That Fail*. New York: Academic.

– 1988. *Constructing the Political Spectacle*. Chicago: University of Chicago Press.

Eisner, M.A. 1993. *Regulatory Politics in Transition*. Baltimore: Johns Hopkins University Press.

Eissler, Rebecca, Annelise Russell, and Bryan D. Jones. 2014. "New Avenues for the Study of Agenda Setting," *Policy Studies Journal* 42:S71–S86.

Elliott, C. 2000. *Forest Certification: A Policy Network Perspective*. Bogor, Indonesia: Centre for International Forestry Research.

Elliott, Lorraine. 2004. *The Global Politics of the Environment*. 2nd ed. London: Palgrave Macmillan.

Emond, D.P. 2008. "'Are We There Yet?' Reflections on the Success of the Environmental Law Movement in Ontario." *Osgoode Hall Law Journal* 46:219–31.

Emmerson, Charles. 2011. *Future History of the Arctic*. London: Vintage Books.

Energy, Mines and Resources Canada. 1973. *An Energy Policy for Canada: Phase 1*. Ottawa: Information Canada.

– 1976. *An Energy Strategy for Canada*. Ottawa: Minister of Supply and Services.

English, John. 2013. *Ice and Water: Politics, Peoples and the Arctic Council*. Toronto: Penguin Canada.

Enros, Phillip. 2013. *Environment for Science: A History of Policy for Science in Environment Canada*. Ottawa: Phillip Enros.

Environmental Assessment Board. 1994. *Reasons for Decision Class Environmental Assessment by the Ministry of Natural Resources for Timber Management on Crown Lands in Ontario*. Toronto: Ontario Environmental Assessment Board.

Environment Canada. 1991. *Canada's National Report: United Nations Conference on Environment and Development, Brazil, June 1992*. Ottawa: Supply and Services Canada.

– 1998. *Environment Canada Estimates*. Ottawa: Environment Canada.

– 2007. *Environment Canada's Science Plan*. Ottawa: Environment Canada.

– 2009. *Canada's 4th National Report to the United Nations Convention on Biological Diversity*. Ottawa: Environment Canada.

– 2012a. *Becoming a World Class Regulator: Final Report of the World Class Regulator Working Group*. Ottawa: Environment Canada.

– 2012b. *Evaluation of Biodiversity Policy and Priorities*. Ottawa: Environment Canada.

– 2012c. *Environment Canada's Response to Environment Canada's World Class Regulator Project: An Assessment*. Ottawa: Environment Canada.

– 2013a. *About Environment Canada*. Ottawa: Environment Canada.

– 2013b. *Canada's Emissions Trends*. Ottawa: Environment Canada.

– 2013c. *Chairs Conclusions from the Arctic Environmental Ministers Meeting*. http://www.ec.gc.ca/international.

Epps, Tracey. 2008. *International Trade and Health Protection: A Critical Assessment of the WTO's SPS Agreement*. London: Edward Elgar.

Etzioni, A. 2012. "Legislation in the Public Interest: Regulatory Capture and Campaign Reform." In Society for the Study of Social Problems, *Agenda for Social Justice: Solutions 2012*, 11–19. New York: Society for the Study of Social Problems.

External Advisory Committee on Smart Regulation. 2004. *Smart Regulation: A Regulatory Strategy for Canada*. Ottawa: External Advisory Committee on Smart Regulation.

"Falling Off a Logo." 1997. *Printing World*, 27 January.

Faulkner, Robert. 2008. *Business Power and Conflict in International Environmental Politics*. London: Palgrave Macmillan.

– 2009a. "Move Infrastructure Funds Fast to Fight Recession, Say FCM Big City Mayors." CNW Telbec, 15 January. http://www.newswire.ca/fr/story/394775/move-infrastructure-funds-fast-to-fight-recession-say-fcm-big-city-mayors.

– 2009b. "Statement by FCM President on Today's Infrastructure Announcement by Minister Baird." News release, 26 January.

Feehan, James P. 2012. *Newfoundland's Electricity Options: Making the Right Choice Requires an Efficient Pricing Regime*. Toronto: C.D. Howe Institute.

Fellows, E.S. 1986. "Forestry's Future Frustrated or a Condensed History of Canadian Foresters' Concern for Forest Renewal." *Forestry Chronicle* 62 (1): 35–50.

Finance Canada. 2010. *Tax Expenditures and Evaluations 2010*. Ottawa: Department of Finance.

Fine, Sean. 2014. "Supreme Court Expands Land-Title Rights in Unanimous Ruling." *Globe and Mail*, 26 June.

Finlayson, C.A. 1994. *Fishing for Truth: A Sociological Analysis of Northern Cod Stock Assessments from 1977 to 1990*. Vol. 52. St John's, NL: Institute of Social and Economic Research, Memorial University of Newfoundland.

Fischer, Frank. 2003. *Reframing Public Policy: Discursive Politics and Deliberative Practices*. Oxford: Oxford University Press.

Fisheries and Oceans Canada. 1998. *A New Direction for Canada's Pacific Salmon Fisheries*. Ottawa: Fisheries and Oceans Canada.

Fitzgerald, E.A. 1991. "Newfoundland Offshore Reference: Federal-Provincial Conflict over Offshore Energy Resources." *Case Western. Reserve Journal of International Law* 23 (1): 133–44.

Fitzpatrick, P., A. Fonseca, and M.L. McAllister. 2011. "From the Whitehorse Mining Initiative towards Sustainable Mining: Lessons Learned." *Journal of Cleaner Production* 19 (4): 376–84. doi:10.1016/j.jclepro.2010.10.013.

Fleury, A.-M., and B. Davies. 2012. "Sustainable Supply Chains: Minerals and Sustainable Development, Going beyond the Mine." *Resources Policy* 37 (2): 175–8. doi:http://dx.doi.org/10.1016/j.resourpol.2012.01.003.

Flinders, Matthew. 2008. *Delegated Governance and the British State: Walking without Order*. Oxford: Oxford University Press.

Floridi, Luciano. 2014. *The 4th Revolution: How the InfoSphere Is Reshaping Human Reality.* Oxford: Oxford University Press.

Foreign Affairs, Trade and Development Canada. 2013. "Foreign Investment Promotion and Protection (FIPAs)." http://www.international. gc.ca/trade-agreements-accords-commerciaux/agr-acc/fipa-apie/index. aspx?lang=eng.

Forest, Patrick. 2010. "Inter-Local Water Agreements: Law, Geography and NAFTA." *Les Cahiers de droit* 51 (3–4): 749–70.

Forest Alliance of British Columbia. 1992. *About the Alliance: Principles.* Victoria, BC: Forest Alliance of British Columbia.

Forest Products Association of Canada. 2011. *Forest Certification in Canada: The Programs, Similarities and Achievements.* Ottawa: Forest Products Association of Canada.

Forest Stewardship Council. 1996. *FSC Principles and Criteria.* Oaxaca: Forest Stewardship Council.

– 1999. "FSC National Initiatives: Contact Details." Oaxaca: Forest Stewardship Council. Accessed 21 August 2007. http://web.archive.org/ web/19990302094042/www.fscoax.org/html/noframes/5-1-2.html.

"Forestry Companies Meet Compliance Deadline for Code of Forest Practices." 2000. Canada Newswire, 22 February.

Forge, F. 2001. *Organic Farming in Canada: An Overview.* Ottawa: Parliamentary Research Branch.

Fowler, P., and S. Heap. 2000. "Bridging Troubled Waters: The Marine Stewardship Council." In *Terms of Endearment: Business, NGOs, and Sustainable Development,* edited by Jem Bendell, 135–48. Sheffield, UK: Greenleaf Publishing.

Fowlie, Jonathan, Scott Simpson, and Jeff Lee. 2013. "B.C. Formally Rejects Northern Gateway Pipeline as Proposed." *Vancouver Sun,* 1 June.

Fraser, Matthew. 1999. *Free-for-all: The Struggle for Dominance on the Digital Frontier.* Toronto: Stoddart.

Friend of the Sea. 2012. "Canada: Mixed Salmon Fishery." http://www. friendofthesea.org/fisheries.asp?ID=32.

Froschauer, K. 1999. *White Gold: Hydroelectric Power in Canada.* Vancouver: UBC Press.

Galaz, Victor. 2014. *Global Environmental Governance, Technology and Politics: The Anthropocene Gap.* Toronto: Edward Elgar.

Gale, R.J.P. 1997. "Canada's Green Plan." In *Nationale Umweltplane in ausgewahlten Industrielandern* [A study of the development of a National Environmental Plan with expert submissions to the Enquete

Commission "Protection of People and the Environment" for the Bundestag]. Berlin: Springer-Verlag.

Gallon, Gary. 1996. "Report Card on Canada for Rio +5." Montreal: Canadian Institute for Business and the Environment.

Galloway, Gloria. 2013. "Nuclear Power Plants to Be on the Hook for $1 Billion in Event of Meltdown." *Globe and Mail*, 10 June.

– 2014. "Ottawa Needs to Lead a Balanced Energy Debate, Canadians Tell Pollster." *Globe and Mail*, 31 December.

Galloway, Gloria, and Nathan Vanderklippe. 2010. "Canada Ties New Emissions Cuts Targets to US Goals." *Globe and Mail*, 1 February.

Garcia, S.M. 1992. "Ocean Fisheries Management: The FAO Programme." In *Ocean Management in Global Change*, edited by P. Fabbri. 381–418. London: Elsevier.

Gatehouse, Jonathan. 2013. "When Science Goes Silent." *Maclean's*, 3 May.

Gattinger, Monica. 2012. "Canada–United States Energy Relations: Making a MESS of Energy Policy." *American Review of Canadian Studies* 42 (4): 460–73.

– 2013. "A National Energy Strategy for Canada: Golden Age or Golden Cage of Energy Federalism?" Draft. School of Political Studies, University of Ottawa.

Gaudreault, Valerie, and Patrick Lemire. 2003. *The Age of Public Infrastructure in Canada*. Ottawa: Statistics Canada.

Geyer, Robert, and Samie Rihani. 2010. *Complexity and Public Policy*. London: Routledge.

Gibbens, R. 1991. "Ottawa Backs Off on Pulp Polluters." *Financial Post (Toronto)*, 4 February.

Gibbon, A. 2000. "Talks Seek Truce in B.C. Forestry Battle." *Globe and Mail*, 20 March.

Gibson, R.B. 1990. "Out of Control and beyond Understanding: Acid Rain as a Political Dilemma." In *Managing Leviathan: Environmental Politics and the Administrative State*, edited by Robert Paehlke and Douglas Torgerson, 243–82. Peterborough, ON: Broadview.

– 2012. "In Full Retreat: The Canadian Government's New Environmental Assessment Law Undoes Decades of Progress." *Impact Assessment and Project Appraisal* 30 (3): 179–88.

Giddens, Anthony. 2011. *The Politics of Climate Change*. 2nd ed. London: Polity.

Gidengil, Elisabeth, and Heather Bastedo, eds. 2014. *Canadian Democracy from the Ground Up: Perceptions and Performance*. Vancouver: UBC Press.

Gillis, Justin. 2014a. "Bipartisan Report Tallies High Toll on Economy from Global Warning." *New York Times*, 24 June. http://www.nytimes.com/2014/06/24/science/report-tallies-toll-on-economy.

– 2014b. "U.N. Panel Issues Its Starkest Warning Yet on Global Warming." *New York Times*, 2 November.

Gladstone, J., Sheena Kennedy Dalseg, and Frances Abele. 2013. "Promises to Keep: Federal Spending on Communications and Transportation Infrastructure in the Territorial North." In *How Ottawa Spends 2013–2014: The Harper Government-Mid-term Blues and Long-Term Plans* dited by Christopher Stoney and G. Bruce Doern. 145–58. Montreal and Kingston: McGill-Queen's University Press.

Global Ocean Commission. 2014. *From Decline to Recovery: A Rescue Package for the Global Ocean.* Washington: Global Ocean Commission.

Glode, Mark L., and Beverly N. Glode. 1993. "Transboundary Pollution: Acid Rain and United States–Canadian Relations." *Boston College Environmental Affairs Law Review* 20 (1): 22–36.

Goar, Carol. 2013. "Hard Time to Be an Environmentalist." *Toronto Star*, 7 November. http://www.thestar.com/opinion/commentary/2013/11/07/hard_time.

Gollner Andrew B., and Daniel Salee, eds. 1989. *Canada under Mulroney.* Montreal: Véhicule.

Gordon, T., and J.R. Webber. 2008. "Imperialism and Resistance: Canadian Mining Companies in Latin America." *Third World Quarterly* 29:63–87.

Gottlieb, R. 1993. *Forcing the Spring: The Transformation of the American Environmental Movement.* Washington, DC: Island.

Gough, J. 2007. *Managing Canada's Fisheries: From Early Days to the Year 2000.* Ottawa: Fisheries and Oceans Canada.

Government of Canada. 2009. Building Canada website accessed July 2009–January 2014.

Government of Canada. 2013. "Oceans Act (SC, 1996, c. 31)." http://laws-lois.justice.gc.ca/eng/acts/O-2.4/FullText.html.

– 2015. "Fisheries Act (RSC, 1985, c F-14)." http://laws-lois.justice.gc.ca/eng/acts/f-14/page-10.html#docCont.

Grabosky, Peter. 2012. "Beyond Responsive Regulation: The Expanding Role of Non-State Actors in the Regulatory Process." *Regulation and Governance* 10 (1): 44–56.

Graham, Katherine, and Caroline Andrew, eds. 2014. *Canada in Cities: The Politics and Policy of Federal-Local Governance.* Montreal and Kingston: McGill-Queen's University Press.

Grant, J.A., and I.A.N. Taylor. 2004. "Global Governance and Conflict Diamonds: The Kimberley Process and the Quest for Clean Gems." *Round Table* 93 (375): 385–401. doi:10.1080/0035853042000249979.

Graveland, Bill. 2013. "Public Trust Has Been Eroded: Pipeline Firms Talk Safety at NEB Forum." *Globe and Mail*, 5 June.

Gray, W. 1962. "Resources for Tomorrow." *Globe and Mail*, 15 January.

Greenpeace. 2005. *A Recipe for Disaster: Supermarket's Insatiable Appetite for Seafood*. London: Greenpeace, UK.

– 2006. *A Recipe for Change: Supermarkets Respond to the Challenge of Sourcing Sustainable Seafood*. London: Greenpeace, UK.

Grubb, Michael, Christiaan Vrolijk, and Duncan Brack. 1999. *The Kyoto Protocol: A Guide and Assessment*. London: Royal Institute of International Affairs.

Gunningham, N. 1995. "Environment, Self Regulation, and the Chemical Industry: Assessing Responsible Care." *Law and Policy* 17 (1): 57–109.

Gunningham, N.K., A. Robert, and Dorothy Thornton. 2003. *Shades of Green: Business, Regulation and Environment*, edited by Stanford Law and Press. Stanford: Stanford University Press.

Guthman, J. 2004. *Agrarian Dreams: The Paradox of Organic Farming in California*. California Studies in Critical Human Geography 11. Berkeley: University of California Press.

Hajer, Maarten. 1995. *The Politics of Environmental Discourse: Ecological Modernization and the Policy Process*. Oxford: Oxford University Press.

Haldane, Andrew G. 2013. "Why Institutions Matter (More Than Ever)." Speech to the Centre for Research on Socio-Cultural Change, Annual Conference, School of Oriental and African Studies, London.

Hale, Geoffrey. 2010. "Canada-US Relations in the Obama Era: Warming or Greening?" In *How Ottawa Spends 2010–2011: Recession, Realignment and the New Deficit Era*, edited by Bruce Doern and Christopher Stoney, 48–67. Montreal and Kingston: McGill-Queen's University Press.

Hall, Peter, and M. Soskice. 2001. *The Institutional Foundations of Comparative Advantage*. Oxford: Oxford University Press.

Hamilton, G. 2003. "Eco-Warrior Wins Battles: Tzeporah Berman Changed the Way We Log on B.C.'s Coasts, Now Sets Her Sites on the Boreal Forest." *Vancouver Sun*, 2 December.

Hancher, Leigh, and Michael Moran. 1986. *Capitalism, Culture and Regulation*. London: Clarendon.

Hanebury, J.B. 1990. "Environmental Impact Assessment in the Canadian Federal System." *McGill Law Journal* 36:962.

Harchaoui, T.M., F. Tarkhani, and P. Warren. 2004. "Public Infrastructure in Canada, 1961–2002." *Canadian Public Policy* 30 (3): 303–18.

Harcourt, M., S. Rossiter, and K.Cameron. 2007. *City Making in Paradise: 9 Decisions That Saved Vancouver.* Vancouver: Douglas and McIntyre.

Harrabin, Roger. 2012. "UN Climate Talks Extend Kyoto Protocol, Promise Compensation." *BBC News,* Science and Environment, 8 December.

– 2015. "Fossil Fuels: The Untouchable Reserves." *BBC News,* 7 January.

Harris, R.A., and S.M. Milkis. 1989. *The Politics of Regulatory Change.* New York: Oxford University Press.

Harrison, Kathryn. 1996. *Passing the Buck: Federalism and Canadian Environmental Policy.* Vancouver: UBC Press.

– 2002. "Ideas and Environmental Standard-Setting: A Comparative Study of Regulation of the Pulp and Paper Industry." *Governance: An International Journal of Policy, Administration, and Institutions* 15 (1): 65–96.

– 2010. "The Struggle of Ideas and Self-Interest in Canadian Climate Policy." In *The Comparative Politics of Climate Change,* edited by Kathryn Harrison and Lisa McIntosh Sundstrom, 169–203. Cambridge, MA: MIT Press.

Harrison, Kathryn, and Lisa McIntosh Sundstrom, eds. 2010. *The Comparative Politics of Climate Change.* Cambridge, MA: MIT Press.

Harter, J.-H. 2004. "Environmental Justice for Whom? Class, New Social Movements, and the Environment: A Case Study of Greenpeace Canada, 1971–2000." *Labour/Le Travail* 6 (1): 83–119.

Haufler, V. 2009. "The Kimberly Process Certification Scheme: An Innovation in Global Governance and Conflict Prevention." *Journal of Business Ethics* 89:403–16.

Hawken, P., A. Lovins, and L.H. Lovins. 2000. *Natural Capitalism: Creating the Next Industrial Revolution.* Boston: Little Brown.

Hayden, Anders. 2014. *When Green Growth Is Not Enough: Climate Change, Ecological Modernization, and Sufficiency.* Montreal and Kingston: McGill-Queen's University Press.

Head, I.L. 1966. "Legal Clamour over Canadian Off-Shore Minerals." *Alberta Law Review* 5:312–22.

Health Canada. 2006. *Blueprint for Renewal: Transforming Canada's Approach to Regulating Health Products and Food.* Ottawa: Health Canada.

– 2007. *Blueprint for Renewal II: Modernizing Canada's Regulatory System for Health Products and Food.* Ottawa: Health Canada.

Heaps, Toby A. 2006. "The Greenest PM Interview: Brian Mulroney."
    Corporate Knights 12:7–9.

Held, David, Anthony McGrew, D. Goldblatt, and J. Perraton. 1999. *Global
    Transformations: Politics, Economics and Culture*. London: Polity.

Helm, Dieter. 2012. *The Carbon Crunch*. New Haven, CT: Yale University
    Press.

Henderson, Chris. 2013. *Aboriginal Power: Clean Energy and the Future
    of Canada's First Peoples*. Toronto: John Denison.

Hendrickson, O., and S. Aitken. 2013. "Statement of Concern regarding
    the Government of Canada's Withdrawal from the United Nations
    Convention to Combat Desertification (UNCCD)." *Biodiversity* 14 (3):
    131–2.

Henman, Paul. 2011. "Conditional Citizenship? Electronic Networks and
    the New Conditionality in Public Policy." *Policy and Internet* 3 (3):
    76–86.

Hessing, M., M. Howlett, and T. Summerville. 2005. *Canadian Natural
    Resource and Environmental Policy: Political Economy and Public
    Policy*. 2nd ed. Vancouver: UBC Press.

Heydon, Kenneth, ed. 2012. *International Trade Policy*. Farnham, UK:
    Ashgate.

Hickman, M. 2006. "Cod Taken Off the Shelves at Asda to Preserve
    Stocks." *Independent (London)*, 28 March.

Hilborn, R., J.L. Orensanz, and A.M. Parma. 2005. "Institutions,
    Incentives and the Future of Fisheries." *Philosophical Transactions of
    the Royal Society B: Biological Sciences, 360* (1453): 47–57.

Hill, S.B., and R.J. MacRae. 1992. "Organic Farming in Canada."
    Agriculture, Ecosystems & Environment 39 (1–2): 71–84.

Hilson, G. 2000. "Sustainable Development Policies in Canada's Mining
    Sector: An Overview of Government and Industry Efforts."
    Environmental Science and Policy 3 (4): 201–11.

Hilton, Robert N. 2007. "Building Political Capital: The Politics of 'Need'
    in the Federal Government's Municipal Infrastructure Programs, 1993–
    2006." MA thesis, Carleton University.

Hilton, Robert N., and Christopher Stoney. 2009a. "Federal Gas Tax
    Transfers: Politics and Perverse Policy." In *How Ottawa Spends 2009–
    2010: Economic Upheaval and Political Dysfunction*, edited by Allan
    Maslove, 175–93. Montreal and Kingston: McGill-Queen's University
    Press.

– 2009b. "Sustainable Cities: Canadian Reality or Urban Myth?"
    Commonwealth Journal of Local Governance 4:122–35.

– 2008. "Why Smart Growth Isn't Working: An Examination of Ottawa's Failure to Deliver Sustainable Urban Transit." in *Innovation, Science and Innovation, Canadian Policies and Performance 2009–2010*, edited by G. Toner, 106–19. Kingston: Queen's University Press.

HM Treasury. 2007. *Stern Review on the Economics of Climate Change.* Cambridge and London: Cambridge University Press and HM Treasury.

– 2008. *Budget 2008.* London: HM Treasury.

Hoberg, George. 2002a. "Canadian-American Environmental Relations: A Strategic Framework." In *Canadian Environmental Policy: Context and Cases.* 2nd ed., edited by Debora L. VanNijnatten and Robert Boardman, 171–89. Oxford: Oxford University Press.

Hoberg, George, and Kathryn Harrison. 1994. "It's Not Easy Being Green: The Politics of Canada's Green Plan." *Canadian Public Policy* 20 (2): 119–37.

Hogarth, D. 1991. "Greenpeace's $3B Threat to Forestry." *Financial Times,* 10 June.

Hood, Christopher, Henry Rothstein, and Robert Baldwin. 2001. *The Government of Risk: Understanding Risk Regulation Regimes.* Oxford: Oxford University Press.

Hood, G. 1995. "Windy Craggy: An Analysis of Environmental Interest Group and Mining Industry Approaches." *Resources Policy* 21 (1): 13–20.

Hopper, Tristin. 2015. "Twenty Years after Kyoto, Preston Manning Has Become Canadian Conservatives' Most Prominent Green Advocate." *National Post,* 2 January.

Horne, Matt, and Karen Campbell. 2011. *Shale Gas in British Columbia: Risks to B.C.'s Water Resources.* Edmonton: Pembina Institute.

Howard, S., and J. Stead. 2001. *The Forest Industry in the 21st Century.* Godalming, Surrey, UK: WWF, International.

Howlett, M. 1989. "The 1987 National Forest Sector Strategy and the Search for a Federal Role in Canadian Forest Policy." *Canadian Public Administration* 32 (4): 545–563.

– 1991. "The Politics of Constitutional Change in a Federal System: Negotiating Section 92A of the Canadian Constitution Act (1982)." *Publius: The Journal of Federalism* 21 (1): 121–42.

– 1998. "Predictable and Unpredictable Policy Windows: Institutional and Exogenous Correlates of Canadian Federal Agenda-Setting." *Canadian Journal of Political Science* 31:495–524.

– 2011. *Designing Public Policies: Principles and Instruments.* London: Routledge.

Howlett, Michael, and M. Ramesh. 2003. *Studying Public Policy: Policy Cycles and Policy Subsystems*. Oxford: Oxford University Press.

Hughes, Thomas P. 1987. "The Evolution of Large Technological Systems." In *The Social Construction of Technological Systems*, edited by W.E. Bijker, Thomas Hughes, and Trevor J. Pinch, 51–82. Cambridge, MA: MIT Press.

Hume, Mark. 2013. "Canada Accused of Ignoring NAFTA Obligations by Environmental Law Association." *Globe and Mail*, 14 August.

Humphreys, D. 1996. *Forest Politics: The Evolution of International Cooperation*. London: Earthscan.

Hutchings, J.A., and J.R. Post. 2013. "Gutting Canada's Fisheries Act: No Fishery, No Fish Habitat Protection." *Fisheries* 38 (11): 497–501.

Illical, M., and K. Harrison. 2007. "Protecting Endangered Species in the US and Canada: The Role of Negative Lesson Drawing." *Canadian Journal of Political Science* 40 (2): 367–94.

Infrastructure Canada. 2007. "Tracing the Development of the Gas Tax Fund." Revised final version, 17 January.

– 2011. "Infrastructure Stimulus Fund." http://www.infrastructure.gc.ca/prog/other-autres-eng.html#isf-fsi.

– 2014. http://www.infrastructure.gc.ca/index-eng.html.

International Energy Agency. 2004. *Energy Policies of IEA Countries*. Paris: International Energy Agency.

– 2013a. *CCS Strategy and Policy*. Paris: International Energy Agency.

– 2013b. *World Energy Outlook 2013*. Paris: International Energy Agency.

International Institute for Environment and Development. 2002. *Breaking New Ground: Mining, Minerals, and Sustainable Development Development – The Report of the MMSD Project*. London: Earthscan.

– 2013. "Mining, Minerals and Sustainable Development (MMSD): Background and Publications." http://www.iied.org/mining-minerals-sustainable-development-mmsd-background-publications.

International Institute for Sustainable Development. 2009. *Biofuels at What Cost?* Winnipeg: International Institute for Sustainable Development.

– 2013. *Natural Capital*. Winnipeg: International Institute for Sustainable Development.

International Union for the Conservation of Nature. 1980. "World Conservation Strategy: Living Resource Conservation for Sustainable Development," with advice, cooperation and financial assistance from

UNEP and WWF and in collaboration with FAO and UNESCO. Gland, Switzerland: IUCN, UNEP, and WWF.

Ireland, Derek, Eric Milligan, Kernaghan Webb, and Wei Xie. 2012. "The Rise and Fall of Regulatory Regimes: Extending the Life-Cycle Approach." In *How Ottawa Spends 2012–2013: The Harper Majority, Budget Cuts and the New Opposition*, edited by Bruce Doern and Christopher Stoney, 127–44. Montreal and Kingston: McGill-Queen's University Press.

Jaccard, Mark. 2006. "Mobilizing Producers toward Sustainability: The Prospects for Sector-Specific, Market-Oriented Regulations." In *Sustainable Production: Building Canadian Capacity*, edited by Glen Toner, 154–77. Vancouver: UBC Press.

– 2014. "Canadians Deserve Honest Climate Talk." *Globe and Mail*, 5 August.

"Japanese and Soviet Whaling Protested by Boycott of Goods." 1974. *New York Times*, 20 June.

Jolly, David. 2013. "Deals at Climate Meeting Advance Global Effort." *New York Times*, 23 November.

Jones, Bryan D., and Frank R. Baumgartner. 2005. *The Politics of Attention: How Government Prioritizes Problems*. Chicago: University of Chicago Press.

– 2012. "From There to Here: Punctuated Equilibrium to the General Punctuation Thesis to a Theory of Government Information Processing." *Policy Studies Journal* 40:1–20.

Jones, Jeffrey. 2013. "Oil's New Arctic Passage to Europe." *Globe and Mail*, 15 August.

Kalfagianni, A., and P. Pattberg. 2013. "Fishing in Muddy Waters: Exploring the Conditions for Effective Governance of Fisheries and Aquaculture." *Marine Policy* 38:124–32.

Kelly, F. 1989. "Rae Rejects Calls to Resign over Temagami." *Toronto Star*, 25 September.

Keskitalo, E., and H. Carina, eds. 2013. *Climate Change and Flood Risk Management*. London: Edward Elgar.

Kinder, Jeffrey S. 2010. "Government Laboratories: Institutional Variety, Change and Design Space." PhD diss., Carleton University.

King, A.A., and M.J. Lenox. 2000. "Industry Self-Regulation without Sanctions: The Chemical Industry's Responsible Care Program." *Academy of Management Journal* 43 (4): 698–716.

Kingdon, J.W. 1995. *Agendas, Alternatives, and Public Policies*. 2nd ed. New York: Harper Collins.

Kirton, John, and Virginia W. MacLaren, eds. 2002. *Linking Trade, Environment and Social Cohesion: NAFTA Experiences and Global Challenges.* Farnham, UK: Ashgate.

Klein, Naomi. 2014. *This Changes Everything: Capitalism vs the Climate.* New York: Simon and Schuster.

Koring, Paul. 2013. "Proposed Arctic Council Treaty on Oil Spills 'Useless' Greenpeace Says." *Globe and Mail,* 4 February.

Lachance, P. 1993. *Canadian Pulp and Paper Association: Changes in Values, Environmental Legislation, and Performance Audits.* Ottawa: Canadian Pulp and Paper Association.

Lafferty, William, M., and James Meadowcroft, eds. 2000. *Implementing Sustainable Development.* Oxford: Oxford University Press.

Landler, Mark. 2014. "US and China Reach Climate Accord after Months of Talks." *New York Times,* 11 November.

Lane, Daniel E. 2000. "Fisheries and Oceans Canada: Science and Conservation." In *Risky Business: Canada's Changing Science-Based Policy and Regulatory Regime,* edited by Bruce Doern and Ted Reed, 261–85. Toronto: University of Toronto Press.

Langman, M. 1992. "Memories and Notes on the Beginning and Early History of IFOAM." International Federation of Organic Agriculture Movements. http://infohub.ifoam.org/sites/default/files/page/files/early_history_ifoam.pdf.

Leiss, William. 1979. *Ecology versus Politics in Canada.* Toronto: University of Toronto Press.

Lenard, Patti Tamara, and Richard Simeon. 2012. *Imperfect Democracies: The Democratic Deficit in Canada and the United States.* Vancouver: UBC Press.

Lester, John. 2014. "Tax Expenditures and Government Program Spending: Reforming the Two 'Expenditure' Worlds for Better Expenditure Management." in *How Ottawa Spends 2014–2015: The Harper Government – Good to Go?,* edited by G. Bruce Doern and Christopher Stoney, chap. 7. Montreal and Kingston: McGill-Queen's University Press.

Levasseur, Karine. 2002. "Commission for Environmental Cooperation: A Timid Step or a Bold New Direction in Institution Building?" Paper prepared for Industry Canada, Industrial Analysis Centre.

Levi, Michael. 2013. *The Power Surge: Energy, Opportunity and the Battle for America's Future.* Oxford: Oxford University Press.

Levi-Faur, David. 2005. "The Global Diffusion of Regulatory Capitalism." *Annals of the American Academy of Political and Social Science* 598:12–32.

Lewis, Jeff. 2014. "Extra-Flammable Bakken Crude Riskier to Ship by Rail Than Other Oil, US Safety Watchdog Warns." *Financial Post*, 2 January.

Liberal Party of Canada. 1993. "Creating Opportunity: The Liberal Plan for Canada" (Red Book 1). Ottawa: Liberal Party of Canada.

Lithwick, N. Harvey. 1970. "Urban Canada: Problems and Prospects." Ottawa: Central Mortgage and Housing Corporation.

Lipp, Judith. 2007. "Renewable Energy Policies and the Provinces." In *Innovation, Science and Environment: Canadian Policies and Performance, 2007–2008*, edited by G. Bruce Doern, 176–99. Montreal and Kingston: McGill-Queen's University Press.

Lucas, A.R. 1977. *The National Energy Board*. Ottawa: Law Reform Commission.

– 1978. "The National Energy Board." In *The Regulatory Process in Canada*, edited by Bruce Doern, 259–313. Toronto: Macmillan of Canada.

Luckert, Martin, David Haley, and George Hoberg. 2012. *Policies for Sustainably Managing Canada's Forests*. Vancouver: UBC Press.

Macdonald, Douglas. 1991. *The Politics of Pollution*. Toronto: McClelland and Stewart.

– 2011. "Harper Energy and Climate Change Policy: Failing to Address the Key Problems." In *How Ottawa Spends 2011–2012: Trimming Fat or Slicing Pork?*, edited by Christopher Stoney and Bruce Doern, 127–43. Montreal and Kingston: McGill-Queen's University Press.

Macdonald, Douglas, Debora VanNijnatten, and Andrew Byorn. 2004. "Implementing Kyoto: When Spending Is Not Enough." In *How Ottawa Spends 2004–2005: Mandate Change in the Martin Era*, edited by G. Bruce Doern, 175–97. Montreal and Kingston: McGill-Queen's University Press.

Macfarlane, D. 2014. *Negotiating a River: Canada and the US and the Creation of the St Laurence Seaway*. Vancouver: UBC Press.

Mackenzie, H. 2013. *Canada's Infrastructure Gap: Where It Came From and Why It Will Cost so Much to Close*. Ottawa: Centre for Policy Alternatives, January.

MacIvor, H. 2006. *Parameters of Power: Canada's Political Institutions*. 4th ed. Toronto: Nelson.

Maes, Frank, A. Cliquet, W. du Plessis, and Heather McLeod-Kilmurray, eds. 2013. *Biodiversity and Climate Change*. London: Edward Elgar.

Mann, H. 2008. *International Investment Agreements, Business and Human Rights: Key Issues and Opportunities*. Winnipeg: International Institute for Sustainable Development.

Marchak, P. 1983. *Green Gold: The Forest Industry in British Columbia.*
Vancouver: UBC Press.

Marine Stewardship Council. 2001. "MSC Announces New Governance
Structure." Marine Stewardship Council, 27 July.

Marx, Axel, M. Maertens, Johan Swinnen, and Jan Wouters, eds. 2012.
Private Standards and Global Governance. London: Edward Elgar.

May, Elizabeth. 1990. *Paradise Won: The Struggle for South Moresby.*
Toronto: McClelland and Stewart.

– 1994. "Endangered Species." 29 November. Accessed 24 August 2014,
http://www.lexisnexis.com.

May, Peter J. 2007. "Regulatory Regimes and Accountability." *Regulation
and Governance* 1 (1): 8–26.

McAllister, M.L. 2007. "Shifting Foundations in a Mature Staples Industry:
A Political Economic History of Canadian Mineral Policy." *Canadian
Political Science Review* 1 (1): 73–90.

McAllister, M.L., and C.J. Alexander. 1997. *A Stake in the Future:
Redefining the Canadian Mineral Industry.* Vancouver: UBC Press.

McAllister, M.L., and G. Milioli. 2000. "Mining Sustainably: Opportunities
for Canada and Brazil." *Minerals & Energy: Raw Materials Report* 15
(2): 3–14.

McCarthy, Shawn. 2013a. "Activists Launch Suit in Federal Court over
Ability to Oppose Proposed Pipeline Projects." *Globe and Mail,*
13 August.

– 2013b. "Aglukkaq Takes Environment Post as Ottawa Seeks to Win
Over First Nations, US." *Globe and Mail,* 18 July.

– 2013c. "Oil Industry Successfully Lobbied Ottawa to Delay Climate
Regulations, E-mails Show." *Globe and Mail,* 8 November.

McCarthy, Shawn, and Jeffrey Jones. 2013. "The Promise and the Perils of
a Pipe to Saint John." *Globe and Mail,* 2 August.

McCarthy, Shawn, and Josh Kerr. 2013. "Coast to Coast: A Power Grid
Stretched Thin." *Globe and Mail,* 14 August.

McCay, B.J., C.F. Creed, A.C. Finlayson, R. Apostle, and K. Mikalsen.
1995. "Individual Transferable Quotas (ITQs) in Canadian and US
Fisheries." *Ocean and Coastal Management* 28 (1): 85–115.

McDougall, John N. 1982. *Fuels and the National Policy.* Toronto:
McClelland and Stewart.

McGlade, Christofe, and Paul Ekins. 2015. "The Geographical
Distribution of Fossil Fuels Unused When Limiting Global Warming to
2 Degrees Centigrade." *Nature* 517:187–90.

McGrane, David. 2013. "National Unity through Disengagement: The Harper Government's One-Off Federalism." In *How Ottawa Spends 2013–2014: The Harper Government Mid-Term Blues and Long-term Plans*, edited by Christopher Stoney and G. Bruce Doern, 114–26. Montreal and Kingston: McGill-Queen's University Press.

McGrath, Matt. 2014. "Fossil Fuels Should Be Phased Out by 2100, Says IPCC." *BBC News*, 2 November.

McKitrick, Ross. 1997. "Double Dividend Environmental Taxation and Canadian Carbon Emissions Control." *Canadian Public Policy* 22 (4): 417–34.

– 2011. *Economic Analysis of Environmental Policy*. Toronto: University of Toronto Press.

McLaughlin, David. 2013. "With Energy East, the Provinces Define National Interest." *Globe and Mail*, 9 August.

McLeod, N. 2013. *Getting on the Omnibus: Bill C-38 and the Repeal of Canada's Environmental Assessment Act*. Ottawa: Carleton University, School of Public Policy and Administration.

Meadowcroft, James, and Matthew Hellin. 2010. "Policy Making in the Indeterminate World of Energy Transitions: Carbon Capture and Storage as Technological Transition or Ehanced Carbon 'Lock-in.'" In *Policy: From Implementation to Ideas*, edited by Glen Toner, Leslie A. Pal, and Michael Prince, 233–56. Montreal and Kingston: McGill-Queen's University Press.

Meadowcroft, James, and Oluf Langhelle, eds. 2011. *Caching the Carbon: The Politics and Policy of Carbon Capture and Storage*. London: Edward Elgar.

Meadows, D.H., D.L. Meadows, J. Randers, and W.W. Behran. 1972. *The Limits to Growth*. New York: Universe Books.

Meidinger, E. 1997. "Look Who's Making the Rules: International Environmental Standard Setting by Non-Governmental Organizations." *Human Ecology Review* 4 (1): 52–4.

"The Melting North: Special Report on the Arctic." 2012. *Economist*, 16 June.

Meyer, Gregory. 2013. "US Biofuel Mandate Change Hits Ethanol Credits." *Commodities* 6 April.

Michleburgh, R. 2001. "Environmentalists Relax B.C. Boycotts." *Globe and Mail*, 5 April.

Mihlar, Fazil. 1999. "The Federal Government and the RIAS Process: Origins, Need and Non-Compliance." In *Changing the Rules: Canadian*

Regulatory Regimes and Institutions, edited by Bruce Doern, Margaret Hill, Michael Prince, and Richard Schultz, 277–292. Toronto: University of Toronto Press.

Miller, M. 1961. "Resources and Development: The 'Resources for Tomorrow' Conference Approach." *Canadian Journal of Agricultural Economics/Revue canadienne d'agroeconomie* 9 (2): 34–53.

Minkel, J.R. 2008. "The 2003 Northeast Blackout: Five Years Later." *Scientific American*, 13 August.

Mirza, S. 2012. "Canada's Looming Infrastructure Deficit." http://economistesquebecois.com/files/documents/b8/95/8mai-saeed-mirza.pdf.

Mitchell, Ronald B. 2013. "International Environmental Agreements Database Project." Version 2013.1. http://iea.uoregon.edu/

Moffet, J., F. Bregha, and M.J. MiddelKoop. 2004. "Responsible Care: A Case Study of a Voluntary Environmental Initiative." In *Voluntary Codes: Private Governance, the Public Interest and Innovation*, edited by Kernaghan Webb, 177–91. Ottawa: Carleton Unit for Innovation, Science and Environment.

Mol, Arthur. 2001. *Globalization and Environmental Reform: The Ecological Modernization of the Global Economy*. Cambridge, MA: MIT Press.

Montpetit, Eric. 2009. "Has the European Union Made Europe More or Less Democratic? Elections, Network Deliberations and Advocacy Groups." Paper presented to the Conference on Bringing Civil Society, Florence, 13 March.

Moore, Dene. 2013. "Kinder Morgan Files National Energy Board Application for Pipeline Expansion." *Globe and Mail*, 16 December.

Morcol, Goktug. 2012. *A Complexity Theory For Public Policy*. London: Routledge.

Morrison, Robert W. 2001. "Global Nuclear Markets in the Context of Climate Change and Sustainable Development." In *Canadian Nuclear Energy Policy*, edited by G. Bruce Doern, Arslan Dorman, and Robert W. Morrison, 34–51. Toronto: University of Toronto Press.

Mowat Centre for Policy Innovation. 2013. *The Politics of Pipelines: Ontario's Stake in Canada's Pipeline Debate*. Toronto: Mowat Centre.

Mulgrew, I. 1984. "Mulroney Pledges Aid for B.C. Forestry." Accessed 4 January 2014, http://www.lexisnexus.com.

Murray, Brian C., Richard G. Newell, and William A. Pizer. 2008. *Balancing Cost and Emissions Certainty: An Allowance Reserve for Cap-and-Trade*. Washington, DC: Resources for the Future.

Myers, Stephen Lee, and Nicholas Kulish. 2013. "Growing Clamour about Inequities of Climate Crisis." *New York Times,* 16 November.

Nagtzaam, Gerry. 2009. *The Making of International Environmental Treaties.* London: Edward Elgar.

National Climate Change Process. 2000. *Canada's National Implementation Strategy on Climate Change.* Ottawa: Government of Canada.

National Energy Board. 2001. *2001–2002 Estimates: Part III Reports on Plans and Priorities.* Ottawa: National Energy Board.

– 2005. *Annual Report 2004.* Ottawa: National Energy Board.

– 2008. *2007 Annual Report to Parliament.* Ottawa: National Energy Board.

– 2011a. *The National Energy Board Filing Requirements for Offshore Drilling in the Canadian Arctic.* Ottawa: National Energy Board.

– 2011b. *Review of Offshore Drilling in the Canadian Arctic.* Ottawa: National Energy Board.

– 2012a. *Annual Report 2011 to Parliament.* Ottawa: National Energy Board.

– 2012b. *Section 58 Streamlining Order.* Ottawa: National Energy Board.

National Energy Board and Canadian Environmental Assessment Agency. 2013. "Joint Review Panel Recommends Approving the Enbridge Northern Gateway Project." News release, 19 December.

National Roundtable on the Environment and the Economy. 2003. *Securing Canada's Natural Capital: A Vision for Nature Conservation in the 21st Century.* Ottawa: National Round Table on the Environment and Economy.

– 2011a. *Canada's Opportunity: Adopting Life Cycle Approaches for Sustainable Development.* Ottawa: National Roundtable on the Environment and the Economy.

– 2011b. *Climate Prosperity.* Ottawa: National Roundtable on the Environment and the Economy.

– 2013. *NRT Reports by Issue.* Ottawa: National Roundtable on the Environment and the Economy.

National Transit Strategy. 2014. "National Transit Strategy." http://www.nationaltransitstrategy.ca/about/.

Natural Resources Canada. 2000. *2000–2001 Estimates: Natural Resources Canada (Part III).* Ottawa: Natural Resources Canada

– 2006. "Canada's National Forest Inventory." Government of Canada.

– 2013a. *Carbon Capture and Storage: Oil Sands.* Ottawa: Natural Resources Canada.

– 2013b. *List of Acts and Regulations.* http://www.nrcan.gc.ca/acts-regulations.

– 2013c. *Shale Gas in Canada.* Ottawa: Natural Resources Canada.

– 2013d. *Tight Oil.* Ottawa: Natural Resources Canada.

Nature Conservancy of Canada. 2013. "Our Story." http://www.nature conservancy.ca/en/who-we-are/our-story/.

Naughton, John. 2012. *From Guttenberg to Zuckerberg: What You Really Need to Know About the Internet.* London: Quercus.

Netherton, Alexander. 2007. "The Political Economy of Canadian Hydro-Electricity: Between Old 'Provincial Hydros' and Neoliberal Regional Energy Regimes." *Canadian Political Science Review* 1 (1): 107–24.

Newall, Peter, and Matthew Paterson. 2010. *Climate Capitalism: Global Warming and the Transformation of the Global Economy.* Cambridge: Cambridge University Press.

"New Certification for Wal-Mart Shrimp Another Example of Environmental Leadership; Adopting Best Aquaculture Practices for Farm-Raised Shrimp Ensures Quality Product for Consumers Around the World – Harvested with Sustainability in Mind." 2005. *PR Newswire,* 17 November.

Noble, K. 1989. "Ontario Pulp, Paper Firms Must Monitor Their Pollution." *Globe and Mail,* 3 March.

Norberg, Jon, and Graeme S. Cumming, eds. 2012. *Complexity Theory for a Sustainable Future.* New York: Columbia University Press.

O'Connor, Don. 2011. "Canadian Biofuels Policies." Presentation at University of Ottawa, 9 June.

Office of the Auditor General of Canada. 2002. *Report of the Auditor General of Canada.* Ottawa: Auditor General, April.

– 2005a. *September Report of the Commissioner of the Environment and Sustainable Development.* Ottawa: Auditor General.

– 2005b. *Status Report of the Auditor General of Canada.* Ottawa: Auditor General, February.

– 2010. *Report of the Auditor General of Canada.* Ottawa: Auditor General.

Ogilvie, K. 2006. "The Emergence of Environmental Movement-Government." In *Sustainability, Civil Society and International Governance: Local, North American and Global Contributions,* edited by John J. Kirton and Peter I. Hajnal, 89–105. Farnham, UK: Ashgate.

Ogilvie, K.B., and E. Everhardus. 2004. "ENGO-Business Partnerships: Lessons Learned." Toronto: Pollution Probe.

O'Hara, Kathryn, and Paul Dufour. 2014. "How Accurate Is the Harper Government's Misinformation? What Role Does Evidence Play in

Federal Policy Making?" In *How Ottawa Spends 2013–14: Harper Government Mid-term Blues and Long-term Plans*, edited by Christopher Stoney and Bruce Doern, 178–91. Montreal and Kingston: McGill-Queen's University Press.

Okereke, C., and C.H. Bulkeley. 2009. "Conceptualizing Climate Governance beyond the International Regime." *Global Environmental Politics* 9 (1): 58–78.

Ontario Forest Industries Association. 1998. *Guiding Principles and Code of Forest Practices*. Toronto: Ontario Forest Industries Association.

Ontario Forest Policy Panel. 1993. *Diversity: Forests, People, Communities – A Comprehensive Forest Policy Framework for Ontario*. Toronto: Queen's Printer.

Organization of Economic Cooperation and Development (OECD). 1977. *The OECD Programme on Long Range Transport of Air Pollutants*. Paris: OECD.

Ostrom, Elinor. 1990. *Governing the Commons: The Evolution of Institutions for Collective Action*. New York: Cambridge University Press.

– 2012. *The Future of the Commons: Beyond Market Failure and Government Regulation*. London: Institute of Economic Affairs.

Overdevest, C. 2004. "Codes of Conduct and Standard Setting in the Forest Sector: Constructing Markets for Democracy?" *Relations Industrielles/Industrial Relations* 59 (1): 172–97.

Paehlke, Robert C. 2010. "The Environmental Movement in Canada." In *Canadian Environmental Policy and Politics: Prospects for Leadership and Innovation,* edited by Debora L. VanNijnatten and Robert Boardman, 2–13. Toronto: Oxford University Press.

Paehlke, Robert C., and Douglas Torgerson, eds. 1990. *Managing Leviathan: Environmental Politics and the Administrative State*. Peterborough, ON: Broadview.

Pal, Leslie A. 2013. *Beyond Policy Analysis: Issue Management in Turbulent Times*. 5th ed. Toronto: Nelson.

Paquet, G., and R. Shepherd. 1996. "The Program Review Process: A Deconstruction. In *How Ottawa Spends 1996–97, Life under the Knife*, edited by Gene Swimmer, 39–72. Ottawa: Carleton University Press.

Park, Chris. 1989. *Acid Rain: Rhetoric and Reality*. London: Methuen/ Routledge.

Parliamentary Budget Officer. 2010. *Report*. Ottawa: Office of the Parliamentary Budget Officer.

Persaud, A. Jai, Uma Kumar, and Vinod Kumar. 2007. "Innovation and Natural Resources: Myths and Realities about the 'Old' Economy versus the 'New' Economy." In *Innovation, Science and Environment: Canadian Policies and Performance 2007–2008*, edited by G. Bruce Doern, 77–97. Montreal and Kingston: McGill-Queen's University Press.

Phillips, Peter. 2007. *Governing Transformative Technological Innovation: Who's in Charge?* London: Edward Elgar.

– 2010. *A Response to the Nuffield Council on Bioethics Consultation Paper: New Approaches to Biofuels.* Saskatoon: University of Saskatchewan.

Pineau, Pierre-Olivier. 2009. "An Integrated Canadian Electricity Market? The Potential for Further Integration." In *Governing the Energy Challenge*, edited by Burkard Eberlein and G. Bruce Doern, 226–58. Toronto: University of Toronto Press.

– 2012. "Integrating Electricity Sectors in Canada: Good for the Environment and the Economy." *The Federal Idea*. Montreal. 1–25.

Pirages, 1978. *The New Context for International Relations: Global Ecopolitics.* London: Duxbury.

"PM: Dion's Carbon Tax Would 'Screw Everybody.'" 2008. CBC News, 20 June. http://www.cbc.ca/news/canada/pm-dion-s-carbon-tax-would-screw-everybody-1.696762.

Poore, D. 2003. *Changing Landscapes: The Development of the International Tropical Timber Organization and Its Influence on Tropical Forest Management.* London: Earthscan.

Potoski, M., and A. Prakash. 2005. "Covenants with Weak Swords: ISO 14001 and Facilities' Environmental Performance." *Journal of Policy Analysis and Management* 24 (4): 745–69.

PPP Canada. 2014. "Overview." PPP Canada.

Prakash, A. 2000. "Responsible Care: An Assessment." *Business and Society* 39 (2): 183–209.

Pralle, S.B. 2003. "Venue Shopping, Political Strategy, and Policy Change: The Internationalization of Canadian Forest Advocacy." *Journal of Public Policy* 23 (3): 233–60.

Pratt, Shella. 2013. "Critics Want Review of Oilsands Steaming Process after Cold Lake Spill." *Edmonton Journal*, 10 August.

Prince, M. 2007. "Soft Craft, Hard Choices, Altered Context: Reflections on Twenty-Five Years of Policy Advice in Canada." In *Policy Analysis in Canada*, edited by Laurent Dobuzinskis, Michael Howlett, and David Laycock, 163–85. Toronto: Toronto University Press.

Princen, Thomas, Michael Maniates, and Ken Comca. 2002. *Confronting Consumption.* Cambridge, MA: MIT Press.

Privy Council Office. 1999. Speech from the Throne. http://www.pco-bcp. gc.ca/index.asp?lang=eng&page=information&sub=publications&doc= aarchives/sft-ddt/1999-eng.htm.

Professional Institute of the Public Service of Canada. 2014. *Vanishing Science: The Disappearance of Canadian Public Interest Science.* Ottawa: Professional Institute of the Public Service of Canada.

Prud'Homme, Alex. 2014. *Hydrofracking.* Oxford: Oxford University Press.

Public Policy Forum. 2014. *Canada's Nuclear Energy Sector: Where to From Here?* Ottawa: Public Policy Forum.

Radaelli, Claudio. 2009. "Desperately Seeking Regulatory Impact Assessment: Diary of a Reflective Researcher." *Evaluation* 15 (1): 31–48.

Radkau, Joachim. 2008. *Nature and Power: A Global History of the Environment.* Berlin: German Historical Institute.

– 2014. *The Age of Ecology.* London: Polity.

Rainie, Lee, and Barry Wellman. 2012. *Networked: The New Social Operating System.* Cambridge, MA: MIT Press.

Raj, Althia. 2009a. "Baird: Not My Job to Track Cash." *Calgary Sun,* 30 July.

– 2009b. "Job Creation Numbers Remain a Mystery." *Ottawa Sun,* 1 September.

Raloff, J. 1979. "Bloody Harvest." *Science News* 115 (13): 202–4.

Ratner, J.B. 1983. "Government Capital and the Production Function for US Private Output." *Economics Letters* 13:213–17.

Rayner, J., and M. Howlett. 2007. "Caught in a Staples Vice: The Political Economy of Canadian Aquaculture." *Policy and Society* 26 (1): 49–69.

Regens, James L., and Robert W. Rycroft. 1988. *The Acid Rain Controversy.* Pittsburgh: University of Pittsburg Press.

Reguly, Eric. 2013. "The Shale Revolution and Its Unintended Side-effects." *Globe and Mail,* 1 June.

Reid, J. 1997. "A Society Made by History: The Mythic Source of Identity in Canada." *Canadian Review of American Studies* 27 (1): 1–20.

Reid, R. 2014. "The Canadian Boreal Forest Agreement: Unlikely Allies Pursuing Conservation and Sustainable Development in Canada's Boreal Regions." *Philanthropist* 26 (1): 21–37.

Revkin, Andrew C. 2014. "A Darker View of the Age of Us: The Anthropocene." *New York Times,* 18 June. http://dotearth.blogs.nytimes.com/ 2014/06/18/a-darker-view-of-the.

Rhodes, R.A.W. 1997. *Understanding Governance.* London: Open University Press.

Ricketts, P., and P. Harrison. 2007. "Coastal and Ocean Management in Canada: Moving into the 21st Century." *Coastal Management* 35 (1): 5–22.

Riddell-Dixon, E. 1989. *Canada and the International Seabed: Domestic Determinants and External Constraints*. Montreal and Kingston: McGill-Queen's University Press.

Rivers, Nic, and Mark Jaccard. 2009. "Talking without Walking: Canada's Ineffective Climate Effort." In *Governing the Energy Challenge*, edited by Burkard Eberlein and Bruce Doern, 285–313. Toronto: University of Toronto Press.

Robinson, Pamela. 2009. "Urban Sustainability." In *Environmental Challenges and Opportunities: Local-Global Perspectives on Canadian Issues*, edited by Christopher Gore and Peter Stoett, chap. 7. Toronto: Emond Montgomery.

Roheim, C.A., and J.G. Sutinen. 2006. *Trade and Marketplace Measures to Promote Sustainable Fishing Practices*. Geneva: International Centre for Trade and Sustainable Development and High Seas Task Force.

Rondinelli, D.A., and T. London. 2003. "How Corporations and Environmental Groups Cooperate: Assessing Cross-Sector Alliances and Collaborations." *Academy of Management Executive* 17 (1): 61–76.

Salomons, G.H., and G. Hoberg. 2013. "Setting Boundaries of Participation in Environmental Impact Assessment." *Environmental Impact Assessment Review* 22 (1): 55–67.

Sánchez, L.E. 1998. "Industry Response to the Challenge of Sustainability: The Case of the Canadian Nonferrous Mining Sector." *Environmental Management* 22 (4): 521–31.

Sands, Philippe, and Jacqueline Peel. 2012. *Principles of International Environmental Law*. Cambridge: Cambridge University Press.

Saner, Marc A. 2002. "An Ethical Analysis of the Precautionary Principle." *International Journal of Biotechnology* 4 (1): 81–95.

Santamaria, Luis, and Pablo F. Mendez. 2012. "Evolution in Biodiversity: Current Gaps and Future Needs." *Evolutionary Applications* 17 (2): 202–19.

Savoie, Donald. 1999. *Governing fFrom the Centre: The Concentration of Power in Canadian Politics*. Toronto: University of Toronto Press.

– 2010. *Power: Where Is It?* Montreal and Kingston: McGill-Queen's University Press.

– 2013. *Whatever Happened to the Music Teacher? How Government Decides and Why*. Montreal and Kingston: McGill-Queen's University Press.

Schneider, Volker. 2014. "Governance and Complexity." In *The Oxford Handbook of Governance*, edited by David Levi-Faur, chap. 9. Oxford: Oxford University Press.

Schott, Stephan. 2004. "New Fishery Management in Atlantic Canada: Communities, Governments and Alternative Targets." In *How Ottawa Spends 2004–2005: Mandate Change in the Paul Martin Era*, edited by Bruce Doern, 151–74. Montreal and Kingston: McGill-Queen's University Press.

Schrank, W.E. 1995. "Extended Fisheries Jurisdiction: Origins of the Current Crisis in Atlantic Canada's Fisheries." *Marine Policy* 19 (4): 285–99.

Schrecker, T.F. 1984. *The Political Economy of Environmental Hazards*. Ottawa: Law Reform Commission of Canada.

– 1991. "The Canadian Environmental Assessment Act: Tremulous Step Forward or Retreat into Smoke and Mirrors?" *Canadian Environmental Law Reports* 5 (March): 22–34.

Schultz, Richard, and Alan Alexandroff. 1985. *Economic Regulation and the Federal System*. Toronto: University of Toronto Press.

Schwanen, Daniel. 2000. *A Cooler Approach: Tackling Canada's Commitments on Greenhouse Gas Emissions*. Toronto: C.D. Howe Institute.

Schwindt, R., and A.R. Vining. 2008. "Conflict and Institutional Reform in the British Columbia Salmon Fishery." In *Canadian Water Politics: Conflicts and Institutions*, edited by M. Sproule-Jones, C. Johns, and B.T. Heinmille, 286–307. Montreal and Kingston: McGill-Queen's University Press.

Science Council of Canada. 1977. *Policies and Poisons*. Ottawa: Science Council of Canada.

Scoffield, Heather. 2010. "Stimulus a Job Flop, Survey Suggests Economic Action Plan Didn't Create Much Employment, Poorly Tracked." *Canadian Press*, 2 December.

Sea Shepherd Conservation Society. 2008. "About Sea Shepherd Conservation Society." http://www.seashepherd.org/about-sscs.html.

Sell, Susan. 1998. *Power and Ideas: North South Politics of Intellectual Property and Antitrust*. Albany, NY: State University of New York Press.

Sethi, S. Prakash, and Olga Emelianova. 2011. "International Council on Mining and Metals Sustainable Development Framework (ICMM)." In *Globalization and Self-Regulation: The Crucial Role that Corporate Codes of Conduct Play in Global Business*, edited by S Prakash Sethi, 161–77. New York: Palgrave Macmillan.

Shabecoff, P. 1981. "Rusty Trawler to Lead Battle against Whale Hunts." *New York Times*, 31 May.

Shane, K. 2013. "Canada Pulling Out of World Timber, Tourism, Expo Groups." *Globe and Mail*, 12 June.

"Sheikhs v Shale." 2014. *Economist*, 6 December.

Shinya, W.M. 1998. "Canada's New Minerals and Metals Policy: Advancing the Concept of Sustainable Development in the Minerals and Metals Industry." *Resources Policy* 24 (2): 95–104. doi:http://dx.doi.org/10.1016/S0301-4207(98)00013-0.

Siddon, T., D. Anderson, J. Fraser, and H. Dhaliwal. 2012. "An Open Letter to Stephen Harper on Fisheries." *Globe and Mail*, 1 June. http://www.theglobeandmail.com/globe-debate/an-open-letter-to-stephen-harper-on-fisheries/article4224866/.

Simon, Herbert A. 1962. "The Architecture of Complexity." *Proceedings of the American Philosophical Society* 106 (6): 467–82.

Simpson, Jeffrey. 2013a. "Ottawa Denies Its Own Emission Stats." *Globe and Mail*, 1 November.

– 2013b. "Still Waiting for Those Emissions Regulations." *Globe and Mail*, 7 December.

Sinclair, Peter R. 2010. *Energy in Canada*. Toronto: Oxford University Press.

Skodvin, T., and S. Andresen. 2003. "Nonstate Influence in the International Whaling Commission, 1970–1990." *Global Environmental Politics* 3 (4): 61–86.

Smiley, D. 1964. "Public Administration and Canadian Federalism." *Canadian Public Administration* 7 (3): 371–88.

SNC-Lavalin. 2011. "Agreement Signed to Acquire AECL's Commercial Reactor Division by CANDU Energy." News release, 29 June.

Soroka, Stuart N. 2002. "Issue Attributes and Agenda-Setting by Media, the Public and Policy Makers in Canada." *International Journal of Public Opinion Research* 14 (3): 264–85.

Sproule-Jones, M. 2003. *Restoration of the Great Lakes: Promises, Practices and Performances*. Vancouver: UBC Press.

Sproule-Jones, M., C. Johns, and B.T. Heinmiller. 2008. *Canadian Water Politics: Conflicts and Institutions*. Montreal and Kingston: McGill-Queen's University Press.

Stanbury, W.T. 1980. *Government Regulation: Scope, Growth, Process*. Montreal: Institute for Research on Public Policy.

– 2000. *Environmental Groups and the International Conflict over the Forest of British Columbia 1990 to 2000*. Vancouver: SFU-UBC Centre for the Study of Government and Business.

Standing Senate Committee on Energy, the Environment and Natural Resources. 2012. *Now or Never*. Ottawa: Standing Senate Committee on Energy, the Environment and Natural Resources.

Stefanick, Lorna, and Kathleen Wells. 1998. "Staying the Course or Saving Face? Federal Environmental Policy Post-Rio." In *How Ottawa Spends 1998–99: Balancing Act: The Post-Deficit Mandate*, edited by Leslie A. Pal, 243–70. Toronto: Oxford University Press.

Steinberg, Jesse. 2013. "The Policies and Politics of Federal Public Transit Infrastructure Spending." In *How Ottawa Spends 2013–2014: The Harper Government Mid-term Blues and Long-term Plans*, edited by Christopher Stoney and G. Bruce Doern, 223–35. Montreal and Kingston: McGill-Queen's University Press.

Stewart, Jennifer, and A. John Sinclair. 2007. "Meaningful Public Participation in Environmental Assessment: Perspectives from Canadian Participants, Proponents, and Government." *Journal of Environmental Assessment Policy and Assessment* 9 (2): 161–76.

Stirling, Andy. 2013. "Why the Precautionary Principle Matters." *Guardian*, 8 July.

Stoett, Peter. 2003. "Toward Renewed Legitimacy? Nuclear Power, Global Warming and Security." *Global Environmental Politics* 3 (1): 99–116.

– 2012. *Global Ecopolitics: Crisis, Governance and Justice*. Toronto: University of Toronto Press.

Stoney, C., and K. Graham. 2009. "Federal Municipal Relations in Canada: The Changing Organizational Landscape." *Canadian Public Administration* 52 (3): 371–94.

Stoney, C., and R. Hilton. 2007. "Dreams, Deception and Delusions: Derailing Ottawa's Light Rail Transit System." *Revue gouvernance* 4 (1): 2–22.

Stoney, C., and T. Krawchenko. 2012. "Transparency and Accountability in Infrastructure Stimulus Spending: A Comparison of Canadian, Australian and US Programs." *Canadian Public Administration* 55 (4): 123–38.

"Sustainable Development Framework (ICMM)." In *Globalization and Self-Regulation: The Crucial Role that Corporate Codes of Conduct Play in Global Business*, edited by S. Prakash Sethi, 161–75. New York: Palgrave Macmillan.

Sutton, M., and C. Whitfield. 1996. "A Powerful Arrow in the Quiver." ICSF. http://old.icsf.net/icsf2006/uploads/publications/dossier/pdf/french/issue_67/chapter463.pdf.

Svantesson, Dan. 2011. "Fundamental Policy Considerations for the Regulation of Internet Cross-Border Privacy Issues." *Policy and the Internet* 3 (3): 66–76.

Swan, G.S. 1975. "Remembering Maine: Offshore Federalism in the United States and Canada." *California Western International Law Journal* 6:296.

Swimmer, Gene, ed. 1996. *How Ottawa Spends 1996–97: Life under the Knife.* Ottawa: Carleton University Press.

Synnott, T. 2005. *Some Notes on the Early Years of* FSC. Saltillo, Mexico: Forest Stewardship Council.

Tait, Carrie. 2013a. "Alberta Revamps Energy Regulator in Bid to Polish Environmental Image." *Globe and Mail*, 13 May.

Temby, O. 2013. "Trouble in Smogville: The Politics of Toronto's Air Pollution during the 1950s." *Journal of Urban History* 39 (4): 669–89.

Thompson, G., J. Frances, R. Levacic, and J. Mitchell, eds. 1991. *Markets, Hierarchies and Networks: The Coordination of Social Life.* London: Sage Publishers.

Tindal, R.C., and S.N. Tindal. 2004. *Local Government in Canada.* 6th ed. Scarborough, ON: Nelson.

Tollefson, C., F.P. Gale, and D. Haley. 2008. *Setting the Standard: Certification, Governance, and and the Forest Stewardship Council.* Vancouver: UBC Press.

Toner, Glen. 1986. "Stardust: The Tory Energy Program." in *How Ottawa Spends 1986–1987*, edited by Michael J. Prince, 119–48. Toronto: Methuen.

– 2000. "Canada: From Early Frontrunner to Plodding Anchorman." In *Canadian Environmental Policy: Context and Cases*, edited by Debora VanNijnatten and Robert Boardman, 59–80. 2nd ed. Oxford: Oxford University Press.

– ed. 2006. *Sustainable Production: Building Canadian Capacity.* Vancouver: UBC Press.

– ed. 2008. *Innovation, Science, Environment: Canadian Policies and Performance 2008–2009.* Montreal and Kingston: McGill-Queen's University Press.

Toner, Glen, and Carey Frey. 2004. "Governance for Sustainable Development: Next Stage Institutional and Policy Development." In *How Ottawa Spends 2004–2005: Mandate Change in the Paul Martin Era*, edited by G. Bruce Doern, 198–221. Montreal and Kingston: McGill-Queen's University Press.

Toner, Glen, and Jennifer McKee. 2014. "Harper's Wedge Politics: Bad Environmental Policy and Bad Energy Policy." in *How Ottawa Spends 2014–2015*, edited by G. Bruce Doern and Christopher Stoney, 108–24. Montreal and Kingston: McGill-Queen's University Press.

Toner, Glen, and James Meadowcroft. 2009. "The Struggle of the Canadian Federal Government to Implement Sustainable Development." In *Canadian Environmental Policy and Politics*, edited by Deborah VanNijnatten and Robert Boardman, 77–90. Toronto: Oxford University Press.

Transport Canada. 2006. "Government Spending on Transportation." In *Transportation in Canada*, 43–55. Ottawa: Transport Canada.

– 2007. *Evaluation of the Strategic Highway Infrastructure Program*. Ottawa: Transport Canada.

Treasury Board. 2008. "Accounting Standard 3.2: Transfer Payments (Grants and Contributions)." Archived on TBS website.

Trebilcock, Michael J. 2011. *Understanding Trade Law*. London: Edward Elgar.

Trebilcock, Michael, Robert House, and Antonia Eliason. 2013. *International Trade*. 4th ed. London: Routledge.

Tripp, D. 1998. "Problems, Prescriptions and Compliance with the Coastal Fisheries/Forestry Guidelines in a Random Sample of Cutblocks in Coastal British Columbia." In *Carnation Creek and Queen Charlotte Islands Fish/Forestry Workshop: Applying Twenty Years of Coastal Research to Management Solutions*, edited by D. Hogan, P. Tschaplinski, and S. Chatwin, 132–47. Victoria, BC: Ministry of Forests.

United Nations. 1992. United Nations Conference on Environment and Development, Rio de Janeiro, Agenda 21. Geneva: UN. https://sustainabledevelopment.un.org/content/documents/Agenda21.pdf.

– 1998. *The United Nations Convention on the Law of the Sea*. Geneva: United Nations.

United Nations Environmental Programme. 2013. "About UNEP: The Organization." http://www.unep.org/Documents.Multilingual/Default.asp?DocumentID=43.

Usher, Peter J. 2000. "Traditional Ecological Knowledge in Environmental Assessment and Management." *Arctic* 53 (2): 183–93.

Vanderkliffe, Nathan. 2013. "Energy Producers Eye New Route to Riches with LPG." *Globe and Mail*, 11 June.

Vander Ploeg, C.G., and M. Holden. 2013. *At the Intersection*. Calgary: Canada West Foundation.

VanNijnatten, Debora. 2002. "Getting Greener in the Third Mandate?" In *How Ottawa Spends: 2002–2003: The Security Aftermath and National Priorities*, edited by G. Bruce Doern, 216–33. Toronto: Oxford University Press.

VanNijnatten, Debora, and Robert Boardman, eds. 2002. *Canadian Environmental Policy: Context and Cases*. 2nd ed. Toronto: Oxford University Press.

Vogel, David. 2012. *The Politics of Precaution: Regulating Health, Safety, and Environmental Risks in Europe and the United States*. Princeton: Princeton University Press.

Volger, John. 2013. "Environmental Issues." In *The Globalization of World Politics*, edited by John Baylis, Steve Smith, and Patricia Owens, chap. 12. London: Oxford University Press.

Waddell, C. 1985. "Ministers Plan Seminars on Forest Management." *Globe and Mail*, 24 September.

Walby, Sylvia. 2007. "Complexity Theory, Systems Theory, and Multiple Intersecting Social Inequalities." *Philosophy of the Social Sciences* 37 (4): 449–70.

Wald, Matthew L. 2013. "New Energy Struggles on Its Way to Markets." *New York Times*, 27 December.

Walker, Gordon. 2012. *Environmental Justice: Concepts, Evidence and Politics*. London: Routledge.

Wapner, Paul. 2003. "World Summit on Sustainable Development: Toward a Post-Jo-Burg Environmentalism." *Global Environmental Politic* 3 (1): 1–10.

Wapner, P.K. 1996. *Environmental Activism and World Civic Politics*. SUNY Series in International Environmental Policy and Theory. Albany: State University of New York Press.

Washington, S., and L. Ababouch. 2011. *Private Standards and Certificaton in Fisheries and Aquaculture: Current Practices and Emerging Issues*. Rome: Food and Agriculture Organization of the United Nations.

Webb, Kernaghan, ed. 2004. *Voluntary Codes: Private Governance, the Public Interest and Innovation*. Ottawa: Carleton Research Unit on Innovation, Science and Environment.

Westell, D. 1994. "Species Protection Proposed Legislation Would Plug Cracks." 23 November. Accessed 24 August 2014, http://www.lexisnexis.com.

Weyler, R. 2004. *Greenpeace: How a Group of Journalists, Ecologists and Visionaries Changed the World*. Emmaus, PA: Rodale.

Whiteman, Gail, Chris Hope. and Peter Wadhams. 2013. "Climate Science: Vast Costs of Arctic Change." *Nature* 499:401–3.

Whittington, Les. 2009. "'Dion's Carbon Tax Plan Was a Vote Loser,' Ignatieff Says." *Star,* 28 February. http://www.thestar.com/news/

canada/2009/02/28/dions_carbon_tax_plan_was_a_vote_loser_
ignatieff_says.print.html.

– 2014. "New Oil and Gas Regulations Would Be 'Crazy' Harper Says."
Toronto Star, 9 December.

Whittington, Michael. 1974. "Environmental Policy." In *Issues in
Canadian Public Policy*, edited by G. Bruce Doern and V. Seymour
Wilson, 203–27. Toronto: MacMillan of Canada.

– 1980. "The Department of the Environment," in *How Ottawa Spends
Your Tax Dollars*, edited by G. Bruce Doern, 99–118. Ottawa: School of
Public Administration, Carleton University.

Wijen, Frank, Kees Zoeteman, Jan Peters, and Paul van Seters, eds. 2013.
The Handbook of Globalization and Environmental Policy. 2nd ed.
London: Edward Elgar.

Wiles, Anne. 2007. "Strategically Natural: Nature, Social Trust and Risk
Regulation of Genetically Modified Foods and Natural Health Products
in Canada." PhD diss., Carleton University.

Wilks, Stephen. 2013. *The Political Power of the Business Corporation*.
London:Edward Elgar.

Williams, Glen. 2009. *Canadian Politics in the 21st Century*. 7th ed.
Toronto: Nelson Canada.

Willick, M.L. 2001. "Forest Sustainability: Ontario Combines Science,
Policy and Consensus." *Forestry Chronicle* 77 (1): 65–8.

Wilson, J. 1998. *Talk and Log: Wilderness Politics in British Columbia,
1965–96*. Vancouver: UBC Press.

– 2003. "The Commission for Environmental Cooperation and North
American Migratory Bird Conservation: The Potential of the NAAEC
Citizen Submission Procedure." *Journal of International Wildlife Law
and Policy* 6 (3): 1–23.

Winfield, Mark S. 2012. *Blue Green Province: The Environmental and the
Political Economy of Ontario*. Vancouver: UBC Press.

Wingrove, Josh. 2013. "Tories Remove Environment Minister from
Economic Prosperity Committee." *Globe and Mail*, 18 July

Wolfe, David. 2009. "Universities and Knowledge Transfer: Powering
Local Economic and Cluster Development." In *Universities and
Research and Innovation: Changing Federal Government University
Relation*, edited by G.B. Doern and C. Stoney, 276–92. Toronto:
University of Toronto Press.

Wolfe, J. 2003. "A National Urban Policy for Canada? Prospects and
Challenges." *Canadian Journal of Urban Research* 12 (1): 1–21.

Wolfe, Michelle, Bryan D. Jones, and Frank R. Baumgartner. 2013. "A Failure to Communicate: Agenda Setting in Media and Policy." *Political Communication* 30 (2): 175–92.

World Bank. 2012. *The Turn Down: Why a 4 Degree C Warmer World Must Be Avoided*. New York: World Bank.

World Commission on Environment and Development. 1987. *Our Common Future*. Oxford: Oxford University Press.

Yergin, Daniel. 2012. *The Quest: Energy Security and the Remaking of the Modern World*. London: Penguin Books.

Young, Oran R. 1999. *Governance in World Affairs*. Ithaca, NY: Cornell University Press.

– 2001. "Inferences and Indices: Evaluating the Effectiveness of International Environmental Regimes." *Global Environmental Politics* 1 (1): 99–121.

Young, R. 2003. "Provincial Involvement in Municipal-Federal Relations." Paper delivered to the Conference on Municipal-Federal-Provincial Relations, Queen's University, Kingston, 9–10 May.

Zarocostas, J. 1995. "ISO: Enviros Say Canadian Forestry Plan Is Too Weak." *Greenwire*, 30 May.

Zililo, M. 2013. "Canada Withdrawing from UN Drought Convention Because It's Too Bureaucratic: Harper." iPolitics, 28 March. http://www.ipolitics.ca/2013/03/28/canada-withdrawing-from-un-drought-convention-because-its-too-bureaucratic-harper/.

Index